Inclinations

Further writings and interviews
by Stuart Morgan

STUART MORGAN was widely regarded during the 1980s and early 1990s – roughly from the period when punk emerged to that when art became more widely accepted and discussed in Britain – as the most significant British writer on contemporary art, and he was an inspiring and engaging teacher, talker and lecturer.

Morgan was born in Newport, south Wales in 1948. He studied English language and literature at Southampton University and completed an MA in American studies at the University of Sussex. He remained in Brighton, working towards a doctorate on Henry James, but began teaching at the art school and thereafter devoted his literary energies to art, displaying from the first a wit, style and a whole approach to art that seemed fully formed. His first essays and reviews appeared in *Arts Magazine* and *Artscribe*, and he was soon writing for *Artforum* in New York, a city he lived in for extended periods. He went on to become the editor of *Artscribe* for a short period in the late 1980s. The aesthetic choices faced by artists in that decade are boldly confronted and re-imagined in his writing, and it is a period on which he is particularly illuminating. From 1990 his writing mostly appeared in *frieze* magazine. From a small flat at the Elephant and Castle, London, where he seemed to possess little more than a radio, books, an ironing board and a telephone, he continued to travel – to Madrid, Athens, Amsterdam, Vienna, Cologne and Auckland – at any opportunity. Along the way he curated ten exhibitions, including 'Louise Bourgeois and Alice Aycock' at the Serpentine Gallery in 1985 and, with Frances Morris, 'Rites of Passage' at the Tate Gallery in 1995. At about that time he began to notice signs of what would eventually be diagnosed as Lewy Body disease, a degenerative neurological disorder affecting both mobility and memory, and by 1999 he could no longer write. He could, for a while longer, continue to look through his work for the making of this book, the title of which is his own. He was cared for in London until he died, in the summer of 2002, at the age of 54. His manuscripts and tape recordings are held at the library at Chelsea College of Art and Design.

His carefully edited interviews with artists, represented in this book as in its predecessor, *What the Butler Saw* (Durian, 1996) form a distinctive part of his work and demonstrate both his rapport with artists and a curiosity to extend and challenge them. His use of interviews and sometimes of a style of diaristic observation coexisted with a continued interest in literature and literary theory as that was allowed to inform the discussion of art through the 1980s. It coexisted also with a robust sense of art's possible social roles and indeed its morality. Stuart Morgan was not naive, though it sometimes suited him to appear so, and what he achieved really did make an impact and a difference, in Britain and beyond, in a way that it now seems rather harder to imagine any single practitioner of the trade of art criticism could.

Ian Hunt, editor of *Inclinations*, was also the editor of Morgan's first book, *What the Butler Saw*. He is the author of *Greenlight*, a book of poems, and writes on contemporary art.

Juan Vicente Aliaga, who contributes an afterword to this book, is Titular Professor in the faculty of fine art at the Polytechnic University of Valencia. He has curated many exhibitions, and his books include *Arte Conceptual Revisado/Conceptual Art Revisited* (1990, with José Miguel J. Cortés) and *Bajo Vientre: Representaciones de la sexualidad en la cultura y el arte contemporáneos* (1997).

Inclinations

Further writings and interviews by Stuart Morgan

Edited by Ian Hunt

Afterword by Juan Vicente Aliaga

frieze

Inclinations
by Stuart Morgan

Published in 2006 by frieze
3-4 Hardwick Street, London EC1R 4RB
Tel: +44 (0)20 7833 7270
Fax: +44 (0)20 7833 7271
www.frieze.com

frieze is an imprint of Durian Publications Ltd., registered in England number 2609458

ISBN: 0 95274148 2
A catalogue record for this book is available from the British Library.

Editor: Ian Hunt
Copy editor: Matthew Taylor
Printed by Butler and Tanner

Distributed in the UK and Europe by Art Data, 12 Bell Industrial Estate, 50 Cunningham Street, London W4 5HB, tel: +44 (0)20 8747 1061, fax: +44 (0)20 8742 2319, www.artdata.co.uk, and in the US by DAP, 155 6th Avenue, New York, NY 10013, tel: +1 212 473 5119, fax: +1 212 627 9484, www.artbook.com

The publisher is grateful for a grant from the Arts Council of England towards this publication.

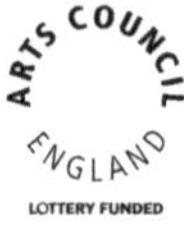

Contents

Editor's introduction and acknowledgments

This book represents a wide selection of writing by Stuart Morgan, and together with its predecessor, it makes a good account of what made his contribution to art criticism particular and cherishable. I cannot say that it is all he wished to preserve, as he left the final selection to me and in the event I have added many shorter articles and reviews from the 1980s, when his writing was at its best. Although he did not especially favour including unpublished work, I have included some notebook entries, including a solitary account of a film by Max Ophüls, and an early essay on Francis Bacon which we eventually pieced together. (He remarked 'I thought it was about me'.) Also here are some unpublished interviews which had the requisite quality of two people listening to one another and engaging with what each is saying. I omitted, in the end, one with John Coplans, and mention instead *Provocations*, the book by Coplans Morgan edited in 1996. There are many manuscripts of his celebrated lectures, but I can mention them here only to say that they have impressed on me how very, very hard he worked, all his life.

As things turned out, a discovered file of quotations provides for *Inclinations* a perfect introduction by its author. But there are some things to say about the groupings latent within the chronological arrangement, and on some of the circumstances of the commissioning. In the earlier period essays for magazines, particularly for Artscribe, were inclined to grow to enormous length – one such, the account of Documenta VI in 1977, is included here, and mostly, I admit, for its beginning and ending. (But then how many of the names encountered in the criticism of Apollinaire are actually familiar now?) Reviews too seem of a length that permits a change of direction or another understanding to arise and allow us to watch a difficult judgment or a spur to our own judgment being formed. Many of these articles are, historians can note, the length of present-day features. Morgan never insisted on long length as a virtue in writing, but in this earlier period, when he had fully arrived as a writer but was not yet fully entrained in his own habits, his work is full of relish for entertaining the reader and for rethinking the critic's role and style of performance. Enjoyment, then a relatively unfamiliar tone in art criticism, is nevertheless not allowed to become the only point of the writing. The swerves to seriousness are always there; those very seriousnesses which some who met him at this time found sometimes forbidding and overwrought. Early on James Faure Walker, editor of Artscribe, encouraged Morgan to forgo some of his academic caution (visible in the Bacon essay) and move his writing closer to the rhythms of his speech. The chronicle accounts of New York resulted, some extracts from which are included here, and they were certainly both influential and a turning point in his development. From the standpoint of the present, however, it seems important to add that he later thought, and said loudly, that the device of the first-person voice was abused by too many critics: that they did not realize what they squandered by turning to it so readily.

At Artforum, where David Frankel became a good friend and supporter, Morgan became an informant initially on less well established media, and on performance, an area in which commissions are never easy to come by. At the same time he developed through a series of reviews, interviews and articles a response to what was happening in contemporary painting that, although necessarily fragmentary, is highly considered and original. The very caution with which ideas derived from literary theory are introduced to the debate, when compared to the way obfuscation could and did become useful as marketing in this period, is exemplary. I have included the Lüpertz interview as an emblem of how strange this episode in art history really is, and two pendents: the theoretically inclined essay 'Drift', and an account of British abstract painting occasioned by an exhibition by James Faure-Walker, in which some memorable asides capture the bewildered response of many British artists to what was afoot internationally, and where some light is shed on the project of early Artscribe. (Anyone looking to make memorials to Stuart Morgan, incidentally, might consider that this magazine has never been indexed, and as a result its resources are not well enough known to art historians.)

There is much of America here, or at least of New York, and Morgan's writing is an intriguing counterpoint to the ways in which British artists of his generation usually leaned in that direction; it had begun with a literary bias rather than an adulation of Clement Greenberg, and continued with first-hand experience of how art, business and social life could be run differently. In discussion, however, he often mentioned an idea of a book of interviews on European art. We discussed also a vestigial 'Russian' section for this book. Traces can be found, including the brief article on Velimir Khlebnikov, a great favourite, and the interview on Ivan Leonidov (these were published in Artscribe, during Morgan's editorship, under the characteristic title 'The Success of Failure'). A lecture on Constructivism and Productivism, not included, is unusually lengthy and detailed; Morgan had studied Russian at school and though his interest in Russian art is that of an orthodox modernist, it kept a place in his teaching and thinking. The brief and rather over the top account of Anthony Wilson's slide sequences (once seen, never forgotten) perhaps belongs here, in an idea of what the Russian experiment in art could yet become.

I looked hard for possible lectures on Vienna, a city Morgan was partial to, but have settled for a short account of Egon Schiele, which he sometimes claimed as his first published piece. (On different occasions that on Smithson would be credited as the first.) An introduction to a novel by Miroslav Krleža brings into the book a fictional artist, amongst the accounts of more substantial ones, and indicates the literary critic that could have been allowed to flourish, had the requests flowed more frequently or Morgan not felt that area already well served by talent in Britain. (About art historians he was not always so kind.)

What else can be said here, briefly? He was once billed at Arnolfini in Bristol (the first art gallery to which he was taken, by his Uncle Gil) with publicity that announced 'Stuart Morgan talking'. He began his art school course on modernism with a lecture on Seurat. For most of his life he had no television. He liked the music of Takemitsu and Charles Mingus, the poetry of Robert Browning and John Wieners. He liked to read aloud, particularly prose – Dickens, Conan Doyle, M.R. James, Isaak Dinesen. Of undone projects, I can mention that he had prepared a detailed bibliography of sources on the short-lived Austrian Expressionist poet Georg Trakl. He also wanted to write on the television careers of Lucille Ball and of Jerry Springer. I encouraged him, too late in the day, to write on Edwin Denby, to whose writings on dance he introduced me and many others. He was keen that one early attempt to write on dance (Simone Forti) should be included in this book. His last published work was an interview with his good friend Ansuya Blom.

But we should not lament what was not to be. While Morgan did experience frustrations in his work through the 1990s, after losing the editorship of Artscribe, these are to be expected in a critic's development. The situation of art was changing too, and no critic can for very many years write from within the middle of the fray. Nevertheless Matthew Collings, in his obituary, was right to say that although the reception of art in Britain has changed in ways that Morgan had always been fighting for, it is not so clear that we can feel entirely comfortable about all those changes. What is clear is that Stuart Morgan's wholehearted commitment to the art and the artists of his time, paying them the compliment that what they did should be written about as well as any other form of art, has made here an unusual achievement in criticism. If some of it appears now properly historical, I hope it is still not easy to predict which.

Acknowledgments

The editor and publishers would like to thank those who have permitted republication of copyright material or material in which copyright is shared. Original sources are given particular prominence under the titles of the selections throughout the book, and these constitute an extension of the copyright page.

For help and conversation of many kinds, I would like to thank Suzanne Hutchinson, James Faure-Walker, Angela Lucas, Juan Vicente Aliaga, David Dye, Darren Leak, Ansuya Blom and Mark Glynne, David Frankel, Simon Watney, and librarians past and present at Chelsea College of Art and Design and at Westminster Reference Library. Matthew Slotover, the publisher of this book as of its predecessor, has been a steadfast and generous presence. Matthew Taylor helped enormously with preparing the texts for publication; remaining errors and inconsistencies are mine, or the author's.

Quotations

These quotations were found in a file called 'Quotations' on Stuart Morgan's computer, and have been printed here in the order in which they were found (excepting the addition of the quotations from Emily Dickinson and Michel de Certeau, which were in a separate file, 'Notebook'). They were probably assembled in the two or so years before he became seriously ill, in 1998.

'Art must become content of life, since only thus can life be beautiful.' [Suprematism's aims] — Malevich in a letter to Dutch artists, 1922, from the catalogue *Transform the World! Poetry Must be Made by All!* (Stockholm: Moderna Museet, 1969).

'Ultimately, photography is subversive not when it frightens, repels or even stigmatizes, but when it is pensive, when it thinks.' — Roland Barthes, *Camera Lucida.*

'And the perfect moments? Where do they come in?'
'They come in afterwards. First there are some annunciatory signs. Then the privileged situation, slowly, majestically, enters into people's lives. Then the question arises whether you want to make a perfect moment out of it.'
'Yes,' I say, 'I understand. In each privileged situation, there are certain acts which have to be performed, certain attitudes which have to be assumed, certain words which have to be said – other attitudes, other words, are strictly prohibited. Is that it?'
'If you like . . .'
'In other words the situation is the raw material: it has to be treated.'
'That's it,' she says. 'First you had to be plunged into something exceptional and feel that you were putting it in order. If all these conditions had been fulfilled, the moment would have been perfect.'
'In fact, it was a sort of work of art.' — Jean-Paul Sartre, *Nausea,* 1938.

'He was forgetting everything else in a half-speculative, half-involuntary identification of himself with the objects he was looking at, thinking how far it might be possible habitually to shift his centre till his own personality would be no less outside him than the landscape.' — George Eliot, *Daniel Deronda.*

'I'm interested in things that suggest the world rather than the personality. I'm interested in things which suggest things which are, rather than judgements. The more conventional thing, the most extraordinary thing – it seems to me that those things exist as clear facts, not involving aesthetic hierarchy.'
— Jasper Johns, interview with David Sylvester, 1965.

'[He] is always absorbed by one problem, that of capturing and bottling the sunlight.'
— Sir Walter Armstrong about Pieter de Hooch in William Orpen, *The Outline of Art.*

'Our imagination is naturally raw and enamoured with absurdity.' — Goethe.

'There are no paintings, just pictures, and as they are not sausages, they are neither good nor bad.' — Samuel Beckett.

'That's all we have, finally, the words, and they had better be the right ones.'
— Raymond Carver, *Fires,* 1986.

'A heart is perhaps something unsavoury. It's of the order of anatomy tables and butchers' stalls. I prefer your body.' — Marguerite Yourcenar, *Fires.*

'Keep me as the apple of an eye. Hide me under the shadow of thy wings.'
— C of E compline service (evening prayer).

'A lesson learned through humour is a lesson retained.' — The Talmud.

'I put a light right in the glass because I wanted it to be luminous.' — Alfred Hitchcock quoted in Peter Blegvad, 'Phosphorescent Milk', *Sight and Sound,* April 1993, p.33.

A party in 1990. Lord Rothermere: 'And what do *you* do?'
Francis Bacon: 'I'm an old poof.' (Daniel Farson)

'He was ugly, with this horrible shepherd's hat, and he smelt of alcohol.' — Madame Calment (age 121) remembering Vincent van Gogh.

'If God were alive, we would go and break his windows.' — Jewish proverb.

'The whole thing is planned on the model of an imaginary walk. First comes the dark wood of the authorities . . . Then there is a cavernous defile through which I lead my readers . . . and then, all at once, the high ground and the open prospect, and the question "Which way do you want to go?"' — Freud, *The Interpretation of Dreams.*

'My business is circumference.' — Emily Dickinson, *Letters*, ed. Robert N Linscott, p.195.

'*Passeur*: one who moves people or things across borders or into forbidden zones; ferryman; taken literally, it means "one who passes".' — Michel de Certeau, 'The Laugh of Michel Foucault', in *Heterologies: Discourse on the Other,* trans. B. Massumi, (Manchester, 1986), p.259, n.1.

'Wallace Stevens remarked that R.P. Blackmur failed as an expositor of ideas "not for lack of ideas, but for not knowing what his ideas are." But I propose to deflect a little the force of that remark by saying that, whether or not Blackmur knew what his ideas were, he took every precaution to prevent that knowledge (such as it was) from becoming too sure of itself. It was not that he despised ideas; though indeed he was more concerned with feeling at a stage somewhat earlier than that in which it settles into the ripe old age (*nunc recondita/ senet quiete*) of ideas. Santayana wrote of Emerson that "he differed from the plodding many, not in knowing things better, but in having more ways of knowing them." Blackmur thought the condition crucial. His poems, like his essays, are efforts not to enlarge the scope of his knowledge but to practice different ways of knowing things. Poetry and criticism were alike for the sake of knowledge, to keep it alive by exercising it in many different forms of life.'
— Denis Donoghue, 'R.P Blackmur's Poetry: An Introduction', in *Poems of R.P. Blackmur,* Princeton University Press, 1977.

'I thought that I might add a postscript to my letter in the previous issue,

explaining that my view of Botticelli's *Primavera* is coloured by early experiences. The picture hung on the wall of our mathematics classroom, where a boy called Hoskins in the back row was attempting to take a surreptitious photograph of the maths master in one of his tantrums. He was discovered and hauled up to the front of the class, where he had to stand below the picture and put his head into a waste-paper basket (a large tea-chest of plywood), and in this position, with his bottom in the air and his head in the chest, he was slowly and methodically kicked (tea-chest and all) out of the door of the classroom. I remember the rasping of the chest as it moved across the floor. All this took place under the picture of the Graces dancing their enigmatic dance under the enchanted trees. Since then for me, as for the rest of the class, sado-masochistic episodes have always acquired a Neo-Platonic penumbra. By the same mechanism, the decipherment of the picture was to be all the more emotionally charged. (Hoskins's own opinion of the *Primavera* was neither asked nor given, though he retained his interest in photography, moving in later years from satirical subjects to landscape.)
Miles Burrows, Al Ain, Abu Dhabi' — *London Review of Books,* 22 July 1993, p.5.

'"A club for gamblers, lords and heroes", Evelyn Waugh called White's. Originating in the 1690s as a coffee-house situated between Piccadilly and St James's, it is apparently the only surviving seventeenth-century club in London, and seventy years senior to its nearest rival . . . "If you want food, go to Boodle's," said Harold Macmillan, "If you want insults, go to White's. . . . There are stories of high-handedness which readers will find magnificent or disagreeable according to taste: Lord Sefton, for example, groping for a word that had escaped him, asking "What's the name of that car I've got" (meaning a Rolls-Royce); or the doubts of Lowell Guiness when the first territorial squadron of the RAF - which had been started at White's in 1924 - needed to stockpile petrol before the impositioning of rationing in 1939: "I think," said Guiness, "That I'm a director of Shell."
"What do you mean, 'think'?" demanded his commanding officer, "Telephone your secretary and find out."' — *TLS*, (18 June 18, 1993).

'What a gay arcadia of happy girlhood!'

'In other schools girls are sent out quite unprepared into a merciless world. But when our girls leave here it is the merciless world that has to be prepared.' 'Sometimes I think it's just the frustrated mother instinct in me that urges me on.'

'This place reminds me of a ladies' powder-room in Port Said.'

'I suppose I'm just a foolish, weak woman' [stuffing cash into the bodice of his dress].
— Alastair Sim as Millicent Fritton in *The Belles of St. Trinians.*

'Talked to . . . Stuart Morgan (who's now totally bald).'
— Brian Eno, *A Year with Swollen Appendices,* (London: Faber, 1996), p.133.

'Is not memory inseparable from love, which seeks to preserve what yet must pass away? Is not each stirring of fantasy engendered by desire which, in displacing the elements of what exists, transcends it without betrayal? Is not indeed the simplest perception shaped by fear of the thing perceived, or desire for it? It is true that the objective meaning of knowledge has, with the objectification of the world, become progressively detached from the underlying impulses; it is equally true that knowledge breaks down where its effort of objectification remains under the sway of desire. But if the impulses are not at once preserved and surpassed in the thought which has escaped their sway, then there will be no knowledge at all, and the thought that murders the wish that fathered it will be overtaken by the revenge of stupidity.'
— Theodor Adorno, *Minima Moralia,* 1951.

Daisetsu Suzuki's definition of *yugen* in Zen philosophy: '*Yugen* is a compound word, each part, *yu* and *gen* meaning "cloudy impenetrability" and the combination meaning "obscurity", "unknowability", "mystery", "beyond intellectual calculability", but not "utter darkness". . . It is like something we feel in ourselves and yet it is an object about which we can talk, it is an object of mutual communication only among those who have the feeling of it. It is hidden behind the clouds, but not entirely out of sight, for we feel its presence, its secret message being transmitted through the darkness, however impenetrable to the intellect.'
— Dore Ashton, *Noguchi East and West*, (Berkeley, Los Angeles/London 1992), p.61.

"Do you think, Mr Bee, that what heppened yesterday will heppen again?"
"It most certainly will, Krazy. History, events, accidents, thoughts, you, I anything and nothing each must repeat itself, everything is just nothing repeating itself – ashes to ashes is the best repeating act we do – so don't worry it'll happen."
— George Herriman, *Krazy Kat.*

Francis Bacon

Undated, unpublished; begun late 1970s, revised and returned to subsequently.

First impressions of a Bacon self-portrait are disturbing; why should anyone embark on such a pitiless examination of his own appearance and character? While continued employment of the triptych has exercised Bacon's interest in mythological and religious themes in the last decade, these more private works have allowed him to push dexterity and distortion to their limits, to investigate the fundamentals of observing the self and the other, and to ask how perception of people relates, if at all, to the creation of art. The evasive quality of the eyes is a constant. Interviews reveal a parallel urge for protection by means of a carapace of witty language. They also provide evidence to suggest that in both paint and words Bacon courts and evades truth by means of a deliberate impregnability. This indefinite stance is important; as the protagonist of his own dramas, a main problem must be that of proceeding with an experiment dedicated to perpetuating painting's 'classic style', but in the form of an arena in which moral certainties are temporarily suspended.

If style in British portraiture arises naturally from social behaviour, Bacon's style is a calculated affront; not only is polite intercourse reduced to absurdity but, like the Fat Boy in *Pickwick Papers*, he wants 'to make your flesh creep'. As Surrealist paraphernalia in his paintings was replaced with everyday objects, and exoticism and imitation were drawn gradually towards the mundane, Bacon referred increasingly to newspapers, posters, film and photography. Slowly, as the outside world imposed its iconography of power on lonely people in rooms, this was counterbalanced by more sophisticated means of registering their solipsism. The growing reliance on self-portraiture cannot have been accidental. Yet accounts of Bacon's painting have laid sufficient emphasis on his obsession with himself, most evident in David Sylvester's book of interviews. Together, the paint surface and the speaking voice offer a coherent set of clues for understanding how Bacon evolved painterly solutions to problems particular to his private beliefs and outlook.

The lapse of classical tragedy into horror and rhetoric, 'shallow', monotonous versions of more complex emotional patternings, provides an ideological backdrop to Bacon's work. Beneath his obsessive image of a cry of pain and his conversational allusions to Baudelaire, Wilde and Nietzsche lies that modern aesthetics of decadence which prompted twentieth-century critics to study 'decline', into Jacobean or Mannerist styles for example. What Bacon offers is a heroic ritual of triumph over adverse forces but (in his own words) 'exhilarated despair', unhealthy nervous excitement prompted by displays of power, not a shared event but a voyeuristic encounter with a vulnerable human being. In the self-portraits he flaunts his own laceration by employing photo-booth snapshots; the embarrassment of being taken unawares is compounded for the artist by the humiliation of studying photographs of himself, though there is an accompanying narcissistic pleasure and an enhanced ability to cope with appearances through an anaesthetized study of his own. As if to deflect the middleman's discomfiture, that of Bacon as his own interpreter, the spectator is distracted by blatant ostentation. A different reading might stress the seductive aspect of the superficies, the shrillness and apparent exaggeration of a tiny area of a total emotional vocabulary. Max Kozloff wrote that the paint 'alienates by its freakish narcissism'. Bacon is no Expressionist, however. The relationship between feeling and medium in his work, enriched by aestheticism, aristocratic disdain, dark humour and an allusiveness which creates density of tone by manipulating context rather than subject-matter, diverts attention from emotional enactment by means of technique. If opera, as Geoffrey Hartman has written, tends toward pure superstructure, 'its form having but an absurd or magical connection with the passions staged', then Bacon's strategies are notably operatic.

Yet the camp dissociation of emotional effect and the vehicle that produces it is apparently at odds in Bacon with any formal definition stressing coherence, integrity, resolution or architectonic disposition of elements. The agonized cry ruptures a closely woven fabric of convention. For Bacon painting is an attempt to carry this breakdown across into life, to transfer it, he would say, to our 'nerve ends'. When Nietzsche complained that Wagner elevated passion above beauty and melody, defining it as 'the gymnastics of what is ugly on the rope of enharmonics', he was simultaneously lodging a complaint against the loss of an integrated mode by which the music achieved meaning, against disintegration into 'life', since passion was cheap and common to everyone. According to this definition, the separation of form and passion in opera would represent only a temporary stasis before the relationship was destroyed by the cry of a real person registering pain, using the medium as a springboard, as a medium to transcend artifice. When Bacon describes road accidents as 'very invigorating, very exhilarating', he is employing that perception which leads past realism to reality, to what Nietzsche considered the degeneracy of passion unsupported by a formal structure. Yet it leads back also to the origins of the modern symbol. Ruskin regarded grotesque as a kind of useful satire arising from sudden, playful realization. 'A fine grotesque', he wrote in *Modern Painters*, 'is the expression in a moment, by a series of symbols thrown together in bold and fearless connection of truths which it would have taken a long time to express in any verbal way, and of which the connection is left for the beholder to work out for himself; the gaps, left or overleaped by the haste of the imagination, forming the grotesque character.' The sight of the accident is a slight example, of course, of Bacon using his painterly eye, sophisticated or jaundiced as it might be, to encompass a 'truth' he must confront. Nietzsche pronounced this vision barbarous. Ruskin argued that its acceptance would be an 'infinite good to mankind' The burden of the past weighs heavily on Bacon, whose employment of such daring visual ellipses can be regarded as a century out of date in terms of a formalist avant-garde. What he chooses to preserve, however, is that entire tradition of Renaissance painting which cherishes the integrity of the objects of the world. His modernity may lie in the precision with which he attempts to overthrow the humanistic assumptions of this tradition. Yet his usual gambit is to hover ambiguously between the stances of Ruskin and Nietzsche, hedging his bets on the power of his paint to delight or shock or persuade. The 'rupture' is unclear in terms of its formal context.

Fascinated by triptychs, Crucifixions and other classic Western genres, Bacon engages in a protracted examination not of the status of the art object but of the social conventions implicit in the act of painting. John Golding called Duchamp's *Large Glass* the 'most elaborately posed' of modern artworks. Aware of Duchampian thinking, Bacon attends not to the 'pose' of the object itself but to the uneasy placement undergone by the subject. A more appropriate description of his method of recording people would not be 'pose' but 'poise'. In his own mind this produces a confluence of form and meaning. 'If my people look as if they're in a dreadful fix, it's because I can't get them out of the technical dilemma', he has stated. His urge to acquire them as specimens and their violent struggle to escape being 'fixed and sprawling on a pin' result in a fight for control as he attempts to wrest truth from them, they to hide it from him. Michel Leiris has described the tussle:

To try to convey a living presence, and try to convey it without losing the life essential to it, is to try to pin it down without pinning it down, to force oneself paradoxically to pin down that which cannot and should not be pinned down because to do so is to kill it.

'Life escapes', as D.H. Lawrence wrote. The obsessive attempt to capture it is pictured by Bacon as a game of chance.

One method of coping with Bacon's literalism is therefore to transfer artistic practice into terms of social behaviour. Like modernist abstraction, his art employs aesthetic distance, but in his case the sign systems he manipulates are aligned with those of daily life. He was an interior designer, and the colour of his rooms is closely identified with those of fashionable surroundings. As for faces, his colours can be compared to those of cosmetics; as important as the activation of a code is the shift of context effected by the initial decision to use it. In one sense cosmetics mean subterfuge or the deliberate perversion of nature. In another, their use is merely a token in an exchange of manners. The wearer apologizes to onlookers for being less beautiful than they expect, or flouts manners by parading an insincere act. And the aesthetic underlying cosmetics has as much to do with animal courting rituals, the formal sublimation of tabooed emotion, as with a 'realistic' cheek equals red theory. Nevertheless, this is the normal excuse for make-up; the barber in Mann's *Death in Venice* asks Aschenbach to be permitted 'to restore what belongs to you'. Realism has the same questionable status in Bacon, who exposes his weaknesses and fights to compensate for this self-inflicted suffering by a hectic surface drama of attractions and repulsions. One paradox underlying Bacon's technique is therefore that an art which deals so openly in humiliation – for this is a portrait, and self-hatred is an indulgent, embarrassing habit frowned on in daily intercourse – should forward itself for our attention in a way that uses glamorizing painterly effects either to apologize for the feelings beneath or to try to conceal them in as insulting or flamboyant a way as possible.

Bacon's discussions rely on a personal set of key words and an account of his own creative process. He tells how, by working from photographs, he is able to let his perceptions 'drift freely', allow memory and knowledge to come into play, then, in an artificial pantomime of spontaneous reaction, record the appearance of the 'new' object, reconstructed by broadening its suggestive range into an area governed by what it is not but could be. 'Could be' is determined by his sensibility, though we are also to understand an absorbent quality that draws one appearance into another, a dark 'other' by which appearances are perceived. The revivified image counters this darkness, straddles two modes of existence. In the *Tractatus* Wittgenstein writes that definitions are rules for translating from one language to another, and that it is exactly this translatability which proves the validity of the sign system. A critical viewpoint based on this meditation would argue that Bacon's paintings occupy a vacancy between languages and that they are committed to persuading the viewer that definition is possible, even that it is occurring, while in effect presenting a series of challenges to the relation between process and system, event and structure, which both languages assume.

Bacon thinks it is necessary to steer a course between two types of painting: 'illustrational', which is designed, ordered, appeals to the brain and does not involve inventing an image, and 'direct', which acts more fully on the nervous system. Direct painting tries to trap the image at its most vital point, works toward remaking it in an irrational way by fusing it with related areas of feeling, finally producing an image that will 'leak back' into fact. Painting in general is both direct and illustrational, impelled by the need for both sides of this dichotomy. At opposite extremes are photography, which is illustrational and lacks immediacy of texture, and pure abstraction, which is direct but presents undisciplined emotion. In an age that emphasized these extremes without devising a middle way, the painter's task is to 'give sensation without the boredom of its conveyance' by letting instinct find a discipline of its own, which is an obsession with something in life, and working this obsession out in direct painting. Here the most useful tool is accident, 'will subdued by instinct', encouraging marks straight from the unconscious. By combining permanently with the medium the image is certain of a potential to defy time and 'thicken' life.

If the term 'image', as Sylvester explains, is to Bacon 'a complex of forms which has an especially powerful or suggestive resonance', the Bacon who tempers this image and stage-manages its distortions is involved in a transfer of potency. Vulnerable at first, he borrows its power and resonance to subdue it, while at the same time probing its life. Paradoxically, a threat has been overcome and celebrated. As an act of confrontation painting parallels memory, recording the surfaces of unrecognizable objects and providing artificial respiration for ontologically weakened images. Yet it is impossible not to regard both painting and remembering as sado-masochistic, and the oblique train of thought which describes images being returned to the world of facts as a means of keeping in suspension the mixture of anxiety and pleasure which is the artist's reaction to the original image. Two processes are evident here. The first is to return distanced images to a world of facts. (Lévi-Strauss describes totemism as establishing a position 'in which signs assume the status of things signified'.) The second is to increase the dynamic aspects of the returned image as it relates to the artist, to achieve a perilously fragile position of stasis, an attempt at permanent postponement, the refusal to believe that a life or an artwork or an act of love has moved past completion into oblivion. Bacon describes his studio procedure as disruption of what can be done with ease; his gambling demands a willingness to abide by any decisions from an outside source, and the creation of a rhythm to cope with the situation.

> Even a pleasurable tension has its natural limits. If it lasts for too long a time it changes its character, becomes unpleasant, and its termination, the discharge, is desired and aimed at. The masochist apparently wants to provide a counter-example for this normal course of things. He wants to maintain the tension for as long as possible and to postpone the discharge or postpone it as long as possible.

Theodor Reik's thesis is supported in Bacon's case; the moments of pure chance, records of meaningless violence, escape Sylvester's questioning and emerge as the goal or discharge towards which Bacon strives. Having mastered his obsessive image after a time of 'pleasurable tension', the feared explosion of painterly activity becomes, in every sense, insignificant. The gratuitous handfuls of paint flung at a canvas to complete a composition simply underscore its fluctuating position between static visual systems. They are no more than marks of externalized frustration, a spilt energy with no function beyond registering its own existence, the only part of the composition completely freed from a burden of meaning, a self-referential signature of utter liberation.

Another main theme tackled in Sylvester's interviews is the damage, real or metaphorical or both, that Bacon causes his sitters. His attitude to others resembles that of his father; he really 'had no friends at all, because he fought with everybody'. Friendship, says Bacon, 'is a situation where two people really tear each other apart'. Injury inflicted in a portrait he therefore regards as creative. An interrupted chain of thought in the third interview links destruction and love – 'so-called love' is his term, since he admits that 'all the people I've ever been really fond of have died'. The only evidence of desire on his part is obsession, leading to a state he calls 'exorcism', or forgetting death. Two powerful phrases make a connection that is crucial to his thinking: 'the whole horror of life – of one thing living off another.'

Bacon's idea of cannibalism is the key to a translation of love as 'an obsession exorcized'. Exhaustion of infatuation, plus feared and postponed climax, leads to total reliance on 'accident', yet an accident that threatens to be insignificant. Dependence on an emotional charge working in one direction, from artist to image – perhaps because the obsessive image is a dead or static 'received idea' – makes the act of painting an exercise in love without reciprocity. Unrequited affection can pay off only when the degree to which all love is a selfish action is discovered and utilized. Shifting 'selflessness' into 'egocentricity' puts the self in total control; the outside world is judged on how interesting it is to the artist's mind, which has absolute power. This position is challenged by outside objects, which impress themselves so fully on the mind that its judgement is impaired. A battle is fought to overthrow this hypnotic alien force, and here the artist's main weapon is vulnerability (or 'sensibility'); by exposing himself as completely as possible to the obsession, he is more able to exorcize it in a work of art. His weapon of vulnerability, however, renders him powerless in the face of other obsessions.

Sylvester uncovers an interesting cluster of associations when he finds that the versions of Velázquez's pope remind Bacon of his father. He regrets this series of paintings, calling them 'very silly', 'distorted records'. When Sylvester indicates the mysterious transfer of excitement from the Velázquez to pictures of the real pope, an elision Bacon makes with no difficulty, links emerge; popes are father figures ('Il Papa') and as a boy Bacon felt a strong sexual attraction to his father. The father–son theme is encapsulated and extended in the 'found' image of crucifixion. In terms of meaning this hovers between accepted categories and definitions – symbolic and actual, death and rebirth, man and god – as well as furnishing an example of an image/son/creation tortured by a different 'father'. Though unreligious, Bacon can love the image in a painterly way. Like Bacon, God can remake Himself in His own image, which is part of Himself. But unlike Bacon, he can withdraw His creation, gather it to Himself by returning it to an amoeboid mass of uncreated world-stuff, as if separation had never occurred. Bacon destroys wilfully. Finished paintings, he says, represent the worst of his work. The best he ruins by over-painting, then discards.

Bacon also cannibalizes photographs, which both fascinate and repel him. He uses them to 'unlock' reality, trigger off undirected emotions that must then, by means of the 'image', be harnessed again for his work. The idea of permission seems important; it is hard to accept his statement that only technical problems prevented his painting people he knew until the early fifties. It is more probable that this coincided with what he calls 'opening myself out' as a character. The opposite of 'opening', destruction of the self by allowing too much to enter, explains his fear of photography, placed low on his scale of values because it involves the viewer too easily. Yet he speaks of being 'haunted' by them; 'ninety-nine per cent of the time I find that photographs are very much more interesting than either abstract or figurative painting.' There is no 'combat' in the relationship a viewer establishes with a photograph. The connection Bacon makes is with the lives of others; 'anyone can enter more into what is called an undisciplined emotion, because after all who loves a disastrous love affair or illness more than the spectator?'

A man who identifies sexual activity with destruction, self-love with self-destruction, risks being misunderstood. If a recurrent metaphor in any examination of his work is that of 'between-ness', of a painter striving to keep his balance amid opposing pressures of system and process, order and fragmentation, 'superstructure' and genuine emotion, this hard-won equilibrium must be construed in moral terms. Morton Feldman said of de Kooning's painting that when he destroyed he was in fact 'making connections'. Destruction in Bacon is neither the debris that remains after a fight nor the incitement to further violence; it is both but also, as in a photograph, an attempt to arrive at a point where accident and design are equally matched. In his own terminology a kind of redemption has taken place, so that the work of art exists as the scaffolding or excuse to prolong a moment of vulnerability and give it the historic serenity of great art. The elimination of obsession, the enactment of a kind of love, is also involved, so that the gesture of painting becomes, in the richest sense, mimetic. 'Acting out' in a ritual sense is of course characteristic of classical tragedy, yet at this point in Sylvester's book Bacon is most evasive, refusing to admit that he ever intended to explore a tragic sensibility. If he is mistaken, or if he means to throw Sylvester off the scent, it might be worth recalling the disputed position of 'deliquescent' tragedies such as *Antony and Cleopatra,* in which waste and a loosening of the actual joints of the drama itself seem to function as the protagonist of the play. (The ripe-rottenness of Bacon's attitude to death and his ability to regard social relationships in terms of a power struggle are typically Jacobean.) More significant, perhaps, is Bacon's concept of blocked catharsis, which is surely more frustrated in the self-portraits than anywhere else in his painting. Both conservative and avant-garde, anarchic, even strenuously anti-social, in these paintings Bacon flaunts his refusals most brilliantly, and shows himself pre-eminent in his private art of thwarted tragedy.

The Skateboard on Middle Ground: 'Looking' at Documenta 6

Published in Artscribe *9, November 1977.*

Recently visitors to London's Hayward Gallery must have looked down from its battlements to the murky depths beneath. Amid the intricate, criss-crossed ramps glide legions of boys with skateboards, like energetic recruits in a fortress on a day when no attack is expected. How many observers must have wondered whether the 'contemporary' works in the gallery above, perhaps produced by artists as old as the century itself, could tell them as much about art impulses right now as the activities of the boys below?

The aim in skateboarding seems to be the simultaneous control of body and board, riding it in circles or straight lines, standing up, lying down, on or off the ground, alone or with others, right side up or upside down. There is no organized competition but rather an establishment and dismissal of private reputations, like the singing contest in *Die Meistersinger*, 'cutting' in jazz or 'flyting' in medieval poetry. With its Zen earnestness, the skateboard aesthetic resembles a dry-land equivalent of surfing. In terms of movement, it looks like the south of England's answer to the last few energetic years of Northern Soul dancing. Like the acrobatic northerner, the skateboard fanatic has an ambiguous relation to those around him, watching them out of the corner of his eye and collaborating with them from time to time on a temporary basis without losing any degree of independence. Yet the most accomplished boarders seem motivated not by narcissism but by the urge to experiment. After traversing, wedeling, click-clacking, walking the dog, hanging ten, doing the gorilla grip, the goofy foot, the coffin, aerial spinners, nose wheelies and Samoan squats, they try new stunts, read books and magazines that keep them in touch with other skateboarders all over the world, advising them on how to care for their bushings, avoid bongos, burgers and going terminal.

The self-presentation of these boys is admittedly ephemeral, like skateboarding itself. Yet the spectator who really wants to know what's happening must wait for the moments when the cogs engage, spirit and technique are fused, when the game – trivial enough in itself – is transcended by pure gesture. For these are also the moments when the cultural cogs unite; a single Nijinksky leap outlives a generation of ballets. Tact will tell him that the gestures of skateboarding are 'wrapped in life'.

'Wrapped in life' is a phrase from Johan Huizinga, the Dutch historian whose yearning for an aristocratic élite is related to the same urge that produced Duchamp's artist-chessplayer or Hesse's *Glass Bead Game*. All three are linked by the brittle apocalypticism of one early modern attitude. Huizinga would have seen artists and skateboarders alike as *Homo Ludens*, man the game player, distilling fundamental emotions such as love and anger into patterns of artifice, arbitrary moves. According to this point of view, individual works of art are like playing cards; what happens to them as a set in the process of being manipulated is more important than regarding them one by one. Jack Burnham calls the entire configuration the 'myth' of art. Myths do not start and stop; they modulate, like music. A later, less assured twentieth-century strain emphasizes such a change of mood, a dying fall. Traditional dance in Satyajit Ray's *The Music Room*, *go* in Yasunari Kawebata's *The Master of Go* and chess in George Steiner's *The White Knights of Reykjavik*, are all presented as pursuits that endure, whereas the context that supports and nourishes them suffers an alteration. Suddenly in a world of young men with bad manners the moves are no longer 'wrapped in life'.

Huizinga's *The Waning of the Middle Ages* describes the festivities at Lille in the fifteenth century in this way:

> Even from across the sea people came to view the gorgeous spectacle. Besides the guests, a great number of noble spectators were present at the feast, disguised for the most part. First everyone walked around to admire the fixed show-pieces, later came the 'entremets', that is to say representations of personages and tableaux vivants. Olivier himself played the important part of Holy Church, making his appearance in a tower on the back of an elephant, led by a gigantic Turk. The tables were loaded with the most extravagant decorations. There were a rigged and ornamental carrack, a meadow surrounded by trees with a fountain, rocks and a statue of Saint Andrew, the castle of Lusignan with the fairy Mélusine, a bird-shooting scene near a wind-mill, a wood in which wild beasts walked about, and, lastly, a church with an organ and singers, whose songs alternated with the music of an orchestra of twenty-eight persons, which was placed in a pie.

Temporary, flamboyant and expensive, Documenta 6 attracted visitors from all over the world to see kilometre-long rods inserted into the earth, honey being pumped around a building, laser beams projected into the night air, a colossal metal structure apparently in danger of falling, and many other wonders. There is probably no reason for what happened either at Lille or Kassel, beyond the service of myths of power and art respectively, the result in each case being an event designed to provoke incredulity rather than contemplation. This stress on boggling makes them both appear trivial, insensitive and overblown, an attack on the genuine purposelessness of art, not 'wrapped in life' like skateboarding but occurring in a period of decline, like Huizinga's Burgundian revelries.

There are two ways to approach both spectacles. The first is simply to look. The second is to try to consider the theoretical substructure on which the choice of objects, themes and artists is based. When Marina Vaizey described Documenta as an 'inchoate, confused, mess', she was adopting the first method, as did most British commentators. They ran the risk of ignoring its status as an event (the fact of 'seeing' is only one way of coping with contemporary art), but most of all of ignoring the conceptual underpinning set out in the untranslated, thousand-page, three-volume catalogue, which contains all you ever wanted to know about the 'hundred-day museum' but didn't dare ask.

In 1975 the theme of the exhibition was 'Enquiry into Reality – Today's Imagery'. In 1977 the focus is 'Media' In volume one of the catalogue Manfred Schneckenburger makes the distinction between enthusiasm for new media in the sixties and the more critical approach of the seventies, citing as an example the 'video jungle' of Nam June Paik displayed this year alongside the 'a-visual' conceptuality of Walter de Maria, whose *Vertical Earth Kilometer* signifies 'an almost therapeutic opposition to the visual totalitarianism of our decade'. As major features of seventies art Schneckenburger lists the shift towards concentration on research into the properties of the artist's chosen medium, the tendency towards 'the analytical transparency of making as counterbalancing the imitation of documentary reality through intermediary manufacturing processes', the move to body experience in sculpture as an alternative to the creation of secondary worlds and the trend towards monochrome canvases as one reply to painterly 'inflation'. These choices of what is important in contemporary art are embodied in the decisions of the working parties assigned to the various media.

Klaus Honnef and Evelyn Weiss, heading the working party for painting, for example, see the painter as involved in a process of testing his own artistic position and adopting various means of approaching his material in ways that reflect this rethinking. Self-examination can take the form of research into the place of paintings as historical objects; Laszlo Lakner paints the last letter of Paul Cézanne, While Enzo Cacciola submits a Venus of 1580 with a text explaining his refusal to rely on a 'fetish' from his own body of work. It can also be distilled into reflexive attitudes. The high proportion of 'reductive' canvases included – Alan Green, Winfred Gaul, Claudio Oliviero, Ulrich Erben, Jerry Zeniuk, Raimund Girke and others – is justified by Honnef and Weiss as an attempt to cleanse visual palates jaded by television and film. Except for Louis Cane and Michael Heizer, bent on a higher degree of complication, most exponents of this approach make it seem stale and unambitious. Palermo, an artist who died this year at the age of 34 and is represented in the catalogue only by drawings and a page of photographs, is notable for his heroic conception of painting as a medium.

'Painting as the Subject of Painting', as the section is called, is bound to point towards the virtuoso piece, where brilliance of execution is called in to compensate for flagging aesthetics. The catalogue makes too little of Jennifer Bartlett's *Rhapsody*, a 998-piece arrangement of enamelled metal sheets one foot square, mounted so that thematic and stylistic variations can be 'read'. Here painting leans towards the effect of strict musical form by the adoption of a cinematic technique. Nancy Graves, appropriately exploring two media at once by basing her sketchy marks on surveys of the moon's surface, seems to be working 'within' an area opened up by Willem de Kooning, who shows a recent painting nearby. Both Graves and Bartlett are made to appear solitary eccentrics, however, while painters who attempt 'masterpieces' elbow them aside. A comparison between the irony and cool hedonism of Americans such as Lichtenstein, Stella and Morley (an English émigré), and the characteristic stolidness of the small East German delegation (including Wolfgang Mattheuer, Willi Sitte and Bernhard Heisig) could be carried out by locating them with reference to co-ordinates: seriousness of subject matter and the connected concept of the place of direct action in politics; leisure; value; the differing relation between public and private that the two sets of works embody; and their approaches to the idea of an avant-garde. The conclusions could be that for completely polarized reasons the idea of 'great painting' is being kept alive, perhaps with an aesthetic of its own, a Renaissance base on which opposing ideologies cannot but choose to be reconciled. It is significant that at least two German reviewers singled out Francis Bacon's remarkable *Triptych* of 1977 as the best of the Documenta paintings.

No disrespect is intended by suggesting that the reason may be Bacon's mastery of a Middle Ground that destroys all attempts to categorize or erect critical barriers, and which regards all artists as engaged in the same (competitive) game for the highest possible stake, a place in history regarded according to the conventions the artist feels it is his duty to prolong. How long sheer stylistic bravura can render whole areas of twentieth-century experimentation null and void is a matter for concern. The flagrant ambiguity of Warhol's glamorous hammer and sickle paintings are a strenuous addition to the dialogue.

David Shapiro, *Artforum*'s representative at Documenta, declared: 'Generally painting seems to be imbricated in a monumental montage of fine incoherence. So despite the theoretical sequestrations of the catalogue, the overall impression is *tohu-bohu*.' You can't say fairer than that. In his introduction to the sculpture section Manfred Schneckenburger finds no unifying styles; sculpture, he suggests, cannot be regarded as a 'medium' like photography and painting. He finds, however, that the 'return to physical experience of forces' ushers in a 'new paradigm' of plastic art, citing Serra as an example of 'the feeling of equilibrium and its frustration'. But this new paradigm also demands a new relationship between body and sculpture, as in the semi-participational work of Trakas, who shows a metal bridge crossing a wooden bridge, and dynamites part of the work. 'Sculpture of the seventies reacts intensely to scenic and spatial considerations', according to Schneckenburger, a trusting soul unversed in the Middle Ground philosophies which everyone knows, no one acknowledges, and for which, like a wise and politic organizer, he has to compensate.

The special conventions of the international art fair demand exactly that blend of interaction with the surroundings, 'scenic' effect and fun that Trakas's *Union Pass* embodies. This is by no means to say that it is a poor sculpture, simply that according to a double grille which Documenta imposes as a place to exercise Middle Ground decisions, it passes both tests. Works with graffiti do not. Neither do those which seek to occupy the spectator's entire attention. When Cage pointed out that the horn player emptying spit from his instrument was as valid a component of the art experience as the end of Beethoven's Ninth, he was rejoicing to concur with the common viewer, who is likely to be more interested (or 'distracted') by the pavement artists in a subway as by Dan Flavin's pretty lights overhead, or by graffiti on toilet walls as much as Brassaï's graffiti photographs. Large scale is important if only because no damage can be done to the work. Jo Jastram of East Germany ignored this rule when he allowed his *Wrestlers* (two bulky male nudes, one with his legs in the air) to be installed out of doors on a shallow base, an open invitation to jolly Middle Grounders to insert an empty beer bottle into the nearest available orifice. Stephen Antonakos and Horst Baumann pass the test with their respective *Incomplete Neon Square* on the north-west façade of the Fridericianum and a Laser Environment, as does the Center for Advanced Visual Studies of MIT with its complex *Centerbeam* project. This 'decoration' of the surroundings leads to some of the great failures of the exhibition. The Haus-Rucker Co. contribute an enormous metal construction placed on the Schöne Aussicht terrace overlooking a celebrated landscape. They make the public climb up steps and along a ramp to arrive at a point from which distant buildings and countryside are framed by concentric rectangles. References to the Jaipur observatory are of no avail; visitors are simply being invited to look at a good view that might have been better if the terrace were not cluttered by a large metal sculpture. Schöne Aussicht *means* 'good view', after all. In the same way Christo, greatly revered in Europe, and Beverley Pepper creator of Amphisculpture, might be found guilty of stating the obvious. Success and failure are closely allied when a double standard is in operation. In bending over backwards to please the visiting crowds Haus-Rucker Co. have forfeited the more usual criteria of excellence. And if all this sounds like a description of sheer philistinism with nothing in common at all with the paintings of Bacon, it is worth remembering that the Middle Ground is concerned with the *reception* of the art object, rather than its appearance.

Alice Aycock's *Project Entitled The Beginnings of a Complex* succeeds on all counts. From the Orangerie her group of sculpted buildings resembles a small town, yet as the viewer approaches, it is evident that these are follies, little more than façades. In the catalogue Nancy Rosen compares it to an abandoned village and notes that shortly before embarking on the *Project* Aycock visited a Hollywood studio. False fronts conceal an eccentric arrangement of platforms, niches and seats. The idea seems to be to scramble up and down over it, from roof to cellar. The psychological equivalent for a mental state which Aycock provides is linked in this case to the entire learning process, yet she means what she says when she uses the word 'complex'; the acquisition of knowledge is obsessive and dangerous, and teaching, or constructing such flimsy houses, is an entrenchment of private, unhealthy states of mind. Rosen quotes from a conversation with Aycock, who connects the work with Gilles de Rais.

> When I think of Gilles, I think of that great stone chimney which stands in the woods, halfway between the towers of the castle Tiffauges. They say that the chimney is connected to another wall, with a door leading upstairs to it . . . you go into a space in which for a long time you have been slitting the throats of peasant children and throwing them into the oven.

Walter de Maria's *Vertical Earth Kilometer* has been justly acclaimed. It takes its place with the small Joel Shapiro sculptures and the plaited canoe of Michael Singer, hidden in the woods, as a 'secret' work, the literal inversion of his Nevada lightning rods. In another sense, it is close to the work of the 'drawing' sculptors such as Alain Kirili, Nigel Hall and Michael Gitlin, yet making no compromises with surrounding space or any other arts, except perhaps mathematics and engineering. Commentators have indicated the 'classical' qualities of such a celebration of measurement. Yet the process of making, the futility of the line itself and the thought of directing it toward the centre of the earth seem to contain elements of threat and the corporate need to 'bury' it. The catalogue quotes de Maria as saying, 'The vertical earth kilometer will make people think about the earth and their place in the universe.'

Though I have concentrated on alterations in ways of looking at object art, reference must be made to video, film, performance and photography as presented by the Documenta catalogue, since approaches to these are at the heart of those shifts. When Evelyn Weiss decided to mount a full-scale historical exhibition of photography, she was taking the medium most 'wrapped in life', lassoing it with the 'myth' of art history and stifling it. One purpose of Documenta is education; it *documents.* The German public is serious in wanting to know about new work. Apart from one or two inclusions, such as Neal Slavin and Eve Sonnemann, however, it is impossible to tell from this section where photography *is* in 1977. A subsection entitled 'Reflection and Extension of the Medium' (Boltanski, Mac Adams, Duane Michals, Ger van Elk etc.,) does not show change in the medium, but simply the medium being used. This should serve as a warning against the formalism that is stifling it. The glamour and elegance of this category are not qualities shown by Les Krims, who should sue for misrepresentation. He does not 'reflect and extend' but is a craftsman staging his photographs for violent effect. (One comparison would be with Weegee in the Documentation section.) The lush colour, fake blood and Hollywood chic of the other members of the section are subverted by Krims, who deserves an 'Unaffiliated', if nothing else. But in Documenta no artist is unaffiliated. Krims chooses to show a man on a pedestal, screaming for all he's worth. The fault with the text on performance by Joachim Diederichs is that it seems to have too little to do with the works (which include Bruce McLean and Reindeer Werk from England and Jared Bark and Joan Jonas from the US). Ulrich Gregor's 'Film of the Seventies' section is compromised by an over-historical approach, veering back to the 'roots' of realism and Surrealism as well as trying to annotate critical terms such as 'deep focus' and 'montage'. One subsection on film and other media (Kubrick's *Barry Lyndon*, Visconti's *Death in Venice*, Rohmer's *Marquise of O*) is particularly relevant to the event as a whole, as is the small sub-section 'Film about Film', more appropriately amalgamated with Birgit Hein's intelligent 'Experimental Film'. Only in the excellent video section was a full-scale investigation into the relationship to TV and film carried out. This was supported not only with material from this section itself (Serra's *Television Delivers People*, a reasoned political argument in the form of a TV 'interlude', Chris Burden's *Promo*, a use of advertisement form, Ant Farm's *Media Burn*, a fake news report of an event in which a 1959 Cadillac drives through a blazing pile of TV sets, William Wegman's *Hopeless Golfer*, a mock 'training' film about his dog Man Ray, and Willie Boy Walker's *Life With Video*, showing how to have sex with a TV announcer while he is still on TV, starring William Walker himself as Captain Video), but also with the felt TVs of Beuys in a nearby museum, Chris Burden's reconstruction of a primitive TV apparatus, and many other references in catalogue texts.

In addition to Wolf Herzogenrath's Videotheque (far preferable to the baroque 'Video Installations/Sculptures' section, with its elaborate technology and eccentrically shaped viewing areas) three sections not only supported the thesis of Documenta 6 in its entirety, but also presented a reasoned and self-sufficient statement on media. Of these the least complex was Rolf Dittmar's 'Metamorphoses of the Book', a full-scale examination of how artists have taken on one form and subjected it to their own vision. Klaus Staeck, whose work elsewhere consists of placards in the streets of Kassel itself, comments not only on the book but on Documenta as a whole with *Art of the Sixties*, the expanding catalogue of the famous Ludwig collection of sixties art bolted and partly buried to resemble a headstone. 'Without a doubt we have entered the age of illiterates', wrote Reinhold

Hohl in *Pantheon*, contrasting these 'books' with their early modern counterparts. Artists such as Staeck prove him wrong, though one floor of a large building completely packed with unreadable 'transformations' of the book (to quote Lucas Samaras, the most notable omission) is a daunting proposition.

Gerhard Bort's 'Utopian Design' focuses on the car and is divided into two sub-sections, 'Construction and Design' and 'Artists' Cars'. Again there are fruitful comparisons to be made with other sections; the General Motors designs are actually drawn with the help of computers, for example. Experimental machines made by Paul Jaray are displayed alongside the futuristic doodles of Syd Mead, a professional designer, and the artists' vehicles, some of which (those of Don Potts) are embodiments of speed, while others the Gianni Piacentino) cannot move. Piacentino's wheel-less wonder is an extreme case, admittedly; more usual is the discovery of shared ground between artist and designer. The Belgian Panamarenko insisted that his car was 'not art' because it was 'logically devised'.

The third of the important 'topic' sections is Gunter Metken's 'Human Archaeology', with the most useful and concise of all the catalogue essays to explain the interplay of disciplined scientific knowledge and 'artistic' intuition found in the work of Nicholas Lang, Dorothee Windheim and others, who explore a number of areas, including geology, ethnology, fresco restoration, biology and physics. The most popular of the exhibits are those of Charles Simonds, a clay landscape for one of his imaginary races of tiny people, and Anne and Patrick Poirier, who have built the town of Ausée as part of their continuing *Domus Aurea*. In semi-darkness the model of a ruined classical island city lies surrounded with water, constructed according to an imaginative but scholarly interpretation of classical texts, a Romantic enterprise of extraordinary scope and power.

One aspect of Documenta that the catalogue cannot include is the stars, such as Beuys, whose face dominates the entire event. He and Serra (who appears in Drawing, Sculpture and Video), Chris Burden (who features in Sculpture, Video and Performance) and Robert Morris (who shows work in Video, Sculpture and Drawing), are the great antidotes to Middle Ground attitudes, forcing us to 'look' at a flexible type of virtuosity, an inventive mind, rather than the eggs-in-one-basket brilliance of a Twombly or a Bacon, the artist as inventor and social force rather than as narrowly 'gifted' individual. It is refreshing to find something that the catalogue cannot contain.

If Documenta offers the choice of gazing thunderstruck at scale or superficies, or devising rickety conceptual edifices, clearly a gap exists between viewers, coerced into the former approach, and critics, condemned to the latter. Both want that lively buzz of effortless triumph over media that properly belongs to artists, mystics and skateboarders. Straining for this by gawping parodies the freedom of a mind engaged in automotor activities, so utterly 'wrapped in life' that self-consciousness holds no sway. The organizers never tire of repeating that the seventies means pluralism. Pluralism's major assumption is that the artists choose any personal game to body forth sheer contemporaneity.

Documenta has a double standard, restating the avant-garde but attracted to the reactionary Middle Ground during lapses of pluralist vigilance. At certain points 'theories' collide. One of these points is individuality. Middle Ground thinking supports a history-book approach to greatness, accompanied by an urge to debunk, while pluralist avant-garders, intent on losing themselves in play, paradoxically sign works to distinguish their games from those of others. The German critic Yvonne Friedrich suggested that the dominance of drawing heralded art's withdrawal into a 'private world'. Is this the result of aping the unapproachability of the Genius, that Middle Grounder *par excellence*, or a device to continue the game despite distractions, a brazen attempt to confront the Duchampian realization that however great, interesting, significant or polysemic a work may be, its meaning can be altered dramatically by context? The East Germans' request to be shown together may be a protest at the rampant individualism of the rest.

Documenta could be seen as the debris of business activities that have ousted art. Huizinga's attitude seems more appropriate – a fascination at the replacement of ordered meaning by elegant kitsch. Huizinga's meditations were nostalgic modernist élitism. Since modernism has ended, perhaps the same repertoire of empty gestures is being ransacked and the Middle Ground is winning. Preoccupation with media may be the remnant of a dead vocabulary rather than a fundamental research. Yet modernism itself rose from the ashes of dead movements.

Could the encroaching 'privacy' be more sinister? The strangeness of Aycock's reference to Gilles de Rais, the punch-drunk quality of de Maria's blank rod, or Serra's charcoal wall is also present as an audience watches Brisley's humiliation, a Paul Sharits film of epilectics having fits, or those desperate washes of Eva Hesse, pierced by scores of tiny nylon threads.

In the Drawing section it is perceptible in the hectic pyramids of Agnes Denes, the horror vacui of Öyvind Fahlström (who died last year), and the superb dragon triptych of Ursula Schulze-Bluhm, as well as in the utopian perfection of Will Insley's imaginary spaces. In Environments it takes the form of paralysing the spectator. Achim Freyer makes us look through a door at an allegorical image of present-day Germany, while Anne Oppermann in *To Be an Artist* imprisons us in a terrifying private shrine crammed with thousands of obsessive objects. Jochen Gerz, another of the best of the German entries, took a sixteen-day journey on the Trans-Siberian Express, remaining in a closed carriage and destroying the notebooks he kept.

One clue can be found in a huge Arakawa drawing, *Sketch for an Anatomy of the Signified or if . . . Part 1*. Pencilled in small letters is 'Isn't it almost that any thought is a form of hysteria?' The avant-garde artist has traditionally identified with the oppressed. (When a visitor to his Free University accused him of acting condescendingly by sitting and talking about minorities every day, and concluded with the assertion 'No-one in this room is a depressed person', Beuys called for the microphone. 'I am depressed, repressed and suppressed', he announced.) In a situation that encourages extreme individualism as well as seeking to enmesh even the most tentative of experiments in terminology and categories, an exhibition that examines the ways that art talks about itself, it is hardly surprising that a leaning towards madness takes the form of a mistrust of rationality. This particular madness is not exciting or heroic but sullen and uncommunicative, numbed by constant sedation. It is as apparent in the art itself as in the reaction it tries to provoke in the viewer. If this is a 'new sensibility', it is a disturbing one, best understood by looking at the work of one British sculptor.

Grey and helpless, the pat-a-cake lobotomy cases of John Davies rest on their haunches in a group that embarrasses the viewer by simultaneously excluding him and appealing for help. Not necessarily docile, they may turn nasty. Luckily there is a protective barrier, as in a zoo. The figures look as if they might play a game, but they do not know any and could not understand the rules. They are simply waiting for a thought to occur.

Once there was a Trip. Hand in hand, they wandered down back streets in their shabby, stinking suits. Suddenly a boy walked up, fit and young, put down a wheeled board, then floated as if by magic. When they can think at all, they want to be that boy, even with their wonky limbs, or at least be there once more, looking with their mouths open. Sometimes no ideas come. The days seem longer now and the nurses don't take them on trips any more.

Translations are by the author from the Documenta catalogue. Remarks originally made in languages other than German are therefore retranslated. The author would like to thank Johannes Weissert of the Goethe Institut, London, for assistance in finding material.

Imogen Cunningham

Review of exhibition at the Photographers' Gallery, London, published in Artscribe *8, 1977.*

Predictably, Imogen Cunningham was a victim of her audience's patriarchal attitudes. Dorothea Lange told her, 'I suppose you'll be remembered for your plant photographs.' The weariness this suggests is underscored by her own comment on *Magnolia Blossom*: 'Some people think I never did another flower.' The recent Photographers' Gallery retrospective naturally contained the burgeoning magnolia, vulnerable and innocent, admittedly, but also ambiguously proud in the display of its centre, with the promise of a deeper revelation within the protected shape we are permitted to see. Forty years before Judy Chicago's analyses of imagery specific to women, Cunningham had conducted her own.

Resistance to sexual prejudice marks her career. Photographs taken in 1915 of her husband, Roi Partridge, nude on Mount Rainier caused such uproar when exhibited that she hid the negatives for over fifty years. In her earlier work mythical gentlemen knelt to unbending maidens in gestures of supplication. An assignment for *Vanity Fair* in 1932 suited her well. It consisted of photographing 'ugly men', and her inclusion of James Cagney and Spencer Tracy prefigured more recent tastes. She is irked by masculine over-confidence; the treatment of Edward Weston is never without irony, and her portrait of Man Ray must have dented his reputation as a ladykiller, even as late as 1960. At the same time her admiration for women is unfeigned, whether simply of their bodies, as in three nudes from 1968, or their intelligence, as in the study of Anna Freud, or both. Gertrude Stein, the most honoured face of modernism, is temporarily docile, without a trace of eccentricity. Ageless as always, she faces the camera passively, the decorative folds of the flowery curtain, the angled pattern of her tweed skirt and the prettiness of the designs on her waistcoat fading into insignificance as the eye is drawn like a magnet to her face – which defies definitions of beauty or ugliness in exactly the way that Cunningham admired. Martha Graham, who called Cunningham the only photographer for whom she could 'create', enacts ritualized gestures that move in a realm far beyond the emotions they symbolize. Unlike Barbara Morgan's shots of Martha Graham, these are not good dance photographs, absorbed as they are with the spectacle of a woman as enclosed in an art of her own devising as any temple dancer. Severely stylized, *Helena Mayer, Fencer* of 1935 alludes to a similar devotion to a disciplined pattern of behaviour, suggested in this case by allusions to medieval chivalry.

The 'straight' approach, wrapping her subjects about with suggestions of their work, the place they have half accepted, half devised for themselves in society, gives Cunningham's productions a quiet but vigilant moral aspect. She is not a plant photographer simply but a woman 'hung up on people', as she herself explained. The density of meaning achieved in *Northwest Native* (1934) is not the result of perfect composition alone but also of a startling area of shadow, as in the famous portrait of Amédée Ozenfant's wife, confusing the distances and angles of the wooden seat in the foreground, a feeling that everything that is important to *see* about this man has been set down faithfully, but, more than any of these, a serenity produced partly by the native himself but more distinctly by Cunningham's willingness to take her own time with him as both person and subject. The poise of the whole study is not 'sensitive' or 'aesthetic', as in her work before the twenties, but is an outward token, an intermediary between photographer and native – and by implication between ourselves and other people we shall know better. More than that, it is pleasurable because of the unusual quality of the emotion it summons up. As Pound wrote of a Joyce short story, it is a 'vivid waiting'.

Bath (1925) holds us by complexity of composition. The central nude presenting her back to the viewer is placed slightly left of centre, framed by two verticals that make a 'stage' for the bath and her slippers beside it. Like a veil, the bare branches in a round pot establish a plane very near us, playing tricks with relative depths beyond, seeming to echo the prevention of the sharply angled wall on the left and leading through one ill-defined room to another on the right, which we are not allowed to see. The balance between intimacy and spare, oriental elegance, between 'staging' and prying, invitation and coolness, makes her seem the guardian of a secret to which we may finally be granted access.

In 1910 Imogen Cunningham was on her way back from Germany when she caught her first glimpse of Alfred Stieglitz at the 291 Gallery. She was too frightened of him to speak. Twenty-four years later she photographed him with his own camera, which he taught her to use. Magisterial as ever in a coat like an academic gown, his white hair curling elegantly and his wire spectacles firmly attached to his face, he flinches at her view, carrying his hands awkwardly and glancing in an embarrassed way at the strange woman who may be making mistakes. We see a precise, unlovable person lacking in humour or fellow-feeling, more at home with objects than with people. This is not the man who wooed and won Georgia O'Keeffe in a series of confrontations unequalled by Bogart, Bacall and a team of Hollywood scriptwriters, then photographed her face and body in a progressive visual infatuation that offered a tangible parallel to the loosening of inhibitions he had masterminded as the self-styled John the Baptist of American modernism. Rather it is the disappointed editor who wandered broken-hearted around his deserted gallery for a year, picking up mail and brooding over the decline of *Camera Work*, the most beautiful magazine of the twentieth century, sold cheaply for pulp when subscriptions dwindled. He has been hurt and is careful not to be hurt again, a defiant spirit broken and prepared at any time to retract and withdraw into silence, his pedantry merely a defence against the real or imagined forces that oppose him. Cunningham herself liked this portrait. 'It has that grim little look in the eye,' she said, 'disliking everything and everybody.' Yet she makes us feel a potential in Stieglitz, a refusal to budge that has to do with sureness and talent and is unshaken by circumstance and the bad weather of daily life. No conflict is taking place before us; with Cunningham as guide we wait patiently for the truth to show itself.

This waiting is essential to Imogen Cunningham's art, so diverse that it forms a history of photography from 1901, when she took her first photograph, to the present. It is no accident that San Francisco, her home, is in so many respects a gateway to oriental culture and attitudes or that, in the context of a retrospective such as this, the *Magnolia Blossom* looks denser and more enigmatic than ever.

Simone Forti: A State of Dance

Unpublished. An account of Big Room*, which toured three venues in Britain, October 1977.*

In October the American dancer Simone Forti was in Britain for the first time, appearing at the Museum of Modern Art, Oxford, Arnolfini in Bristol, and the Third Eye Centre in Glasgow. Despite her distinction as a pioneer in avant-garde performance, press coverage was minimal during her week-long tour. Was this because she neglected London? Could it have been sheer rudeness on the part of the reviewers? A third, kinder reason could be that although what Simone Forti does is wonderful, the problem is to explain its power, or even to describe it. Consisting as it does of movement she herself has discovered, trained her body to perform, then perfected by constant practice, her dance is marked by a humility that resides in function, a complete subordination of style to method. Her opposite would be Twyla Tharp, whose idiosyncratic stylization is imposed like a grille on pre-existing choreographic languages. Whereas Tharp's style is about control, Forti's is about liberation. 'I think there's a state of dancing,' she wrote, 'like there's a state of sleeping or a state of shivering.'

Sixties prentice-work led Forti to regard the dance state as a means of holding rational thought in abeyance. For the duration of a piece called *Rollers* two singers sat in open boxes with swivelled wheels and ropes attached, with a group of people tugging them violently in all directions. Though 'excitement bordering on fear', the phrase used to describe the singers' feelings, hints at a dispersal of concentration, the dance experiments served rather as a way of winning through to a heightened awareness of sense impressions. In *Accompaniment for La Monte's Two Sounds*, a man rode in a loop of rope, staying in it until it had wound and unwound itself completely. By the end of the ride he had undergone his ritual preparation and hung still, listening to the tape of La Monte Young's music.

For Simone Forti dance is not only a release from the constraints of rationality but also a method of leading the body towards a state of heightened awareness of both internal and external stimuli. In *Handbook in Motion*, published in 1974, she explains some of the sources of her present style, with its use of systole/diastole rhythms and obsessive repetition of 'play' gestures. The wish to run into the centre of whirlwinds, the employment of T'ai Chi and drugs, her experience as a nursery school teacher and her patient study of animals in zoos are all brought together in a type of dancing that depends on a hotline from body to mind, and on a concentration different from that which day-to-day perception demands. She found that both children and animals could unfocus their minds so that 'feedback' from gestures was allowed to direct their bodies; passive awareness of movement permitted them to lapse into a condition where their 'automatic pilot' took over. They would repeat simple movements again and again, like the polar bear rocking from side to side as he sits. 'It seems to me', she writes, 'that when the polar bear swings his head, he is in a dance state. He is in a state of establishing measure, and of communication with the forces of which he is a part.'

Big Room, the piece performed in Britain, demonstrated how the establishment of measure pervades Forti's conception of her art. A series of exercises to cover, occupy and inscribe the available space is offered as a private attempt to attain that state of equilibrium, that central axis of sincerity which Pound so admired in *The Unwobbling Pivot* of Confucius; a clarifying activity which is 'the great root of the universe'. The dance does not exist to show 'steps' or to present the dancer as individual, though it would look different if anyone else were to perform it. Purpose overrides personality. How well the movements are carried out is immaterial; their beauty arises from constant use, the wearing away of everything unimportant. It is unified only by the place and the performer. Music is not strictly necessary since percussive effects are produced with the bare feet. Yet because it involves an activity akin to prayer or self-hypnosis, the music is there to inspire the dancer, or persuade her into a mood of willing sacrifice of identity. In an elementary way the buzzing, tingling aural effects of Peter Van Riper's music tell the audience something of the processes of the dance. My guess is that, because of basic similarities of approach, Simone Forti's collaboration with Charlemagne Palestine may have resulted in a more integrated creation. In a recent interview Palestine described his whole career as an alchemical transmutation into a 'golden sonority'. There will also be a magic quality of perfection in the absolute measure at the heart of Forti's movements, an abstraction most easily defined not as an essence arrived at by penetrating superficies to reach a core of idea, but by meditating on the aura surrounding the gestures.

Simone Forti is a short, dignified figure. She enters and prepares herself, sitting patiently while four notes are repeated in varying keys and patterns, first on one instrument, then another. After a while she rolls across the room from end to end, forcing us to notice the momentum of the upswing. Then she runs to and fro, slowing, retreating and turning at the ends of the room but gathering impetus at the centre, as if dangling from a rope that hangs from the ceiling. Describing the perimeter of her space at a fast walk, thumping her feet flat on the floor, she lengthens her stride, heightens the swing of her arms and falls into a Groucho Marx lope which reaches down to the floor as her paces become too large for comfort. Then, taking the longest step possible, she holds it for a time, like a fencer's lunge, before toppling over sideways. Spiralling ever faster towards an imaginary centre, she employs one hand to push aside obstacles, while the thumb and forefinger of the other keep tight hold of an invisible string. Suddenly breaking away from this vortex, she reverses, turning her motion into an infinity symbol, and repeats the exercise. A musical phrase of eight notes is answered with a leaping movement in eight paces, danced quickly from end to end of the room as well as diagonally across it, finishing at an 'edge' which tips her on her back, jerking her legs spasmodically like a galvanized frog. Animal parallels are plentiful. Plunging the mind back into the body, Forti has found out how to forage like a pig, crawl on her belly like a snake, shake her mane like a horse, spring like a kangaroo, circle endlessly like a fly. The heart of her dance is the source of these movements. As the music reaches a vivid luminescence, holding single notes while a furious continuo is maintained, utilizing the acoustics of the big room so that the notes echo and re-echo, new ones rebounding off the old to create an active wall of sound and its after-image, she seems to attain a state of absolute immersion in her body, so that particular movements can expand according to innate rhythms and inherent patterns, those (perhaps) of physical being itself. Thus, what Simone Forti shows is not movement *by* the body but *of* it, movement embodied. Circles, spirals, surges to and from a central point are intrinsic to her work, conveying 'cyclical momentum', a term that seems so obscure in her writings yet so obvious when her work is experienced. She is exploring the energy centre itself, the mid-point of equilibrium where hovering and stillness, inner and outer measure, are one.

Forti's approach to dance seems so stripped of theatre and rhetoric that it resembles no other. The polar bears she watched were bored; their walks led nowhere. Similarly, her works lack catharsis, 'point' or conclusion, all part of a cluster of profit-based Western attitudes that she deliberately ignores. In a famous poem Rilke saw the perfection of a Greek torso as a permanent rebuke. 'Du mußt dein Leben ändern', it tells him: 'You must change your life.' Whether intention or not, the presence of spectators weaned on the assumptions of rationalist thought makes *Big Room* didactic, an anthology of survival techniques instructing us in what dance could be if we let it change our lives.

Egon Schiele

Review of an exhibition at Serge Sabarsky Gallery, New York, published in Arts Magazine, *vol. 53, no. 2, October 1978.*

Personal vanity is part of the Schiele legend. Abjectly poor, he would wear imitation starched collars cut out of paper. Teachers dismissed young Egon as affected, noting with disapproval the way he knotted his long fingers. More sympathetically, Heinrich Benesch described those 'large, dark, astonished eyes', 'the earnest, almost sad expression, as if he were suffering from an inner grief' and 'a personality of such markedly pronounced unusualness that its mere presence might not be pleasing to everyone'; not even to its owner, perhaps. One photograph shows him contemplating his reflection in a full-length mirror, half suspicious, half afraid.

Schiele carried the mirror from one shabby lodging to another. Confronting it, he would screw up his eyes – ironically, 'schielen' means 'to squint' – maintaining an uneasy compromise between the isolation of unseeing and the titillation of being observed. Naked before it, he would preen and dance, whipping his black hair from side to side. His self-absorption resulted in drawings in which he paraded as the outward cipher of deep emotions, so fully indulged that for a moment he became a monk, an angel, an odalisque, an aristocrat or a martyr, drawings in which he flinched with pain beneath an imagined lash or lay swooning, the idealized object of his own desire, exhausted from self-love. Intensely private, flagrantly public, it was a strategy to seduce himself.

Despite Schiele's undeniable good looks, narcissism alone scarcely accounts for the plethora of self-portraits in his brief career. As a child, he was compelled to watch his father going insane; Schiele *père* contracted syphilis, refused to have it treated, then infected his wife, whose first three children were stillborn. Perhaps the ravages of an intangible disease that claimed mind and body alike left Egon on the lookout for symptoms and for ways of preventing decay. Sometimes he painted himself as a raddled, screaming crone. Perhaps it also made him regard sitters as patients humiliated by a prying surgeon; he was allowed to visit Erwin Graff's clinic to sketch pregnant women, sick young girls and babies. It is possible, however, to attach undue importance to a 'degenerate' Schiele. At the age of twenty-one he wrote eloquently of the co-existence of growth and destruction. He is neither a Kafkaesque hunger artist whose death coincided with the decline of the Austro-Hungarian Empire itself, nor a stern realist enamoured of nature and organic growth, but both, regarding his own position as subject to unceasing change.

The self-portraits assembled at the Sabarsky Gallery to honour the sixtieth anniversary of Schiele's death display all the characteristics of his draughtsmanship: violent foreshortening, the omission of supports for figures, a tendency to encircle figures with 'astral' light, a deployment of empty spaces derived from Japanese prints, an incessant emphasis on physical and emotional tension and a puzzling application of colour. One major style is etiolated and arthritic, with bones protruding from beneath taut skin. Another, the prototype of his late, ignored, near-Matissean method, consists of thick strokes punctuated by tufts of hair and decorative scribbles. New approaches to anatomy are discovered – vertebrae as an open seed pod or the lower spine as a laced corset. Despite such particularity of vision, terse, infrequent titling suggests a universal frame of reference.

These were underground drawings. During his lifetime Schiele was the victim of hypocrisy and prejudice, jailed for offences against children and forced to watch a judge burning his work. In the self-portraits he regards masturbation as both a theme and a metaphor for the gesture of creation. The spectator adopts the role of voyeur, watching Schiele make love – discovered sitting on the floor in a state of undress, as a young god gazing dolefully over the shoulder of a doting nymph or, in a startling reversal, at the point of sexual climax, with a girl peering out from below, he oblivious, she angry at our intrusion. Yet part of the motivation for the works is to allow their maker to pre-empt our situation of excited meditation. As always, his approach is selfish; we are persuaded to allow him to return to his place in front of the mirror. In return he lets us look over his shoulder and glimpse our own reflection.

Pie-slicing and Small Moves: a conversation with Morton Feldman

Published in Artscribe *11, April 1978; republished on the Morton Feldman study site, www.cnvill.demon.co.uk/mftexts.htm and in* Morton Feldman Says, *Hyphen Press 2006*

'I don't know what a composer is', said Morton Feldman two years ago. 'I never knew as a young man, I don't know now and I'm gonna be fifty next month.' Feldman (at present Edgard Varèse Professor of Music at the State University of New York at Buffalo) studied composition with Wallingford Riegger and Stefan Wolpe. In New York in the fifties he met John Cage and joined a circle that included Earle Brown, Christian Wolff and pianist David Tudor. A second major influence was painting; friendships with Rothko, Kline, Pollock, Guston and de Kooning are commemorated in his music. 'What was great about the fifties,' he wrote in 1971, 'is that for one brief moment – maybe, say, six weeks – nobody understood art. That's why it all happened. Because for a short while these people were left alone. Six weeks is all it takes to get started.' Interviewed five years later, he made the same point but reduced the period of time to a week. 'But the week was important . . . we began to listen . . .' Operating at the edges of the audible, his music seems to re-create this process of composition by listening. Interviewers have compared it with his conversation; long silences occur while he puffs hard at a cigarette and patiently unravels an idea that suggested itself because it needed to be said. Hesitantly, repetitively, he allows it to emerge. Serious talk is a pleasure for him, but a private pleasure. He uses his interlocutor to prompt an even denser monologue. 'Everybody has to learn what it is to be lonely again . . . That's why, WHO said it recently? I think it was Paul Valéry, that when something is beautiful, it is tragic. And I think the implication for me as I see it is that something that is beautiful is made in isolation. And tragedy in a sense is a kind of psychic flavour of this loneliness.'

Feldman admires hard work. 'If Cage comes to stay he will wake you up at 7.30 to ask if you have a dictionary. It will take us ten years to catch up with the things he's doing now.' Titles such as *Routine Investigations* and *Elemental Procedures* focus on the 'small moves' of a daily life in art. In his private pantheon Seurat, Giorgione, Rembrandt, Piero della Francesca are guided towards exact measurement and precise judgement by means of 'total sensuousness . . . total intuition', exemplified in the twentieth century by Mondrian. Tact informs Feldman's art criticism, which is meditative, daring and partisan. (See, for example, 'Some Elementary Questions', *Art News*, April 1967; 'After Modernism', *Art in America*, December 1971; and 'The Anxiety of Art', *Art in America,* September/October 1973.) A heightened sensitivity to time and the gradual progression of artistic careers underlies both his reminiscences ('Give my Regards to Eighth Street', *Art in America*, March/April 1971) and an eloquent tribute to his friend Frank O'Hara ('Frank O'Hara: Lost Times and Future Hopes', *Art in America*, March/April 1972). A preoccupation with images of life and death is evident in his images of creative work. 'What it really amounts to is whether you want to be in the work, in the medium or outside it . . . I feel that Cage and myself are in the work . . . Stockhausen and Boulez are out of it.' (Alan Beckett 'Morton Feldman', *International Times 3*, 14–27 November 1966). Later he elaborates: 'Secreted in Frank O'Hara's thought is the possibility that we create only as dead men . . . Death seems the only metaphor distant enough to truly measure our existence . . . Only the artist who is close to his own life gives us an art that is like death.' For Feldman, being 'in the work', 'close to life', seems to entail loss of some kind, perhaps a shedding of personal feeling. 'For the work to succeed, the artist must fail.'

Feldman's talk has been reported frequently and well. (See, for example, Gavin Bryars and Fred Orton, 'Morton Feldman', *Studio International*, November/December 1976, which covers both music and art; also Walter Zimmerman, 'Desert Plants', ARC Publications, Vancouver, 1976, pp.4–20.) Nevertheless, on a visit to London late last year he was reluctant to consent to an interview.

* * * * *

Stuart Morgan: *Why don't you like interviews?*

Morton Feldman: One of the things about interviews is that I made some remark in *Studio* about Rauschenberg's cardboard works, how chic they look, and I was very, very unhappy about it because it was to some degree out of context with what I was talking about and the interview didn't get into it. I think we have to talk about the history of the galleries sometimes as well as the history of art. What were the first galleries? I mean public galleries, not the Louvre which was a palace. I think the great economist Veblen talks about official architecture. In other words the campus where I'm teaching with the Greek columns, the pompousness of the official look of buildings and the whole history of the National Gallery or the Metropolitan Museum .... At the old Guggenheim, Sweeney framed every picture the same way, with a certain type of stripping no matter what. I like the look of the Tate – it's pretty seedy. The Whitechapel's a disaster, a caricature of a private place, and here we put art into it.

It's a problem that needs some discussion. And when I saw that Rauschenberg's cardboard art looks a little too chic on those walls, I feel it *does* look a little too chic. You get some kind of swank Milano gallery and you hang this thing there. It looks fantastic but it also robs from it. That's what I meant in that interview. Not that Rauschenberg was making chic art but what happens to the art when these sharpies get hold of it and start packaging. Orchestras are like galleries. A certain type of orchestra has a pretentiousness within its tone before it plays *your* tones. Its own delivery, its own attitude. That's like a gallery. I'm writing a lot of big pieces now. Even when they play softly, quietly, nicely it's still lost a lot; it's hanging in this streamlined gallery where you can't have an ashtray in the room because it would kill the room. You're fighting an insidious packaging conspiracy. At the same time I don't like that funky 'I-am-an-artist' look and 'This is an artist's painting so let's just slop it on the wall'. That's another kind of attitudinizing.

We're talking about intimacy, aren't we?

Which is non-existent in England. Most art in England is public art. England never really had a tradition of private art. Even someone like Anthony Caro would be a reduction of the monumentality of the English sculptural tradition of artists like Moore.

What is the relation of scale to intimacy?

No matter how smart we are, we still see things in clichés, we feel that something big is monumental. That's a delusion. I feel that scale is no barrier to intimate art. Just the other day I saw that gorgeous Watteau in the Wallace Collection, a large-scale painting that reaches unparalleled intimacy. A lot of people went into the big picture in terms of its design potential. It's as simple as that. Or just in terms of its look divorced from any other kind of connotation. I don't feel it's in Al Held's mind to make monumental paintings. You could have a big American painting and it could be intimate. It's very hard to have an intimate big European painting.

Is this intimacy what you've tried for in your music?
Always.
Do you still look at painting a lot?
It's very difficult for me to look at painting now without having a personal concern about the artist. I haven't been in anyone's studio for ten years. Without the personal involvement of the artist it goes into another – I wouldn't say criterion, but another . . . kind of ballpark.
But you have a remarkable feeling for Piero della Francesca, for example, or Mondrian.
Yes, but that's the other ballpark. I was looking at Piero again yesterday. I wonder what happens to the work when it goes into a gallery or a museum. It's confusing because it gains somehow.
Because it's out of time or because the mind is free to attach any meaning at all to it?
I think because it's dead. If we love someone and they die, they mean more because we've lost them. You understand how someone would love something from the past, if only because it's dead.
In your statements about music you talk a lot about 'dying away'.
Well, since I was a young man I always tried to work like a dead artist. How else can you get the objectivity?
Don't you feel this opposes any idea of modernism as contemporaneity, what Baudelaire talks about in 'The Painter of Modern Life', the feeling that you can enjoy something because it is of the present, like clothes or design?
I'm not exactly on Baudelaire's side.
What's the opposite side?
There isn't any.
But you're on it whatever it is. I would envisage the opposite side as someone like Greenberg, perhaps?
What would that be?
Greenberg seems to want to erect a perimeter around paintings. In 'Modernist Painting' he seems to want the same as Baudelaire. Baudelaire sees art as going on all the time. Greenberg seems to say 'Here's the perimeter. This is what modern art has decided it's about, which is its own conventions, its own set of rules. Having discovered this, artists in the future are free to do as they like.' This is obviously very paradoxical, as people have pointed out, but I feel that it's not Baudelairean. Baudelaire wasn't talking about fences.
But Baudelaire was also at the very early stages of a kind of art idealism and

didn't realize that the greatest danger to art is the artist. He didn't realize that the potential of the artist, especially in America, is to become like a Watergate lawyer.
Why?
Loopholes. It happens more and more as artists become educated. They become their own historians. After the fifties artists suffer from a historical consciousness. Picasso ingeniously cut up the rectangle. They ingeniously cut up the artistic space in which to fit. They were pie-slicing. They figured everything out perfectly and were too brilliant to become mannerists. Every era has a mannerist period and if they were living in another age they would move towards it but it's too difficult. You can't do that any more.
But after mannerism what?
You have to go on. Where I don't know. You just have to go on cutting up that pie.
But you're blaming *them for pie-slicing.*
I'm not really blaming them. They gotta do it or else. To realize that historical destiny, do it. Slash or else. What's annoying about it is knowing that you have to go on. Which brings us to an overly conscious period and the misreading of consciousness. It's very hard to understand what consciousness is; it's a double-edged thing. By being conscious you could see that the work appears to be going one way.
Consciousness of historical tradition?
Everything. It's not so much history as the nature of the work itself, the problem that you give yourself. You could see that it's going one way but because of the consciousness – the *it-ness* of consciousness – you then take it another way. One might call it a focus on the problem, or as John Cage would say, to ask the right question. And when you ask the right question of the work, you're conscious of the problem and then the work proceeds and consciousness has a decision. It decides whether to go on with what appears to be where it's going or whether to divert it somewhere else. Now everything I say is not a negative. I'm not attacking anybody. Unlike my time when I was a young man a level of consciousness was more concerned with directing it on the right path. So, say, in painting the placement would be elegant, the space around it would be just right. Everything about it would have a feeling of 'This is it', which is the fifties.
So the fifties meant focusing on a completely new set of problems?
But it took it on the right path. I feel that now there's a fork in the road and

the choice could be to divert it.
Is that the choice facing you?
Yes, actually.
What are you going to do?
Well, for the last few years I'm involved in diverting it. I feel we have no control any more over the whole aspect of problem-solving even though the problems are invented by ourselves and solved by ourselves.
Why is this?
The father of cybernetics, Norbert Wiener, has a phrase, 'the hardening of the categories'. Things are neither open the way Baudelaire idealized it and neither are things going around like . . . I think Clem Greenberg was too influenced by the structure of the London subways. A well-working loop, wouldn't you say? (Actually it was invented by an American.) There is a discrepancy between what appears to be an open situation, a situation in which Baudelaire and Greenberg happily meet, and on the other hand a situation where, if you want to do something else, you're forbidden. I'm not just talking about the opening up of new problems. I mean problem-solving going in the right way. Barney Newman's line was just in the right place. Motherwell's shape was absolute perfection. Tworkov left open just that which should be left open. Guston had an incredible repertoire of the open picture and the finished picture. I think what they had in the fifties was that right amount that individual pictures should have, which really couldn't be said of any other period in history. It had to be a very personal painting that had that in the past. The fresh pictures are like the fantastic picture I saw the other day, the Giorgione with the two saints. It could be an Abstract Expressionist picture in terms of amounts.
You're not afraid of using taste terms such as 'elegant'. Although modernism seems to bring with it an aspect of destruction, your words seem always to refer to creation, building things up, realizing a personal consciousness.
I think there's very important work that never destroyed. Seurat never destroyed. And his twentieth-century counterpart, Jasper Johns, never destroyed. Rauschenberg never really destroyed. But 'destroy' is the wrong word. When a painting looks as if it's being destroyed, the painter is really looking for something.
What's he looking for?
For the painting. Like de Kooning.
Is this the function of violence in de Kooning?

You're watching him make connections.

You wrote of de Kooning that part of his greatness lay in his ability to do six different things on six different days.

I compared him to Matisse. He found a life in art rather than getting up and doing that same thing. Cy Twombly is another example. I was with Twombly recently in Rome. I spent three days there and saw a lot of his work. I was just knocked over. Just knocked over. I have a student who is very interested in horse-racing. I'm just convinced that Twombly is the big long-shot of our era. I feel closer to Twombly and Johns and Rauschenberg than I ever have in my life.

You wrote an opera recently.

It's not really like an opera. It's a little over an hour, to a gorgeous poem that Beckett wrote for me. And it's that classic Beckett theme . . .

. . . which you almost paraphrased earlier when you spoke about 'going on' after mannerism.

The theme interests me tremendously because it's very close to my own thinking. The poem is called 'Neither' and if I may paraphrase it, it has to do with the fact – it's not a narrative, it becomes like a narrative – that there is no understanding of the self or the un-self; nor is there a synthesis. They're both on the outer shadows. We go back and forth between them. We keep on going back and forth. It became a narrative in defining a musical proximity to this thought. It was a lot of fun watching the production. Pistoletto did the . . .

Sets?

I don't know what you'd call them. He did something. A different situation for each production, I saw too. There were about six. The first one I didn't like. He said it looked better without the audience. He had people walking at a distance, back and forth on the stage. A little too fancy. A little too sixties. All these people discovering their own space, about 25 or 30 of them.

How many characters?

One. It was great fun. The audience was screaming and booing for an hour. They couldn't stand it. Actually, the orchestration is crazy and quite scary. I was freaked out a little bit when *I* heard it. But after ten minutes, as soon as the girl sang – and she's the most beautiful part of the orchestration – they associated the female voice with opera and started to boo. And every time this lovely singer sang, which I thought the most accessible parts of the opera, that's when they went berserk. Martha Hanneman has a very sad effortless voice without too much colour in it, evoking some kind of lost world. She's simply tremendous. Lisa Wertmueller was at the opera and I was very happy that she caught the dichotomy between this lost world of the voice and the more ominous world of the music.

How long have you felt close to Beckett's writings?

Late. Again he was an aspect of . . . you see, I was such a modernist myself that I kind of avoided anything . . . even though he's twenty years older than me, in New York we felt he was a contemporary because he was published at the same time as we were all growing up. In Grove Press. So he was very much a part of our life. After meeting him in Berlin I didn't know if he was going to send me anything or not. When I got back I was at the University of California, Los Angeles with John Cage. And Jasper Johns was there. It turned out that Jasper Johns had just written a book with Beckett which is a whole series of prints and Beckett writing the commentaries. So it was actually 'in the air'.

There's a recurring theme in your writing. You say that the only thing necessary for a complete change in art is to have a short period when no one knows anything. Is this how you felt about your experience in New York in the fifties?

I took the open environment very seriously. But it's impossible now. The over-educated attitude I've described spoilt that. After all, art is a life of small moves. And unless one has the kind of tolerance to watch Motherwell's small moves, you've had it after five or ten years. Mondrian's was a life of small moves. There's unbelievable change in Mondrian's work, his repertoire was very, very important to me. Now we see the brushstroke, and now we don't. Now we reveal this much, now we don't. Almost like a public and a private look and a schizophrenia between the intimacy and some kind of idealism. I've learned a lot through his life. My biggest complaint – and I have to quote Nietzsche on this one – 'The world of distinction is lost'. We no longer get concerned with distinction about the individual artist we are allegedly concerned with. We see big broad issues on an art magazine level.

So you feel a loss of creative openness?

When I'm teaching, one of the ways I always get a laugh is to say, 'Let's sit for a minute and concentrate where half of us is open and half of us is closed'.

Two interviews with Alice Aycock 'A certain image of something I like very much'

Published in Arts Magazine, *vol. 52, no. 2, March 1978.*

Stuart Morgan: *'Projects', your current exhibition at the Museum of Modern Art, consists of one new, finished work plus drawings and photographs of others, sometimes built and sometimes not. What is the status of a 'project' for you?*

Alice Aycock: There has always been a close relationship between the state of the carpentry or engineering skills I have and what I envision. Usually the drawing precedes the pieces, sometimes by as much as two years, but I try to catch up with them in some way. They also operate as a nudge; in each new work I try to take a little more in. Also – I'm a little bit schizophrenic about it – I feel it's a very humbling process. You can dream about it an awful lot but if you don't bring it into being, then you don't really know all the things that happen along the way and you also don't verify whether or not something really works. And because so many of the things have had historical references, when I go to build them I'm not in the same position as a great architect with infinite money and equipment at his disposal. I feel very serious about trying to bring it into being . . . . If it took someone thirty or forty years to build a pyramid with all the resources available to them, then they needed to do that awfully badly.

So the drawing exists in a state of desire and can be read as a sketch of the mental processes you're in control of at a given time.

Which I lose control of when the piece is built.

Did you invent the term 'psycho-sculpture'?

I started saying 'psycho-physical spaces' a couple of years ago, because it was the only way I could think of to describe the fact that the physical experience set off a psychological one, or that it was a combination of the two.

You're trying to isolate the phenomenological element in architecture, then, which would account for the clean look of your work; it doesn't have rust or dirt and it doesn't look medieval or classical, despite its connotations.

Right. To do that would be *too* self-conscious, though I feel I am getting more self-conscious. I feel I have to stay honest.

Is there a possibility that your work will grow more and more complex?
Yes, but I think it has almost reached the state where it will not get too much more complex. But now the writing adds a whole other element to it, and I'm trying to get as much going as possible.
Do you regard the storytelling as enmeshed with the work or as another thing entirely?
Meshed into it. There are three things going on now – the drawings, where I'm very conceptual; then there's executing them, where all kinds of pragmatic things happen and where you make decisions based not only on aesthetics but on millions of reasons, which often influence the next set of drawings; then there's the writing, which occurs both before and after and which kicks off more pieces too. If I start fantasising about a certain piece of architecture and then verbalize it, I often isolate an element which I use in another piece.
In the captions for the current show you keep going back to the same phrase, in which you say that you have been led by association to a completely new point. So as well as the sketches being impelled beyond their real state to one of desire, the physical existence and documentation of your pieces push the viewer toward associations. You act as a storyteller in an abandoned world, always ready to sit down and unlock your word-hoard, a pessimistic rigmarole. Is this too dismal an interpretation?
Well, I suppose that the feelings that motivate it are often very strong, at one time euphoric and deeply, deeply depressive – not tragic but melancholy.
You want to work directly on your viewer by inspiring him with fear, even with doubts about his sanity.
There is a state of free fall where you don't know up, down, left, right, backwards or forwards; they're totally confused. Those seem to me to be the six ways of orienting yourself. (That's taken from Borges.) What I would like to do is probably just disorient all those sensations. On the other hand, that also can be a very euphoric state; it can be very pleasing and people engage in all kinds of activities that involve this titillation (skydiving, amusement parks) . . . what are they all but ways of titillating yourself? They always have to do with whirling in space, for pleasure as much as for fear; you make yourself frightened so that you can enjoy it. For me things have that aspect.
Have you ever been an architect?
No, but it was all-pervasive; my father was in construction and from the time I was small I watched him. He wasn't a construction worker, he was a construction engineer, and I was just surrounded by all that. It was a first

imprint. So I never had any formal training; I was a *naïve*. I didn't hang around or go on jobs with him, but it was everywhere. Also, the concept of 'house' was very strong, a place of origin, a place where things occur that are somehow very deep and serious.

What feelings are most deeply involved with your process of creation?

I try to find a relationship between the way I might feel about something, not a piece of architecture but just an event, and use that as the basis for making something that I might love. But I have always loved the game of history and a kind of control exists. When you're looking at something two or three hundred years ago or a thousand years ago or even twenty-five years ago and you're sitting at your desk examining why Hitler did something and Stalin didn't, fear is kept out, held back. But also, when I have gone to archaeological sites, there's my experience of it and there's remembering. If I go to Mycenae I think of Agamemnon. They were people who had a life not so different from the life we live now. I find associations with my own life in what I've read. As a child, the best way to escape issues I didn't want to deal with was just to read, lose myself in a character.

The irony you mentioned is present in another of the terms applied to your work – 'pseudo-architecture'. Is that yours or someone else's?

Someone else's, and I think they meant it derogatorily. I decided that it wasn't and so I co-opted it. I'd been having a hard time describing what I wanted to convey, and was using the words 'true' and 'false' a great deal.

In Poetry and Science *of 1926, I.A. Richards suggests the term 'pseudo-truth' to describe the way that (as he saw it) science deals with real issues while truth in literature was true only within the perimeters of the work. Is it the same emotion I feel watching* Lear *as I'd feel watching my own father on a moor, half-naked and mad? In work like yours the very thin line between 'truth' and 'pseudo-truth', real and fictional feeling, is operating for us in a frightening way, because whenever we are unsure of where the line is to be drawn we are frightened. The state of uncertainty is also present in dreams.*

Titillation is present there too; at a certain point you don't want to be in that state. When I studied *King Lear* at college for an examination, I dreamt that play for eight nights in a row. It hounded me. I used literature to mediate. I was raised on Alfred Hitchcock and Poe. If I could distance myself enough I could use that to mediate certain kinds of terror in my own life. I was taught that if you can conceptualize it, concretize it in an idea or a character, outside yourself, you can handle it. Someone like Yvonne Rainer does that. Bachelard talks of Poe, who is also there in a way.

Smithson wrote parodies of Poe, Nauman drew underground rooms like those described in Poe . . .

At one point something underground is a protection, is secure, and at another point claustrophobic and has both those associations. The same is true of heights: a wavering between a euphoric, titillating state and a sensation of accessibility, being able to see everything and be above it, and a fear of throwing oneself over, falling, being out of control, and vertigo. The constant ambiguity between the two poles fascinates me.

Ortega y Gasset defined love in terms of movement toward a desired object. Your pieces are thrown up in your mind as a token of love which involves desire and movement towards an object. The work implicit in your sculptures is a labour of love. The sketches are only the signals of the state of your mind at that point. If the sculptures are tokens of work and love around work, they also seem to show the forces that can undermine love.

Undermine and underpin at the same time. I think what you say is true. I also try very hard for each piece to have a certain image of something I like very much. I call it a treat. It's a thing I want to have myself. And if I don't start a piece with that feeling – it's like a good book you want to have or a beautiful piece of jewellery, something good to eat, things you want very badly to own just for a while – then the piece doesn't work. I don't mean it's the whole piece; it might just be a part of it that organizes the rest somehow. I throw something out unless there's a treat somewhere in the piece.

The thin line we've been talking about, in terms of love for a person, would be the danger of wanting to possess them.

Well, there is one passage I love very much and it's what Oscar Wilde wrote to Lord Alfred Douglas from prison. It's very melodramatic: 'For my own part the only thing I could do was to love you. I knew that if I allowed myself to hate you, then in the dry desert of existence, over which I would have been forced to travel and am travelling still, every rock would lose its shadow, every palm tree be withered, every well of water prove poisoned at its source.'

What does that mean to you?

At that point in his life he was compelled in various ways beyond anything he knew was rational or sane toward self-destruction. But, morose and totally despairing as he was, he couldn't help betraying his delight. He had an enormously rich sense of the world which comes through despite it all.

'The Wonderful Pig of Knowledge'

Published by the Arts Council of Great Britain for the exhibition 'Alice Aycock and Louise Bourgeois', Serpentine Gallery, London, 1985

Stuart Morgan: *What was your first feeling of being you?*
Alice Aycock: The first sense of consciousness I had was standing in my crib – I must have been a year and a half old. I opened a drawer and there were all these socks inside. I'd pick up each one and suck the colour out. It was a glorious experience, as if I could suck it out with my eyes and it would ooze into my body. When I'd finished, I'd throw the remains on to the floor. There was always another sock. Then my mother came and started screaming at me. It was hard to feel guilty; the whole thing was pure pleasure. It was sensory and aesthetic simultaneously.
What was your first intellectual experience?
There was a certain point when I was about eleven or twelve when I began to know things intellectually for the first time. I thought that if I read enough books I would discover the secrets of the universe. I put myself through a concentrated effort to synthesize every piece of information that came in, to add it to the stream.
It seems that when you started to make art you brought the two together somehow. You once said that every work of yours had to contain a treat, an image of something you wanted very much. That accounts for the sensuality. Then there is the constant urge for intellectual synthesis, in the form of cross-referencing in your work, the compounding of one piece with another and the fact that every so often you manage to tie all the strands of your thinking together with a single work, like your The Machine That Makes the World *in 1980.*
Yes, that combined imagery of machines and texture and a house, and a maze, institutions and an amusement park . . . I have always been haunted by the Tempietto of Bramante. At graduate school I wrote a long paper on it, starting with the *tholos* tomb and moving up to it slowly. And I went to Greece and Italy specifically to see these things. Bramante made the Tempietto as a solidification of Renaissance ideas. I have a need to make something that clear and synthesized. Recently I feel like going back to the *Gestalt*. It's time to bear down on it. But you really have to travel though a lot before making something that crystallizes so many different ideas.

Oddly, in 1980, when your work reaches a high pitch of synthesis in one sense and you are able to sum up all your previous interests, it takes a quite different turn with the first of the 'How to Catch and Manufacture Ghosts' series. Who was the ghost in that machine?
The character who was N.N., from Geza Roheim, who seemed at home rambling through history, through walls, through matter and was not ashamed of his needs and desires. He was like a jellyfish, he could suck in and absorb a lot. I wasn't frightened of him. There is another character who is always at the back of my mind, in Calvino's *T Zero*, where there's a single-celled animal in the primal ocean. He wanders the universe as a unit of DNA, which somehow has a consciousness and never becomes inanimate.
Concentrating on what it means to be an individual, in the simplest possible way perhaps, must result from some anxiety of yours.
It is the death of consciousness that most frightens me.
Presumably this accounts for the real danger of your early works?
Those pieces recalled terror from a secure plane. Later I felt I had to let the self go to see what would happen, and tried to deal with that explicit moment in which you came face to face with a mindless force which I think of as a whirling that moves through the universe, almost like a vortex. (There's a lot of validation for this.) I call it 'the glance of eternity'.
What is it destroying?
Often nothing, but when it comes into contact with hard matter it reduces it to particles.
The whirling blades in your recent work must also relate somehow to the plough, one of the results of your investigations into the origins of the Industrial Revolution.
With the later work I became more and more convinced that killing and eating were irrevocably locked together, however much you want to whitewash it. Settling down in an agricultural community to secure your survival by knowing if the crops would come on a regular basis was also the invention of the bomb. The blade that tills the soil can also kill.
The blades are destructive but hypnotic too. You're deliberately thinking about oblivion and enjoying it.
It is seductive to bring this feeling on and it is the root of the work.
It is the work that stops you dwelling on it?
Usually.
This idea and lots more crop up in the novel you're working on, which is a

synthesis of all of those new stories that go with the art.

Something like that idea occurs in a chapter called 'The Wishbone Years', in which the characters ask the question Leonardo asked: 'Why did nature ordain that one animal should live by the death of another?' This is the chapter where we get 'In the beginning was the Word and the Word was made flesh'.

The book ends with a debate, doesn't it?

Between the Organ of Corti [*part of the inner ear*] and the Pig of Knowledge.

Who or what is *the Pig of Knowledge?*

He's the diagram of how Doges are elected in Venice – he's got that crest on his head; he's an attack system for a medieval fortress in Europe, he's a fan, he's the 52 decks of cards, he's the chicken story. Especially the chicken story.

He can't be all those things.

He is. He and Corti discuss the whole situation. The Pig is fluttering in the corner like birds do when they are in a room and they knock themselves against a wall.

Pigs don't flutter.

He's not a pig: he's a bird. He's really a bird. But he's a pig because he's so hungry. When you're ravenous for information you're a Pig of Knowledge. Einstein was a Pig of Knowledge – he wanted it so bad . . . . You know how birds keep knocking themselves against walls when they're inside rooms and they want to get out? Someone walks in and says 'I want to hear the vast flapping of the soon-to-be-belated bird.'

Are there any people *in the book?*

The only real character will probably be Sally Hemmings, Thomas Jefferson's black wife. She was also his first wife's half-sister. When Sally was sixteen Jefferson took her to Paris – it was at the time of the French Revolution – and they became lovers. For ever afterwards she …

Stop, stop. You promised to tell me about your dance dream.

It happened when I had come back from Europe and was on jet lag. Instead of going home to bed I went to the Roxy and stayed up all night dancing. And about three in the morning they started to play older music, rock music from a twenty-year history. I was feeling really good. They would change the music very rapidly, the way they do with break-dancing so that one tune would suddenly turn into another. It wasn't chronological. One time you were in the 1950s, the next time you were in the 1970s, then all at once you were in 1962. Quick quick quick quick quick. Each time I would have to change my body to remember those old dances and rhythms. It was fun to see how versatile I could be.

Then I went home and had this dream that I was dancing, but instead of its being the history of rock it was the history of all music throughout all time. And again it wasn't chronological and the periods kept changing. Every time the music altered, it was as if the whole physical and chronological structure of my body shifted, as if I was literally transformed each time. In my dream, of course, I could dance just effortlessly. So I thought really there *is* something to this because it's almost as though the rhythmic system of the brain or the nervous system is different from culture to culture, from one time to another, and that I was at the root of it – the physical, visceral root – when I was dancing, I felt no sense of tradition or nostalgia.

That got me back to the idea of what are the root structures of art. So one night I asked the I Ching what the root structure of art was and it came up with this fortune that said there were sounds in the air and those sounds were birds and trees and things like that. Then people began to move their bodies according to what was in the air. Then they began to make up rhythmic systems and dances, and from those dances they made music, and from the music they made theatre. And somewhere you get into the interlocking between language and art, between the action of the hand and the thought in the brain, between word and the feeling inside yourself, which is another sort of root structure.

This is where magic signs are particularly interesting. I have lots of books on magic signs, angels' and devils' handwriting, but you can find them in any standard alchemical manual. The ones I chose were the most curious and complex. They are desire first and foremost – pure feeling and pure need. Then they get made into a symbol which becomes the root of a certain kind of language that allows you to attain this desire. Then that started to get me back into thinking about making architecture out of hieroglyphs, which was something that interested me around 1980 – taking a hieroglyphic and literalizing it. The palm drawing is like that. Like looking at clouds and seeing images in them. What I did was to look into my hand and see different sorts of magic signs to start off with and then to see . . . Well, this one has palindromes; Solomon's seals; Mesopotamian devils' whirls, which have bits of Mesopotamian writing on them; another cabbalistic sign, Cleopatra's sign;

the angel Gabriel's handwriting. That's the Pythagorean theorem. That's the trench system in World War I. That's the Organ of Corti. This is the I Ching three-dimensionalized. This is a diagram of how the Doges are elected in Venice. There is the Big Bang theory and here is Tic-Tac-Toe. I kept throwing more and more in, as if I was going to see the entire universe in my hand.

In your MA dissertation on the definition of the American highway system you had three epigraphs. The first was from Joyce's Portrait of the Artist as a Young Man, *and it was the game children play when they write their names. 'He turned to the flyleaf of the geography and read what he had written there: himself, his name and where he was.*

Stephen Dedalus
Class of Elements
Clongowes Wood College
Sallins
County Kildare
Ireland
Europe
The World
The Universe

...Then he read the flyleaf from the bottom to the top, till he came to his own name.' Aren't you just involved in a similar exercise – defining and redefining yourself, in a body, in a place, in civilization, in history, in the universe. Surely you can carry on doing that again and again, reading from top to bottom, then back, over and over.

No. There's that indulgent part of me that makes the work to pacify a terrible fear and there's another part that makes the pieces to find something out, much as Piaget did in his kind of research. Or Foucault. Or Barthes. Or Galileo, even. And now I want not just to define me but to find the root of verbal and visual signmaking. That does not have to do with me as an ego. It's much more of an experimental intellectual pursuit. The art always has to pose a larger question, almost in the way science does. Otherwise I'm not interested.

‘A Wiry, Electric Force’: Dennis Oppenheim interviewed

Published in New York Arts Journal *12, November/December 1978.*

Stuart Morgan: *Bearing in mind your knowledge of World War II military strategy, it has always seemed that a major factor underlying your artistic decisions has been an intention to comment on or modify or even change the entire direction of avant-garde art, creating works that are simultaneously manifestos and correctives. Your pieces from 1966–7 in the recent New Museum ‘Early Work’ show were certainly of this kind.*

Dennis Oppenheim: I had a lot of malignant training as a young art student and a lot of poisoned interference in the early sixties. Some of those things were made after I left the West Coast in 1966. Armed with a masters degree, I taught high school that year and made those works, including the *Site Markers*. I show them a lot because they didn’t get displayed during that early period and I’ve extrapolated from them to produce other works. They have sometimes been seen as attacks on Minimalism, and I think that what’s behind the avant-garde is that feeling of distaste for what occurs in the artist’s own time-structure, his real disbelief in this and his desire to disprove it. Strong as these drives may be intellectually, they should operate in a zone where impulses are conjured at really subliminal levels. To try to investigate an impasse or disprove Minimalism intellectually is not as rich as to find a flow that naturally ties in with some subterranean need to agitate. In that agitation you just naturally disprove what is ahead of you or frustrate, improve, clarify.

What decisions were involved in the shift to marionettes in the seventies?

The marionettes were originally conceived as a post-performance activity which would include some of the elements of sculpture, that is, the constant physical placement of sculpture, *and* some elements of performance – movement, duration and so forth. So the first piece, *Theme for a Major Hit*, is a small figure in my own likeness. It dances continuously, so it can be installed in a space and function almost as a rigid object. But it also qualifies in terms of performance, an activity that travels through time. Part of the impetus behind these surrogates was of course the dissipating energy behind personal performance, doing it yourself. I think this was most noticeable in the early seventies, when there was so much performance behind us and there was so much use of individual artists having to perform in real time themselves. In the minds of many of those artists the supposition that this performance would continue became more and more implausible. *Theme for a Major Hit* has a soundtrack played by artists; friends of mine. The lyrics, which are constant, are, 'It ain't what you make, it's what makes you do it', repeated over and over again. The words are about the belief that virtuosity can really breed any number of visual instruments. Any kind of skill laboured at year after year will give an individual a wide range of almost mindless, dextrous abilities, but what makes him do it is still a problem. What fires this virtuosity at deep levels is unknown; even the most intellectually coralled artists are not totally in grasp of what propels them to exude this energy, to manifest form for communication So *Theme for a Major Hit* is really almost a gesture on my part, saying 'It's not what you make, it's what makes you do it and I'm going to tell you that that's what I think is important'. Now a higher level of this act would be in the confines of an individual work, in the methodology from origination to completion, in the structure that dwells between these two points. One level is in actually originating or crystallizing or making evident these drives in the work that becomes concrete. The completed end is a recapitulation of the drives that instigated the work. So we are using art as a form that can make solid the roots from which it is precipitated. I think that this is what occupies my time. One is left with the suspicion that much of what I've done is based on intellectual and historical virtuosity, mere art school training and exams that give a certain sense of what to do based on what not to do. We can all look at works developed through pain or formal manipulation, but they're often vastly removed from individual impulses within the artists. What art needs now is to bespeak its origins, to see that it's not led astray by effective distractions but does come to echo some substratum. What I would like to make is art more tuned to root impulses.

Works like the one in which magnesium flares were arranged across a hillside to spell RADICALITY *for a few seconds indicate a wish to go on trying to communicate despite powerful forces of loss.*

The whole art-making process is subject to an evolutionary scale. We begin, we exert, we surface, we become focused upon, and within that focused-upon range we eventually, unfortunately, deteriorate. Part of the artist's goal within his lifetime should be to ward off any kind of interference that will refract or ricochet his content. Ageing is one problem, a process that will interfere with whatever content you can register. No matter how much you want to do a thing, it takes longer to get up in the morning, longer to energize yourself. These goals will become more and more extreme. These physical things and other manifestations of evolution will eventually curtail your content. On the one hand we're guarding our integrity, our consciousness, our ability to home in on certain necessary areas, and on the other we're trying to perpetuate ways of making this possible, making finances available, openings within the art world available. All this peripheral instrumental activity is separating our compulsions. Artists spend something like 80% of their time in these activities and are fortunately equipped with this talent for separation.

How does your belief in forces of deterioration affect your methods of working?

Art has a family of uses, one of which is to venture into things that are seen to be sidetracks to other disciplines – science, philosophy, zones that for some reason aren't as erratic. Art is a wiry, electric force in its contradictions and its ability to counter, then counter the counter. It has an irony nothing else seems to have, and with this one is well equipped to survey any kind of terrain. Part of the priority would be to sense the place most in need of art as a scalpel, of art as a device to probe it. But for me to deliberate focused attack is not as viable a state of mind as scanning new territory. Given an individual's prospective lifespan, one of the dangerous things as an artist is to be backed into a corner and unable to reverse. I could never believe in an instrument that deserves a lifetime to propel it, instigate it and present it to others with conviction. Things are much more given to constant disruption, interference and questioning. Dissipation and entropic loss of sensory abilities make it difficult to get through to the content. So what I've always wanted was a large arena.

In your latest installations you employ a large 'arena' by combining a number of elements – sight, space, sound and a kind of theatre. Could you describe one of these pieces?

Recently I made *Dayton Falls* in Dayton, Ohio, in a room with a catwalk around it and an open area in the middle. Four steel structures were built, varying in height from five feet to twenty, and as they increased in height their construction became more complex. They looked like electrical towers or derricks, but also like snowflake crystals, all geometry, and they had this energy about them. The soundtrack was awesome. It went on for thirty minutes, calling for people to jump off the towers. This was mixed with all sorts of verbal tracks and the sound of water falling. Being kind of formal as I am, my notion of falling is like sculpture. Falling is probably the most profound experience an artist can have. Falling, entering, emerging or submerging are things that are constantly at the back of my mind. I've seen the body – I'm sure Chris Burden has also – as an instrument to pass through or receive or enter into the material. A number of works would suggest that he is considering his body as the tool that can engage in these sometimes traditional acts. Essentially, falling would be like pressing a traditional tool into a soft substance. So here we are again back with the chisel and the marble. But *Dayton Falls* is a condition whereby the individual meets with a situation in which the ground itself falls – although this is verbiage on the soundtrack so that one can't hit it. In other words Dayton, which is in the Midwest, is dealt with as a pocket that couldn't strike or bounce back its energy. As one jumped, a surface descended so that one would be caught, would drift, in this kind of vacuum. The sounds were re-recorded, always acknowledging the recording equipment; as I spoke into the mike I would make tests and constantly refer to the sound man. Then we ventured into this fantasy where the sound system was falling, we couldn't keep the plugs in the walls and the mikes were falling out of our hands into this vortex . . .

Do you feel conscious of developing a new aesthetic to match your uses of such sophisticated techniques?

There is a tremendous disparity between what I do and what I want to do, and between what is done and what is communicated. One would hope that when the urge comes it's not going to be bothered by conscious manipulation – where things go, where the spectator should stand and so on. We know these things exist, we know we're all of varying abilities to manipulate them . . . It sounds very romantic, but I believe the best art rushes to consume all the fussiness that goes into designing the work, that planning you're in control of. I think the best stuff you ARE in control of. Sometimes it gets out and it's very bad and you can't cure it and it doesn't make sense, but there's a pure core we're all trying to get to no matter what abilities we may have.

What kind of art will prevail in the eighties?

Lots of young artists are opting for music now, which means they're choosing something more immediate. An art context is feeding into rock or punk rock and I would speculate that this is our new stuff. I don't know if it will, but it could become a backdoor entrance into the gap that will displace all that we're used to. Although art at present is disturbingly morbid and is not showing the power it has available to it, artists are usually equipped to practise their profession at astonishing levels. Given the cathartic energy of the late sixties, which sparked off Conceptual art and earthworks and Process art, given the riches that we had before in Abstract Expressionism, the way that art uses and submerges aspects of this nucleus is what is breeding eighties art. We're capable of amazing things not only in what we can do but also in what we know not to do. It really is time for art to practise magic. And if 'magic' can be pinned down, it's a condition in the hands of the individual who is able to operate in an infinite matrix, somehow within an infinite table of possibilities conjuring a sound or a structure that bypasses its own precipitative instrument, the sender, the artist, and truly expands to meet many people. We can give it dimensions, but it's not available often.

Extracts from The State of Idea: New York Chronicle

Published in Artscribe *11, April 1978.*

[on John Cage]

Mystic *manqué*, Wizard of Oz, John Cage also indulges his whims in order to put his status in question. I braved the cold on 22 December to attend the second of his concerts at The Kitchen. Whatever he had been up to, he was up to it again. The previous night he had presided as a patient pianist, and had devoted 90 minutes to his *Études Australes Books I and II*, created by superimposing a grid over star maps and converting the result to traditional notation. Then for a full half-hour he had 'played' an amplified cactus. (An empty half-hour, his detractors would say.) At 65 John Cage is too old to care what people think. The next night he gave a completely different concert.

The first piece, *Cheap Imitation*, was written when French copyright-holders refused permission for an arrangement of Satie's *Socrate* for two pianos to accompany Merce Cunningham's *Second Hand.* Subjecting Satie to the I Ching, Cage made a piano solo, then an orchestral work, and lastly a piece for violin, specially requested by Paul Zukofsky, who gave it its première on the 22nd. Classical in tone, its regularity and cool seriousness made it suitably ironic. Satie's mode was retained, though the actual notes were changed. After mapping a space, establishing temporal expectations, Cage allowed the listener to experience a parallel to the clean attraction of logical thought, incorporating romantic swoops and dives that would have been heartbreaking if indulged. Again and again the music snubbed them and our tears were stifled; Socrates died as he lived, and lived as he argued. The audience, which included Cunningham, Rauschenberg and Morton Feldman, received Zukofsky with rapture.

Benign but slightly dotty, Cage himself played in *Inlets*, first performed in September 1977. Three musicians (Cage, David Tudor and Takehisa Kosugi) sat behind tables covered with conch shells of different sizes. Choosing one shell at a time, each man partially filled it with water and made it gurgle around the interior while sensitive microphones picked up the noise. Large conches sound like bathwater going out, tiny ones like birds gargling. They are played by sensing where the water is lying, then turning the shells at the correct speed to obtain a suitable slurp. Large ones come conveniently equipped with spindly ends which lend them well to such treatment, while smaller versions have to be cradled, and giants rest on the floor. There is always the danger that in turning your shell the wrong way you might tip water down your leg. Mr Kosugi did this, but mopped up so inscrutably that no one laughed. From time to time they played a recording of pine cones on fire, and a little over half-way through a man stood up and blew a conch shell very loudly. Sometimes all these things happened together. In no way directed by Cage, the performers collaborated in a real sense, earnestly but wittily engaged in tasks that demanded their entire attention and made for constant aural interest.

[On Dennis Oppenheim]

Always read graffiti; they will tell you what you should already know. Early in January I spotted an inscription in the men's room at the Lower Manhattan Ocean Club: DENNIS OPPENHEIM AND THE IRANIAN TORTURER, it said. Rooted to the spot, I read it again: DENNIS OPPENHEIM AND THE IRANIAN TORTURER. There was a poetic rightness about it, like the title of a novel no one had bothered to finish. It meant nothing to me. Any of the artists upstairs could have written it; they all knew Oppenheim, the Conceptual conquistador who proposed projects as small as a fingernail or as large as a mountain. Intent during the sixties on his body and its possibilities, in the seventies he had involved himself in statements about radical aesthetics and the machinery of power. They all knew also that while he showed galleries full of stolen hubcaps or dragged his video equipment across the floor to spell out four-letter words, Oppenheim was a shrewd businessman, respected for having outsmarted the gallery system.

Only a few days earlier I had interviewed Oppenheim. Stepping from the elevator into an apartment the size of a field, I was surrounded by music so loud I could almost feel and taste it, coming from speakers big enough for Madison Square Gardens. Dotted around the room were guitars, an organ, microphones, cameras, plus other ware, hard and soft. Far in the distance stood two men by an open hearth. I was greeted, poured a drink, invited to lose myself in an enormous settee and did so, submitting to the noise. One of the men was quiet and blonde and laughed a lot. He was Dennis Oppenheim. The other, who lived downstairs, was talking about clams and as he talked he became so excited that he broke into a little dance. He was called Red.

Somewhere in the settee I came across a girl with glasses but contented myself with mouthing politenesses, expecting no mercy from the sound system. 'They're new,' Oppenheim explained, without flinching.

'I'm just testing them. Too strong really.'

'WHY? SO? BIG?' I screamed.

'So I can wire them up for the group.'

'DO? YOU? PLAY? THE? ORGAN?' (*pointing to it*)

'No.'

'GUITAR?' (*pointing again*)

'No. I figured I might if they were here.'

The girl seemed to have fallen asleep. Red's wife had appeared. He was shouting 'Whoowee! Clams!' and jigging up and down. I decided I was being European and uncrossed my legs, though I refrained from putting my feet on the table. Later I interviewed Oppenheim, who talked about art, punk rock, his latest work (a combination of sound and architecture), artists he admired . . . but not a word about his Middle Eastern torturer. Afterwards we ate Red's clams.

Back in Britain in mid-January I received a letter containing two pages ripped from the *Voice*, with a scribbled message from a friend in New York: 'Stuart – What is an artist once he has abdicated his conscience.' The absent question mark left no doubt. He was annoyed. The enclosed article, 'Dennis Oppenheim's Dilemma' by Richard Goldstein, was illustrated with not one but two photographs of the great man frowning faintly and looking vague. Goldstein explained that after talks in Tehran, Oppenheim had been approached by the Shah himself to supervise construction of one project, with the option of proposing six more for the same price, 54,000 dollars each. Oppenheim's private export drive had aroused such fury from fellow New Yorkers with low opinions of the Iranian regime that he said he was reconsidering, that he might even break the contract that he had already signed. Enraged at the Shah's encroachment on the New York art scene, Goldstein wrote: 'The world's most absolute monarch intrudes into our lives, but softly, like a suppository.'

Cage, the work the Shah accepted, consisted of a huge wire-mesh cone covering a pit in which a live bird would be placed. For its construction the help of the army had been promised. Though at first it seemed that only two possibilities existed (to make *Cage* and face the reaction in the United States or back out and forfeit the cash) later in the article Oppenheim discussed a third – to make a politically engaged sculpture expressing solidarity with the oppressed Iranian peasants. 'The big question is, can we make art in the land of our enemies,' he asked Goldstein, 'and can it ride above the political structure in which it was created?' Honouring his contract would permit him to create a large-scale symbol of freedom from within the stronghold of power. But the money would be the Shah's and the Shah's soldiers would build it on the Shah's land. What more compromising background could there be for a gesture of liberation? Whether or not an artwork can transcend its immediate occasion depends totally on its 'greatness' in traditional terms, or on the impact and topicality of its message, in terms of a quasi-political aesthetic such as Oppenheim has espoused in recent years. One solution to his problem is to make *Cage* significant in every way, yet the idea is already there and to suppose that the Shah would choose to buy a subversive work is simplistic.

Oppenheim's political scruples came a little late in the day. From the cynical Old World it is difficult to regard his concern for the poor of Iran as anything but a joke. Yet in Europe it is well nigh impossible to imagine the artist as a Faustian man, daring enough to think he could change the world, put the torturer in irons. My friend was wrong; Oppenheim has not abdicated his conscience, but this does not mean that he will break his agreement with the Shah. Once in a while a genuinely moral problem arises. I read about them on walls. Meanwhile, the stereo is turned up a notch and Red is cooking more clams.

Donald Judd, Andy de Groat, Bob Carroll

Review of Judd's exhibition at the Lisson Gallery, and of performances at Riverside Studios, London, published in Artscribe *19, September 1979.*

The story so far. For ten years Don Judd has been marooned on a desert island with nothing to read but published volumes of his own drawings, his *Complete Writings* and Roberta Smith's definitive catalogue. What happens to a Minimalist once post-Minimalism is over? Suddenly a British frigate is sighted in the distance. Now read on.

Nicholas Logsdail's clean, well-lighted place was the perfect setting for a homage to Judd. Upstairs were wall pieces, blocks and progressions, wooden boxes with the familiar recessed lip, now with bases painted surprising colours, and drawings for exhibited works as well as for adobe-style buildings. The quality was as high as ever, but these were the potboilers famous artists make to keep dealers happy. Downstairs Judd had created a single large sculpture specially for the space and the occasion.

Midway along the far wall nine long rectangular copper tubes protruded at right-angles, one above the other, hollow but with a layer of blue Plexiglas five inches from the mouth of each. The dappled metal, the cloudy depths of the Plexiglas, the viewer's partial reflection in that blue, the changing distortions by which the eye registers equal measurements all combined to make the sculpture seem distant and reticent. Upstairs there was no way of keeping the whole of the base of that wooden box in view or of seeing the surrounding frame of the copper wall piece; the mind extrapolated from visual clues. Downstairs the viewer was made to doubt the initial evidence; as the light from an open door struck the blue surfaces they suddenly dissolved and leapt back to twice their usual depth. It was easy to understand why one reviewer hailed the work as a masterpiece and called for its immediate purchase by the Tate.

Sophisticated trickery has always been present in Judd, qualified by a compulsive return to first principles of mensuration, such as counting or the relation of part to whole. The new sculptural language he invented in the sixties had similarities with the American language itself, distinguished, according to certain commentators, by flat assertion, monosyllabic phrasing and the distillation of meaning into key words rather than larger units of syntax. In the seventies the use of language has changed. At this moment it seems orotund, polysyllabic, periphrastic. The gratuitous beauty of the new piece is a sign that Judd senses the mood.

Whether or not the rescue takes place depends on what Judd himself wants to be. He can choose to shore up a history-book reputation by ringing as few changes as possible on ideas that have made him famous, or he can experiment and perhaps fail miserably. ('Move,' cries the heart. 'Stay,' yells the pocket-book.) No rescue is needed; the island is in his head.

Andy de Groat is best known as the choreographer of Robert Wilson's *Einstein on the Beach* and *Letter for Queen Victoria.* In June his company gave a single performance at Riverside Studios presenting three works, *Rope Dance Translations*, *Angie's Waltz and other Dances* and *Red Notes/Get Wreck.*

The 'rope' in *Rope Dance Translations* (1974) consisted of three connected ropes of different lengths, the 'dance' on the dancer's own axis. The 'translations' were gradual and compelling. Four dancers arranged their ropes on the floor, stepping inside the circle they made, then grasping them with both hands. In ritual fashion each dancer lifted the rope and, to the accompaniment of a violin continuo, began to turn inside it, lifting and dropping it at will, first taking solos then moving in orbit together, like planets, gaining speed before the lights dimmed. In silence a film was shown of de Groat doing the same dance alone. Then, again in silence, he did the rope dance live, moving faster and faster, making his rope a net, a dress, a lasso, a flail, finally a weight pulling him upwards. As the lights dimmed a second time his figure was succeeded by a vivid after-image. And, as if to prolong even that, one member of the company, Ritty Ann Burchfield, continued to spin like a top throughout the evening. The dance seemed to be intended as a manifesto, a prescribed activity in a prescribed time with no special 'steps'; each dancer tackled it differently. The relationship between the prop and the movement was as close as that between the dancer's personality and the choreographer's needs.

Angie's Waltz and other Dances (1977), which involved all nine of the company, raised the question of the extent to which distinctive gesture should be sacrificed to overall conception. The dancers' personae were obviously based on personality, skill and physique: Sheryl Sutton, naturally graceful;

Harry Sheppard, wiry, with a preference for intricate, self-absorbed gestures; Kathy Ray, all hair and eyes and innocence; Gary Reingenborn and Michael Kuhling, one classically inclined, smiling as he danced, the other elegant and gawky in equal proportions; Frank Conversano, a bearded man with a sense of humour, moving like a sportsman. The 'character' of each gradually assumed as much importance as the composition itself. A song was sung. A poem was unfolded from the ceiling and Mr de Groat danced prettily in front of it. A wobbly waltz took place in foam rubber costumes. In a sequence for couples, *Come Dancing* combined with callisthenics. Though the Balanchinesque Boy Meets Girl, Boy Loses Girl atmosphere kept it all together, *Angie's Waltz* was the least compelling of the three items.

In *Red Notes/Get Wreck* (1977–9) any hint of 'narrative' was abandoned. It was best regarded as a collage, with music by Michael Gallasso and texts by Gertrude Stein and Christopher Knowles. As an epigraph a slide of an oriental painting was shown, its 'mountains and rivers without end' suggesting that there would be no particular reason for the dance to start and stop, since, as Gertrude Stein would be heard to say, 'The History of anyone must be a long one.' Essentially *Red Notes/Get Wreck* offered a series of dances employing props such as shoes, fans and cigarettes. The set was simple – a white gauze backdrop, a table with glasses of water and, leading up to it, a set of converging lines marked on the floor. Two dancers also seemed part of the set, a sequence of Stein texts or the unmanageable number of shoes Kathy Ray struggled to collect and hold in her solo, the dignitary clothed in newsprint, crossing very slowly and solemnly behind the gauze, attended by a girl with an electric lamp. As the elements of the dance piled haphazardly, the audience was reminded of the ways events fall out in life, well or badly, according to a pattern too difficult to fathom. To the personal styles and the time divisions was added a concept of being 'onstage'; though the dancers walked 'for ever' towards the central table, never arriving, they dropped out of the dance periodically, went to the table and drank the water. Similarly in a sequence with cigarettes they stopped from time to time to smoke and look at each other.

Individual versus group identity was a thematic as well as a technical preoccupation in all three dances. If a dichotomy existed between loss of the self and the unimportance of groups in *Rope Dance Translations* and traditional ways of mixing with others in *Angie's Waltz*, the climax of *Red Notes* reconciled the two. Wearing red uniforms and carrying fans, the company moved to and fro in a stately, ordered way, pausing to dance alone. The persuasiveness of this final consort was due to the social metaphors it celebrated, referring to a court celebration and the tailor-made self-expression of popular dance. De Groat's achievement was to take what could have been an unworkable paradox and to turn it into rich ambiguity.

On the floor at the side of the stage lie a haversack and a bottle of wine. Carroll seems to have wandered in off the street. He starts gently, drinking from a paper cup, addressing newcomers, establishing eye-contact, posing, flirting, chancing his arm. Even born show-offs need to get into the mood. He makes the audience feel at home. 'You can leave any time . . . . If I put somebody to sleep I don't feel I've performed in vain.' *The Bob Carroll Salmon Show* is odd enough. It consists of his account of the life history of the salmon. Carroll himself sounds like an ageing drag artiste in mufti and moves . . . well, words fail me. The sight of a middle-aged man wriggling lasciviously, clutching his genitals and – 'Pretty cheap, eh?' – probing his rear end with one finger in an attempt to simulate the spawning of fish is best described as 'Rabelaisian' and left at that.

Carroll improvised within a circular, repetitive structure, gathering rhetorical strength from what he calls his 'integrity of metaphor'. Gestures are used for emphasis and as the show proceeds they are shifted ironically from one section to another. So, for example, a feeding motion, *Big Fish Eat Little Fish*, is shifted from a passage on piscine sexuality to a description of cash flow in a diatribe on the world financial situation. Carroll is shifting constantly from one level to another, breaking in mid-sentence to deliver asides, answer critics, explain what he's doing or has done or is going to do, or how he feels, appealing to the audience to interrupt or correct him. ('The next section's gonna be hyper. If I start getting too hyper too quick feel free to yell out "hyper".') The 'show' itself is delivered in a rhythmic Captain Beefheart manner, with long babbling lines and half-hidden puns. Sometimes it is a struggle to find it; Carroll's self-reflexive remarks are like an undergrowth that needs pruning. Yet pruning would mean cutting some of the funniest parts of the evening. Half-way through a vain attempt to do the splits he wipes the sweat out of his eyes. 'In an otherwise rave review *New York Times* critic Mel Gussow said that the actor appeared not to be in the best physical shape.' Striding into the auditorium he pauses. 'Marlene Dietrich choreographed every exit out of the orchestra pit. In later years, having drunk too much, she would sometimes fall *into* the orchestra pit and break a bone.'

Slowly the strands are pulled together and the audience realizes that the clowning has a purpose. The point where the metaphors converge is the long speech about George Jackson. Just as a single salmon, swimming free, travelling 1,800 miles in its lifetime, is prey to human sharks who mean to tin and sell it, George Jackson was assassinated by the vast business corporations that control the State of California. Imprisoned in a five by eight cell for most of his adult life, he too was doomed. The really admirable part of Carroll's show is his expert grasp of everything he discusses, whether politics, economics or ecology. He makes it all seem so easy that the audience scarcely realizes that a lecture is in progress. This man is not a scholar; he speaks too well. He is an informed layman with complete faith in the significance of his theme, willing to go to any lengths to communicate. His show is a superb example of inspirational speaking which shows up most 'education' for the wretched thing it is. At the high point of the show he simply recites excerpts from Jackson's prison writings. As he does so Bob Carroll – fat and scant of breath, playing with his long, blonde hair – himself becomes a metaphor worthy of comparison with the black misfit and the peaceful salmon: the lone individual using every means in his power to make us see the forces threatening our freedom.

The Writings of Robert Smithson

Review of Nancy Holt, ed., The Writings of Robert Smithson *(1979), published in* Art Journal, *New York, vol. 39, no.3, spring 1980.*

Seven years after his death nothing has been decided about Robert Smithson. No biography or monograph has been written. Essays have differed widely in emphasis, overstressing single periods of his working life. While a fine early study by Lawrence Alloway argued that the 'non-site' experiments lay at the heart of Smithson's theory, most of the contributors to a special issue of *Arts Magazine* in 1978 concentrated on the later landscape works. If Smithson's paintings are ignored, so also are his final excursions into industrial design. Despite the obstacles, however, Smithson's career is best regarded as an amalgam of finished works, drawings and writings. This volume of writings is therefore a keenly awaited addition to primary sources on Smithson, providing easy access to all the published essays and also to interviews and previously unpublished typescripts.

Complaints are few. A fragmentary interview with P.A. Norvell included in Lucy Lippard's *Six Years* does not appear, and, sadly, there are no photographs of the paintings shown at the Galleria Lester in 1961, though a catalogue was printed. One problem bothers me. The decision to republish articles as they first appeared is both laudable and irritating. Essays such as 'Ultramoderne' and 'Strata: A Geophotographic Fiction' were written around a visual idea. Altered, they would lose much of their meaning. Yet Smithson punctuated poorly, could not spell, and made up words that did not exist. Editors should have corrected many of these errors at the outset. Reprinted now in a definitive text, they have become a monument to editorial sloppiness.

Two main preoccupations underlay the six years of Smithson's writing. One was the urge to break down Greenbergian formalism, most evident in his treatment of Michael Fried in a series of drubbings unparalleled in twentieth-century art since Barnett Newman confronted Erwin Panofsky. Fried's essay 'Art and Objecthood' was the perfect springboard for Smithson. It represented the apotheosis of a pseudo-objective, ultimately prescriptive view of abstraction, attacking what Fried called 'theatre'. Smithson, a natural mannerist, fought strenuously for the right to be as flamboyant and shrill as he wished, for the right to load his own strange objects with a burden of meaning that only historical relics – those museum pieces he both admired and detested and to which he returned so often in his thinking – have to support.

The second preoccupation underlying Smithson's writing was with leading sixties art out of a diluted Duchampianism. Between 1966, when he used a photograph of a Robert Morris pastiche, and 1973, when Moira Roth's interview was published in *Artforum*, Smithson lost patience with the cult of the disappearing art object. Nevertheless, it is difficult not to suspect a knife beneath the cloak in the latter attack on Duchamp's lack of humour, his alchemy and his 'mechanistic' attitudes: Smithson could admire the apocalyptic statements of Flavin while ignoring the science fiction of *Encore à cet Astre* or the forces preventing the *Nude*'s descent. Though priggish, his disillusionment with Duchamp, and incidentally with Warhol, so pervasive in the essays written in the sixties, was genuine and moral. 'My view is more democratic,' he said, striking out at Duchamp's pseudo-aristocratic stance and the 'dream world' of the occult that obsessed him. No mention was made of eroticism. Leo Steinberg wrote that in America love was replaced by work, and the sublimations involved in David Smith or in Smithson's earthworks are among the most impressive proofs of his point. Perhaps America will always be hostile to an art that acknowledges its own masturbatory motives.

'No ideas about things, but the thing itself', wrote William Carlos Williams. Behind Smithson's antipathy to Caro and to Conceptualism was a determination to deal with 'real' space. The Fried issue was simpler than it appeared. A man at a desk read Tony Smith's report of a night drive on the New Jersey Turnpike, gave it a C+, then invented a theory to disprove what a sculptor had seen with his own eyes. Smithson, like Duchamp, would have read through the entire 'Perspective' section in the Ste. Geneviève library, but he would not have sacrificed his common sense at the altar of other people's systems: ultimately verbal representations of individual experience. The unfamiliar juxtapositions of mood and vocabulary in Smithson, the leap from Captain Beefheart to Parmigianino, indicate an expanded vocabulary that writers of the period employed more than critics. (Someone, somewhere, must be writing a thesis on obscure references to the comic strip in Pynchon and Ashbery.) But the dichotomy between the apparently improvised, free-wheeling essay and the extended conceit, between 'A Tour of the Monuments of Passaic' and 'A Cinematic Atopia', reveals a more deeply felt distinction in Smithson's mind between the picaresque and the parable, the mud and the crystal. His journeys and his concepts, the *Swamp* movie and the drawings of imaginary countries, were equally attractive and equally perilous. Smithson, a romantic, needed new objects in the universe to ratify the patterns of imagery that were his equivalent of Fried's thought systems. He then engulfed these new experiences, deepening and complicating the patterns they affirmed. The images of the vortex and the black hole fascinated him because of the increased 'de-differentiation' they offered. As for language, the paragraph on William Empson's *The Structure of Complex Words* in a previously unpublished essay 'From Ivan the Terrible to Roger Corman, or Paradoxes of Conduct in Mannerism as Reflected in the Cinema' comes as no surprise. The effect of a key word in a Shakespeare sonnet, Empson contended, is to unleash all of the dictionary meanings of that word and to permit them to operate simultaneously. Focus, definition and control versus bewilderment, free fall and loss of equilibrium have verbal counterparts in the texture of Smithson's prose. The precision of the sentences that read like parodies of proverbs and the imprecision of others that trail and hang like tropical growths have their theoretical underpinning in statements such as the press release 'Language to be Looked at/ and/or Things to be Read'. Smithson's late remark that language is 'matter and not ideas', the thing itself and not 'ideas about' the thing, is disingenuous, however, because the spatial patterns that directed his thought demanded both and made of both a temptation. 'We wander between the towering and the bottomless. We are lost between the abyss within us and the boundless horizons outside us', he wrote, his cosmology that of the naughty puritan. Smithson claimed he was a self-taught writer, though from the first his stance seemed considered, his tone confident. Published in *Artforum* in 1966, 'Entropy and the New Monuments' was a radical departure from available modes of criticism. In Italy, not long after its publication, Ettore Sottsass jun. described the piece perfectly: 'Since an artist wrote the article it is a mess, but a mess with everything; ideas transformed into images, the images themselves, words interchanged to express new meanings, new concepts arrived at by the way things are said.' Smithson would have been flattered; that 'mess' is usually called poetry. 'Art critics,' he wrote, are 'generally poets who have betrayed their art.'

It is time to deal with Smithson as literature, despite the fact that issues he introduced are still being debated. Like Gorky's letters and Hesse's diaries, his writings transcend immediate occasions and achieve significance as the products of an original, gifted and startling mind. The fight will not be easy.

Artists' writings belong to a neglected literary genre that is no genre at all. His editors' refusal to work at correct texts indicates that artists, when they write, are thought not to warrant even the most elementary considerations a textual critic allows a poet, though Smithson has been more fortunate than most.

The combination of that emotional logic with which he replaced reasoned discourse and an exhilarating mental rapacity that pushed him constantly towards the edges of charlatanism gives Smithson's prose a curiously driven quality and a melancholy aspect, which are the result partly of a failure of confidence in the deductive powers of the mind, partly of a desperate need to encompass every field of human knowledge. His literary ancestors are the 'dark' romantics of nineteenth-century prose – Poe, Melville and De Quincey, plus to some extent Dickens and Hoffmann. The lists in Dickens and Melville, the bogus scholarship in Poe and De Quincey, the view from Todger's, the mounting hysteria of 'The Revolt of the Tartars' and 'The English Mail Coach', the taste for grotesques and icy humour, the romantic irony of *Kater Murr* – all have their Smithsonian counterparts, though Smithson may not have known it. Pre-eminent is Poe, venerated at one remove through the movies of Roger Corman and directly in references to *The Narrative of Arthur Gordon Pym* and 'The Fall of the House of Usher' and in an inset dialogue in 'Incidents of Mirror Travel in the Yucatan', a parody of Poe's 'Colloquy of Monos and Una' and 'Conversation of Eiros and Charmion'. 'Quasi-Infinities and the Waning of Space' contains a diagram from *Eureka*. Poe's schizophrenic insistence on hectic ratiocination and coolly applied Longinian aesthetics, his almost operatic style of presentation and, above all, his sense of evil are also integral to Smithson's literary imagination. In Nabokov the 'doubles' and exotic etymology appealed, and Smithson was capable of a Nabokovian flourish: ''The sky was a subtle newspaper grey', he wrote in 'A Tour of the Monuments of Passaic', referring to Jules Olitski, 'and the clouds resembled sensitive stains of sweat reminiscent of a famous Yugoslav watercolourist whose name I have forgotten.' The sense of space in Borges and the scientific esoterica of Burroughs also held an interest. The science fiction of John Taine, Henry Kuttner, Brian Aldiss and others, however, provided the cosmic scale Smithson sought, as did the writings of some of the artists discussed in 'A Museum of Language in the Vicinity of Art'. There were few kindred spirits in criticism. Closest to his own tactics is the hectic cross-referencing of Northrop Frye, whose mystic method offers one of the classic 'dream worlds' of the sixties, or the strategies of Empson's *Seven*

Types of Ambiguity, virtuoso analysis so self-intoxicated that it undermined its own methods and proliferated into nonsense. Smithson had read George Kubler as early as 1964, as the note on 'The Eliminator' shows. Like Poe and Reinhardt, Kubler entered the pantheon of undoubted influences, minds to be answered back rather than simply absorbed. Kubler's anthropological approach to art-historical questions and his command of metaphor seem to have made Smithson single him out.

Reinhardt, like Poe and Kubler, was interested in time. (He reviewed Kubler's *Shape of Time* for *Art News*.) All three were intent on shuttling back and forth in time in exactly the way Smithson desired; Max Kozloff wrote of the non-site sculptures that they gave 'a stutter to the categories of the infinite'. The key to Smithson's treatment of Reinhardt, with whom he exhibited in a show called 'Ten' at Dwan Gallery, is emotion. Instead of regarding Reinhardt's negative tactics in terms of non-style or anti-art, Smithson concentrated on his ability to explore degrees of boredom in the painting and uncontrolled laughter in the cartoons, like a pianist disenchanted with middle C. These were precisely the emotions that Smithson wanted to inject into his own sculpture. The cartoons are apocalyptic, showing the art world of New York as infinitely small and classifiable. Like Pope's dunces, the faster the artists ran and played silly games, the nearer they would be to the day when the universe was extinguished and swallowed by a cosmic yawn, and the reign of Dullness was begun.

Smithson's work, like Reinhardt's, pleads for spiritual, if not religious, interpretation. Future critics, convinced of the American-ness of Smithson's writing, may leave the heights – the superb passage on the genesis of *The Spiral Jetty*, for example, in the essay of the same name – and analyse the footnote to 'A Sedimentation of the Mind: Earth Projects'. While 'Arcadian improvers', as Smithson called them, wanted a return to lost paradises, Smithson advocated a temporary pact with opposing forces of time. In his footnote, tempted more than ever by the sheer beauty and perfection of Eden, he recognized the effect on his dialectics of the concept of original sin. It is a moving moment as well as a major contribution to the oldest debate of all in American thought. Smithson's running battle with the idea of the fenced art work, the framed painting, the 'confined' museum, the formal English garden and the formalist American critic was not only part of a private foray into the origins of sculpture and language but also a critique of the 'radical innocence' that resulted in a prolongation of misplaced Adamic thinking in American art,

Emersonian optimism having by the sixties dwindled into what John Barth called 'a cheerful nihilism'. Suddenly, unexpectedly, Smithson found he was out of control. Perhaps this was the abyss he had feared so much. Perhaps evil was not the opposite of some perfect good that no one could envisage, but the absence of any such opposition. In a variation on the paradox of the Fortunate Fall, one of the greatest theological 'stutters', Smithson confronted the dimension he had stumbled into, like an astronaut in one of the science fiction stories he avidly read.

Robert Smithson's Early Work: A Resurrection

Published in Artforum, *XXIII, 8, April 1985.*

In 1961 George Lester, who owned a gallery in Rome, put Robert Smithson on a stipend to make work for a one-man exhibition there. Early this year Lester helped to mount an augmented version of that Italian show at the Diane Brown Gallery in New York, with the result that 40 'new' paintings have come to light and a brief, crucial phase of Smithson's development can be discussed for the first time.

Not unexpectedly, genres range from conventional second-generation Abstract Expressionist *Sturm und Drang* through to proto-Pop collage. Somewhere between the two are cross-sectioned landscapes, showing above- and below-ground areas, and a hieratic figuration as tortured as the vegetable studies are relaxed. Apparently disparate works are connected emotionally and thematically. This is a vision of the City and the Plain, of Baroque cathedrals and desert agonies. Time is infinite; a diving apparatus resembles an Egyptian mummy case, while a space capsule looks like a prehistoric burial chamber. Figures are both more and less than human, varying between the grotesque and the sublime: mermaids, chimeras, walking trees, even Christ Himself. Creatures of myth and legend are in a struggle for survival. An angel topples into an abyss to be eaten by a giant insect, while both Jesus and a chimera display their stigmata, the tokens of eternal suffering. The pervasive sensation is of threat.

Vulnerability demands protective tactics. Apparently doubting his medium as a means of revelation, Smithson uses pigment as camouflage; his *horror vacui* is countered by an uncompromising presentation of vacancy itself. This may result from a broken connection. For Willem de Kooning an equation between flesh and paint seemed as natural as breathing. Smithson felt otherwise – his figures seem never to have arisen naturally out of swirls of pigment, or from casual wrist actions, but to have been introduced artificially. In *Purgatory* (1959), one of Smithson's own favourite paintings from this period, faces cower behind a roughly worked grid that imprisons them. An implicit critique of Jackson Pollock's *Eyes in the Heat* (1956), it is a warning against anthropomorphic abstraction. Smithson's iconic alternative, at its most extreme in his religious subjects, offered a way out. But at what price?

Smithson's train of thought culminated in the experience he described in the essay from 1972 on the *Spiral Jetty*: the complete paradox of a simultaneous heightening and eradication of pure consciousness. This frenzy was brought about by sheer intellectual overload and a condition of delirium induced by years of dialectical perception. Either this or boredom was the state he expected would intervene after a ceaseless attempt to fuse elements of his theorizing. Repetition was vital; the high decorative quotient in the paintings implies ceaseless change and paralysis caused by an inability to choose. Smithson's aim may have been to convert paradox into a workable 'dialectic'. In fact, his progress consisted of hovering ceaselessly between opposing but equally attractive alternatives, only to reject both. It is a sequence evident in his first great dilemma – a confrontation with what he regarded as the unwarranted anthropomorphic basis of New York School abstraction. For Smithson, Pollock's dependence on myth and submerged figuration was 'eating him up inside'; his fatal flaw was a refusal to reject 'the sensuous, anthropomorphic pantheism of Renaissance humanism'. Did this smack of European decadence to the 23-year-old Smithson? In Rome he had been reading Ezra Pound, who described Europe as 'an old bitch, gone in the teeth', and T.S. Eliot, who envisaged it as a cross between Dickensian London and the barren land of Ecclesiastes. One method of redefining abstraction was to return to Wilhelm Worringer's (and T.E. Hulme's) talk of a hard, classicizing impulse. In future his attempts to bring this about would mean employing crystalline structures. At present he turned to figures influenced by Byzantine art and Celtic decoration. Perhaps this was the first of many occasions on which he experienced attraction and repulsion in equal measure. The group of English literary modernists around T.E. Hulme, a group he was still puzzling over in his last essay, 'Frederick Law Olmsted and the Dialectical Landscape' (1973), had developed a decidedly antidemocratic turn of mind. Wyndham Lewis even wrote a book on Hitler. If a young man impressed by Catholic ritual and the classic architecture of the Eternal City felt drawn to religion, was this urge for spiritual direction somehow linked with a more worldly attraction to authority? Perhaps he had read Eliot's *After Strange Gods* (1933).

The religiosity that beset Abstract Expressionism in its late days was Smithson's inheritance. Only in the light of his subsequent work is it possible to measure the force with which it had to be discarded. Perhaps he already deplored the rejection by Worringer and Hulme of what he called the 'nature dialectic'. The truth is probably that he felt an act of faith would solve his problems too soon; he may have sensed correctly that his would be a career in which the journey, not the arrival, mattered, or that his masochism demanded more scope. Certainly, any non-religious reading of the naked male figures flaunting their wounds would have to acknowledge a certain paranoid tendency. Or could the turn from religion have arisen simply from a need to deal with problems in more worldly terms? Worringer had regarded Egyptian and Byzantine art as an escape from 'nature'. Perhaps mysticism would have served as Smithson's escape; Christ may be above and beyond human 'nature'. Was Smithson feeling guilty of blasphemy for making religious art because of merely theoretical considerations? All that can be suggested with any measure of certainty is that his crisis may have an equal and opposite attraction to Catholicism, and a need to overthrow it.

As art-historical documents, these paintings could hang in major museums. As new art they could take pride of place in any East Village gallery. But categories matter less than impact. In some measure these works possess the obscure scholarship, the morbidity, the humour, the perverse eroticism, the taste for emotion so high it may unbalance the mind or so low it may make it subhuman – indeed all the creative and destructive power that made Smithson the most troubling, subversive American artist since Pollock.

Theatre of Mistakes

Review of Homage to Morandi, *performed at the University of Southampton and at Goldsmiths College and St Martin's College of Art, London; published in* Artforum *IX, 11, September 1980.*

On a bare stage three men dressed in brown, white and green are matched with props of their respective colours. In time these props decrease in number. As they disappear, they are replaced by the actors themselves, who can also be summoned by fellow performers to represent missing items. As usual in the work of the Theatre of Mistakes, time, space, action and language are governed by systems of rules. The result resembles a choreography for words or a game too difficult to fathom. Repetition is used to heighten awareness of decision-making processes while offering a vision of some Pavlovian purgatory where what is learned holds sway over what is freely decided. Yet freedom is precisely the issue in a language so codified that it has become second nature. The 'mistakes' in their theatre could result from a failure of intellect, which in past pieces has been construed as a sin and punished accordingly; from some concept of elegant variation which the laws do not permit, from innovation, from art itself.

In a straight-faced bid for abstract theatre, as removed from storytelling and characterization as music or algebra, the Theatre of Mistakes could not be further from randomness. Yet it is called to mind in *Homage to Morandi*; amid a welter of codes something akin to freedom may appear when agreed structures collapse. The piece is disturbing because it calls to mind areas of life where rules no longer apply or matter, at fringes scarcely reached by our ordering procedures or so totally compelled by them that they constitute emblems of mere vacancy. Thought, instruction, law, are all devices for caring. The deep sadness of *Morandi* arises from considering – for longer than a second – that point where total power and total freedom are indistinguishable, where anything approximating consciousness is irrelevant or annihilated. It considers those lapses with a tenderness that our taxonomies will not permit us to redeem.

Homage to Morandi is a companion piece to the earlier *Homage to Longhi*, is shorter, has fewer actors, and conceals its structural principles. While *Longhi* featured slapstick, fainting fits, masking, and allusions to paintings themselves related to the comedies of Goldoni, *Morandi* elaborates on the motif of acting by means of constant play between animate and inanimate, and the bearing this fluctuating definition may have on ideas of being watched or of being on- or off-stage. *Longhi* and *Going* (based on the act of saying goodbye) suggested studies of etiquette. *Morandi*, not surprisingly, is a 'still life'. If relationships can be inferred between actors and the furniture they carry, these, it is hinted, arise from the viewers' inferences alone. The real Morandi concealed 'metaphysics' in naturalism. Transposed, his remedy resembles English irony, that indispensable survival kit containing both rose-coloured spectacles and wool to be pulled over the eyes. These succeed for a moment. In that moment an ideal universe is adumbrated; effects are dissociated from those who caused them, works of art never bite their feeders' hands, and by that terrible logic we desire without comprehending, those with 'powre to hurte' use it, and 'onlie begetters' are recognized as the open secrets they were always intended to be. Where precisely does the homage to Morandi lie? Not in distances but in codes that determine distances, not in the display of codes but in the understanding of them and the mute agreements they manifest, perhaps. We are wrong to think so; the homage lies in demonstrating how a self-regarding art of conventions can achieve a relevance so powerful it shakes our fixed beliefs. Saying it is insufficient; the Theatre of Mistakes enacts it.

At each point of 'incident', the actors will tell you, what the audience sees is decided by what was once a counting system and is now a complex code based on concepts of identity – singularity, repetition, inconsistency and frequency (or addition) – and how one of these is the device for arriving at position, gesture, remark. The piece has four acts, six scenes in each act, but runs without break. In Act One there are four chairs, three cases and two wardrobes. In Act Two there are three chairs, two wardrobes and one suitcase. In Act Three there are two chairs, one wardrobe and no suitcases; in Act Four there is one suitcase, no chairs and no wardrobe. Another act is suggested and not shown. In that act there would be no furniture at all. They will tell you that the reason the actors seem to turn to a sudden corner when crossing centre-stage is that there are two different rooms there – one passionate, the other dispassionate – and that a perspective distortion takes place as we look at the invisible rooms. And there comes a point, perhaps after pondering for an hour the diagrams governing each incident, when you are told that different parts of different systems are in fact juxtaposed, when you realize why linguistic philosophers understand Lewis Carroll, why Bergman or Fassbinder can legitimately, persuasively, make us believe that

God is a madman with a travelling repertory company. 'We use systems to defeat their own logic and create something which transcends those systems', says Anthony Howell, referring to the company's work. Then, sighing and smiling at no one, 'I think we use systems to defeat ourselves.'

Meredith Monk

Published in Artforum *XVIII, 6, February 1980.*

From the first moments of *Recent Ruins*, when six singers in formal dress apply their impressive technical skill to something like plainsong, the theme of sophistication versus primitivism is explicit: *Recent Ruins* is an experiment in pastoral. In an elaborate 'worked example' in which paired figures in the costume of different historical periods work towards the same discovery, chalking and rechalking the floor as they search, a pair of contemporary archaeologists slowly grasp the truth that a life's work may be devoted to documenting one part of a cheap souvenir or vacuum cleaner. Suddenly their labours are interrupted by the appearance of a small group of Ellis Island immigrants. A film is shown of a reconstruction of their lives; charades give way to more fragmented, oblique methods of perceiving their existence – their hospital treatment, food and living conditions are violently and unscientifically approximated. A lengthy set piece concerning a tribe called the People in Yellow shows their customs and journeys, and as the viewer senses parallels with other, more recent 'tribes', he also feels he is near the heart of myth. Finally, Monk conjures up a vision of a world beyond recorded time, a dark civilization that combines animal worship and odd, ritual play.

Recent Ruins is a chamber work in which limitations of space and form permit a gentle stress on the ironic repetition of faces, gestures, props and music. Monk's medium is operatic, unified emotionally with music, visually by the action. Though highly organized, it allows for 'interpolations' such as the sacred wrestling match between two women in section 111 or the powerful image of an 'Earth Mother' throwing heavy pieces of timber from one end of the space to the other. Details gather strength; the sudden dashes from spot to spot to avoid the camera eye in the Ellis Island film are a fixed part of the life of the People in Yellow. Sand falling from the roof marks the end of sections and is dramatized at first, then gradually begins to take place in darkness, forgotten. What sticks in the mind is not the startling visual moments or the *coups de théâtre* – the immigrants having their eyeballs examined, the violent courtship games of the People in Yellow, the electronically powered tortoises in the finale – but the gathering rhythms that bind the movements and correspond to a private, emotional dialogue with history.

Despite Monk's statement that the work is 'about the notion of archaeology as a way of seeing', the discipline itself is little more than a focus for her rhapsody on the themes of knowledge and time and how they are perceived. Robert Lowell wrote that history was what 'cannot be touched'. If 'touch' implies measurement and location, Monk would agree; what is lost in daguerrotypes or reports of excavations is quite simply 'life', the hum of a Viennese ballroom, the chit-chat of Regency bucks, what immigrants ate. Our daily lives are affected by tribes we have never heard of, in places we may never know, at periods before recorded time. Only song, dance, fighting and other social rituals can call them to mind. But they are not known; they are intuited. The very humour of reducing an intellectual discipline to an enactment of kindergarten activities, the possibility of giving 'history' a peremptory summons by concocted pseudo-ritual, the inescapable fact that our conception of historical period is comically, pathetically limited by who and where and what we are is not simply asserted, but acted out. Pastoral is a form as old as civilization itself, perhaps. Monk's contribution is a felt realization that art and archaeology may be more nearly aligned than we had ever expected.

Two Views of East London (Ian Bourn, Gilbert & George)

Extracted from a review – also reporting on Roberta Graham's work on the Kray brothers – of Helen Chadwick's 'ancillary section' of the Hayward Annual, Artforum *XVIII, 3, November 1979; followed by a review of Gilbert & George's Whitechapel Gallery exhibition,* Artforum *XX, 2, October 1981. Morgan returns to the question of Leytonstone in his essay on Jeffrey Dennis.*

[On Ian Bourn]

Eleven p.m. in Leytonstone, closing time in a London suburb. A key sounds in a lock, a light goes on and a young man sits down at a desk in his den, lights a cigarette, opens a can of beer and gradually begins talking to himself. Lenny is writing a documentary about his life in Leytonstone. As we eavesdrop he begins a 45-minute monologue, trying, and failing, to collect his thoughts. Stuck in a dismal place with no prospect of escape, Lenny struggles to find a voice. By turns he is an after-dinner speaker ('Who better to talk about Leytonstone than Lenny. Take it away. Lenny. Thank you, my son. What can I say that hasn't already been said . . .'); a satirist ('Geographically, Leytonstone is just a case of in one end and out the other. It's not the end of the road like Whitechapel or the beginning of the end like Southgate. Leytonstone, if it's anything, is the urethra of London') or the narrator of a travelogue ('This, my friends, is one of the northern approaches to Leytonstone over here. To my mind the only advantage of living in high-rise flats is that one can, if it is one's bent and one happens to have an air rifle, take pot-shots at the arses of old ladies below . . . I get a bus to see my friends in Leyton. Leyton is but a stone's throw from Leytonstone, and Wanstead Flats are within flobbing distance. Which reminds me, there's another thing you can do off the top of a block of flats'). Memories and confessions take over, imitations of pub conversation and Frank Sinatra singing 'Just One of Those Things'. As the documentary is forgotten only the impossibility of communicating remains. His stories, about the local mental hospital and the dirt kitchens in the high street cafés, drunken escapades and retarded people, become more grotesque. Lenny is clever enough to know he is trapped but not clever enough to know how to escape. His speech lapses into obscenity and incoherent litanies. As he struggles for coherence, one last sentence emerges: 'I believe that I have it in me to become a normal person like everybody else.' As Frank Sinatra sings 'I've Got You Under My Skin', the camera shifts to the driver's seat of a car travelling down a Leytonstone street.

Ian Bourn wrote, shot and acted *Lenny's Documentary*, best regarded as a video record of a remarkable private performance. Despite apparent improvisation, the lines were learned; before turning to video Bourn wrote poetry and fiction. At his degree exhibition at the Royal College of Art earlier this year two Bourns were evident, one a tangled Borgesian, writing about writing about writing, the other a neo-realist, dispelling the 'narcissism' of which critics complain and making fresh unselfconscious narrative video. His most recent work showed that the neo-realism persisted. *From the Junkyard* (1979), featured an unrecognizably different Bourn as Billy, a young junk dealer, talking to his uncle Bert on a quiet day. Again a strange, sculptural set was used, and while Lenny's speech was punctuated with captions showing the time that elapsed ('Five Minutes Later', 'Ten Minutes Later'), the junkyard dialogue was interrupted with exterior shots of a bleak area with punk and reggae posters covering the walls.

Bert fears for Billy, whose friends he considers crooks. Though Billy lacks his uncle's social ease, he respects his talk about 'the old days'. Bert's nostalgia has made him a National Front supporter and Billy's refusal to march with him may stem from self-absorption, loss of face or moral disapproval. Music symbolizes the rift between generations. Though he thinks his uncle's songs peculiar, Billy likes hearing them, dimly perceiving a more cohesive social order that underlies them. Perhaps some of Bert's love of the past rubs off on Billy as his uncle sings 'The Winkle Song' or plays records which are lying about; the tune which begins the tape – 'Dreaming', by Billy Reid and his London Accordion Band – has become a leitmotif by the end, accompanying him as he walks down the street at the end with his girlfriend Christine.

Lenny's Documentary and *From the Junkyard* are concerned with the state of Britain now, especially the loss of sensitivity and direction in young people. The crucial issue, as Bourn sees it, is caring. Billy is unable to distinguish his uncle's valid criticisms from his bigotry. His only answer is a fantasy life and an uneasy shrug. ('Leave me alone, let me wander' sings the piano-accordion band, 'A roving vagabond am I.') Lenny cares desperately and, like some late seventies Prufrock, is unable to take action. Maxim Gorky described the audience crying with recognition at a Chekhov play and said that watching it was like being sawn in half with a blunt saw. Video may turn out to be a digression in Bourn's writing career. Meanwhile, it was possible to turn up at the Hayward Gallery and feel just a little of Gorky's reaction.

[on Gilbert & George]

Appropriately, Gilbert & George's photo-piece retrospective ends its European tour in the East End of London, not far from the artists' Fournier Street home, from which the collaboration has been stage-managed for the last fourteen years. Around 1968 the posh but dilapidated pair, silly-ass comedians in old school ties, began an energetic expansion of the term 'sculpture' by insisting that their every action qualified for the title. Strolling nonchalantly down country lanes, they dedicated themselves to Art and to a life of 'artistic-ness', basing their satire on the values and beliefs of the middle classes. With a series of works about drinking, the jokes acquired a disturbing intensity, yet between landscape and the bar they had set up a pastoral dichotomy that would continue to serve them well. By the mid-seventies the funniest artists in Britain had turned sour. After the drinking bout came a prolonged hangover. Rolling in paper and debris they grimaced in postures of 'human bondage', surmounted by crosses and swastikas, or wandered endlessly through empty rooms gazing at dark shadows and dusty corners, musing on their imprisonment. Repetition had begun to pall. Their threadbare, nonsensical titles became nursery rhyme rigmarole, while their poses seemed no more than vacuous and inexpressive masks. After bucolic, alcoholic and just plain colic, Gilbert & George's vitriolic period had begun.

Giant photographs, assembled in grids like stained-glass windows, show blacks, Indians and Pakistanis, the unemployed queuing in grey crowds, skinheads, drop-outs, vacant public spaces, Victorian Gothic skylines, policemen, marching soldiers and the sculptors themselves, disillusioned and shabby, refraining from comment. As political comment on the state of the nation this work is simplistic and offensive – in *Paki* (not in the exhibition) the two Gs look down on an immigrant; an antique caricature of a woolly-headed black is magnified to wall-sized proportions; working-class boys are hailed as 'knights', 'patriots', 'angels' or, in one case. 'Britisher'. Women do not appear.

Trapped by their own personae, Gilbert & George have turned into the period gentlemen they once impersonated. Admittedly, prejudices are aired and confronted in *Modern Fears* and more recent works; but they have not been challenged or overcome. Britain in general is seen in terms of the Whitechapel locale – a sordid web of power struggles, the depression relieved by rough trade. Snobbery, lack of human warmth, political naivety, ambiguous application of obscene language, and above all a spurious concern for the underprivileged, coalesce to form a truly right-wing art, aestheticizing and self-indulgent. During the exhibition's run a prolonged outbreak of rioting, looting and burning occurred in cities all over the country; art like this can only make matters worse.

A Rhetoric of Silence: Redefinitions of Sculpture in the 1960s and 1970s

Published in British Sculpture in the Twentieth Century, *ed. Sandy Nairne and Nicholas Serota, Whitechapel Art Gallery, 1981.*

Between Bryan Robertson's 'New Generation' in 1965 and Anne Seymour's 'The New Art' seven years later 'new' sculpture in Britain changed beyond all recognition. That much at least, is certain. Whether it remained sculpture, whether it destroyed the possibility of ever defining sculpture again, or whether an orgy of rule-breaking was halted once and for all by a conservative backlash in the mid-seventies are all contentious issues. So contentious, indeed, that, although by the end of the sixties, thanks to Germano Celant's book *Arte Povera*, published in 1969, and Harald Szeeman's exhibition 'When Attitudes Become Form' of the same year, Britain was a recognized participant in an experimental community spanning America, Germany, Italy and the Netherlands, no detailed art-historical model for the art of this period has yet been proposed.

Perhaps there are good reasons for this omission. Flavio Caroli can maintain that in order to defeat consumerism the Italian avant-garde committed tactical hara-kiri in 1968.[1] Similarly, Robert Pincus-Witten can defend 1968 as the year that rivalled any in early modernism.[2] In Britain no comparable *annus mirabilis* can be found. Perhaps the battles were fought elsewhere. Already in Kynaston McShine's 'Primary Structures' exhibition at the Jewish Museum, New York, in 1966, for example, Caro, King, Tucker and other St Martin's sculptors had met decisive opposition. Decorative elegance influenced by hard-edge abstract painting, in which modernity was interpreted as novelty of form or colour, proved no match for the leaner approach of Carl Andre, Sol LeWitt, Robert Morris and Don Judd, in whose work craftsmanship and composition played little part, and neither modernist reductivism nor Constructivist theory had served as precedent.[3] Research on the British equivalent to Robert Pincus-Witten's 'post-Minimalism', the only soundly argued historical explanation of turn-of-the-decade art, would begin with a paradox.[4] Is it possible to identify a post-Minimalism without an initial Minimalism? One's first reaction is to look for opposition to Caro and his disciples. Predictably, it came from their students at St Martin's School of Art.

On the vocational course there through the sixties were David Bainbridge, Jan Dibbets, Braco Dimitrijevic, David Dye, Benni Efrat, Barry Flanagan, Hamish Fulton, Gilbert & George, Tim Head, Gerard Hemsworth, John Hilliard, David Lamelas, Roelof Louw, Richard Long, Bruce McLean and others. They were taught by Tim Scott, David Annesley and Michael Bolus, writers such as Alexander Trocchi and Raymond Durgnat and visitors including Clement Greenberg, Max Kozloff, Barbara Reise, William Burroughs and Kenneth Noland.[5] It has been said that Caro's students learnt 'not a style, not a dogma, but a discipline of doubt and enquiry'.[6] Traditions deteriorate. 'The St Martin's sculpture forum would avoid every broader issue, discussing for hours the position of one piece of metal in relation to another', Bruce McLean remembered, 'Twelve adult men with pipes would walk for hours around sculpture and mumble'.[7] Characteristically terse, Gilbert & George said, 'We were not in favour of people standing around talking about sculpture'.[8] Something of the prescriptive tone of senior staff, most of them trained by Caro himself, can be gauged from the writings of William Tucker. In 1975 Tucker defined sculpture as 'subject to gravity and revealed by light'. Free-standing, 'its constancy, in time and space, springs from its fundamental availability to perception'.[9] Reviewing Tucker's book *The Language of Sculpture*, Albert Elsen suggested that Tucker was becoming 'the Charles Blanc or Adolf Hildebrand of his era, spokesman for an academic abstract art'.[10]

Every one of Tucker's precepts had been violated long before. Constancy in time and space had been denied by Bruce McLean's photographs from 1967 – *Vertical Ice Sculpture* (a sheet of ice standing upright on a frozen pond) or *Splash Sculpture* (a stone hitting the surface of water). Richard Long's records of travel challenged fundamental availability to perception, showing temporary arrangements of on-site materials as the sole reminder of some transient human presence. After stressing the aggressive potential of sculpture with a set of obstacles blocking the St Martin's corridors, John Hilliard constructed a luminous line around the perimeter of his ceiling at home, a work revealed only by darkness. Certainly floor-bound installations by Long or Flanagan could be seen as extending the Caro innovation of abolishing the base. Perhaps in other media ex-students' concerns were persistently sculpturesque. The very fact that McLean, Long and Gilbert

& George clung to the term 'sculpture' to describe their activities, however, suggests that no theory of head-on confrontation at St Martin's can ever apply. The likeliest rationale for student reaction is provided by a letter from Barry Flanagan to Anthony Caro dated June 1963, published in *Silence*, a student magazine he co-edited: 'Rejection has been a motivation for me . . . Am I deluded . . . or is it that in these times positive human assertion, directed in the channels that be, leads up to the clouds, perhaps a mushroom cloud. Is it that the only useful thing a sculptor can do, being a three-dimensional thinker and therefore one hopes a responsible thinker, is to assert himself twice as hard in a negative way . . . I might claim to be a sculptor and do everything else but sculpture. This is my dilemma.'[11] To be or not to be a sculptor was not the question. Rather, how to conduct a career during a time of elected silence. 'Since the artist can't embrace silence literally and remain an artist,' wrote Susan Sontag, 'what the rhetoric of silence indicates is a determination to pursue his activity more deviously than before.'[12]

In 1966 John Latham reduced Greenberg's *Art and Culture* to a test-tube of goo and was fired from St Martin's as a result. The same year the Tate mounted its 'Almost Complete Works of Marcel Duchamp' retrospective. A year later in America Michael Fried published his essay 'Art and Objecthood'.[13] Possibly the three events are not as unrelated as they seem. Dissatisfaction with formalism was increasing. In what Victor Burgin later called a 'pseudo-debate' inside the formalist camp Fried distinguished between 'literalism' (Donald Judd) and 'modernism' (Anthony Caro), favouring the latter.[14] His division, seen in terms of life versus art, exposed the very issue that had exasperated Flanagan. To want to make 'sculpture' without accepting the 'rules' laid down to ensure that an object constituted an *art* object – in other words, to behave as Latham did and call it art – was impossible given existing terms. Duchamp was the necessary catalyst for *new* terms. In particular the readymade – which Octavio Paz described as '*an*-artistic' – became crucial.[15] Michael Craig-Martin's tour de force *An Oak Tree* (1973), a single glass of water on a shelf in a vast gallery with a leaflet purporting to be an interview with the artist, later summarized the pros and cons of a belief that 'it's art if I say it is', hinting that nomination was the infinitely thin knife-edge separating Flanagan's 'sculpture/not sculpture' paradox. Similarly Art & Language, a collective working in Coventry, and John Stezaker published lengthy deliberations on the readymade, successfully resisting a Duchampian initiation their American contemporaries had taken more lightly. In 1970

Greenberg, who regarded Duchamp as a phenomenon rather than an artist, sounded the alarm, denouncing the audience for his works in a lecture called 'Counter Avant-Garde'. By that time it was too late.[16]

The flirtation with use implicit in Duchamp was shared by some of the new art. Invited by Cedric Price (who was under the impression that they were an offshoot of Pop design), David Bainbridge and Harold Hurrell staged an exhibition called 'Hardware' at the Architectural Association. Later Bainbridge found that his 'sculptures' – such as a design for a crane for a children's playground in Camden – made useful topics for analysis for the Art & Language group.[17] Both James Collins (who taught Basic Design in England before moving to New York in 1970) and Stephen Willats focused on an art of social behaviour, Collins with his *Introduction Pieces* of 1970 and Willats with his shift from a preoccupation with audience response to sociological field-work.[18] Accompanied by a lengthy text, 'Beyond Art for Art's Sake', John Stezaker's *Mundus*, (1973), a perspex and wood construction, contained an electronic apparatus by means of which the participant played a game. By answering questions and pressing two control buttons it was possible to illuminate panels containing diagrams of four ideas – Action, Custom, Learning and Law. The status of *Mundus* ('world') was that of a diagram, summarizing Stezaker's theories.[19] In *Robin Redbreast's Territory* (1969) Jan Dibbets altered a robin's territory to correspond to 'a form that pleased me', laying out the new domain with poles like a drawing. 'The sculpture was comprised by the movements of the bird between the erected poles.'[20] From street theatre in which the movements of the 'audience' directed the 'actors', the Theatre of Mistakes proceeded to impose complex artificial codes of behaviour on comparatively simple activities such as pouring water (*The Waterfall*, 1977) or saying goodbye (*Going*, 1977). Interplay of behavioural patterns regarded as taxonomic systems provided tension as well as lyricism, and later a Mannerist repression of high emotion.[21] The behavioural model could be seen as one side of Pincus-Witten's American post-Minimalist dichotomy – 'epistemological activity . . . engaged in the study of knowledge as its own end'.[22] His other pole, 'ontological activity', which 'tends . . . to emphasize the self-referential; and the theatrical gesture' is certainly paralleled in British art.[23] In *Lecture Sculpture*, a collaboration with the Royal College of Art in 1969, for instance, Gilbert & George sat on the stage applauding politely while Bruce McLean acted out the work of famous sculptors. McLean repeated some of these imitations in *King for a*

Day, his thousand-piece, one-day, book-form Tate Gallery retrospective in 1972.[24] 'Theatre' was a term used already by Michael Fried, who defined it as the area between traditional modes. The concluding section of 'Art and Objecthood' described the impression given by 'literalism' and 'theatre', both to be avoided. The experience was that of 'an object in a situation – one that, virtually by definition, includes the beholder', extorting some special complicity as another person did.[25] It conveys perfectly the impression given by certain works of Stuart Brisley, notably *ZL 65 63 95 C* or the celebrated *And for today . . . nothing* (both 1972), in which the artist himself was discovered in a filthy room, motionless in a wheelchair or sitting in a bath full of cold water and rotting meat.[26] Here 'situation' was equal in importance to 'object', a person functioning as one element in a totality.

Duchamp's influence served to deflect attention from the internal properties of works of art to their context; what had previously been considered support systems for art rather than the art itself were now emphasized. One major innovation, and the most common replacement for object-making, was the marriage of language and photography, particularly in books. By the mid-sixties concrete poetry had become a thriving international movement. 'Conceptual' photo-texts or titled drawing opposed the concrete poets' belief – dating, perhaps, from the publication by Pound of Fenollosa's *The Chinese Written Character as a Medium for Poetry* – that words in Western languages can function happily as visual configurations and denotative tools. Like illustration titles, the words in a Long photograph or a Tremlett book do not trespass into a visual medium, but function as in magazine layout or advertisements. Later Stezaker, Burgin and Hilliard were to embark on analyses of exactly these subtexts, Burgin becoming a major critic of photography.[27] Yet despite increasingly scholarly examinations of words and images, the relationship between space on a page and space on a wall, between those two-dimensional spaces and the 'white cube' of the gallery, was seldom if ever mentioned by critics. Without requiring theoretical supports, such as Oppenheim's for his 'removals' or Smithson's for his 'non-sites', the viewer needs to feel some balance between the possibilities of each, and reassurance that in the work of given artists not only general principles but specific manipulations of space are connecting different media. In future commentators may connect the reading process with the duration that characterizes performance, and appreciate contrasts between the two. Gilbert & George's page by page, line by line rehearsal of 'Underneath the

Arches' in their book *Side By Side* (1971) evokes not only the measured precision of one of their performances but functions as a reminder of the self-perpetuating, endless devotion they proclaim to Art. Long's use of folksong ('John Barleycorn') or Country and Western music ('Corinna, Corinna') indicates a reliance on regular rhythms and unpretentious content. It also relates to travel and to the relaxed perception David Tremlett has claimed that his pieces demand. Tremlett's own graceful calligraphy in *Some Places to Visit* (1974) or his sign language in *On the Border* (1979) are the nearest that this schizophrenic medium gets to the concrete poetry of (say) Ian Hamilton Finlay. An entire Arapaho legend reprinted at the conclusion of Hamish Fulton's *Hollow Lane* (1971) offers no direct key to the photographs. Paradoxically, as his journeys become more picturesque, in *Nepal 1975* or the title piece of *Skyline Ridge*, words diminish. The suggestion is of a loss of identity in the face of alien experience. Like an epigraph in a novel by Sir Walter Scott, the Indian legend acts as a key or talisman while adrift in strange places, among other ways of life. At the other extreme from such loose evocation is the methodical testing of language against picture in John Hilliard, intent on discovering whether his chosen medium can be a vehicle for truth.

Uncertain of how to find terms to cope with the new art, critics isolated its most obvious property. Alarmist phraseology such as 'dematerialization' or 'de-objectification' hinted at some apocalyptic exhaustion of forms.[28] The term 'Conceptual art', unveiled before an English audience in the first edition of *Art-Language* in 1969 in an article by Sol LeWitt as well as in the magazine's subtitle, 'A Journal of Conceptual Art' (later discarded), stressed that art's concern was change of consciousness, an approach supported by Charles Harrison in his new essay for the London showing of 'When Attitudes Become Form' at the ICA in the same year. Yet since 'object' can be regarded as the opposite of 'concept' the danger always existed that one side of a false division would banish the other. (Harrison and Barbara Reise, the most sensitive critics of the time, avoided such black and white dichotomies.) Characteristic of artists' preoccupations was the desire to exploit an 'object's' potential to ricochet interminably between fixed systems. One entire *trompe l'oeil* sub-genre demonstrates this well. Jan Dibbets's *Perspective Correction* (1967–9), Bruce McLean's *Mirror Work* (1969), Richard Long's *England* (1967) and Keith Arnatt's *Invisible Hole* (1968) all provided 'proof' of imagined edges separating levels of reality. Claes Oldenburg's contribution to a 1967 'Sculpture in Environment' exhibition was a hole dug by gravediggers and then refilled. He called it an underground sculpture and 'a conceptual thing'. Arnatt said, 'Although the idea of a sculpture that you couldn't see intrigued me considerably, I was sceptical about the notion of a sculpture being a "conceptual thing". There is at least a clear distinction to be made between the concept of a filled-in hole and an actual filled-in hole and it did worry me at the time that one had to take someone's word for it that such a hole had been dug and filled in.'[29]

Arnatt's hole, mirrored on the sides and with the turf removed from the surface of the ground replaced on the bottom, isolates his confusion, states the paradox he perceived and does nothing more. Yet he notes the paradox that Flanagan had already described to Caro; 'sculpture' defined in the terms they both inherited, was unworkable unless definitions of all kind could be shelved or altered or confused.

As a typical 'sculpture' of the period Arnatt's *Invisible Hole* exemplifies one especially appealing quality – an underlying desire for anonymity. Similarly, Braco Dimitijevic, in a funny, Warholian series, made monuments to the 'casual passer-by' he met in the street at a given time and place. They could be in any medium from hoardings to public sculptures. Finished and installed, they proved indistinguishable from other hoardings or monuments to allegedly 'famous' people, a situation that permitted the artist to claim that works could have been made by him. In an urban setting he was making his own human parallel to the activities of Long, disturbing the landscape then passing on. Gilbert & George's assumed personae, identically clad gentlemen from an earlier age, finally led to charges of snobbery and insincerity. *Art-Language* magazine proposed a continuing dialectic by which guidelines could be established for an art not yet in existence. Unlike Stezaker, who claimed his essays as his art, they offered only inconclusive dialogue, the record of a search. Fulton and Long avoided publicity. Such apparent modesty befits an art *povera*, stripped to the bone as a protest against the economic system. Yet humility too can satisfy the media. Richard Cork noted the movement's 'abject failure' to bypass the art market.[30] Anne Seymour wrote that 'instead of being quite unusable within the sinister structure of the art market an enormous amount of money has been made out of Conceptual art.'[31]

Sadly, ten years later the explosion of activity that post-Caro sculpture represented has been all but forgotten, the product of an episode in which criticism may have outrun original creation. Permission has been granted for a certain type of performance and a precedent has been set for artists to fluctuate between media. The almost Georgian naivety of approach to nature may continue to charm, but grotesqueries of jargon and ill-informed borrowing from other disciplines have worn badly and exerted little influence. Vicarious experience of other people's emotions through 'documentation' was also a feature of the time, it seems. It has not persisted. Yet the virtues of a 'moratorium on objects' were undoubted and in future may seem a moral, if Pyrrhic, victory.[32] Above all, it dented formalist formalist doctrines once and for all, as well as warning against a surplus of objects in the world. What terms art employs to describe its manifestations is of no concern to me. But my lack of concern was fortified, if not engendered, by this period. It seems inconceivable that sculptors cannot use its findings to enrich their practice in future, finding time amid the din to listen to a rhetoric of silence.

1 Flavio Caroli, 'Before the Flood', *Nuova Immagine* (Milan: 1980), p.12.

2 'I think 1968 and 1912 are parallel moments in the twentieth century.' Robert Pincus-Witten, unpublished interview with the author, 14 August 1978.

3 Cf. Arts Council's 'Pier and Ocean' exhibition at the Hayward Gallery, 1980.

4 Robert Pincus-Witten, *Post-Minimalism* (New York: 1977).

5 See *Studio International*, January 1969, special St Martin's issue and Charles Harrison, 'Some Recent Sculpture in Britain', *Studio International,* 26 (January 1969) (Dibbets, a Dutch student researching coloured sculpture in Britain, only used the library.)

6 'Norbert Lynton, 'Latest Developments in British Sculpture', *Art & Literature,* 2 (Summer 1964), p.196.

7 Nena Dimitrijevic [diacritic on c], *Bruce McLean* (London: Whitechapel Art Gallery, 1981), p.7.

8 Anne Seymour, 'Gilbert & George', in *The New Art* (London: Arts Council of Great Britain, 1975), p.7.

9 William Tucker, 'Introduction' to *The Condition of Sculpture* (London: Arts Council of Great Britain, 1975), p.7.

10 Albert Elsen, 'A Review of William Tucker's *Early Modern Sculpture: Rodin, Degas, Matisse, Brancusi, Picasso, Gonzalez* (the title of the American edition), in *Art Journal* (Winter 1975–6), p.138.

11 Barry Flanagan, 'A Letter and Some Submissions', *Silence,* 6, (January 1965), pp.2–3.

12 Susan Sontag, *Styles of Radical Will* (London: Secker & Warburg, 1969), p.12.

13 Lucy Lippard, *Six Years* (London, 1973), pp.15–16; *The Almost Complete Works of Marcel Duchamp* (London, 1966); Michael Fried, 'Art and Objecthood', *Artforum* (June 1967), reprinted in Gregory Battcock, ed. *Minimal Art* (New York, 1968), pp.116–147.

14 Victor Burgin, *Work and Commentary* (London: 1973), n.p.

15 Octavio Paz, 'Marcel Duchamp or the Castle of Purity', trans. D. Gardner (London, 1970), reprinted in Joseph Masheck, ed., *Marcel Duchamp in Perspective* (Englewood Cliffs, N.J.: 1975), p.84.

16 Clement Greenberg, 'Counter Avant-Garde', *Art International,* XV, 5 (1971), pp.16–19.

17 For *Art-Language* see Lynda Morris, 'Do You See What They Mean?' in Martin Attwood ed. *Artists'*

Bookworks (London: British Council, 1975), pp. 88–97; *Studio International* (October 1973), Art Theory Supplement; Art & Language 1966–1975 (Oxford: Museum of Modern Art, 1975).

18 Sarah Kent, *James Collins* (London: ICA, 1978), pp.13–14; Stephen Willats, *Concerning our Present Way of Living* (London: Whitechapel Art Gallery, 1979), pp.13–17.

19 John A. Walker, 'John Stezaker at Nigel Greenwood Gallery' *Studio International* (December 1973), p.248.

20 Jan Dibbets, *Robin Redbreast's Territory: Sculpture* (Cologne/New York: 1969), n.p.

21 Nick Wood, 'The Theatre of Mistakes: Anthony Howell Interviewed', *Artscribe* 10 (January 1978), pp.11–14.

22 Robert Pincus-Witten, op. cit., p.89.

23 Ibid.

24 *Gilbert & George: 1968 to 1980* (Eindhoven: Van Abbemuseum, 1980), p.47, and *Bruce McLean*, op. cit., p.21.

25 Fried, op. cit., p.125.

26 'Chronology' in *Stuart Brisley* (London: ICA, 1981), nos. 57 and 59.

27 See, for example, his *Two Essays on Art Photography and Semiotics* (London, 1976).

28 Lucy L. Lippard and John Chandler, 'The Dematerialization of Art', *Art International* (February 1968);edited version included in Lucy L. Lippard, *Six Years: the Dematerialization of the Object* (London: 1973), pp.42--43. Ursula Meyer, 'De-objectification of the Object', *Arts Magazine* (Summer 1969), pp.20–22.

29 Quoted in Richard Cork, 'Sculpture Now: Dissolution or Redefinition?', Lethaby Lectures, Royal College of Art, 11 and 12 November 1974, *Audio Arts Supplement* 1975.

30 Richard Cork, *Arte Inglesi Oggi 1960–1976*, vol.2 (Milan: British Council, 1976), p.314.

31 Anne Seymour, 'Introduction', op. cit., p.6.

32 Victor Burgin, 'Thanks for the Memory', *Architectural Design* (August 1970), p.388.

Cold Turkey

On the exhibition 'A New Spirit in Painting' at the Royal Academy, published in Artforum XIX, *8, April 1981.*

A woman decides to hold a dinner party and hires a maid to wait at table. All goes well until the servant steps into the room carrying a huge turkey, trips and drops it on the carpet. 'Blanche,' says the hostess, her voice quivering, 'take that away and bring in *the other turkey*.' 'A New Spirit in Painting' isn't just a turkey – it's the same old turkey dusted off and disguised. Cold, mangled and covered with fluff, it may stick in our throats, but the day is saved – any turkey is better than no turkey at all. Unless of course, you prefer the truth. The most provocative part of 'A New Spirit' is the word 'new'; every major point in the catalogue text has been made before, and the average age of the artists is 50. By London standards this is a very large, very expensive show indeed, and publicity for it has been unusually immodest. Unfortunately, magnitude has led to a loss of coherence. 'A New Spirit' is a chance to think about the possibilities of painting; it is a clarion call to born-again painters, an attempt to consolidate some current critical stances and a ratification or revision of existing traditions. Inside it are entire sub-exhibitions trying to get out – for instance, a survey of contemporary German painting and a group of late modern masters. Altogether it is synthetic, symptomatic, even representative. Not 'new'.

The selectors seem to disagree. Christos Joachimides writes, 'This exhibition presents a position in art which conspicuously asserts traditional values such as individual creativity, accountability, quality, which throw light on the condition of contemporary art and, by association, on the society in which it is produced.' Wait for the catch. 'Thus, for all its apparent conservatism the art on show here is, in a true sense, progressive.' Britain, a country with extraordinary continuity in its cultural history, is easily fooled by such paradoxes. But 'backwards equals forwards' isn't a paradox; it's an untruth. Any major public display of this kind demands an accompanying statement. And to paraphrase Pound, exhibitions should be at least as well organized as critical essays. Here theory is replaced by appeals to traditional aesthetic uplift. It is the last straw when Joachimides recommends a recapitulation and then claims that this will renew the avant-garde.

According to the selectors, 'A New Spirit' is a manifesto but not a prophesy, an 'area for assertions to be tested' and 'a reflection on the state of painting now' – an anthology and an art work in its own right. The main confusion is between description and prescription. Why are the paintings there? Are they slides for a lecture or counters in a Leavisite power struggle? Why is New Image painting banished, or at least restricted? Why is pattern painting ignored completely? Why drag in performance artist Bruce McLean or Jannis Kounellis just to prove a point about the flexibility of the medium, while Conceptualists engaged in examining the philosophy of painting (such as Michael Craig-Martin) are omitted, to the detriment of the show and its argument? Why, above all, does the show exclude John Walker, the single artist in the country whose entire output for the last ten years is relevant to the matter at hand?

One thing is clear. 'The New Spirit' was intended to make exciting juxtapositions and propose new historical relationships. Its failure to do both can be attributed to a scatter-shot thesis, and to the nature and brevity of the catalogue texts. Yet it is just possible to spot connections without knowing whether they were deliberate. It is like imagining a small city block where by chance Frank Auerbach and Willem de Kooning are neighbours. Hockney and Warhol might also live near to each other. At times they pop up to de Kooning's to borrow a cup of sugar. Balthus and Kitaj talk politely from time to time in the elevator, united by a distant family relationship. The Minimalists would keep themselves to themselves: the landlord rented them an apartment but no one knows why. One of the mysteries of 'The New Spirit' is why all these artists are hung together. Gothard Graubner seems to draw on the German Romantic tradition; while projecting the warmth of physical presence, his stuffed canvases heave with the *Sehnsucht* of overweight contraltos. Alan Charlton is site-specific, dividing and inflecting the space he finds. Robert Ryman is an inventor, determined to begin again as if no one has ever made paintings before, conscious of the fact that after thirty years he may have only redesigned the wheel. Are imageless paintings included as an indictment of the bankruptcy of means? At the boundaries of the tradition of abstract formalism, Brice Marden should qualify as a key figure in any debate surrounding 'The New Spirit'. There is no clue that he has been singled out, though two recent works are included. On the subject of abstraction in general, it is difficult to piece together an argument. The importance of German Expressionism is hammered home, but the fate of Abstract Expressionism is less easy to discern. Philip Guston's change of heart, and an aspect of late de Kooning, hardly provide material for an answer. But we can see A.R. Penck's vast hieroglyphics recall early Adolph Gottlieb and David Smith's drawings. Someone in Sweden must be writing a scholarly article about Per Kirkeby and his connection to the New York School. Kirkeby is that art-historical rarity, the artist who revives a defunct movement and kills it off again almost immediately. In his case he does it in the same painting. Mimmo Paladino's *Rosso Silenzioso* – it sounds better in Italian – has me completely foxed; it is either a deep and moving cry from the unconscious or a piece of flim-flam too silly even to hang on the wall.

Abstract Expressionism, then, seems to have vanished or been abandoned, though there are whiffs of it here and there. In the US it may be difficult to mount a major show that is optimistic about the future of painting without constant reference to the fifties. (Barbara Rose's 'American Painting: The Eighties' is a good example.) But in Britain an unbroken line of realist art, which Kitaj calls 'School of London', can be used as a spine. The main figures are represented here: Bacon, Hockney, Kitaj himself, Auerbach and Lucian Freud.

The link between the three major groups represented – the British realists, the German Expressionists and America in the sixties – remains a secret. What can be learned from 'The Greats'? From the final paintings of Picasso, a lonely abandon, with the colours of decay and a quicksilver style that is second nature, the rules of a game he had almost forgotten; from Hélion, bathos. How to paint a fish head severed by an axe and call it *Holocaust*; from Guston, the guts to look at R. Crumb and steal from him; from de Kooning, the courage to be a child again; from Balthus, the strategies of a *pasticheur* with too little to say; from Bacon, an obsession with right-wing iconography. 'The Greats' are their own captors, who at worst provide object lessons and at best provide a private virtuosity that disciples cannot emulate. Like family gods, they exist to be cajoled and chastised, as if we really know them. We do not. What is to be learned from Shakespeare's final plays, or Beethoven's late quartets? Everything and nothing. Behind the bars they do not think of us at all and ignore the nuts we throw.

In contrast, 'the youngest' artists here seem to address themselves to less private issues; their headaches are caused by poise, taste, reconciliation of styles, the mechanics of facing an audience and entertaining. Rising from a wilderness of broken crockery in Julian Schnabel's *St Francis in Ecstasy*, a black-faced martyr looks puzzled as a male torso flexes in mid-air. Sandro Chia's smoker farts as he puffs. Malcolm Morley's *Lone Ranger* has wandered on to the set for *Fantasy Island*. Faux naïveté is to the late seventies what camp was ten years before: a recoil from feeling, from history, from accountability. Despite its artificiality, it reveals a distaste for devices, an impossible desire to present pleasure directly, to escape pre-existent languages and express an affinity with the purely fictional. Marooned in a historical doldrums, its exponents try to make the best of their situation; they strive for a new behaviour, not a new technique – a way of accepting, even flaunting, poor expedients and hand-me-down styles. Dressed in tatters, they make tatters fashionable. To those who argue that realism in painting is a neglected vehicle for expressing ideas – ideas from the world outside – faux naïveté must seem a betrayal, a way of dismissing the problem. And from any point of view this exhibition assumes an aestheticism with which many will disagree, finding the ivory tower of Balthus, or Warhol's obeisance to the privileged, offensive and irrelevant. All three selectors – Norman Rosenthal, Nicholas Serota and Christos Joachimides – write that in some of his last works Picasso 'achieved a synthesis born from the sense of the history of painting and also a wild disdain of his own place within it. The last paintings have a freedom of expression which allies them to the youngest paintings of this exhibition. In the end the only care is about the act of painting itself. That we think is true of all the other artists in the exhibition, each in their very own way.'

Perhaps the real problem is expressed in the small room of Twombly drawings, skittish and excitable yet, after all, only variations on a sigh of regret that history can no longer meet and fertilize, that time runs on while myth, and traditionally art, try to halt it. The classic modernist invention was not the fixed style of 'The Greats', but the collage, which spoke of change, of the smell of the air in the street, outside the studio. Collage has been banished from 'The New Spirit' yet has found its way in through the back door, as the only visual equivalent of the historical model that governs the present.

There were no grounds, runs the conclusion, for deciding that a direction was evident in 'The New Spirit', no grounds for saying that the true avant-garde lay in unsaying the avant-garde. One style, and its justification, is here. Another is there. A third lies nearby. At the Royal Academy I can connect nothing with nothing. Frustrated that painting can't be life and relieved that this is so, the faux-naive, with their quasi-suspension of time, become easier to acknowledge. Their subject-matter arises from boredom. Roland Barthes wrote: 'Ennui is not far removed from delight; it is delight seen from the shores of pleasure.' The combination of ennui and delight is a combination that has been used before. In *The Will to Power* Nietzsche characterized modernism as 'the opposition between external mobility and a certain inner heaviness and fatigue'. With the painters of pleasure, total recall is subject to forgetfulness as they doze in the sun, living comfortably off the interest from their modernist investments. At the other extreme is Teutonic gloom. Rivalled only by some of Bernd Köberling and Dieter Hacker, Anselm Kiefer wants us to look at bogs of dark impasto. Markus Lüpertz paints three almost identical versions of a gigantic World War II monument against a battlefield setting, calls them *Black, Red and Gold Dithyramb* and hangs them side by side, a work with all the subtlety of a visual gang-bang.

If any poetry resides in sheer murk, it emerges in K.H. Hödicke's *Against the Light* and Rainer Fetting's *Large Shower I* and *II*. Though Fetting's fantasies exude an air of Crucifixions and concentration camps, both he and Hödicke can produce large, fluent neo-Expressionist works without relying on bombast. Does some proportional relation exist between external mobility and inner fatigue, between the nervous brushstroke and the burden of the past? Hockney's new landscape paintings suggest that one does. Quirky, oversized, they look like a cross between Dufy and Hundertwasser. The colours are uniformly bright and the composition has disintegrated into a collection of motifs. There are signs that subject-matter no longer interests him, nor the problem of finding visual devices; he may be content to string together cheerful Hockneyesque passages. His *Mulholland Drive* (1980) is an allegory describing the directions the whole exhibition takes: realism, threadbare and giggling with embarrassment, prepares to come to terms with an avant-garde it claimed it never wanted to join. 'What the hell,' Nietzsche would have said, 'it's all modernism.'

From the shores of modernism one can only look back. The four main points of 'A New Spirit' – the return of figuration, the neglect of the Northern Expressionist tradition, the increased subjectivity of the artists and the need to reconsider 'old masters' – give way to a different, dominant theme: the difficulty of establishing a relation with the past that involves neither continual homage nor deliberate ignorance. The problem is less a debate than a family quarrel in which logic has no place. In his poem 'The New Spirit' John Ashbery described such a vacancy: 'So that we must despair of all realism now, because it is there, it is totally adequate for what was being represented, only we cannot feel it as such, but that is our tough luck.' There may come a time when talking won't help, and when it will be impossible to move forwards or backwards. Worse still, that time may already have come. Unable to face it, we sent Blanche out for the other turkey. We have only ourselves to blame.

Becoming Arshile Gorky

Published in Artscribe *31, October 1981.*

> Once in a dramatically illuminated exhibition in a museum he appeared suddenly conspicuous beneath one of the spotlights. A woman crossed herself, then apologized.
> 'For a moment,' she said, 'I thought you were Jesus Christ.'
> 'Madam,' he said, drawing himself up to his towering tallness, 'I am Arshile Gorky.'[1]

For most New Yorkers there was no mistaking Arshile Gorky. 'A nice manly face,' said de Kooning, 'very handsome, with rough, big hands, beautiful physique, lean beautiful body, very masculine.'[2] His painting style has been harder to define. Unashamedly imitative of modern masters in his early career – he spoke of being 'with' Cézanne or Picasso – he confused even the experts.[3] After his death, for example, Greenberg published an apology for having thought him 'a slave to influences'.[4] Labels for his art proliferated, some contradicting others: Abstract Expressionist (Rosenberg), Abstract Surrealist (Levy), late Cubist (Greenberg), Biomorphic Surrealist (Ritchie). Only Breton, it seems, wrote of 'an entirely new art'.[5] Today critics hedge their bets and content themselves with detailing rifled sources. Yet the writing of Julien Levy, Gorky's dealer in the forties, hints that with him neither purity nor sincerity was a straightforward issue.

Announcing his forthcoming course at the Grand Central School of Art in 1942, Gorky claimed that some knowledge of camouflage would be an advantage to painters. Taking up the theme, Levy called him 'the camouflaged man'. Reasons are not hard to find. Deprived of house, inheritance and aristocratic status, a displaced person seeking refuge in the United States set to work remaking himself like a monster without Doctor Frankenstein. First he needed a different name – 'Arshile', one of four possible spellings of 'Arshak', had connotations of royalty.[6] If it sounded French, all the better; he sometimes told people he had studied in Paris. 'Gorky', Russian for 'bitter', he purloined from Maxim Gorky. Luckily the name was familiar; later he was to claim that the Russian writer was his cousin. A need to make and remake identities for himself is evident from photographs, which show a fleshy, clean-shaven aesthete becoming a rangy, moustachioed exotic. In ten self-portraits he adopted other men's features, among them Picasso, Cézanne and Matisse. Even his love letters contained plagiarized passages from Gaudier-Brzeska and paraphrases of Éluard.[7] The progression from filching other men's styles and faces to an acceptance that he was, after all, a culturally displaced person seems an outrageous paradox. Fusing existing styles can be regarded as an activity appropriate to exiles, patching together scraps of culture, condemned to persist in their new beginnings as compensation for what they have lost. That, at least, is one argument. What confuses it is one assumption underlying Abstract Expressionism – the predominantly immigrant movement of which Gorky is frequently claimed as a pioneer – that elements from existing historical styles may be subjected to infinite cross-fertilization in order to form an independent 'American-type' painting. Another approach would be to suggest that Gorky never discarded his masks; perhaps the process was too painful. Levy has suggested that meanings are subjected to a complex veiling and unveiling in Gorky:

> The unconscious is, so to speak, the domain of camouflaged objects, and Gorky was soon to discover that if the realistic object can be camouflaged, so can the unreal or 'surreal' object be coded and decamouflaged.[8]

The nature of his 'coding', however, may itself be construed as an even greater act of concealment; he seems never to want to divulge secrets, demanding from his viewers permission to drift, to rhapsodize on the elements suspended with the picture frame. Illusions are always stage-managed by Gorky. If, as Yeats pointed out, lyrics are overheard, then Gorky is pre-eminently a lyric painter.

Most Gorky criticism has fallen into two categories: biographical information and complex analysis of stylistic features. If Gorky was in any meaningful way 'the painter of his own legend', as Elaine de Kooning declared, it is surprising that they have not been successfully combined.[9] His mature style corresponded with much that is reported of his social behaviour. Stuart Davis described his conversation as 'extremely remote from accepted English usage'. He spoke with an accent, of course, but the effect was the result of 'earthquake-like' rearrangement of sentence structure and a 'savagely perverse use of words to mean something they didn't'.[10] It could be a description of the style of the late paintings. Unrestrained exoticism, dislocation of pictorial structure and point blank metaphor – *The Leaf of the Artichoke is an Owl*, one title announces – coalesce to form a 'code' that may have been as much a manifestation of social procedure as the prosecution of some inner search. (Perhaps deliberately, André Breton misspelt another metaphorical title. *The Liver is the Cock's Comb*, wrote Gorky. *The Liver*, Breton misquoted, *Is the Coxcomb* – paraphrased, 'Everyone alive is a dandy'.[11]) Yet suggestions of this kind do not imply that Gorky was anything other than obliquely biographical in his art. Investigating the nature of that obliquity and its mysterious operation involves some risky meditation, less on the subject-matter and style of his art than its genre and sustained tone.

* * *

> The most potent elements in a work of art, are, often, its silences.
> – Susan Sontag[12]

His wife, Agnes, testified that the mid- to late thirties were the worst period in Gorky's life; his own words were 'bleak' and 'spirit-crushing'.[13] Poverty and lack of direction affected other artists too. In the last years of the decade Pollock was consulting Joseph Henderson. In 1944 Barnett Newman destroyed all his work. Gorky's *Portrait of Master Bill* shows his colleague as amiable but vacant and non-committal, like a puppet waiting to be manipulated. The self-portraits reveal more potential activity. The air of nobility in decline has given way to a hurt expression, puzzled rather than resentful, alarmed at the indecision that besets him. A drawing in the manner of Ingres reveals a permanent shrug and the resigned hands-in-pockets attitude of a man forced to take charity. But those hands and those unseen pockets are worth a second look.

One of the most quizzical of the self-portraits, of around 1937, shows the artist pale, thin beneath his clothes, about to speak or perhaps recoiling from an attack. His hands are heavy, the fingers not distinguished, the movement limited. In short, they look more like clubs or stumps than a sensitive apparatus for making art, and the rendering is brushy, unfinished, like the panel behind him, which could well be a painting. The odd, fussy brushing, a way of indicating that something doesn't matter by making a shorthand cipher of erasure, is frequent in Gorky, and stands at an apparent extreme from his other gesture, the sudden manifestation of core or viscera. Or is he making it plain that there are things that *do* matter but they cannot be embodied?

Art about boredom has to reveal truths about boredom, to dramatize it for the onlooker in some new way. Here Gorky makes a token connection with those hours and weeks and months spent scraping off paint, changing his mind, wavering between abstract and figurative modes, dreaming of a new 'Armenian' style. Yet the mark on the canvas does not incorporate that experience or pass it on to the spectator. A friend, Ethel Schwabacher, wrote of the portrait that it resulted from 'a mixture of potency and impotency – the potency of the inquiring eye and the impotence of the hand which, though it suggests endurance and contained energy, is heavily frozen, immobilized'.[14] Metaphors of the transfer of power in Gorky's art are deceptive, however. Previously, utter obedience to European masters had been accepted as a moral duty. Now the pull of Europe was too strong to inspire. One story, 'apocryphal perhaps but significant nonetheless', is that some time in the mid-thirties he called meetings to plan a team effort painting by eight or ten artists, including Lee Krasner and de Kooning, in order to produce some native opposition to Europe on the only basis that seemed workable.[15] Could the reason for the play between potency and impotence, correctly sensed by Schwabacher, be explicable as the product of a belated need to achieve creative independence as an artist at a time when choices were limited? ('In 1940', wrote Barnett Newman thirty years later, 'some of us woke up to find ourselves without hope – to find that painting did not really exist.'[16])

Similarly, both paintings titled *The Artist and His Mother* – one dated 1926–36, in the Whitney Museum collection and the other, dated 1929–42, at the National Gallery of Art, Washington – shy from what painting can do by not forcing technique to a point where meaning will be fully evident, by tending towards either representation or symbol. Only the original photograph on which they are based explains that the boy is holding a bunch of flowers, for instance. And in the Whitney variant his mother's hands are concealed by pockets that did not exist in the photograph. In both pictures the apron is the largest 'empty' area in an arrangement made more poignant by incompletion. The Whitney apron billows like a cloud, defying perspective, while the mother, in keeping with her expression of suppressed anger, has her hands stuck grimly into her pockets. The later painting shows her drained of life, hands free but muzzy, the apron deep enough to make a lap for her dutiful favourite son. Much of the emotional tension of the Whitney composition arises from the nervy grey divide created as the son, needing to be prepared for life, is separated physically and emotionally from his dying parent. For the Washington revision, in which the pair are proportionally larger and placed closer together, the sleeve of his coat touches her right sleeve and the entire apron – a mixture of pinks, rusts and lavenders – is the only part to approach that yellow which affected Gorky deeply, a reminder of the colour of dandelions boiled during childhood summers on the shore of Lake Van, which he shared with his sister Vartoosh.[17] The tonality of the later picture has shifted; instead of greys and blacks the range is nearer a fleshy pink. Lady Shushanik, Gorky's mother, died of starvation in his arms, after having refused food to ensure that her children had enough. Her death, following the abandonment of their family home to escape the invasion of the murderous Ottoman armies, left the young Gorky and his sister Vartoosh alone in the world. A meeting with his father in America was not a success, and for whatever reason he subsequently considered the family atomized.[18] Once more the drama in Gorky's view of himself lies in his feelings of sorrow and apprehension when independence is thrust upon him. Did he regard his painted image as getting younger as he aged? Certainly he does not try to hide his dependence on the reassurance his mother's apron could provide. Unable to imagine a time when his hands would provide art and food, wanting both yet fearing the challenges they entailed, he avoided thinking about them too hard in the *Self-Portrait*. His mother's apron, painted in that same nervy, slapdash manner apparently denying painting, whistling in the dark, was truly a taboo subject, an expanse too exciting even to countenance, defying description yet continually inviting it.

* * *

> I recover my tenderness by looking.
> – Theodore Roethke[19]

Gorky had discovered that the emotional focus he had been needing was there from the start. From now on nostalgia, sentimentality, a fear of being vulnerable, and a counterbalancing desire to be made to feel more vulnerable, were released into his work. And now, perhaps, he could see that his problem had not been poverty or the limited range of approaches available to him, but understandable apprehension. He told pupils to find something they loved before starting to paint. But in a touching letter Vartoosh had told him to stop pining for the Armenia of his childhood, his obsessive, enduring love; it no longer existed. The agony of confronting a loss of home, culture, language, family, mother and name, and confronting it deliberately day after day was as necessary for the artist as it was unbearable for the man. Style and genre were to provide the only protection he could muster.

For *The Garden of Sochi* paintings – four with that title and one untitled study – Gorky wrote a poetic statement of which this is part:

> About 194 feet away from our house on the road to the spring my father had a little garden with a few apple trees which had retired from giving fruit. There was a ground constantly giving shade where grew incalculable amounts of wild carrots, and porcupines had made their nests. There was a blue rock half hidden in the black earth with a few patterns here and there like fallen clouds. But where came all the shadows in constant battle like the lancers of Paolo Uccello's painting? This garden was identified as the Garden of Wish Fulfilment and often I had seen my mother and other village women opening their bosoms and taking out their soft and dependent breasts in their hands to rub them on the rock ...[20]

Fact is not at issue here. (In a remarkable statement Edouard Roditi stressed the significance of the text as 'individual mythology rather than as collective folklore'.[21]) Nor is the obviously Freudian translation of the name of the garden. Light, colour, movement, sound and atmosphere combine to make a transposition, not a description, of the picture. Yet Gorky's verbal Armenia seems theatrical and affected, only a hair's breadth away from the cute exoticism of (say) Yasuo Kuniyoshi. Surely this must be the element of 'charm' that so irritated Greenberg, the theoretician of kitsch as well as the avant-garde.[22] Gorky had planned to paint in a hieratic, 'Armenian' figurative style, as in the *Portrait of Vartoosh* and *Portrait of Akko*, his younger sister and older stepsister. Commentators are usually generous but vague on the subject of the Armenian influences on Gorky's mature abstract style. The central shape, which appears in all but the 1941 gouache, a kind of pointed Disney buskin, may owe as much to the illuminators of the School of Van as to Miró, however. More obvious is his constant association of his childhood with a dream of Armenian femininity. Previously he had been searching for a type of beauty. Now he remembered or fantasized a fertility ritual of which he was the only male witness. Any power this may have given him is undercut by the fact that he is a child; the only aggressively male image, Uccello's lances, turns out to be a trick of the light.

It could be said that both Gorky and de Kooning possessed powerful anima components, yet while de Kooning's was attacked and symbolically destroyed in the *Woman* paintings later, Gorky's remained ideal and unquestioned. (Marny George, whom he married in 1935 and soon divorced, said 'Arshile wanted to form and mould me into the woman he wanted for his wife.'[23]) The woman he wanted was Armenian, yet Gorky's Armenia no longer existed. *Portrait of Myself and My Imaginary Wife* demonstrated that his ideal woman would also function as muse. In that painting the figures stare into the middle distance, facing the same way and taking no notice of each other. His downcast gaze has been explained as a reference to medieval Armenian sculptures of Christ.[24] The truth is simpler than that. Certainly Gorky is adopting one of his favourite poses – of the man of constant sorrow, marked by destiny for a life of 'endless pursuit' and subsequent torment'.[25] But the intersection of spaces occupied by the figures, which are suspended in space on the canvas with no attempt at realistic reconciliation, demonstrates that while she is watching over him, he is *imagining* her. The establishment of a 'feminine' atmosphere for his contemplations, the habit of organizing his pictures in untethered sections, separated by a wandering Armenian decoration, lines both spiky and bulbous that contain their own private realities like cartoon bubbles; the thematic preoccupation with the motif of floating, blowing, dangling in space; most of all the progress of the final version of the *Garden in Sochi*, a scrubbed playground for his chosen units, says everything about Gorky's idea of abstraction. For him it worked precisely as he had described it: *The Way My Mother's Apron Unfolds in My Life*.

Her apron was not the only trigger to his imagination. The sequence of paintings he called *The Plough and the Song* celebrated two others. Gorky loved carving wooden ploughs for friends. A few survive.[26] 'What I miss most are the songs in the fields,' he told an interviewer, 'No one sings them any more . . . And there are no more ploughs. I love a plough more than anything else on a farm . . .'[27] Nor did he forget his native dances. At parties he would bring records, turn his jacket inside out so that the lining resembled a peasant costume and dance alone in traditional style. Because singing and dancing, doodling or whittling wood did not absorb the whole of the concentration, they left part of the mind free to improvise and play. They were also ways of acknowledging the fact of being an Armenian without directly calling to mind the undesirable concomitants. If he had stopped there he would have become a painter of idylls. His achievement in the early forties was to redefine pastoral.

* * *

> Tout l'univers chancelle et tremble sur ma tige.
> – Paul Valéry[28]

Disagreement about the role played in Gorky's development by the Newark Aviation murals may simply be because their 'rescue' did not take place until 1977.[29] Still unclear is Gorky's own view of the technological subject matter forced on him by the WPA. Yet it is certain that after concentrating on unfamiliar problems Gorky seems to have been relieved to drop them completely and return to his private Armenian world. How he challenged his right to that world and registered what Erwin Panofsky called a discrepancy 'between the supernatural perfection of an imaginary environment and the natural limitations of human life as it is', is the study of how he became Arshile Gorky.[30]

One method was to allow his earnestness to lapse. The utter seriousness with which art was to be taken was part of Gorky's doctrine that he shared with John Graham. Later too he was to blame the Surrealists for their lack of seriousness. Another way was to cultivate the habit of reverie, a state of daydream set off, perhaps, by his triggers. Bachelard emphasized the crucial parts taken both by childhood and a powerful sense of anima in populating a state between dreaming and waking, lacking the violence of total dream. Much has been said about the influence on Baziotes of Poe and Baudelaire. In comparison, the lyric tone in mature Gorky seems to approach a post-Symbolist sensibility, to have arrived at a position beyond subjective idealism, where the self seems total and omnipotent. In Valéry it is

> the state between dreaming and waking, when images of peculiar significance and brightness melt into an undifferentiated and nebulous background, when at moments we seem to have a peculiar understanding of matters of great import only to sink back into the half-conscious confusion of dream . . . . In such a mood we may well see ourselves in a new light, as figures of cosmic import. And this happens in *La Jeune Parque.* The poet transposes the movements of his consciousness into a strange milieu. He sees himself as a divine figure who has left a serene superterrestrial dwelling for the chances and passions of mortal life. So may a man dramatise himself who is torn between his thoughts and his actions. In this state the ordinary limits set to our powers seem not to exist. We feel that we are the centre, if not of

> the universe, at least of some enormous scheme, and that anything we do or that happens to us is pregnant with huge issues.[31]

By 1942, the date of his trip to Virginia, Gorky had perfected the style Alloway calls 'polymorphous fabulism', which insists on 'the identity of everything with its simultaneous phases of seeding, sprouting, growing, loving, fighting, decaying, rebirth', presenting a single indivisible object that defies scale.[32] It is tempting to regard this image creating itself as a product of what Bachelard called 'cosmic reverie'. The quality he finds in Rilke's *Sonnets to Orpheus* 13 and 15, in which the poet 'dances' the orange, dares 'to say the name Apple', and is consequently borne away by their potential for expansion, parallels Gorky's habit of lying face down on the ground and putting his face into the grass, then drawing the effect. Yet 'cosmic reverie' is discernible in Gorky in other ways too. 'For any human being, man or woman, it is one of the feminine states of the soul . . . in general the dream issues from animus, and reverie from the anima.'[33] 'We dream at the frontier between history and legend.'[34] Most notable is Bachelard's assertion that the dreamer is always present in his own reverie. ('Je me voyais me voir', says Valéry's Young Fate: 'I saw me seeing myself'.) And Bachelard insists on the domination of childhood memory in reverie. A state that helps the dreamer to escape time, it 'bears witness to a soul which is discovering its world, the world where it would like to live and where it deserves to live.'[35] For Gorky, of course, liking and deserving had nothing to do with it. His painting would have to help him situate himself in America, or be abandoned. The state of reverie was more than just a mental exercise to get him in the mood to paint; it was to be communicated to the viewer with as much of its raptness and bliss as possible. Yet it also had to be opposed, not on moral grounds – there are no 'shoulds' or 'should nots' in Gorky – but for sheer survival.

Both major styles used in the Virginia studies show a concern with registering the process of facture. The pullulating polymorphs throb obscenely, like portions of raw guts that have decided to go it alone. Often they are drawn with magic realist precision. Yet the other style – that of *Virginia Landscape*, *Composition I* and *Composition II* – seems rushed in comparison, with trees in hot red wax crayon, applied powerfully and inaccurately like a whore's lipstick, while the rest of the composition hangs in an elegant Calderesque tangle. The exactness with which Gorky balances speed of apparent movement of the subject with a drawing rhetoric pitched differently, suggests the middle ground he wants to establish, as a way of reconciling opposing pressures. The impulse to devour the landscape visually, make it serve one's own purposes without respecting its separate existence. The slower, inescapable analysis is part and parcel of perception taken further and performed by the painter, who stills his subject matter, dissects it, then gives it back its freedom again as a new object in the world; there is even the impulse to simplify and tidy the unruly landscape until it becomes no more than a function of one's own sorting mechanisms. Above all, the pressure to exhaust the emotions utterly, as quickly as possible, secure in the knowledge that there is always more landscape there, that any chosen part will be arbitrary and make us feel 'mere midgets in the wide universe but masters of our particular planet'.[36] For Gorky it was vital that his paintings as statements of identity should cope with the opposing claims of such drives. By 1943 it was possible for him to enact his drama of personal definition in totally visual, perhaps totally 'abstract' terms.

That, at least, was the prevailing view until this year. Ironically, at exactly the time when Diane Waldman was mounting the most comprehensive Gorky retrospective ever, at the Guggenheim Museum, New York, Harry Rand's *Arshile Gorky: The Implication of Symbols* was attempting to undercut one entire view of the artist. Essentially, Rand takes an assumption that is usually shelved – that the iconography of Gorky's later career consists of abstractions from life – and moves relentlessly through the entire oeuvre, 'reading' each work. Results are as spectacular for the critic as they are demanding for the viewer. According to Rand, *Water of the Flowery Mill* contains two women and a man in a landscape, while *Agony* focuses on Gorky himself, already hanged. *The Betrothal* – considered by Ethel Schwabacher, William Seitz, Gail Levin, Robert Reiff and others to be a stylised version of a horse and rider from Paolo Uccello's *Battle of San Romano* – is a bride and groom with their little dog. The same approach has entered Pollock criticism in recent years, with mixed results. Few commentators will support all of Rand, but many will sympathize with at least some of his arguments. Perhaps the fault of his book – and it is a magnificent 'fault' – is that it is so provocative that it demands a rejection of most other criticism of Gorky. Take his interpretation of *Waterfall* in the Tate Gallery collection.

> In the upper centre, at the right base of a triangle near the top rests a dark blue-green circle that denotes the head of a man; and Gorky, never one to use

> disembodied symbols, attached the head to a fully described figure. Beneath the head are two arms, green oblongs, that rest horizontally on the shoulders of a woman; simply a man and a woman in an embrace. The woman's body, mainly white and high-value warm tints, can be distinguished if the triangle in the very centre of the painting is seen as the space between her waist and left arm. She is wearing a dress, and its skirt bells out and away from her full figure.[37]

There seems to be no alternative but to accept or deny these phantoms.

Waterfall was part of a sudden leap forward for Gorky. 'Despite some vagueness and possible misrepresentations in the date of his paintings through 1942, there is no question that he was working in his personal style by the end of that year', wrote William Rubin, 'that he was creating masterpieces by the following year.'[38] The motif of tears – the 'raining down of tears' mentioned in a poem called 'Thirst', for instance – has already been noted: Gorky is always present inside the subject-matter, wanting to feel for it. Here his technique of unfixity, allowing the subject to hover between as many known attitudes as possible, wishing it to preserve its quality of strangeness, is overwhelming. Gorky's desire is to save it, always to have its potential there.

These, of course, are exactly the reasons artists paint waterfalls. But for Gorky experiment with 'given' subjects – the pots of flowers and torsos he had always made in the twenties and thirties, for example – presented a challenge because they so adamantly resisted expression in terms of his private world.

Gorky's five years of unquestioned greatness began with *Waterfall*. He still made use of reverie, as in the *Plough and the Song* series. Yet violating it, allowing reality to encroach, had helped to establish a genre – pastoral, sophisticated play on the difference between wildness and civilization, nature and culture, simplicity and sophistication. Schwabacher claimed that the main theme in Gorky's art was the relationship of love and death. It certainly is, though a less general definition would stress 'love' as desire without fulfilment, 'death' as either ageing or loss through memory. It could be regarded as the constant attempt to amalgamate two irreconcilable modes of vision or to locate and experience a sensuous present tense between a powerful past and future. Also involved is a complex of paradoxes concerning independence and potency as well as nagging doubts about influence and identity. In short, his art so far had been about becoming Arshile Gorky.

1. Julien Levy, 'Foreword', *Arshile Gorky: Paintings, Drawings, Studies* (New York: Museum of Modern Art, 1962), p.7.
2. Willem de Kooning in *Ararat*, vol.12, no.4, Fall 1971, p.51.
3. Julien Levy, *Arshile Gorky* (New York, 1966), p.15.
4. Clement Greenberg, 'Two Reconsiderations', *Partisan Review*, May/June 1950, p.513.
5. André Breton, 'The Eye-Spring: Arshile Gorky', *Arshile Gorky*, Julien Levy Gallery, New York, March 1945, n.p.
6. Karlen Mooradian, 'Chronology' in *Arshile Gorky: Drawings to Paintings* (Austin, 1975).
7. Nick Dante Vaccaro, 'Gorky's Debt to Gaudier-Brzeska', *Art Journal*, vol.23, Fall 1963, pp.33–4; and Harry Rand, *Arshile Gorky: The Implications of Symbols* (London, 1981), pp.5, 9–10.
8. Julien Levy, 'Foreword', *Arshile Gorky: Paintings, Drawings, Studies*, p.7.
9. Elaine de Kooning, 'Arshile Gorky: Painter of His Own Legend', *Art News*, January 1951, pp.38–41.
10. Stuart Davis, 'Arshile Gorky in the 1930s: A Personal Recollection' [1951], repr. in Diane Kelder, ed., *Stuart Davis* (New York, 1971).
11. Rand, pp.183–6.
12. Susan Sontag, *Against Interpretation* (London, 1967), p.36.
13. Diane Waldman, *Arshile Gorky* (New York, 1981), p.41.
14. Ethel Schwabacher, *Arshile Gorky* (New York, 1957), p.35.
15. Dore Ashton, *The Life and Times of the New York School* (Bath, 1972), p.61.
16. Barnett Newman, 'Jackson Pollock: An Artists' Symposium Part 1', *Art News*, April 1967.
17. Waldman, p.34.
18. While Schwabacher quotes a letter from Vartoosh Mooradian explaining that Gorky no longer associated with his father after his second marriage (p.151, n.19) Robert Reiff (*Arshile Gorky's Art from 1943–1948*, New York, 1977, pp.122–5) implies strongly that snobbery prevented Gorky from properly acknowledging any of his family in America.
19. Theodore Roethke, 'What Can I Tell My Bones?'
20. Maurice Tuchman, *The New York School* (London, 1971), p.60.
21. Reiff, pp.131–3.
22. Clement Greenberg, 'Art: Paul Gauguin, Arshile Gorky', *The Nation*, no. 162, May 4 1946, p.552.
23. Schwabacher, p.61.
24. Hayden Herrera, 'Gorky's Self-Portraits: The Artist By Himself', *Art in America*, vol.64, March 1976, p.64.
25. Karlen Mooradian, 'The Philosophy of Arshile Gorky', *Armenian Digest*, September/October 1971, p.54.
26. Hayden Herrera, 'The Sculptures of Arshile Gorky', *Arts Magazine*, vol.50, March 1976, pp.88–90.
27. Ibid., p.88.
28. Paul Valéry, 'La Jeune Parque'.
29. Newark Museum, New Jersey, *Murals Without Walls: Arshile Gorky's Aviation Murals Rediscovered*, 1978.
30. Erwin Panofsky, 'Et in Arcadia Ego: Poussin and the Elegiac Tradition', *Meaning in the Visual Arts* (New York, 1955), p.300.
31. C.M. Bowra, *The Heritage of Symbolism* (London, 1943), p.24.
32. Lawrence Alloway, 'The Biomorphic Forties', in *Topics in American Art since 1945* (New York, 1975),

p.20.

33. Gaston Bachelard, *The Poetics of Reverie* (Boston, 1969), p.19.

34. Ibid., p.101.

35. Ibid., p.15.

36. Schwabacher, p.86.

37. Rand, p.88.

38. William S. Rubin, 'Arshile Gorky, Surrealism and the New American Painting', *Art International* 7, February 1963, p.28.

Who Chicago?

Review of exhibition at Camden Arts Centre, London, published in Artscribe *27, February 1981.*

Most of 'Who Chicago?' consists of paintings from the seventies by artists who surfaced in the late sixties, notably the Hairy Who group (Jim Nutt, Gladys Nilsson, Karl Wirsum, Art Green, James Falconer, Suellen Rocca) plus the Chicago primitive Joseph Yoakum, Ray Yoshida (a teacher from the Art Institute), H.C. Westermann and some members of ad hoc groups – Ed Paschke from the Non-Plussed Some, Roger Brown, Christina Ramberg and Philip Hanson from the False Image and Barbara Rossi from Marriage Chicago-Style and Chicago Antigua.

Highly coloured, raucous and obsessive, the work of the Hairy Who soon shed its urban rawness and gave way to a more private stylism distinguished by complex surface incident, an emphasis on craft, a penchant for sexual themes and a shrill use of colour. The group identity of the Chicagoans matters less, perhaps, than the values they have supported – those of mannerist figurative stylization in an era of formalist preoccupations. By 1966, the date of the Hairy Who's first show at the Hyde Park Center, native Chicago art had been flourishing for twenty years. The 'Monster Roster' – Leon Golub, George Cohen, Cosmo Campoli, June Leaf – had been augmented by a new group of artists who emerged from the Art Institute in the mid-fifties. While the Monster Roster were expressionists, Irving Petlin, Robert Barnes and H.C. Westermann created private fantasy worlds. If history decides that the Hairy Who and their disciples did more than continue this nay-saying, anti avant-garde holding action, they may be considered not as pioneers of a completely new movement, as Dennis Adrian and Russell Bowman suggest in the catalogue, but as part of a larger School of Chicago comparable to the New York School. Among the important questions this raises are those of the nature of change within such a regional or provincial trend, the gradual decline of a historical awareness on the part of the artists, the progressively greater articulation of perverse and neglected areas of the psyche and the communicability of visual idioms.

Elaboration of flat surfaces and absence of implied movement – a characteristic of all the artists except Nilsson and Nutt – combine to produce iconic presences that may seem alive and terrifying in their jittery excitement

(Wirsum) or coldly meditative (Brown). For European viewers colour is an immediate problem. Whereas Green's high-keyed acidity at least serves to orchestrate an entire colour range, Yoshida's murky mosaics and Rossi's plastic pastels rely on such wilful elision of treble and bass registers that their relational systems seem arbitrary, despite the evidence of careful planning. Something similar may be true of content. In Green's work subject matter is unanchored, imported; comparison with, say, Stephen Posen indicates the limits of a style that is all muscle and no brain. Green's are the largest paintings in the show. The almost uniform canvas sizes are nothing to do with the fact that this is a travelling exhibition; lacking loft spaces available to their New York contemporaries, the Hairy Who and others scaled their work down. Choices of surface – Wirsum's work on plastic, the metal studs hammered into an early Nutt, the fake thread and welding in Green, the beading in Rossi and the *trompe-l'oeil* lattices of Christina Ramberg – hint at a relationship with sculpture that is evident in Brown's shaped paintings and Wirsum's wooden figures, Margaret Wharton's chairs in the Mayor Gallery exhibition and the uninhibited use of colour in Westermann. If painting and sculpture tend toward a mid-area, verbal play is also almost obligatory. Puns, misspellings, words written on the canvas in paintings and even (in Westermann) on the sculpture or its box constitute another level of significance, playful but far from accidental.

Of the Hairy Who, two (Suellen Rocca and James Falconer) stopped painting. Two others (Karl Wirsum and Gladys Nilsson) were 'naturals' so gifted that it was hard for them to improve, though Wirsum's talent for design can be extended over an unexpectedly wide area. (At Halloween in 1979 I was led into a darkened room at the Phyllis Kind Gallery in New York to watch a slide show of a hundred pumpkins he had carved.) In the last few years two more artists, Jim Nutt and Ed Paschke, have developed into major painters. With Paschke 'develop' is the wrong word; it is hard to see how the crass sensation-seeker of ten years ago curbed his taste for vulgarity and exaggeration, refined his sense of colour and located an emotional area which was at once chic, banal, evil and sad. Featureless 'Invisible Man' figures pose against luminous backgrounds while electric flashes zip across the picture like encephalograph readings. The effect far exceeds the sum of the parts. Theatrical yet self-absorbed, these Watteau-esque dummies suggest a historical awareness lacking in Paschke's peers. Could he be the next Leon Golub? Jim Nutt's subject matter, the emotions lurking beneath social intercourse between men and women, is presented with almost animal violence. Yet for Nutt the act of painting itself represents the normalizing processes of daily behaviour. Like some Japanese courtier, Nutt has ritualized this process; alternate shocks and seductions form a set of 'good manners', symbolically delivering the spectator from his fears and temptations. The grace with which embarrassment and hatred are deflected appeals on a level of sheer aestheticism. Yet Nutt's work, though exquisite and cultured, is openly mendacious. Working within the system, he has shown what art is capable of and finds it insufficient, at best a means of preoccupation. If, as Frost pointed out, it is a 'momentary stay against confusion', for Nutt that confusion consists of discovering who we really are.

Peter Greenaway: The Falls

Published in Artforum *XIX, 7, March 1981.*

Peter Greenaway has written documentaries about defenestration and people struck by lightning. He has also written pseudo-documentaries about fictional characters such as the polymath Tulse Luper. *The Falls*, a marathon three-hour-long movie made with the support of the British Film Institute, employs, extends and ridicules his pseudo-documentary conventions. It examines the results of a mysterious occurrence – the Violent Unknown Event (VUE) – discussed but never explained by the characters. Of the 19 million victims of VUE, a random selection from the new, fictitious Standard Dictionary yielded 92 surnames beginning with the letters 'Fall . . .'. Case histories of these 'Falls' are presented in alphabetical order. The Event changed their lives completely: vision, height and weight altered as mutations took effect. Four new genders came into existence and 92 languages were acquired by the VUE victims: Alowese, Agreet, Abcadafghan, Betelgeuse, Candoese, Cathaginian, Cathanay, Curdine, Egalese, Entree, Foreignester, Glendower, Glozel, Ipostan, Itino Re, Karnash, Mawdine, Mickelese, Untowards, Upthalian, Vionester, Wringer. Physical mutations included skin discoloration, contracted intestines, splayed or retractable thumbs, six-part hearts, incontinence, loss of fingertips, bone-marrow deficiency and wings. The stricken are fascinated or terrified by water, darkness and flight. The most disturbing change is that sufferers seem to be immortal.

Evidence is often confused. Some of the Falls are simply typing errors, names of places not people, fictional rather than 'real' characters. Others are involved in court cases, have escaped or been killed, have no fixed address or are too shy to speak. Interpreters are needed, as well as interviewers and narrators.

The three VUE epicentres were the Boulder Orchard on the Lleyn peninsula in North Wales, the Temple of Piety in the grounds of Fountains Abbey in Yorkshire and the Queen Charlotte Maternity Hospital in Goldhawk Road in London, all real, totally unremarkable sites lovingly filmed by Greenaway. Theories of the Event are topographical, ornithological or religious. For instance, Agostina Fallmutt's thesis that, ousted by mankind, birds took their revenge by alienating the human race, is greeted with derision by experts and laymen alike; Usbian Fallicutt is convinced that the VUE was a hoax devised by Alfred Hitchcock to resolve the unsatisfactory ending of *The Birds*.

Compromised though it may be by sheer self-interest, for Greenaway historical reconstruction – a compound of pedantry, anger, logic and perversity – exists in an almost operatic domain. Nabokovian in its narcissism, Pynchonesque in its Manichean morality and manipulation of infinitely detailed subcultures, *The Falls* has been compared to Laurence Sterne, though manic cross-reference and linguistic *tours de force* bring it closer to James Joyce. It is an encyclopaedia of avian mythology; an encapsulation of Greenaway's own fiction, illustration, painting and cinema; a scrapbook containing pieces of old newsreel, tatty animated collages, a complete avant-garde work based on the construction of the Royal Festival Hall and studies of still photographs from family albums; a guidebook to a lost Britain; and a compendium of British humour, blending irony and smut, eccentricity and schoolboy puns. A taste for grotesques and proliferation also make it a contemporary bestiary: Tasida Fallaby, the malodorous naturist with black-and-white vision and a double menstrual cycle; Aptesia Fallarme, the 'Waterfall on Legs'; Ipson and Pulat Fallari, the twin trapeze artists; Vacete Fallbutus, the *petomane* (a man who farts for a living) who can wiggle his ears, blow smoke rings from his nose and spit 80 yards; Arris Fallacie, the lice-ridden Dutch kite salesman; Carlos Fallantly, the murderer who had an affair with a turkey; Afracious Fallows, the scrofulous ex-headmaster with enlarged genitals and a chip on his shoulder; Pollie Fallory, who before the VUE worked as a bird imitator and after it learnt English again in order to become a woman imitator – all exist in the foreground of *The Falls*. The background is a directory to the lost and neglected. A single shelter on the promenade at Barmouth, a cooling tower in Goole, a yellow door on the Lleyn peninsula, the word 'clout', a photograph of a Hereford wash-house and hundreds of other ordinary details are suddenly shot through with significance by their involvement in a plot that, like gossip, has no plot at all. The burden Greenaway places on the viewer's shoulders is heavy, but no heavier than what a reader would expect from a post-Joycean novel. In return Greenaway's audience is rewarded with the materials for an entire alternative system of thought.

Stuart Sherman

Review of performance at AIR, London, published in Artscribe *29, June 1981.*

In walks Stuart Sherman, carrying his props in a suitcase. They are cheap and ordinary – a telephone receiver, a newspaper, a hat, strings of neckties, folding tables, tape measures, children's toys. Sometimes they are home-made. In bursts of movement, each with a title, he pulls out combinations of objects and performs a sequence of actions with them. Sometimes clumsy, invariably too quick to think about, they are gestural conundrums, a cross between the brain-teaser and an automotor activity, a kind of physical nonsense. Yet they are propositions too, announced in this way with no questions from the floor.

Critics, theoretically ideal spectators, have failed to define Sherman's art of intimate pantomimic haiku. Berenice Reynaud called it 'object ritual'. Sherman himself coined the phrase 'visual object music', a species of kenning that parallels as well as describes what he does. His chosen generic title is 'spectacle', however, and in at least one important sense it resembles circus, or formation swimming; Sherman displays himself only as a person proficient in certain activities. Nothing more. Alarmed by a performer humble enough to deflect a personality cult, audiences wait with bated breath for acknowledgement or claptrap. They are disappointed. Not even smiling, Sherman goes about his demonstrations like an absent-minded brush salesman who has forgotten to deliver his doorstep spiel. And implicit in his short films is the impulse to serve his material without wasting his or our time.

It is difficult to overstate the oddness of seeing a grown man concentrating hard on intricate manoeuvres with no purpose, though no odder, perhaps, than watching any rehearsal of a set of rules you have no hope of comprehending from a purely intellectual standpoint. *The Twelfth Spectacle (Language)* contained recurring motifs – toy people and animals, guns and limbs, the equation of reading and looking – for a passing Martian to grasp the idea that the talk was of codes in general. Yet though the set pieces moved in a straight line and Sherman himself has compared the procedure of his spectacles to writing on a page, the argument was far from sequential. Much of the humour had to do with the seriousness of the subject; like an enthusiastic but incomprehensible lecturer, Sherman will go to any lengths to prove a point no one can understand. The sight of a grown man rolling on his back with a globe of the world on his forehead is irresistible. *The Tenth Spectacle (Portraits of Places)* contained less repetition; each set piece seemed more independent. As he began each sentence he spoke its title. 'Harper, Kansas.' Out of the suitcase came a plastic corn cob, a tape measure and a set of clacking clockwork teeth. A miniature tape-recorder played the noises of a party. The party was extended, then drawn into alignment with the teeth. 'Istanbul.' The props were a black bag, a loaf of bread with a candle stuck in it, a knife and a tape-recorder playing market sounds. After lighting the candle, he drew the knife through the flame, cut the bread and turned the bag upside-down so that some white boxes fell out. The difficulty was to notice everything and, because digressions, if any, were indistinguishable from dominant motifs, to know what was important. Images began as ambiguities – the polystyrene with rectangular cuts for 'Copenhagen' could have been windows or deep snow – and gathered more ambiguities as they unfolded. One thing was clear. Easy references such as weighing drugs in 'Istanbul' were denied rather than confirmed; what interests Sherman more is the *state* of a metaphor, like that of a 'red-light' district at the end of 'Amsterdam', when the props are covered in red cellophane. Social comment (Harper) and realistic detail (Istanbul) may occur incidentally, but impressionism is far from the aim. 'I'm afraid I haven't been to a lot of the places you portrayed', I said, trying to make conversation. 'Neither have I', he replied, sipping his Coke. Language took up where *Places* stopped, with fictional clusters such as 'St Petersburg, Russia-Los Angeles-Eden'. The titles in *Language* – Ears/Nose/Hands, 'Fearful Symmetry', Hair Piece, Mirrors, Finger, Hello/Goodbye, Airplane, Wind/Breath, Magnet, 'Balloon', Records, Baseball/Yoyo, 'World/Word', Four Colours of Black, 'Wealth of Words' and Measuring tape/Filmstrip – were for his own use, written as usual on a box-file card hidden in his top pocket and consulted after each stage of the action. In *Places* the titles were one element of the total effect, whereas in *Language* every part could profitably have been called 'Untitled'. Each was an abstract poem in itself.

In Britain the idea that poets invent words died out with Robert Browning. But American writers, from Emerson to Pound and beyond, inherit a preoccupation with language as a tarnished instrument to be redeemed by each generation in the cause of truth. 'No ideas but in things', wrote William Carlos Williams. 'Say it.' But saying doesn't make it so. 'There is an idea for every object', said Sherman, perhaps equally innocently. The earnestness of his acts of work, mental not physical gymnastics, is not a by-product of eccentricity or some private world, but the hard labour that invokes linguistic deliverance. The ideal may be a state where language, like a restless fly, never settles. The reality may be that we have swatted it already.

Fortunately matters are not that straightforward. From the simple visual pun in films such as *Fountain/Car* or *Flying*, Sherman goes on to test various ways in which words, objects and events co-exist. As in all linguistic theory, change must be accommodated. In Sherman's case change of context (*Hand/Water*) or magical changes of state (*Skating*) are explored. Yet he is no scientist, attempting tangible proof of his hypotheses, but a matchmaker, arranging happy marriages between his various components and striving to state the result as clearly and wittily as possible.

Home Truths: Laurie Anderson

Published in Artscribe *32, December 1981.*

Darkness. Two engineers wait at a console. Gently three working areas are illuminated in red, with mikes, lecterns, lights and keyboards. Behind them is a dais, behind that a screen. As the music begins, a slide of the Statue of Liberty appears. Aerial shots in negative of Central Park follow, then dissolve. The rhythm persists, the volume builds, the key changes and a grid falls like a curtain over the entire screen. Only after the overture are we aware of a small figure in black, with cropped hair. 'Lately I've been doing a lot of concerts in France', she says, in a voice not entirely her own. Cool, androgynous, removed, she performs without apparent anguish. Nothing has been left to chance. Yet somehow slickness itself comes to resemble a force that may overwhelm her. Entering the spotlight, dwarfed by background images of Fifth Avenue skyscrapers, she seems frail and alone, in keeping with her pose as an alien. The shots of Manhattan lack warmth. Built by a Frenchman, the Statue of Liberty is an ideal – unassailable, incomprehensible. Perhaps she refers to them later in a parody of the old Harry Belafonte song: 'I took a trip on a sailing ship, and when I reached your country I made a stop.' Or maybe that was Columbus himself. *United States*, Laurie Anderson's set of four three-hour performances due for completion next year, had another title once. It was called *Americans on the Move*.

Two situations recur in Anderson's script. One is a felt conjunction of word and image, like the times when you're at the breakfast table early, you're 'not quite awake' and you're 'just looking'. Then suddenly you 'snap to attention' and realize that 'what you're reading is what you're eating'. The same thing may have happened to Wittgenstein when, after seeing a courtroom mock-up of a car accident, he hit on the idea that propositions were essentially pictures. Another situation, announced at the outset, is the feeling of a complete dearth of languages. 'Unfortunately I don't speak French . . . I realized I couldn't speak a single word.' Anderson once mentioned 'nomadic voices' in a press release on her own work.[1] In one of her sleeve notes she wrote, 'Iisnow, for me, asifI am allways inaforeign country and listening to speech.'[2] She adopts the point of view of the permanent foreigner, 'reading' visual cues – in 1974 at the Clocktower, New York, she 'read' a sandwich – and cutting her American to the core.[3]

'Only he who is not truly at home in language uses it as an instrument', Adorno wrote of Heine.[4] Displaced both literally and metaphorically – by means of sound filters her voice can become that of a man, woman or child – Anderson achieves a clear-sightedness based on objectivity or alienation. Craig Owens argued that her dependence on the electronic media marked a new stage in the history of performance, taking it beyond the experience of pure presence and uniqueness implied by Minimalism, to a point where directness was prevented by an armoury of devices that magnified her own feelings of estrangement and ruptured the mythical bond between star and audience. Yet as he says, 'while an author is supposed to speak through his characters . . . Anderson's characters appear to speak through her.'[5]

Eager to reveal Brechtian influences, Owens neglects Anderson's native roots. In *USA* John Dos Passos used disturbance of narrative logic and a 'camera-eye' technique to show Americans turning into automata. But another older ancestor should be considered. 'Both in and out of the game', Walt Whitman's persona in *Leaves of Grass* expands to include the entire population of the United States: '(I am large, I contain multitudes)', he says in a famous aside. The humanity and patriotic pride of Whitman, expanding his ego to an impossible extent, furnishes a less dehumanized model for Anderson's epic approach. 'The United States themselves are the greatest poem', he wrote, swelling with pride.

Both men asserted that words were their main concern. 'But mainly *USA* is the speech of the people', Dos Passos decided in the preface to the one-volume edition of his trilogy in 1938. And late in his life Whitman said, 'I sometimes think the *Leaves* is only a language experiment.'[6] Anderson too begins with talk. In her hands clichés multiply alarmingly and turn into threats. 'Every man for himself', says a voice in one song, 'It's cold outside. Don't forget your mittens.' And an animal is seen foraging in the snow. 'There's safety in numbers', 'Don't forget to turn out the lights . . .' One key to Anderson's intentions is a slide of two quotations one above the other:

> 'If you can't talk about it point to it' – Ludwig Wittgenstein
> 'Throw that crutch away' – Reverend Ike

Anderson, conducting at the time – pointing at music or just at thin air – is indicating the most mysterious language of all, total structure or total expression. Wittgenstein was enough of a musician to be able to whistle entire concertos or conduct a symphony orchestra, while the Reverend Ike may talk nonsense, as a series of carbons of a sick man discarding his crutch and ending up in a coffin prove. But he sings up a storm. Having resorted to gesture and sound at this point – using her head as a percussion instrument or pointing a gun at it – Anderson may be hinting that 'talk' is a crutch. And by inference the 'ladder' Wittgenstein told his readers to discard at the end of the *Tractatus* is equated with the necessary aid.[7] A third proposition emerges: that art, theorizing about truth, might be inescapable, a kind of dead end. If, as the tile of an earlier song suggested, 'Ethics is the Esthetics of the Few-ture' (from a remark by Lenin), how is it possible to escape language, so dishonest a servant that the simplest statement admits an inexhaustible variety of interpretations? 'Language is a virus from outer space', wrote William Burroughs, and Anderson uses that too as a song title. One escape would be music, that 'pointing' to the ineffable which Anderson, with her quirky German translation, finds preferable to 'remain silent', or poetry, at best a miracle of ducking and weaving to avoid the obvious. Much of her time is spent 'pointing' to examples of visual languages – sign language, lines on graphs, musical staves, video games, maps, clocks, street signs, strip cartoons, a telephone dial, television graphics, computer graphics, computer print-outs. There are analyses of the limitations of media, like the story about the newspaper strike when television networks asked writers to read their columns on the air and they did it all wrong: '"They squinted into the lights. They wore ruffled clothes.' Subtler still are the characters who express themselves in specialized terminology, such as the deep-voiced man whose talk consists of political jargon, or conversations that seem created by the medium itself rather than by two people, like the short but disturbing telephone call by a woman waking up a man to invite him to a 'kindof party': 'I know you're asleep . . . Whyn't you come down? . . . No, he's not here . . . What's the difference? . . . Call a taxi . . . I know it's expensive but what's a few dollars?' Or a list of words appearing one at a time on the screen:

> Talkshow. Uplink. Update. Phrasebook. Downtime. Hotline. Aftermath. Upshot. Dropout. Nosecone. Headset. Hotshot. Heatwave. Domehead. Flashback. Feedback. Wetback. Crossfire. Jetlag. Meltdown. Earshot. Backbeat. Hyperspace. Gridlock . . .

And that grid returns, flowing down the screen like a wave breaking, less like an

Agnes Martin than a sheet of graph paper, maintaining a tight grip on nothing at all, dramatizing emptiness, a cipher denoting absence of language.

Linguistic unhousing is not the only type Anderson isolates. One key word is 'home'.

> I came home today and you were all on fire.
> Your shirt was on fire,
> Your hair was on fire,
> And flames were licking around your feet.
> And I did not know what to do.
>
> I came home today and I opened the door with my bare hands and I said 'Hey. Who tore up all my wallpaper samples?'
>
> I came home today and you had rearranged all the furniture and you had changed your name and I had never seen you wear that pinstripe shirt before.

Despite the appearance of 'professional barbecuers' on balconies, with 'smoke rising from their little fires' or the possibility that your mother will start cutting out animal pictures from magazines and gluing them into picture frames, home is still where the heart is. In *Walk the Dog* home is seen as a cartoon confection with Dagwood Bumstead relaxing in his chair while Blondie cooks a meal. The prospect is ordinary but comforting. Their dog is not 'made entirely out of light'. You only see things like that when you're alone and do not know what to do. Reject convenient fictions. Don't say, with Dolly Parton, that you 'just wanna go home now' to Mom and Dad if you don't mean it. Tell yourself lies. 'Close your eyes and imagine you're at the most wonderful party.' It may help. The distance between home with Mom and Dad and 'home' you make yourself is miserably great. Yet both are imperilled. A wordless sequence accompanied by sounds like animal noises features an anthology of slides of electric sockets, circular, with holes in the shape of two triangles, points downward, and a third, circular, below them. Caked with paint, they look like a pack of howling animals. And in 'Oh Superman', the most sinister of Anderson's songs, with shadowed hand signals, the answering machine's message from Mom ('Are you coming home?') is contrasted with an anonymous speaker announcing that 'the planes' are coming, the start of a sequence of events the narrator finally welcomes. When Mom reappears –

'Hi, Mom' – she is at one with her technological warfare, her 'automatic' arms all the better for hugging her children to death, a fate they accept willingly.

'Home' is a necessary fiction, whether it is Dolly Parton's 'Tennessee Mountain Home' where her Mom and Dad may be forced to walk the dog without her, or Manhattan, where Anderson begins and ends. The recital spans the history of America from discovery to cataclysm. The Statue of Liberty, at first a symbol of welcome and hope, is seen at last in negative, with a superimposed film of an American flag rotating in the drum of a spin-dryer. The tone of the preceding stories has darkened. Russian parachutists whose 'chutes didn't open in World War II plummeted so far down into Finnish snowdrifts that they found themselves at the bottom of holes fifteen feet deep. Before long farmers whose land they were on were aiming shotguns down the holes. During the 1979 drought farmers in the Midwest rented land to the government to use for missile sites. There is a possibility that grain silos are now connected by hundreds of miles of railroad. By the finale nothing less than atomic disaster is foreshadowed, and in that combination of infantilism and worship of a superpower for its own sake we are made ready to accept the presence of a death wish in ourselves.

Yet such unambiguous significance is resisted; ideas are enmeshed in the fabric of the performance, a slowly developing web in which each element qualifies and changes the others.

> In all my work I've ever done, my whole intention was not to map out meanings but to make a field situation. I'm interested in facts, images and theories which resonate against each other, not in offering solutions.[8]

Removed from this dense mesh, ideas polarize instantly. Black and white, good and bad. We are persuaded into resisting the temptation not only by an impression of totality but also for a communicated distaste for imponderables. 'I fear those big words which make us so unhappy', Stephen Dedalus tells Mr Deasy at the beginning of *Ulysses.* Anderson fears big concepts for which there are no words. She is fatally attracted to them too. Though *United States* may have no proper climaxes, they will come when, in her self-appointed role as outsider, she expresses her own response to symbols of power. The feeling she engages so often might be a frisson of excitement or a touch of guilt. Perhaps it is a little of both. After such rabbit punches argument is futile. She has seen the future and this is it. Her job is to make audiences think about emotions they would prefer not to acknowledge, truths they would rather ignore.

1. Laurie Anderson, 'From Americans on the Move', *October* 8, spring 1979, p.45.

2. *Airwaves*, One Ten Records, New York, 1977.

3. Alan Sondheim, *Individuals* (New York: Dutton, 1977), pp.xvi–xvii.

4. Quoted by George Steiner, *Extraterritorial* (Harmondsworth: Penguin, 1975), p.15.

5. Craig Owens, 'Amplifications', *Art in America*, March 1981, p.123.

6. Whitman's (and Emerson's) ideas about language bear comparison with Anderson's. Cf. 'Only a Language Experiment', chapter of F.O. Matthiessen's classic *American Renaissance* with Anderson discussing the teaching of vowels in a Steiner school in John Howell, 'Interview with Laurie Anderson,' *Live* 5, p.6.

7. Wittgenstein's prose style and Anderson's bear close comparison. Of Wittgenstein Norman Malcolm wrote 'The style is simple and perspicuous, the construction of sentences firm and free, the rhythm flows easily. The form is sometimes that of dialogue, with questions and replies; sometimes, as in the *Tractatus*, it condenses to aphorisms. There is a striking absence of all literary ornamentation . . . . The union of measured moderation with richest imagination, the simultaneous impression of natural continuation and surprising turns, leads one to think of some of the other great productions of the genius of Vienna. (Schubert was Wittgenstein's favourite composer.)' Norman Malcolm, *Ludwig Wittgenstein: A Memoir*, (London: Oxford University Press, 1967), p.21.

8. John Howell, 'Interview with Laurie Anderson', p.6. Cf. John Howell, 'A Few Things We Know About Her', *Art-Rite* 10, fall 1975, n.p.: 'The thing that takes the most time is letting myself feel something and then letting the piece be about that without getting lost in the structure, without wrenching the structure into a certain formal order, which may be very interesting, very strong and you may be able to talk about it in intellectual terms, but without that core, we're just talking about surface technique, not the real feeling behind the work.'

Jonathan Borofsky

Review of an exhibition at the ICA, London, published in Artscribe *32, December 1981.*

Half light, half empty, half public, Borofsky's urban no man's land was flyposted and strewn with garbage. Where or what it was remained a mystery. The roar of traffic, the flicker of light on a gridded patch on the ceiling, a grey 'dead' area at one end, a television screen and table-tennis table suggested a subway tunnel or a seedy street-level bar, places of uneasy relaxation. Ironically, it was a gallery too, with pictures 'acting' pictures, all surface and no substance: a green fish painted on the ceiling, an elliptical mauve light falling half across a raised white lozenge, a painting of a ruby, a more abstract painting of tumbling tubular solids, standing at an angle to the wall. In the threatening film noir atmosphere, with shadows of fleeing giants on one wall and a sinister grey gangster on another, with a dustbin lid timed to bang on the floor periodically, the viewer was kept in a state of permanent indecision. Discontinuities were calculated; not 'ambiguity' but 'contradiction' would best describe the effect.

It is easier to remember a Borofsky installation than to stand inside one. Like daily life, their state is too random for easy reading. Something always escapes – an animated video cartoon of a dog walking the tightrope or the fact that the crumpled papers littering the floor all bear anti-littering pleas. Oddly, works are based on the numbers of the dreams they illustrate. Yet the numbers are not for cross-reference; they are simply part of an unending catalogue from which Borofsky feels at liberty to draw. And somehow any therapy involved in telling his dreams is short-circuited. The intention could be a continual remaking of the self. As if to confirm this, a fibreglass Borofsky lookalike hovers high above the ground, like a perplexed putto pausing momentarily to check details before zooming off somewhere else. It all takes place with a minimum of introspection. If Surrealism minus Freud equals visual muzak, Borofsky may be guilty of wasting his audience's time, risking sheer superficiality in his decision not to settle or repeat motifs or analyse his own dreams, worst of all in his determination to continue to ramble in future. His obsessive return to images of heads – his own is seen with an electric light bulb, like a signature on an otherwise abstract canvas – hints that the entire anthology is an equivalent of his mind. Looking further is futile; the recurrent motif of the running man indicates that 'depth' is to be avoided.

Borofsky's view of the world refracted through his dreams – and the Kunsthalle Basel and the ICA have published a book of these to accompany the show – reflects the violence, panic and exhilaration of urban life. Most importantly, it is an artist's life in New York, with walk-on appearances by Paula Cooper, Ed Ruscha, Roman Opalka, Diane Waldman, Barry Le Va, Picasso and others. Like Jennifer Bartlett, who wrote an autobiographical book called *The History of the Universe*, Borofsky is not modest about his desire to become a representative man, and the cosmos seen from SoHo may seem totally irrelevant to a European. The attempt to connect with the political situation in Ireland (the dustbin lid) and world power-politics (the table-tennis table) was sheer trivialization. Most disturbing was the damage the entire idea of an installation may do Borofsky. Tom Lawson recently accused him of 'mystification', by which he meant the desire to pile up objects without 'composing' or just the implication that his graffiti are deep, when he allows no opportunity for analysis. If the essential Borofsky is in the dream narratives, the effect of redelivering these by means of altered perspective and good packaging is surely to detract from them, dealing with copies of memories of jottings of dreams. Was Plato right after all?

The other side of the argument is that at last we have a sculptor capable of translating – not 'reproducing' – the effect of street awareness, the consciousness of walking in a big city with no focused thought in your head, obliquely aware of external stimuli, the job in hand, the wishes and emotions that make you you, most of all of the possibility of blending what (if you were to think it out) would be quite separate layers of experience – of becoming something different, achieving a wish or extending a little further. There is no such thing as 'person'. We are not bags of guts on legs. There is no such thing as Jon Borofsky; he is part of other people, his character is sometimes beyond his control, sometimes so clichéd it's hard to distinguish it. Yet it's there and it moves through material, keeping some, losing some, transforming some. The issues in Borofsky are touched skilfully and brilliantly in a way no one else touches them. They are points of definition between thought and action, public and private, decision and passivity. No, he isn't 'deep'. He's trying to be representative, and most people don't meditate like Rodin's *Thinker*. They go shopping or jog around the park and thoughts strike them obliquely, like invisible particles whizzing around in the atmosphere. The effect Borofsky has is ultimately bracing and optimistic, because it is about awareness, openness and activity. It's like meeting a new person or visiting a strange place. Forget the objections. He knows what he's doing.

Joseph Beuys: Dernier espace avec introspecteur

Review of exhibition held at Anthony d'Offay Gallery, London, published in Artforum *XX, 10, June 1982.*

While the location of Joseph Beuys's thinking varies between street and study, thematically his sculpture seems to be undergoing some alarming temporal fluctuation. This recent installation, *Dernier espace avec introspecteur* ('Last space with introspector'), features his *Fettstuhl*, an artist's stool covered with wax, now 24 years old, as well as childhood reminiscences of the Schwanenburg Castle in Kleve, reduced to rubble during the war. At first the dating of the piece, '1964–1982', suggests a Proustian reminiscence, a desire to fox art history by doubling back while remaining within an avant-garde, or simply an old man's gathering senility. (Already Beuys is considering death; the trees he intends to plant at this year's Documenta will outlive him.) Perhaps it is more interesting than that: in making a site for the *Fettstuhl* Beuys is researching his own career, providing a rationale for his earlier stance, while expressing doubts about the possibility of an emotional return.

The *introspecteur* of the title is another relic. On a tripod, camera-like, is a rear-view mirror, the only part of a car left undamaged in 1967 – in French, a *rétrospecteur*. It reflects the sculpture before it, though in a personal manner; Beuys's stamped cross prevents a direct image. Indeed, the function of the mirror seems rather to be to make a 3-D representation of a photograph of itself behind it on the gallery wall. Rammed gracelessly into holes in the walls are two double lengths of felt, one along the floor, the other making a slight arc as it hangs from the roof. The core of the installation consists of two differently angled models of roofs in moulded beeswax, with chimneys added at the four corners. The moulds for the roofs have been broken open and left in their debris, their plaster wings dangling. On one stands the *Fettstuhl*, the didactic symbol Beuys made to inspire his students long ago.

It all sounds such a mess, an anthology of junk with sentimental value, thrown together anyhow in a dumb formalist spoof. Why then, is the effect so moving? The answer may lie precisely in 'formal' failure, in the fragility of metaphoric superimposition. Thus striking open a mould of a destroyed building produces artificial (yet ideal) newness together with a sad rubble of its own; creation is an eternal return and an index of the impossibility of such a return; habits of obliquity alone can help free art from immediate temporality, yet obliquity demands an underpinning that may itself be regarded as one of the relics in *Dernier espace*. Distanced from his own work, Beuys, looking back blankly, even ironically, sees his attempt at reconstruction of the German mind as limited by its role in repairing irreparable personal damage. Atop the rubbish, the *Fettstuhl* resembles a throne; the effect is tatty and flamboyant, at once pathetic and grand. Like certain works of Georg Baselitz and Anselm Kiefer, Beuys's 'last space', a forlorn museum parading as a public monument, expresses complex, significant feelings about the role of the intellectual in contemporary Germany. And if not overtly political, it indicates a wish to explore the motives underlying political action. Its paradoxes are realistic, even hopeful.

Joseph Beuys: Plight

Extract from 'Letters to a Wound: An address prompted by recent exhibitions of work by Joseph Beuys, Eric Bainbridge and Julian Schnabel', published in Artscribe *55, December/January 1985/6. The exhibition* Plight *was held at the Anthony d'Offay Gallery, London in 1985.*

W.H. Auden's *The Orators* contained a prose poem called 'Letter to a Wound'. Writing to it in the way that most people speak to a lover, the narrator tells it about the difference it has made to his life, recounts the history of their relationship and looks forward to their living together for many years to come. Critics have racked their brains to find allegorical interpretations for the wound. But in vain; the answer is too simple. In communicating with the pain in this way the man is addressing his own identity.

The wound remains a secret. In life, most do. In art, almost all do. The only exceptions are images of the Crucifixion, where the blood of Christ streams visibly from rents in His flesh, the outward and visible sign of a catharsis that involves the fate of the whole of mankind. Nowadays catharsis goes on in private. People talk about their analysts and try to estimate their own progress towards some lost unity. In art, it would be surprising if new schools of wound painting were to spring up overnight. The fact is that some things can be more easily suggested than rendered; they can be summoned up by avoiding the entire topic or even by changing the subject. That does not mean that wounds are not there, even as subtexts; simply that our relationship to our bodies is obscure. But they can be discovered, even in the oddest places. Admittedly motif-hunting is out of fashion. These days no one writes essays called 'The Egg in Art'. But how easy it is to crave the reader's indulgence when one's subject is so concealed, so fugitive, so literal an absence.

The atmosphere is oppressive. A gallery has been lined with felt – two tons of it, brought from a factory in Bavaria and prodded into place with pitchforks. With the windows and doors covered, the place resembles a prison or a bank vault. Light, freedom, sonority have all been reduced. In spite of this the space is safe and warm. If it looks like a padded cell, it is also, in the true sense of the word, an asylum. Three other objects complete the installation: a grand piano with the lid closed, and on it a thermometer and an empty blackboard.

As his ubiquitous hat demonstrates, Joseph Beuys and felt are inseparable. At least two monographs offer biographical reasons for this relationship. When his fighter plane crashed into the snow of the Russian steppes during World War II, Beuys has explained, he was rescued by nomads who coated his burns with honey and wrapped his body in felt. Whether or not this is true is irrelevant; Beuys makes and unmakes his life-story at will. What is undeniable is that he has made a felt television, a felt suit (based on his own size but with the arms and legs extended), a series of *Fond* structures – piles of felt with thin metal covers – and actions such as *Infiltration homogen for grand piano: the greatest contemporary composer is the thalidomide child*, in which a piano, the instrument Beuys would always choose to play at Fluxus concerts, was wrapped and sealed in felt in order to prevent its being used and, symbolically, at least, to block its sound. Yielding yet resilient, matted but chaotic, felt insulates, warms and muffles. Above all, as in the plane-crash legend, it heals.

The concept of breach or rupture occurs frequently in Beuys's thought. As might be expected of a soldier who earned the Golden Stripe medal after his fifth set of injuries, the word 'wound' has a heightened significance for his art; '1921 Exhibition of a wound drawn together with plaster' is the first entry on his fictional *curriculum vitae*. If it is to heal, the wound must not remain a private hurt; as in psychoanalysis, reciprocity may provide an answer. Yet Beuys does not underestimate the problem of urging people to reveal their frailty.

> It must be made properly acceptable to people that it is interesting to expose themselves fully with all their failings. I only want to encourage people not to wait for an ideal state of consciousness. They should begin with their present means – to begin with their mistakes.[1]

The phrase 'Show Your Wound', used on blackboards made at the ICA in London in 1974, recurs three years later as the title of an installation made in an underground pedestrian area in Munich. Both this and the present felt-lined room can be regarded as studies in sickness, excursions into what Beuys has called 'the death zone'. Beuys seems to regard illness not quite as a punishment for, but certainly as an inevitable accompaniment to living.

> As Nietzsche said: man is an ill being. That's a definition of humanity. The human being is ill and can be ill. Because of his freedom the human being always trespasses into areas that threaten him or her.[2]

It is characteristic of his thinking not only to regard illness as exemplary, a kind of initiation or threshold experience, but also to give equal weight to the process of recovery:

> You really do get into a zone of death when you become conscious of our contemporary civilization, of the concept behind it. but this dark mood can provoke the opposite mood in people, you know. I've always though that it was better to use colourless materials, for instance . . . I use this grey to provoke something in people, something like a counter-image – you might even say to create a rainbow in people's minds . . .'[3]

The title *Plight*, then is an apt one: both a catastrophe and a pledge or bond. The place is designed to serve a dual function; sensory deprivation, an internalized experience, compels viewers to take stock, to realize a feeling of community in sickness. Gathered together in silence, they may turn that silence into some hymn or protest; may measure – hence the thermometer – their own capacity for life. And, because a piano will only emit a sound if it is struck, they can estimate their willingness to involve themselves in the situation that embodies such threat. The readiness of the room, the emptiness of the blackboard, bodes well for the future.

Plight presents a setting for a private ceremony: the enforced withdrawal into the self and the re-emergence into a larger community: a recuperation after a period of trauma. As in the fictional wound exhibition from the year of his birth, the subject is separation, a separation that can be overcome. The almost religious air of his work is an aspect he has never denied. Critics who have adopted the idea of transubstantiation to describe the operation of the elements he employs have done so with good reason.[4] The immediate meaning of the parts may be based on their properties as matter in the world, but a cross-referencing as well as the inevitable repetition has raised materials like felt and fat to symbolic status without damaging their objective immediacy. They have been absorbed into a process that has rightly been compared to ritual, with Beuys as priest or shaman, exorcising his own fears, perhaps, but also supervising a collective ceremony, in this case a recovery from sickness, a consolation after grief, a change of heart and even a resolution.

1. Quoted in C.M. Joachimedes, *Joseph Beuys: Richtkräfte* (Berlin: Nationalgalerie, 1977), p.50.
2. 'Questions to Joseph Beuys Part II' in Jörg Schellman/Bernd Klüser, *Joseph Beuys: Multiples* (Munich: Schellman u. Klüser Verlag, 1980), n.p.
3. Joseph Beuys, Heiner Bastian, Jeannot Simmen, 'If Nothing Says Anything, I Can't Draw' in *Joseph Beuys: Zeichnungen* (Berlin: Nationalgalerie, 1979), p.95.
4. See Martin Kunz, 'Christus, Kreuz und Braunkreis' in *Joseph Beuys: Spuren in Italien* (Luzern: Kunstmuseum, 1979), p. 95.

Joseph Beuys: The End of the Twentieth Century

Review of exhibition held at Anthony d'Offay Gallery, London, published in Performance *62, December 1990.*

Since Joseph Beuys's death remounted versions of his work have acquired a different status. It is no use remarking, as one hapless reviewer did, that the arrangement of 31 floorbound basalt chunks that make up *The End of the Twentieth Century* is reminiscent of the way the sleds cascade from the van in Beuys's *The Pack*; he is comparing the artist's own version of the latter with a revival of the former carried out in the artist's absence. Saying so may seem to violate all the assumptions on which the genre rests, but nowadays any installation of Beuys's sculpture must be regarded as a critical interpretation of the 'original'. Photographs of Beuys's own version of *The End of the Twentieth Century* at the Galerie Schmela in Düsseldorf in 1983 show the viewer's gradual approach to the work down a staircase. In a basement space the basalt lozenges – 39 of them, at least – were ranged in rows, the circular incisions on the upper part of one end, where a face would be on a body, all pointing in the same direction except where one seemed to have toppled over another. In London 31 of these were placed in a space level with the incoming visitor, who suddenly made intimate contact with a set of forms now less reminiscent of sarcophagi and more of petrified tree trunks that may have fallen that way thousands of years before, but with that flowing motion the reviewer mentioned.

Making the arrangement appear haphazard encouraged one particular emphasis in interpretation. Much of the visual interest of the work lies in the difference between each stone, achieved by slicing away a circular section from each and replacing it. After this, each disc sits differently because of the addition of felt and fat, usual symbols of energy, warmth and transformation in Beuys's thinking, plus clay, perhaps the most ancient symbol of fertility. However slight the indentation, the stones have become sealed vessels. The body in general, not only the human body, has turned inwards, perhaps as a response to attack. They seem to exist in a state of suspended animation. In the past the millennium has been synonymous with the sense of an ending. If reports of the year 1000 are to be trusted, the end of this century, which is also the end of the millennium, will bring a heightened sense of an ending. Beuys's *End of the Twentieth Century*, however, is concerned with neither resurrection nor afterlife, but with a dichotomy between spirit and its vehicle, a division it has become impossible to entertain in a 'me'-orientated society. (Two friendships blossomed during the eighties: with Andy Warhol, who had reduced his own presence to a cipher so that a team of imitators could double for him at parties, and with the Dalai Lama, whom Buddhists believe to be the thirteenth consecutive incarnation of the same spirit.) In the London reconstruction of Beuys's installation the idea of death as sleep – regarded by Ariès as an archetype of medieval Western Christian thinking – has been replaced by the suggestion of a voyage, which squares well with Beuys's interest in shamanism. Is a defensible alternative interpretation the sole criterion for a successful revival of a classic installation? The success of the London exhibition might suggest that it should be.

Ian McKeever

Review of exhibition at Walker Art Gallery, Liverpool, published in Artforum *XX, 6, February 1982.*

After hovering between drawing and photography Ian McKeever has turned to painting with his 'Night Flak' series, organized with the discipline of a Conceptual piece. For his six paired panels, inspired by the *Hymns to the Night* by the German Romantic poet Novalis, he chose canvases as large as he could encompass with arms outstretched. Then he prepared himself like a method actor. To accustom himself to dark spaces he learned pot-holing; Novalis had been a student of mining. He got into the habit of painting at night, working from dusk to dawn without lights. The intention was not to learn to manage without daytime vision, but rather to exploit the emotional vulnerability caused by disorientation and lack of sleep. The second panel of *Solitary is the Place* suggests a testing of perimeters, like the prowling of a caged animal. Yet help is at hand. 'Aside, I turn to the holy ineffable Night,' wrote Novalis in his first hymn, 'far below lies the world, sunken in a profound pit: waste and solitary is its place.' In the first panel the paint skids as it is flung in curves; mapping seems to have given way to rhythmic activity. The contrast between a first painting in thick impasto, perhaps with incipient forms in brighter colours, and a second, more graphic 'drawing' against a white ground is maintained throughout the series, a reminder of the different responses that day and night demand.

Despondent at the death of his sixteen-year-old fiancée, Novalis experienced a vision at her graveside, recounted in a straightforward flashback to his third hymn, corresponding to McKeever's *Twilight Shudder*, the only one of the series not shown in Liverpool. From that time onward he welcomed night as his link with the lost girl, finally as his means of accepting her death and death in general. *Evening Dawn Shows Grey*, with its second panel of hanging blossoms, and the first panel of *Mark Glad Departure's Day*, in which Novalis's intoxicant poppies burst forth from the gloom of a dark composition, both convey the shudder of excitement the poet feels as he rhapsodizes on death in the final hymn. Panel two of the latter, resembling a mapped cave or the ample curve of an absent bedmate, shows how far McKeever has come. By *There Was But One Thought* – from Novalis's fifth hymn, a meditation on the age-old fear of death – sheer happiness surges through both panels, as natural images rise unbidden and the distinction between diurnal and nocturnal is entirely overthrown.

No narrative can be discovered either in the order of the paintings or the process of their making. The 'representation' that informs them hinges on an act of faith which does demand reference to the spine their chosen text provides, however. The relationship between the emotions and the paint on one hand and the developing spiritual awareness in the *Hymns to the Night* on the other is far from straightforward, something like the physical and mental aspects of yoga. It would be unfortunate to regard this rethinking of mimesis as a lapsed belief in what paint can embody; a more fruitful approach might emphasize the ability to question the terms of existing arguments altogether. Whether the 'Night Flak' paintings are the by-product of some hackneyed sensory-deprivation performance or a type of visual programme music, or even illustration (the final taboo) is less important than their power to prove that a raddled tradition of British neo-New York School formalism, often misunderstood from the outset, can be sabotaged and renewed by the acceptance of Conceptual armatures.

Markus Lüpertz

Review of exhibition at Waddington Gallery, London, published in Artforum *XX, 8, April 1982.*

Inspired by *Alice in Wonderland*, Markus Lüpertz made 48 paintings during a six-month period in late 1980 and 1981. In spirit, if not in appearance, they combine that blend of the absurd and the pompous stressed by Sir John Tenniel with elements of secrecy and terror that are Lüpertz's own addition. The contrast in Lewis Carroll's book between implacable authority and a natural order in which flux seems the dominant principle yields two distinct styles in Lüpertz's rendering. In the first, a type of Surrealist portraiture, shapes like deserted buildings are situated in landscapes; the Caterpillar, the White Rabbit, the Mock Turtle and the March Hare are among the characters dealt with in this way. The second style, an Abstract Expressionist throwback, improvises on snatches of songs and poems – a line from 'You are old, father William', 'Twinkle, twinkle, little bat', the barking chorus of the Duchess's lullaby – or registers violent actions.

Instead of establishing a direct narrative correspondence between painting and title, Lüpertz employs a stock of images to create the atmosphere of the original. Figures are masked; faces emerge only in number 40, *'You don't know much,' said the Duchess*, and *'How fond she is of finding morals in things'*, a study of Alice herself. More responsive to menace than to humour, Lüpertz transfers his attention away from people and towards actions, words and objects. This is a valid method – the Queen's slogan 'Off with his head!' has more impact than the Queen as a 'person'; the Mouse's tail becomes its own life story; and, rendered as it appears in the book, the March Hare's house is both brain and emblem, a thing in itself, as vivid with significance as Charles Bovary's cap. Lüpertz's tendency to crowd together the colours of his palette makes the pictures (literally) more obscure than is necessary; number 42, *'Found it,' the Mouse replied rather crossly*, with its Beckmannesque crown, flying Easter egg and early Clyfford Still effects, lightens and varies the palette slightly and restores confidence in his abilities as a colourist. Yet style in itself is scarcely the main issue. The most successful of the series resemble three-dimensional structures, suggesting sometimes heads, sometimes buildings, sometimes sculptures, but always some unseen interior space or entrances to caverns. The tight-crowded tones suggest that Alice, who dreams it all, actually is all the spaces she confronts and enters, and that this haze of meditation constitutes an attempt to distance the facts about her own body. And since Alice is Lüpertz's own persona, it might be possible to regard him as a painter dedicated to (symbolic) abstraction, defiantly attempting to conquer the two (non-symbolic) modes current figuration permits – the erotic and the grotesque.

The text is well chosen. Alice is taught what it means to be an adult by a team of playing cards and talking animals, while Lüpertz, torn like her between good manners and unedited emotion, experiments with approaches to artistic identity in an attempt to produce some new historical synthesis. 'You've no idea how confusing it is, all the things being alive', Alice tells the Cheshire Cat; but later, 'Why, they're only a pack of cards after all. I needn't be afraid of them.' Varying between the bland and the blockbuster, Lüpertz's parable of contemporary painting skirts the issue of faux naïveté by examining a case of true naïveté. That Alice refuses to grow up at the end of the book was Carroll's triumph; this is part of the text that Lüpertz dare not render. Alice postpones her development into a woman by learning to sing songs and tell stories to the strangers she meets. The same is true of Lüpertz, who in this work outlines the current international debate on modernism, without resolving it. Conceivably, he raises its stakes.

An interview with Markus Lüpertz

Published in Artscribe *47, July/August 1984.*

'Of my generation', Markus Lüpertz said last year, 'I am one of those who set up laws to end pluralism, so that revolutions can take place.' Not everyone would agree. His apolitical stance and his proclamations of the amorality of art have been interpreted as retrogressive products of a genuine, deep-rooted conservatism rather than an irritant anti-avant-garde pose. Yet champions and detractors alike must now recognize that from the mid-sixties onwards Lüpertz's theoretical position has rested on a career in painting, a career of dramatic paradoxes. 'Picture-making is disgusting', announces a post-Conceptual Lüpertz, nevertheless allowing maximum scope for virtuosity. Purists of either persuasion – Conceptual or painterly – find it hard to repress a shudder at the spectacle of *peinture-peinture* dragooned, of impastoed pseudo-masterpieces goose-stepping in interminable single-file series with high-sounding titles. None of this is accidental; Lüpertz thrives on artistic provocation. As his career continues it develops echoes, internal ruptures, that sense of dialectical manoeuvring which characterizes his treatment of thematic devices. This could proceed from largeness of mind or from sheer flippancy. No use expecting straight answers from the man himself, despite the fact that in his own work he is never far away: as the sum of the fragmented wholes he manipulates, as the wearer of the empty clothes, as that sheer authoritarian impetus which first summoned them into existence. Never far away. Far enough not to be vulnerable, far enough away to offer the alternatives of irony or evasion. His complexity of authorial distance betokens the subtlety of Lüpertz's changing approach to the real, the most available key to his rethinking of abstraction. But what does it all add up to? A prolonged meditation on an idealized artistic persona? If this is the case then it must be admitted that Lüpertz also presents that person in terms of his actual identity: cultured, in its correct etymological sense. Lüpertz is a creature of artifice. 'I work at my good looks', he has admitted, defending this attitude as 'aggressive' and deliberately public. ('We live in a period of truth when everyone confesses whether they have piles or not.') Aggression is not something he is in the habit of avoiding, I decide as he introduces himself. His handshake would paralyse a navvy. We exchange pleasantries for a while; the interpreter has failed to appear. Finally an apology arrives. There will be no interpreter. Shrugging and laughing nervously, we agree to carry on as best we can.

* * *

Stuart Morgan: *Tell me about the first dithyrambic paintings. You began in 1964 . . .*

Markus Lüpertz: A little later actually. This was the time of the first influence of Pop painting and in Germany it was the end of the influence of the École de Paris. The big painter in Germany before the arrival of Pop was Nay, who was part of Tachisme. This was the finish of European painting – perhaps not quite the finish, but it became a little decadent. The new wind in painting was Pop. It was ugly, aggressive, it came from advertising and PR. And this idea swept Europe. Even Scandinavians were making Pop art. Five or six painters, my friends and I, had problems with it. Our understanding of art was philosophy, intelligence, what lies behind things you can see. For us painting was not just about entertainment. Our big love was the tradition of painting and a special kind of nationality. I don't see in the same way as Americans see, or the French or the English. Tradition is something in your brain, and it's a good thing. So my friends and I were flying in the face of the official art, which at the time was Pop. It was popular, unintellectual, normal, direct and uncritical. So I said 'Well, that's not what I want.'

What did you want?

I value tradition in art and want to make a classic, as Newman did. A 'gift of God', you understand? When you see a classic Greek figure, it's as if he has come direct from the sky to stand there. This is the old fascination, the idea of what art is. When I make a really fine painting it's as if it's more than me; it's bigger than I am. And I see the painting with the same surprise as anyone else looking at it. This is the ideal. I thought, 'This is what I want – this idea in my life which is larger than my own self.' While I was eating and sleeping and doing all the things people do, I was thinking, 'What is an artist?' The artist has an idea which is not for everyone but something more. The point of art is not feeling or heart or politics or social problems for all the people but a meeting of the sky and the earth. Pop was OK in its time. It was journalism. It was not art.

Your dithyrambic paintings had no sex, then, no ideas.

Well they had sex, I hope, and were entertaining. But not in a direct sense.

You have to find it. It's not for me to say, 'This is sex. This is entertainment.' If you look at art you must be in a very free position. This was the idea when abstraction first began. Abstraction was freedom from dogma: having ideas for yourself. When you look at a painting you have to say, 'What are the possibilities of this painting?'

If the artist gets his ideas from God but is neither a god nor one of the other humans what is he?

Maybe he is an angel.

And the word 'dithyramb'?

I used it at the time I was thinking 'What is it that I'm doing?' It's the Dionysian form of intensity, like the position I occupied – 'drunken', 'inspired'. It meant a formal translation of a movement of the brain. The dithyramb was a new object. You paint apples. I find a new object for that apple – a new object with expressive content, a special new object in the world of art. The dithyramb gave me security. It marked my first separation from the art of that time. Once this was established, I thought 'What is possible in the way of abstraction and realism?' From there I started the playing way. That is the way I'm still following today.

The playing way?

Playing. Joking.

You talk about your special position, your originality. But your paintings are full of references to Picasso and early modernism. Is this a form of play?

Picasso is a great artist. But he is not only that; he is a man who introduces forms. Look at the forms of tables, chairs, wallpaper, cups, suits. These are our direct line to fifty years of abstract art. Seeing these abstract forms is my connection with Picasso. It is not to do with painting; it is to do with reality. You may say the same when you look at Pollock. Pollock paints Picassos. He paints fantastic Picassos. He paints better Picassos than Picasso because he paints them wrong. It's the same with Arshile Gorky; his Picassos are better than Picasso's. So it's not a question of originality; it's to do with the times in which you live. Not Picasso himself but the time influences me.

Could we discuss an issue that may be related: the use of repetition in your art?

One problem for many of my friends was what to do when you paint a real object with your abstract ideas in your head. Baselitz's upside-down image was a very simple, brilliant solution. For me it was a little more complicated; it was a question of timing, like in the movies when you have thousands of little paintings one after the other. So if I paint you, then I paint you the same two, three, five times, it is abstracting abstraction, negating the 'original'. The same negation occurs when you paint the image upside-down or make stick figures, as Penck does; this is the idea of abstraction in a small way. We understood abstract painting but we also had a feeling for the traditional – the figure, the head, the portrait, the conventional things about painting. Cubists abstracted from a glass until it just consisted of three lines. But you can't do that again next day.

Why did you choose to paint about Hölderlin?

Hölderlin represents a worthwhile position for the artist to assume. But I never do Hölderlin alone; every time there is a part of Hölderlin which is Heine for me.

But they are so different. Heine is such a cynic.

Heine is an aggressive critic and a real artist with only a little poetic feeling. Hölderlin is just poetry with no understanding of reality at all. Together they form a model of what is possible today for artists.

The difference between them is their irony.

Irony. Yes, I like Hölderlin; he was crazy for reality, a 'poor' artist only for Romantic people. Heine is hard-hearted, fighting in reality for poetic people. He was an angry critic, an ironist. My own position lies between these two alternatives, like a discussion. On the one hand we have a classic, aggressive form, positive for art; on the other, Hölderlin, who is positive for life.

Presumably in painting your series based on Lewis Carroll you were choosing an author who has facts and figures pitted against stuff and nonsense, both Heine and Hölderlin simultaneously. What about your series on the Amor and Psyche legend?

It's my playing with the classic theme of women and men and my relationship to that theme. Cupid, for example, is featured as a cactus. There is the hard and the soft – the abstract idea, the line and the volume and it occurs throughout my painting both technically and thematically. Maybe Amor is hard and Psyche is soft. But perhaps Psyche is hard-headed while Amor is the opposite. Similarly, I've made a sculpture called *Standbein-Spielbein*, 'standing leg' and 'playing leg', my paraphrase of the classic position in Greek sculpture, like Michelangelo's *David*.

Critics have found a certain egocentricity in your work. Are they correct?

The problem is the same for anyone who writes about art. It's not possible to understand the art of your own time, either for the critic or for the artist himself. We can only do two things: feel and believe. And in the world at present belief is very hard. People are saying we are tough and looking only for money. The believing position is very hard. But when you have an interest in art you must have a feeling, a sensitivity and a certain belief. I have to speak in the frame of mind of the lover, from the security of the lover. When the lover understands, he is finished; you only love when you don't understand. It's the same with art. Everyone says, 'He is a good painter. I understand him.' But when it's possible for everyone to understand your painting, then I think you are a bad painter. The problem with the new painting now is that these are pictures with which everyone can identify. Too often when you have a homosexual painter viewers say, 'Good, a homosexual painting'. But that's too 'normal', too directly understandable. It's not really a critique either of homosexual life or of ordinary life seen from the homosexual's point of view.

Are you most yourself in your painting or least yourself?

When you ask me that way I can't say yes or no. I have my eyes and my hand. I can do what I want. I am not disconnected from my personality or my originality. This is the freedom I see in art now. I'm not fighting for the world; I'm not Robin Hood. I'm not a political artist. My only problem is of finding the moment of greatest intensity in my life. I may go this way or that, but I'm still an artist at every moment. I'm not sleeping, I'm not finished. I'm always beginning again. An artist is like a boxer. He trains every day and then he has the fight. It's possible to stay with a particular way of working, make something of it and say 'Look, I'm famous.' But I have an idea of the last, the best, the greatest. I want to think of myself alongside the best artists of my time. It's my fight against death. I think to myself that I have only one life.

Are you afraid of dying?

No. I'm not frightened in that way. Or preoccupied with my own death. Angst is not one of my problems.

* * * * *

The conversation continues, with Lüpertz talking about his feeling that artists are different because of their duty to make art, that talent which imposes a kind of morality. Yet the morality of an artist is based on freedom, he argues. He rails against misery and apocalypticism in art, ways of giving a public exactly what it wants. I lose track of his talk about capitalism and socialism and am not entirely sorry.

Certainly we don't agree on very much. Why, then, do we get on so well? Having to grope for words in either English or German? A shared respect for irony? More probably it is a joint disregard for closure, which would force a distinction between experiment and play, which eradicates the middle ground between polarities, or destroys conversation.

As he leaves we shake hands. A little more warmly this time.

Quotations from previous interviews are from Dorothea Dietrich, 'A Conversation with Markus Lüpertz', *Print Collector's Newsletter*, XIV, 1, 1993, pp.9–12; Oswald Wiener, 'I Paint More than I Look' in *Markus Lüpertz: Bilder 1970-1983* (Hanover: Kestner-Gesellschaft, 1983). Easily the best introduction to Lüpertz in English is Richard Calvocoressi's essay in *Markus Lüpertz: Ohne Titel* (Zurich: Galerie Maeght, 1983). A bibliography is in *Expressions: New Art from Germany* (St Louis Art Museum/Prestel Verlag, Munich, 1983) pp.168–9.

Sandro Chia

Review of an exhibition at Anthony d'Offay Gallery, London, published in Artforum *XX, 9, May 1982.*

In Sandro Chia's *Fratello*, one of 42 drawings and paintings in this show, a muscular man stands with arms akimbo, steam shooting from his cranium, and the bulging material of his apron proclaiming a massive erection. In *Speed Boy* a hefty youngster, with muscles in places where most boys don't even have places, wears roller-skates and seems powered by the violence of his own farting. The mysterious protagonist in *Confidential Declaration* fires a cannon at nothing, for no apparent reason. Chia's preoccupation with presenting energy hints at his conception of painting. An explosion exists at a threshold of visibility; while the impulse itself is impossible to discern, its passage is marked by vapour or smoke. In drawing the force itself may be suggested by haphazard graphic billows or lines of force, which appear in Chia's work as decorative marks resulting from a painterly *horror vacui* and as the arbitrary definition of some immeasurable power. In the absence of that power protagonists pass their time restlessly. Excited by prospects of activity yet alarmed by the incomprehensibility of the universe, Chia's juveniles seem overcome with weariness or confusion. They could be observing the underlying order of the world and perfecting a science of mapping it, like the *Heroic Botanist* or *Young Stone Age Painter*; instead, a boy stumbles over a giant's causeway of black cylinders ('barrels', it seems) in *Accident*, while in *Temples and Guns* a well-dressed gent is alarmed by a De Stijl design.

Existing fully in neither two nor three dimensions, the barrels and the abstract geometry loom disagreeably, apparently able to materialize or dematerialize by magic. *Courageous Boys at Work*, *Meditation*, *Anaemic Courageous Boys*, and *Doubts about Colour and Form* show the hulking juveniles occupying the lower portions of predominantly abstract works – the abstraction suffusing the air that surrounds them as well as the works of art that confront them. *Idiots* seem isolated, unable to change their condition; *Anarchist Crowned* employs an Anton Bragaglia-like double image to suggest nervous disorder. Between foolishness and aggression, then, passivity is the safest course. If change occurs, it will do so in its own time, out of the air. It will have the qualities of an announcement of the self, a release of pent-up energy, a sexual thrill – even of a spiritual experience. And it will change the world. *Speed Boy* and *Everything is Going Well* show the modern city in ruins, as Futurism so often pictured it. How far the individual is responsible is unclear.

Chia's content bears an allegorical relationship to his method. Waiting to be summoned from the ether is an allusive Mannerism in which only figure and ground exist, both raised to a high level of tension and complexity. That the painting style strains under its burden is not surprising. It must maintain the force of caricature while orchestrating a limited range of colours, must conjure figuration out of thin air while simplifying figures severely, must quote textbook modernism, outdo it and make it unfamiliar once more. In addition to this, it is subjected to a mysterious deprivation. In an excellent catalogue essay Anne Seymour suggest that Chia leaves everything to the last minute, then uses a contradictory gesture to call into question what he has painted so far. It may be a mistake to regard apparent spontaneity as a device for grasping that ineffable X-factor around which he circles; perhaps, after all, his allusive Mannerism is intended to dramatize the failure of painting in its present form, to emphasize the bankruptcy of modernist traditions. Yet if this were all he did, the result would be too arty for words. The new monumentality, the odd combination of wonder and satire, the desire that aestheticism should be hard won – all of these make Chia's chosen genre a kind of spiritual burlesque.

Georg Baselitz

Review of exhibitions at Anthony d'Offay Gallery and Waddington Gallery, London, published in Artforum *XXI, 6, February 1983.*

'In my eyes you will see the altar of nature, the sacrifice of flesh, the remains of meals in the lavatory pan, exhalation of bed sheets, blood on stumps and aerial roots, oriental light on the pearly teeth of flecks of shadow, parades of epileptics . . .' At the time of his first 'Pandemonium Manifesto' Georg Baselitz saw dismemberment as a function of the grotesque. To focus on remnants, protuberances and fleshy paraphernalia, all with the appearance of independent life, was to force painting to act as 'conciliatory mediation', a means of defusing the threat these objects presented. The air of nervous exhilaration in pictures such as *P.D. Foot* (1963) also pervades the 'idol' series of 1964, which treats the head as an independent, ponderable entity. 'The most beautiful thing in the world is always to work a face, a head, to pieces', Baselitz concluded in his 'Letter to Herr W. of August 1963'.

But, he added, 'Perhaps something else is involved.' Gradually his alternation between extremes of action and suffering was becoming more evident. And though Christian patience supplanted sado-masochism in Baselitz's work in 1965, when the '*neue Typ*' prints followed explicit images of crucifixes and castration, an involvement with emotional polarities remained. Opposing views of repression were shown, a desire to suspend intellect or morals being compromised by a pressure to employ accepted patterns. Suspicious of Tachisme, Baselitz had begun by rejecting easy metaphors for liberation, and felt compelled to retain figurative content; yet he could not resist the urge to un-make it.

The '*Frakturbilder*' ('fracture paintings') tended gradually towards increased formal dismemberment. In some of the earlier of these works motifs were halved, then one half was shifted sideways; in others different motifs were arranged like photographs on a page. By 1967, in such pictures as *Curlyhead*, shapes formed a seething, entirely unexpected unity. Only variations in scale indicated that fragmentation had taken place. By 1968 *Alsatians* and *Three Dogs Upwards* revealed a taste for ornament, the logical extension of grotesque, pushed into a decorative, figurative variation on the all-over Jackson Pollock works that Baselitz had seen ten years earlier in Berlin. Three large 'Woodman' pictures from the same year demonstrated his most intricate system of facture to date. Already, in the 'Woman with Whip' drawings, he had borrowed the child's trick of stretching the outline of a hill up the side of the paper, then standing figures on it at right angles to the 'base'; now blocks of wood hung in mid-air, men in pieces dangled upside down, one picture plane set diagonally inside another. As usual, Baselitz moved forward by opposites. Dry, matt surfaces with raw canvas showing and plenty of overpainting suited his new, celibate foresters. If the argument was not advancing, it was deepening emotionally. Fluctuating between formal dissection and moody hacking offered Baselitz a personal dialectic, a way of isolating irreconcilable attitudes towards partial figures. The decision to reverse motifs permanently in 1969 encapsulated the whole debate and shifted it to a higher ground.

In Baselitz's recent pictures all the painting is overpainting, in a graphic drawing style. Shouting heads, anguished figures in rooms, a harlequin, are set against windows which tussle for authority, resembling paintings within paintings or scrolls with oriental hieroglyphs, revealing artifice before reasserting it. Only a roundabout way of asserting impact is possible; these enormous walls of canvas are sometimes covered in only two colours. But an impact is felt. Where it comes from, how it reaches us, is all called into question by Baselitz – not the aesthete European curators have taken him to be, but a painter content to tell the truth about conventions we have been taking for granted. The heads are shouting messages we are unable to hear; their scream is a figment of art. It takes place inside art. Endlessly sympathetic, always inclined to take an anthropomorphic approach to these painted units, we are led to conclude that they scream because they are locked in.

Critics agree that painting images upside down is a way of distracting attention from content. But viewers have trouble here. The effort of twisting your head around, just out of curiosity, to see the pictures right side up – men in some recent drawings twist their heads around to get a good look at you – is like including the word 'dog' in a poem and expecting readers to forget about hairy domestic pets with four legs and a tail. It is a simple solution to a less simple problem. Perhaps the reversed people are intended to be read neither as content nor as non- or anti-content, but as springboards for thinking about other things. Three of the latest canvases are reworkings of Edvard Munch; perhaps these historical references are a red herring too. A whole range of perhapses extends to the horizon.

In the post-1969 inversions of image Baselitz was trying to simplify his art, to isolate its main features and to help the viewer concentrate on relationships between image, content and style by keeping them separate. One parallel could be deconstructive criticism: just as Jacques Derrida located latent contradictions in Fernand de Saussure's arguments about the relative priority of 'spoken' to 'written' language, Baselitz found obstacles in the path of painting and set himself to show their existence. The belief that present emotion can be re-presented by means of churned pigment and the simultaneous faith in painting as a vehicle for sensuousness, the question of whether content or 'originality' matter – these are areas where it would be wise to seek Baselitz's aporia. He has moved from a preoccupation with recording experiences of the self and the other to operating within the terms of art, experimenting almost scientifically with Derridean *différance* to create a form of painting close to traditional art and yet so isolated from it that the two are related in the same way as the terms of a pun.

Just as deconstructive criticism barely conceals its complicity with the texts it worries, Baselitz's former assumptions and present aims cannot be seen apart. In the same way that the pre-1969 fractures generated visual events, the dissociations of the later work may be thought to 'create origins', as Theo Kneubühler has suggested. Oddly, the success of Baselitz's enterprise may depend on the points at which he fails. Perhaps he has stopped trusting his chosen medium and abandoned personal exploration only in order to erect a superstructure, a meta-painting with a specific didactic point and nothing else. Perhaps the idea of art about difference is so attractive that we take the thought for the deed. Whatever, Baselitz the exemplar is unmistakably the invention of Baselitz the morbid introvert, the man who made the *Frakturbilder*. Painting for him is still a hatchet job.

Drift

Published in The Fifth Biennale of Sydney, Private Symbol: Social Metaphor, *edited by Leon Paroissien, 1984.*

Two shapes are sketched broadly in black paint on a tarpaulin. Each is grotesque in its way – the female figure cactus-like with a blooming headpiece and clinched waist, the male a cross between a printing press and a hammerhead shark. They stand side by side, presenting themselves ceremonially to an audience like Punch and Judy, their retinue and emblems of office behind them. And their royal stance is mimicked by a layer of superimposed cream gloss paint, daubed into parodies of human figures. Though they are silhouettes they seem to suffer, if only by feeling the effects of gravity, as the royal pair do not, with their fixed identities of tool and vegetable, the woman an ascending organic spiral which the male is designed to flatten. But titles too are part of a painting. '*JULIAN SCHNABEL*', the label reads, '*Memory and the Stimulus for Memory*'. That play of revelation and concealment recalls the way memory solidifies impressions into caricature, while continually questioning its constancy.

It may be possible to interpret a picture of this kind only by rethinking the very word 'interpret', rethinking the interference the interpreter makes between it and its viewer, suspending the need to unpick simply because the artist has already indulged that urge: as might be expected of a painting about memory, it creates and uncreates as it goes, changing and editing like memory itself. Fixing the precise denotations of marks is far less important than noting the emotional resonances between layers of paint with private histories of their own. The double curve of the left-hand cipher, on display like a sculpture on a pedestal, occupied prime position in an earlier painting, *Procession (for Jean Vigo).* It resembles the double helix structure of a DNA molecule, a life force, though the regal desert plant is reminiscent of a form in Mark Rothko's *Slow Swirl by the Edge of the Sea.* While the background evokes tidal eddies, the two superimpositions, barely more than alphabet letters, are flattened, clinging on to the top and bottom edge, recalling the theme of another recent door painting, *Christ in the Bay of Naples*, in which the crucified body seems to have been crushed into the icon He became. A hieroglyph for a dangling man and a Greek X, the symbol of Christ, have been added to complement the central figures, all the stranger because of the air of judgement they bring to a painting that began life as a kind of epithalamion.

'Began life'? A work of art begins life when the viewer catches sight of it. Since catching sight of this picture, its constituent parts have assumed now one relationship, now another, resisting solution in the mind. Samuel Beckett said that Joyce's writing was not about anything; it was that thing. This painting is that thing and is about that thing too, and, like the superimposed flow of housepaint, another duality is offered if the viewer wants to make the connection: between present and past, sound and echo. It rings in the mind like a remark you thought you had forgotten.

And, of course, it quotes as it shifts in the mind. While Salle, with his ready stock of images, is praised for the aptness of his quotation, Schnabel is blamed for the same reason. If Rothko *is* present somewhere in the painting in question no more appropriate reminiscence could be imagined; *Slow Swirl*, sometimes described as a wedding portrait of the artist and his wife,[1] is indebted to textbook diagrams of cell development.[2] Schnabel's weird tree hints that his couple are Adam and Eve. Rothko was determined to take the story back to blobs of protoplasmic slime. But Schnabel is interpreting Rothko – translating him. (There was a time when the two words meant the same.) Perhaps he is even measuring himself against a great artist – or at least a great painting – and seeking to overthrow by misreading, letting the mind wander. Freud used the word *Bedeutungswandel*, 'wandering signification'.[3] Bringing the two together in his own theory of creative misreading, Harold Bloom has rethought terms such as 'influence' and suggested that what poets and critics do with a poem is deeply connected.

A tradition-minded modernist would object that Schnabel was simply situating himself historically; whom you quote is what you want to be. T.S. Eliot knew what culture was: a row of books on a shelf, in chronological order. These days the canon is out of fashion. Of more use to us is Walter Benjamin's habit of arranging his book collection by means of impossible taxonomies: large next to small, and so on. Systems collapse, and a man who so enjoyed getting lost or drugged must have known this better than most. The late writings of Barthes describe such a state of collapse. In *The Pleasure of the Text* he remembered a night when, half asleep in a bar, he tried to count all the languages he could hear and in doing so became 'an exemplary site', a public square in Tangiers through which fragments passed without congealing into a sentence.[4] The experience of the here and now, the 'performative' tense, would occupy him more than once in his last writings.[5] And he had a word for that state of mind in which no sentence formed. 'Drifting', he wrote, 'occurs whenever I do not respect the whole'.[6] For Barthes it was also present in writing and desire.

Writing is an act, while desire is a state of mind. Barthes might have disagreed. 'Drift' an intransitive verb, may be a state of mind, but to begin to drift involves consenting to passivity, allowing will-power to fall into abeyance. Certainly this may be exciting but it is a private sort of excitement. Sensitive, secretive men, both Barthes and Benjamin – in most of their writing at least – seem far removed from that declaration which activity presumes. Their pleasures entail loneliness and childlike selfishness. If not entirely capable of being willed, pleasure is wilful. Little wonder that the word 'drift' enters the vocabulary of Achille Bonita Oliva as a way of appreciating the skittish poetry of Italian figuration.[7] And little wonder that a habit of distraction, an involuntary unfocusing, should be so prized when models of culture itself have changed. Culture, Abraham Moles remarks in his book *La Sociodynamique de la Culture*, is a table of magazines in a dentist's waiting-room.[8]

Drifting, by definition, is aimless. Plural, paradoxical, pleasurable and provocative, the ideal text proposed by French poststructuralists such as the late Barthes was also aimless; its direction was not 'here' or 'there' but 'between', as his definition of intertextuality demonstrated:

> Any text is a new tissue of past citations. Bits of codes, formulae, rhythmic models, fragments of social languages etc. all pass into the text and are redistributed within it, for there is always language before or around the text. Intertextuality, the condition of any text whatsoever, cannot of course be reduced to a problem of sources or influences: the intertext is a general field of anonymous formulae whose origin can scarcely ever be located: of unconscious or automatic quotation, given without question marks.[9]

By 1980 it seemed that intertextuality was such a main assumption of art practice that it had become the pivot of entire works, such as Laurie Anderson's *United States*, which deliberately dramatized what Barthes saw as a universal condition. Anderson perfected a way of allowing media to ricochet off each other, the complete antithesis of traditional notions of *Gesamtkunstwerk* or synaesthesia. It could serve equally well as a worked example of other post-structuralist conventions: the shift from 'work' to 'text', for instance, or the 'death of the author'.[10] Anderson's functional, *Neue Sachlichkeit* disguise, deliberately asexual and ironic, stressed a rift between creator and creation. It was one of the most perfect of many experiments with the self in eighties art: Clemente's chameleonism, Sherman's identikit females, Borofsky's dream refractions, Kiefer's representative German.

Though the death of the author was a major assumption of literary theorists, the conclusions to be drawn from it were debated. Foucault urged that it was crucial to reverse the traditional role of the author in literature, imagined as a genius from whom meaning proliferates precisely because we fear the proliferation, using the concept 'author' as the image of the creator as a roly-poly Santa Claus who is great because he is good, or vice versa.[11] In suppressing the male stereotype Father-God-Author relationship to their own production, artists – as Foucault would see it – are attacking a mode of discourse intimately connected with property and power. His thesis may be borne out by the evidence of power as a dominant preoccupation in recent art. Or perhaps not.

For every period there exists an accepted apology for the relationship of art to politics. Clement Greenberg looked at the time when artists who had previously been WPA members retired to their garrets to paint Abstract Expressionist pictures and decided that their new-found bohemianism was 'heroic'.[12] Michael Fried explained that for artists technical decision-making both paralleled and subsumed decision-making in the moral sphere.[13] The contemporary art critic who tries to find 'the' answer for 1980s art will have to ask first how compromised a reputedly avant-garde art is by pricing, the gallery system and, most of all, by the sheer power of the dominant 'official' culture to reveal its sting. One solution, in the practice of Hans Haacke or theory of Thomas Lawson, would be to challenge the system from within. Their opponents in this – and to oppose their theoretical solutions is not necessarily to disagree with their diagnosis of the problem – would reply that such single-mindedness is needed for the fight that to oppose the system is all that their art is able to do. As artists they might choose to address themselves to more individual matters. Indeed, a return to the studio has been remarked by commentators, basing their findings, perhaps, on the resurgence of interest in painting. Yet the studio provides a good hideout for the *agent provocateur*.

An ideal site for painting, said Sandro Chia, is the outside wall of a building, facing the street. Certainly a main structural model for recent art is a wall of graffiti, the visual equivalent of that Moroccan square or a mind in the process of wandering. Anonymous underground figures hovering between public and private domains, graffitists are fresh kids who scrawl what they wish. Gradually what they do hides, then transforms the building, or makes a mobile painting out of a subway train. Neither bohemians not business gents, 1980s artists often seek such cultural interfaces, translating, interpreting, then leaving their work drifting in a condition of cultural intertextuality. So the political statement they make will be putative at best; even though they might be writing their names over and over again, graffitists really say nothing on walls. They perform a therapeutic activity, allowing aesthetic decisions to be made in an improvisatory way. Name has become image. But that image is camouflage, concealing and transforming as it pretends to 'express'. There is only one way to signal the impotence of the artist in such a situation: to engage with images that are beyond hope of control – not images we understand, as David Salle has said, but images that understand us.

There is certainly a danger of being misunderstood by making such choices, and a related danger of being unable to fight the chosen images. Charles Jencks pictured postmodern architects as switchboard operators plugging and unplugging a set of wires, each with a label and a textbook signification.[14] Sometimes the board jams. Commenting on 'Fascist' elements in Aldo Rossi's architecture, Jencks decides that these are not yet sufficiently neutral to be used, but that given time they will be. (Did Fascist references in Philip Johnson escape comment simply because of his flippant manner?) After years of posing as eccentrics Gilbert & George adopt the stance of average Englishmen in photocollages that juxtapose studies of racial minorities, self-portraits of the artists and obscenities scrawled on London walls. The large split photographs naturally take their place within the private odyssey the artists have pursued for so long, a return to the streets after the crisis of *Dark Shadow* but a disorienting one in which stability is promised only by emblems of patriotism – union jacks, bronze warriors on memorials, the stuff of Falklands war talk as well as National Front aggression pursued by precisely those skinheads who figure as objects of desire for the two besuited middle-aged bachelors. Outside the terms that any artist's 'world' seems to create for its parts, the picture of Whitechapel promulgated by these works is so loaded that it is hardly surprising if British critics attacked them on moral grounds. Yet Gilbert & George are, after all, engaging with images that fascinate them, like Anderson or Longo, and pushing the equivocation in their working method to a limit.

Any answer to the question of possible political engagement in art should bear in mind first the assumptions that art makes, isolated here as a cluster of ideas from French poststructuralist thought. It should also take account of three paradoxes. First, that neo-Expressionism, the myth of the liberated brushstroke, is locked in a deadly embrace with that of the artist as image processor. Second, that just as French poststructuralism itself has been regarded as a reaction to the failure of 1968 student revolution,[15] a tacit decision that henceforth subversion would be carried out on paper by a process of continual analysis of language itself, the return to the studio could be interpreted either as a resurgence of interest in the methods and lost causes of late sixties Conceptualism or an admission of defeat. Third, that Barthes and Benjamin may have been performing a service by forcing us to see that what had been regarded as an interiorized activity has public significance, that in the condition of 'drifting' lies the possibility of subversion. Arising from thoughts of the collapse of the systems, it treats that collapse as a permanent, above all enjoyable, state in which creative alteration can take place.

1. Diane Waldman, *Mark Rothko 1903–1970: A Retrospective* (New York: Guggenheim Museum, 1945), p.45; Robert Rosenblum, *Mark Rothko: The Surrealist Years* (New York: Pace Gallery, 1981), p.8.
2. Stephen Polcari, 'The Intellectual Roots of Abstract Expressionism: Mark Rothko', *Arts Magazine*, September 1979, pp.124–34.
3. Harold Bloom, *A Map of Misreading* (New York: Oxford University Press, 1980), p.89.
4. Roland Barthes, *The Pleasure of the Text,* trans. R. Miller (New York: Hill & Wang, 1975), p.49.
5. Roland Barthes, *Empire of Signs,* trans.R. Howard (London: Cape, 1983), p.6: 'The Dream; to know a foreign (alien) language yet not to understand it . . .', cf. Elias Canetti in *The Voices of Marrakesh* (London: Marion Boyars, 1982): 'A Dream: A man who unlearns the world's languages until nowhere on earth does he understand what people are saying.'
6. Roland Barthes, *The Pleasure of the Text*, p.18.
7. Achille Bonita Oliva, *La Transavangarde Italienne* (Milan: Politi, 1980).
8. Edgar Morin, *New Trends of study of Mass Communications* (occasional paper of the University of Birmingham Centre for Contemporary Cultural Studies, n.d.).
9. Roland Barthes, 'Text, Discourse, Ideology', in R. Young, ed., *Untying the Text* (Boston and London: Routledge, 1981), p.39.
10. Roland Barthes, 'From Work to Text' and 'The Death of the Author', in *Image – Music –Text*, translated by S. Heath (London: Fontana, 1977).
11. Michel Foucault, 'What is an Author', in J.V. Harari, ed., *Textual Strategies* (London: Methuen, 1980), pp.141–60.
12. Clement Greenberg, *Art and Culture* (London: Thames & Hudson, 1973), p.230: 'Some day it will have to be told how *anti-Stalinism*, which started out more or less as *Trotskyism*, turned into art for art's sake and thereby cleared the way, heroically, for what was to come.'

13. Michael Fried, *Three American Painters* (Harvard: Fogg Art Museum, 1965), pp.9°10: 'This means that while modernist painting has increasingly divorced itself from the concerns of the society in which it precariously flourishes, the actual dialectic by which it is made has taken on more and more of the denseness, structure and complexity of moral experience – that is, of life itself, but life as few are inclined to live it: in a state of continual intellectual and moral alertness. The formal critic of modernist painting, then, is also a moral critic: not because all art is at bottom a criticism of life but because modernist painting is at least a criticism of itself.'

14. Charles Jencks, *The Language of Post-Modern Architecture* (London: Studio, 1977).

15. E.g. Terry Eagleton, *Literary Theory* (Oxford: Blackwell, 1983), p.142.

In Pursuit of Savage Luxury: an interview with Edward Alllington

From a catalogue published by the Midland Group, Nottingham, 1983.

Stuart Morgan: *When did you become interested in Greek culture?*
Edward Allington: As soon as I could read. First it was the usual stilted children's version of the myths. Then I started reading history books, popular archaeological works and translations of Greek literature and philosophy. The problem was how to sort out what was meaningful to me.
Why did that present a problem?
There were so many versions of the truth that instead of accepting or rejecting evidence I found I had to pick it to bits. A similar headache arose from having to study the Bible as a child and realizing that it was a translation. It's supposed to be translated from original manuscripts. Which manuscripts? Where are they? And if they are God's word – which is the fundamentalist view – what validity does editing have? It seemed important to try to work out what was happening.
Important in a moral way?
Well, my studies were in the context of a kind of religion known as The Truth, so rejecting that meant courting eternal damnation. Reading Plato was a big step. It was fascinating finding something that seemed to relate to the way Christianity developed.
Plato, of course, had his own way of differentiating between alternative 'truths'.
I pictured the truth as Plato presented it as the difference between a blueprint and an engineered product. The engineering drawing, immaculate and perfect, is the Concept. Then there is the Form, which is never as immaculate as the drawings, no matter how wonderfully engineered it is. It's often a crude representation of what those drawings sought. Reading Plato gave me the idea that a blueprint in the heavens was superimposed on things that were real. I came to see that this wasn't true; for me things that are real are *in* nature. I realized that in culture itself it is impossible to prove that one level is more important than any other. As an artist it would be irresponsible to omit what I began to see as the larger part of culture. I had to learn and understand not only 'high' art but also 'low' art. That would be how a word like kitsch

operates.

Could you define kitsch?

Historically, kitsch is one result of Romanticism. Romantics brought hitherto exclusive things into the realm of the commonplace. Love, for instance, which had previously been considered as transcendental, became thought of as very common indeed, though before this it may not have been available to the masses at all. Beauty was similarly debased. One prerequisite for kitsch was these Platonic blueprints, very complicated notions ready-packaged.

So kitsch is an attempt by the middle classes to bring high and low taste together.

It's a way of trying to resolve a difficult paradox – like gluing over a crack. One suggestion is that kitsch was how the newly powerful bourgeoisie assimilated high culture without abandoning their own Puritanism. They wanted the cultural attributes of the aristocracy without the libertinism they felt went with it.

When did kitsch become a big issue for you?

Probably after my first visit to Greece. As a holiday-maker I found it impossible to see the real Parthenon for the souvenirs and distorted depictions of it. Confusion about versions of the truth reared its head again. Finally I decided that the 'real thing' just wasn't there.

By doing that you were turning your back on Plato, who saw it as a moral duty to intervene in a universe of copies in order to decide which were good and which bad. Did you rebel against his thinking in other ways?

Yes I did. One of my main objections was to his idea of the present in relation to the past and the future. As in Christianity, it seemed to me that this was denying the present, trading it in against the future, a format that as well as being the metaphysic of Christianity is also that of capitalism and Marxism. Put in a simple way, Plato's aim was to achieve the good through reason, a sort of Jacob's Ladder where the student works now for promised gains in the future. In Christianity this is worked into a complete denial of the body and earthly existence for promised salvation. And with both capitalism and Marxism we're all supposed to suffer now so that one day we will enjoy equality before the cornucopia provided by industry. Denying the fact of being here this minute was something I could never accept. I also realized that Plato was a cheat. In a dialogue such as the *Gorgias,* where Socrates lays into Gorgias about oratory and his being a Sophist, Socrates uses rhetorical tricks to beat him down. He is using the same tool he condemns Gorgias for using. My strongest objection to Plato is that he was always trying to bury both the Sophists and the cult of Dionysus.

Why does that worry you so much?

Reading about it or gazing at dislocated fragments in museums we can catch a glimpse of another way of living which was orgiastic and physical, even almost bestial. What we need now is a new understanding of what was lost then.

There's always hot debate whenever people talk about varying degrees of savagery or civilization in Greek culture. Nietzsche argued that an old idea of the Greeks as noble and serene was only one side of the coin – the Apollonian side. In sharp contrast was the Dionysiac side, which focused on ecstasy and suspension of moral values. He saw the two as being in continuous conflict. If there is something terrifying about the savage side of the duality it must lie in its contempt for reason. As punishment for trying to reason with Dionysus, Pentheus in Euripides' Bacchae *is made to dress as a woman, then taken to the mountains where the women of his city are already dancing ecstatically in homage to the god. There he is tied to a tree, shot through the air and as he falls to the ground is ripped limb from limb and devoured by the crazed women, including his own mother.*

The point at which Pentheus weakens and falls in with the Stranger's plan, the point at which he is touched by the divine madness of the god, is when he conceives a desire to watch the women on the hillside. One aspect of reason in its guise as science – which we recognise as a great Greek achievement – is the desire to investigate the world. Euripides obviously regards that as sheer folly.

The authorities might have felt unhappy about the fact that Dionysian (and Eleusinian) rituals took place in private; like politics, religion in ancient Greece seems usually to have taken place in public.

All the mystery cults were élitist, caste-oriented. In contrast, Robert Graves wrote that the success of Christianity lay in its being the first mystery cult open to everybody.

If he was right, then Christianity flourished because of its kitsch elements.

Clement Greenberg proposed something similar in his essay 'Avant-garde and Kitsch'. He argued that mass literacy was a major contribution to kitsch because people deprived of their own original culture, which was oral, had moved from rural areas into the city and were faced with empty leisure time. But it wasn't enough time to enjoy 'real' culture, as Greenberg defined it. The result was a mass mystery religion of art – in other words, kitsch.

In both cases the issue is one of translation: the transmission of images and their changing contexts. For you this figures as a dilemma about beginnings and endings. Do you try to purify the successive versions of the truth by returning them to some unfallen state? Or do you settle for living with intolerable paradoxes?

I've reached the point where all the oppositions within me aren't resolved. Trying to resolve them would be kitsch. My way of working allows me to reclaim and reconstruct.

You seem to have moved steadily toward myth, which stands at the end of any search for originals. Some scholars cling to the notion that there was a neolithic period when Greeks walked around speaking myths. But myth as a term surely incorporates the suggestion that there is no end to that receding line of images. A more useful definition would be that myth is always a story others have told; it is always *already in circulation. If there is a trick in this, the same trick can be found among recent French thinkers who fall back on the idea of the 'eternal return' and so annihilate the whole question of origins or goals. But I'm still not certain that I understand your view of history.*

Most sculpture denies the past totally or recycles it into new products. So the past is considered as old junk that the artist recycles into new junk. Instead I try to reclaim the past for the present. Archaeologists waste time trying to reconstruct the past. They say 'In 504 BC this was going on . . .' By adopting this attitude they create a third kind of time; archaeological time as a product to be sold. My motive is quite different from this type of restoration. It's a way of making connections. I can't remember much about my childhood, for example, so I find through my dream diaries that something comes back to me. It doesn't matter whether that connection is true or not. And the same is the case with the idea of Greece. While reclaiming the past I am trying to accept that it never existed. And – whether or not it makes sense – in doing this I am reclaiming my own life.

Edward Allington: Resting Form

Review of Allington's participation in the TSWA 3D sculpture project, published in Artscribe *66, 1987.*

Of British sculptors Edward Allington is probably the least likely to be chosen to work out of doors. Or the least likely to want to do so. Perhaps it was his distaste for public art in general that gave his TSWA entry its particular edge. Indeed, apart from the drawing itself – of a leafy ornamental scroll – everything about his construction in the portico of St Martin-in-the-Fields was unexpected. In two dimensions rather than three, it hung at a diagonal to the right of the main entrance, avoiding floor and walls. Not a hindrance, nor exactly a convenience, it seemed more of a white elephant than an embellishment.

Seeing an Edward Allington work of any kind now has become a rare occurrence in London. Although the drawing style is recognizable as his, the frame of reference of the St Martin-in-the-Fields structure is as unusual as its situation. His choice of site reflects a recent interest in graves and temples, but the fact that this church in particular is a popular tourist attraction harks back to his original concern with the fate of Greek civilization, a theme that at one time inspired images of Greek busts as picture postcards, printed on his ceramics. That predilection for *trompe-l'oeil* which was a feature of past work relates to childhood stories about the acceptance or rejection of illusion. To expect all these preoccupations to coincide in a single work would be asking a lot. But by now, when some of the patterns of Allington's career have become apparent, it can be seen that instead of moving from one point to the next, he keeps a number of different concerns in play simultaneously, colliding from time to time without ever meshing fully. Motifs are pursued until they dwindle into decadence, like the open shell which moved gradually from Baroque to Rococo and finally floated into space in a bliss of erotic self-absorption, a 'debasement' of a different kind from the degradation of the impossible Platonic ideal which has been a major concern of his work for so long.

Made at a time when his sculpture has never seemed so severe and cerebral, *Resting Form* might pass for a kind of corrective. Interviewed at the ICA, Allington explained that this was in fact how it was intended. Yet the correction was not to the building itself or to a trend in his own work but rather to other people's visual perception of St Martin's as a monument, especially tourists with cameras. For the six weeks of its installation, he explained, his intervention would ruin thousands of tourist snapshots; only when they had returned home, perhaps, would they become fully aware of an alien element collaged into their experience. And because tourism exists as a perception at one remove, as a vicarious alternative to a full life, the unexpected may jolt them into some richer expectation. But perhaps Allington only half-believes his own explanation. Since the time he showed domestic repairs as sculpture, he has been concerned with exhibiting damage as a way of emphasizing a healing process just beyond our capabilities. As in the case of the giant scroll itself, the role of the purely visual in Edward Allington's art is to act as a kind of bookmark. Opening the book we discover some complex juxtapositions, the old incommensurables in some revised order. And the way is opened again to Allington's changing train of thought about time and the object, the real and the fake, the gradual curtailments of experience and the consequent yearning for the recovery of lost ideals. Each exhibited fault, every disjuncture exposed as if it will heal, poses a larger, grimmer dilemma: whether history is corrigible or whether the question fades into oblivion the more it is repeated, perpetuating an *idée fixe* that becomes more debased as it is indulged.

Pina Bausch: 1980

Notebook entry, 1984.

Seeing this 'piece' (her word) again it seemed just as wilful in formal terms – a 'loose baggy monster', as James described Tolstoy. Yet even more powerfully it appeared that this was a woman who knew exactly what she was doing. The emotional impact was full, unerring and with great range; the music was faultless; the actors/dancers/performers were unique.

A stage with a dais. A man climbs on it with a bowl, adjusts a microphone and sits. Then, slowly he eats what is in the bowl, dedicating each spoonful 'Pour papa', 'Pour maman', inaugurating the theme of childhood, its games, fears and delights, which permeates the work. Bausch's ability to link childhood sexuality with a punishment system and to see both sublimated in games that continue through our lives is a constant in her work, it seems. *1980* is pre-eminently a work for a *company*, and as the tableaux alter the relations between members do too, as if the company is a changing social microcosm. The members hold competitions, give each other orders, stage battles of the sexes . . . Only in the very odd moments are they together, yet even then they are individual, as in the sunbathing scene or in the scene in which they sit in relative darkness and stillness listening to a girl singing to a harmonium. Then they are lost in their own thoughts; although they are relaxed they are profoundly serious. (And this emotion, achieved also at the end, is Pina Bausch's triumph in *1980*: a deep sadness through happiness, a knowledge of pleasure and a way of setting its loss in perspective, an acceptance that things will never again be as they were. Her use of the Shakespeare song 'O willow willow' is perfect. The tenor of *1980* is not at all unlike that of *Twelfth Night*.) Often it is these set-pieces one remembers. Equally often it is the beauty of the transitions – crowds breaking up steadily to move elsewhere, with all the dignity their formal clothes demand. Bausch is a master of walking and walking dances, like the unforgettable comic line that is formed every now and again, snaking through the audience, or the part when sets of three performers walk steadily forward down the stage while the rest of the company panic and shout (to the music of 'Land of Hope and Glory'). Bausch's concept of dance is social, then, and not surprisingly she wrings every nuance she can out of posing for photographs, parlour games, jazz dance, smoochy cheek to cheek dances, etc. Whether 'dance' is quite the term for what takes place is doubtful. These are public shows which can be inflected with private meaning. Bausch frequently brings private weaknesses into public view. Perhaps the most tedious parts of *1980* are the sequences of questions and answers, the leg competition in which each tries to get hold of the microphone to advertise his/her legs. Though none has secrets, it seems, all of them are private, surprising people, as their responses to the question on dinosaurs demonstrates. Yet people are born exhibitionists.

The pastoral setting – turf and a toy deer – helps the *fête champêtre* atmosphere Bausch sometimes conveys, the sense of a round of social pleasure which is transient. We can never return to childhood though we are doomed to repeat its patterns and fears, such as having to lie in a bed where the bedclothes are too short, or being made to recite in public. Only one girl dances in anything like a traditional way. We see her alone in front of a water-sprinkler in one part. But this, indicatively, is for her a fantasy, an escape.

Most haunting is Bausch's use of time. It is as hard to tell whether events are starting or stopping in *1980* as it is in a piece of Balinese gamelan music. There are repetitions, the whole final sequence surely being the longest of these. And there are leitmotifs: Merryl Tankard's alternate panic and total self-sufficiency. Yet in general we are at sea, not even knowing when pauses in the action correspond to traditional 'intervals' or not. So when the lights come up and dancers serve tea to the audience or a conjuror comes on and does tricks is it permissible to leave the auditorium or not? Even the conjuror reappears, with everyone taking an over-reverent interest in his old tricks, as they do in the activity of the old athlete on the parallel bars.

What, then, is *1980* about? The company constitute different microcosmic societies as the action proceeds. They all seem to be required to work equally hard, and their weaknesses and natural urge to compete are played on by Bausch. Yet it is always suggested that in some way *they* make their rules, that the movements and words and songs and games which occur come from a common 'myth-kitty' (Auden's term) but that this kitty has individual areas of eccentricity, respected by the others as 'private', inviolable.

Saul Steinberg

Review of an exhibition at Waddington Gallery, London, published in Artforum *XXII, 7, March 1984.*

Start with the signature. It's always there, plus a date and sometimes a copyright symbol. Abbreviated to 'ST', 'Steinberg' even becomes a brand name on products in the work. This apparent monomania extends to the creation from scratch of a world that resembles the real one. Pencils are carved and painted, a camera is a block of wood with a pushpin for a button and the screw top from a soda bottle for a knob. There are signs that the world outside Saul Steinberg's studio consists of landmarks like hotels and banks – Miami and Istanbul are Miami and Istanbul because trains stop there; Steinberg shows stations and nothing more. Cairo has oriental architecture, which is cracking. It also has 'International Style'. That is cracking too. These blank places seem to exist only because they are there and have names.

Yet the opposite is also the case. A Steinberg signature is a line on vacation, capable of endless metamorphosis. Similarly his artistic persona is mercurial, eclectic, multilingual, as totally dependent on the world as any tourist. A piece of fruit, a label in Arabic, a box, an Algerian banknote, a 50-lire ticket to visit the dome of a building in Florence, a Ugandan trademark, an enamel clock-face that looks French . . . like passports the drawings bear the impressions of rubber stamps. The Steinberg myth takes over. Another album of fragments: fear of labels that could have led to denunciation in his native Romania, hints of forged documents. The real Steinberg never stands up; or if he does, there is a brown paper bag over his head. His signature becomes a trademark like any other. Perhaps his real signature is the visa stamp in gibberish.

The more that stamp is used the more sinister it seems, a monogram that is specific to him but not unique – immediate but passionless, both public and private. As some commentators argue about Jackson Pollock or Arshile Gorky, Steinberg stage-manages a skirmish between camouflage and expression. There the comparison with Abstract Expressionism ends. If theirs was a language problem, he has made his a strength, and in doing so has distinguished himself as a dissenter. Were those late Adolph Gottliebs or Ad Reinhardts really so different in motivation from the manic repetition of a graffitist who inscribes one name – his own name – over and over? Never certain of his status as an artist, Steinberg disposes of the 'aura', ritual and uniqueness Abstract Expressionists so cherished, making an identity crisis the pivot of his art. Travel, translation and reproduction form his triple theme, all being ways of transferring something to another place.

In some cultures reproducibility and heresy are closely allied. Steinberg would sympathize. His favourite device, the signature, combined with his other favourite, the impress or seal, is a conceit that displays his sensitivity to infinitesimal degrees of difference, the change incurred by each transfer from original to copy. An open box contains Rorschach blots, more faded on one side than on the other, an entire 'printed' blot returned to its origin as a real blot. In other works this simple gesture of replication becomes increasingly complex. A (wooden) book lies open to reveal an etching plate of a woman looking through a grille at the opposite page, from which, in the etching itself, the same woman looks back. Identicalness is always spurious; one's *Doppelgänger* is a disappointment. Looking more closely, it is possible to see that the grille is a Mondrian in perspective. 'Art' is that still point at which the change between image and original is generated. And at that very point Steinberg can intervene, using the wafer-thin distinction between things and versions of things as a vast area of activity.

Far in the distance in *Rainbow Reflected* (1974) is the rest of the world – in shorthand terms, an opera house, some trees, a windmill, the Eiffel Tower and a pyramid – while a series of puddles between the horizon line and the bottom of the drawing become a sea, a river, an estuary, then at last a sidewalk puddle. A rainbow, reflected in the water, becomes more fragmented the nearer it is. Far away, ships drop anchor. Settlers with wagons trek around the edge of a lake. A man flies a kite, another fishes, a third (the older man and his cat from George Caleb Bingham's *Fur Traders Descending the Missouri*, c. 1845) floats aimlessly along, and at the base of the picture a bird on the edge of a bird-bath contemplates its reflection. All this is mirrored in the water. The sketch is a reflection in a puddle and a reflection on that reflection. Though a rainbow has as little tangible about it as a reflection, the latter verifies our existence while the former gives that existence a reason. The pursuit of happiness is every bit as important as life and liberty; together the rainbow and the puddle almost produce an image of eternity, a complete circle of light.

Schoolboys write their names, then long addresses that end 'The Solar System' or 'The Universe'. Steinberg too sits in one place, makes his mark, considers it, then uses it to improvise complex philosophical games, ways of locating the terms by which he exists. His work may not permit us to know him better. Rather, it allows us to eavesdrop on a debate that is only ever semi-public.

James Faure Walker and British Abstraction

Review of an exhibition at the Whitworth Art Gallery, Manchester, published in Artscribe *54, September/October 1985.*

If the Whitworth Art Gallery at Manchester University looks like one person's collection, it is because one kind of perception overrides history and geography there; the choice of Japanese prints and William Morris wallpapers, oriental costume and textiles reveals a high degree of respect for abstract design and decorative values. Surprisingly, the twentieth-century British painting section, which doubles as a teaching aid, reveals the same qualities. In one narrow, unpromising space, for example, a 1950s Alan Davie, as hot and uninhibited as they come, is mounted alongside a complex, muted William Scott, and a recent pastoral idyll by Gillian Ayres. Facing all three, like a framed vibraphone solo, is a William Henderson. And suddenly a dull corridor hums with colour – as refulgent in Ayres as it is restrained and reticulated in Scott, as much a tell in Davie as it is an orchestrated whisper in Henderson. Each is full; each has found a language appropriate to its emotional needs. And each, in a different way, is the heir to a tradition of abstract thinking all the more available in this place because here the past seems to have been remade to fall in with it. What became of that tradition? Advance further into the South Gallery and the problem is pushed to a crisis point.

The question of what happened to British abstraction provokes strong feelings. Whether you loved it or hated it, the answer lies in how nearly your definition of 'abstraction' is aligned with formalist theory. For a decade the two had each other in a stranglehold. But that was only the culmination of a longer flirtation. By 1985 the affair is long over. Boozy, muscle-bound ladies' men have stopped bloodying each other's noses in pubs and are sitting in libraries debating points of structuralist theory. Their dyslexic comrades may console themselves with the idea that Julian Schnabel is a big boy who probably likes a drop, but it won't do and they know it. Everything has changed. For most of them the solution has been to start painting hairy animals with erections, which only goes to show that they didn't have a clue in the first place. Luckily a small band of aware artists, of whom Henderson and Ayres are two, has continued, not as monks keeping learning alive but as people for whom the job of strengthening their painting does not necessarily mean the reversal of their previous tenets. Always something of an outrider, commenting on this position as he goes, is James Faure Walker, for whom a solo exhibition at the Whitworth was an example of the right man in the right place at the right time. Pre-eminently British, as his leaning towards the Braque-ish phase of Patrick Heron and reminiscences of sixties Bernard Cohen reveal, Faure Walker nevertheless succeeds in escaping categorization. Is that a pinch of Stuart Davis? Could that palimpsest technique refer to David Salle? As a major critic for over ten years, Faure Walker was in an ideal position to take stock of both national and international developments. That he has not lost touch is demonstrated by a remarkable *tour de force*; for the Whitworth selection he wrote his own catalogue, a mixture of theory, reminiscence and plain good sense in a lean prose style that never reveals the hard work underlying it. And as a vociferous defender of formalism he has grown as that formalism has grown. This is not to say that he has rejected his past; he has not. But it should not be forgotten that Faure Walker single-handedly led the debate on formalism to a new stage in Britain by devoting half of one issue of *Artscribe* to a lengthy, revealing interview with Clement Greenberg, outlining his failures as well as his continuing concerns. While T.J. Clark and others are prepared to bring the old boy out for a bit of rough and tumble, only Faure Walker in that interview showed him as a human being – fallible, involved and as acute as ever. The fate of formalist critics was that they ran further and further into dogmatism. Compare Faure Walker's position with that of William Tucker, for example, blind to any values but formal ones even in a Duchamp bottlerack. The comparison falls apart. Faure Walker wrote about Japanese kimonos, sculpture, football, more recently people queuing at a bus stop, in a constant attempt to find a visual foundation for each. None of this has been wasted. His new paintings show the extent to which he was thinking in public during those ten years of writing reviews and essays. Each stage of his development as an artist has been thought as well as felt through.

The sketches that accompany the paintings show two apparently divergent tendencies – one a kind of organic process of development, an accretive doodling, the other a fixed repetitive decoration. It is hard to imagine the working process of a large painting such as *Heron Island,* but it must be somewhere between the two. Overwhelmed by complex, even contradictory messages, the eye is kept mobile. *Heron Island* is a response to a coral reef as seen from underwater, yet it is also quite simply a painting and a sprawling, difficult one at that, with colours inlaid or tangled and brushstrokes ranging from long ribbons of vermilion trailing across the surface to areas of scuffed blue that barely conceal the canvas below. Most of all, the entire project resembles a game in which improvisations take place but repetition or redundancy are against the rules. *Variation on Thai Themes* separates the levels into a dawdly linear overpainting and a patchwork texture below, its colours creating different spaces. Unlike *Heron Island*, which could be either an all-over painting or a parody of Claudian perspective, as you prefer, *Variations* can be read as a set of hanging rectangles, connected by the ciphers over them, too sketchy to form distinct outlines but bearing no relation to calligraphy. In short, it resembles a scroll which might continue forever, though a set of resemblances or a language may emerge from the marks on top. Faure Walker's either-orness is not a desire for tasteful compromise; he is prepared to risk not having his cake or eating it – the total escape of a 'painting' in any recognizable formal sense. It is hardly surprising, then, that *Sea Passage* works like a play of light, a study of reflections. Sometimes these look like crenellations repeated at different levels. But the ways in which they occur are more important than the marks themselves. The invention of an unstable line that thickens or thins alarmingly as it goes, like a stick reflected in gently moving water, comes in useful here; its passage is of more interest than its fixed identity.

The only painting that 'works' properly is *Painting in D* (1984), a perfectly achieved study in rusts, blues and greys. It comes as no surprise when Faure Walker refers to it as an accident, however. In his catalogue he says 'its implications veer off the path' he supposed he was taking. Still appreciating the style he is leaving behind, he knows better than to reject it but sets no store by it either. The others may be cluttered; certainly, some are clogged to a degree where they tend to undo themselves. But with their inbuilt uncertainty, their deployment of a large number of colours, their insistence that balance should be wobbly at best, they testify to a new set of preoccupations: not with easy representation or the trickery of illusion but a state of perceptual discontinuity where metamorphosis is the norm and alternative versions of the same states of affairs multiply in the mind. Am I speaking of the paintings? Or the position in which they place their viewers? 'Disorientation', 'disinformation': if the terms that echo through the catalogue are negatives, they are tantalizing negatives. The very genre Faure Walker has developed – a jumpy rumination – suggests a third word: 'disbelief'. His temporary suspension of faith in the conventions that underlie British abstraction could be a way of playing for time or a simple blocking tactic. Like Joyce's latter-day Hamlet, Stephen Dedalus, he walks along the beach pondering 'the ineluctable modality of the visible'. His paintings are far from being solutions to a problem; they are evidence that that problem exists.

Abstraction in art is no more outdated than abstraction in thinking. Both fairly and unfairly, British abstract painting is under pressure. Fairly because of a general air of staleness about many of its 1970s adherents; unfairly, because as the direct product of a critical paradigm so recently displaced, it has lost any status at all in a general discourse. Postmodernist even-handedness may be less even-handed than it appears. Decentred, abstract practice has turned in on itself and has become a closed debate (like British Constructivism). From this it has gained in focus and strength. Faure Walker's paintings show that it is high time to weigh the consequences of 'New Art', with its academy of contemporary masters. His doubt may lead to one of those careers which bridges older and newer practice, and which opens more doors than it closes.

Open Secrets: Identity, Persona and Cecil Beaton

Published in Cecil Beaton, *ed. David Mellor, Barbican Art Gallery/Weidenfeld & Nicolson, 1986.*

Both more and less than portrait, Paul Tanqueray's study of Cecil Beaton reveals, but refuses to analyse, a tangle of fictions that sustained him. The most obvious is concealment; surrogates, in the form of photographic portraits pinned to his suit, are employed as camouflage, or even armour. Of equal importance is display – not only done but seen to be done, as Beaton makes eye-contact with the viewer while permitting himself an expression of bored superiority. If he appears disdainful of his audience, he is just as disdainful of the squads of sub-Cecils he commands. While calling attention to his own creativity, the ability to summon a multitude of alternative selves, he deprecates it too. Retention and expenditure, production and consumption, release and repression are kept in perfect equilibrium. And the result is a prodigy: a Burning Bush of a man whose capacity for the proliferation of images keeps pace with the rate of their natural dissolution, a man who exists by virtue of a process of constant renewal, defying time by mastering the very operations of time itself. The tone of Tanqueray's portrait is ambiguous. Is it satirical or complimentary? One thing, at least, is certain. As the viewer becomes aware of the overlay of images by which Beaton is defined, the picture slips into another mode completely. In Shakespeare's *Henry V* an actor appears as Rumour, in a costume covered with tongues. The man in this photograph may also be an allegory of something. But what? The search for an answer involves an analysis of the creative act as Beaton saw it.

Beaton's reports of his early years reveal divergent attitudes to his own identity. 'I want only to be Cecil Beaton', he commented, on seeing his initials on a box he had to take to school.[1] Yet this sense of ineradicable difference from others was countered by 'a secret feeling of inadequacy' physical, social, sexual and financial – which preyed on him for the rest of his life, and was accompanied by an unusual eagerness for change.[2] ('I'd like to change my whole self', he wrote after seeing Fred Astaire.[3]) In the first volume of his diaries, *The Wandering Years*, the conflict between these alternatives is heightened by the need to find work, a point at which *Bildungsroman* ceases and picaresque begins. Gradually the debate on selfhood takes the form of a discussion of the appropriate way of life for an artist. Having renounced frivolity, Boy Le Bas reminds his erstwhile devotee that the self brooks no alteration. But young Cecil thinks differently and they part forever. 'Life is deeper than thought', he wrote much later.[4] In his case choosing 'life' meant opting for change and levity, but above all for a histrionic metaphor that would eventually come to dominate his entire aesthetic.

When Beaton decided to tour North America as a professional speaker in 1953, the lecture he chose to deliver again and again was one with a venerable history on the lecture circuit. It concerned the problem of vocation. Given the dilemma of having to preserve selfhood at all costs while never ceasing to adjust the presentation of that self, Beaton drew on his deepest instincts when faced with the need to survive. Masquerades had provided the occasion for his best early photography. Already Beaton had found his medium. Later he was to use the phrase 'living picture' to describe his own theatre designs. But it was something resembling tableau vivant in its proper sense that preoccupied Beaton for his entire career. As described by Goethe in *Die Wahlwanderschaften* and Jane Austen in *Mansfield Park*, the tableau vivant was a household entertainment, sometimes highly elaborate, in which sets, costumes, poses and lighting were employed to create a sculptural rendering of a given painting. The proscenium arch was crucial to such reconstruction, enabling two dimensions to turn into three, the effect of depth being dependent on a frame. Theatre was referred to merely in terms of setting; the participants were no more than life models. One object of the exercise was to stimulate thought about the complex relationship between life and art. In a more worldly sense it provided social lubrication. Ironies in casting would be noted, unexpected groupings might be assessed on their potential in real terms. Performers would be thrown together unexpectedly and the audience was given permission to discuss them. Suddenly relations between people were sharpened and changed.

Beaton's own tableaux were constructed in free space. Framed by his camera, imaginatively illuminated and developed by trial, error and experiment, the scenes appeared totally deliberate. The product could be regarded as a flattering portrait, and 'abstract' illustration in the Pictorialist vein or simply a souvenir of one form of improvised fun. Yet each of the best of these photographs has the potential to be more than the sum of its parts. As in the boyhood works of Lartigue, the secret lay in that sense of heightened possibility experienced in play, captured by making the act of photography one element in the game. At its peak, tableau vivant was the true heir of the defunct court masque. As in the masque, an image of an ideal community lay at its core. The rhetoric that served to convince spectators of that social perfection succeeded at an aesthetic moment when each separate unit could be regarded in its own terms yet, by 'willing suspension of disbelief', acted also as part of a totality with perfect political, as well as artistic, justification. When distinctions between children and adults, men and women, contemporaneity and history, reality and fiction imploded, and for a second it seemed that anything was possible, Beaton's camera not only captured that carnivalesque moment; it also transmitted and perpetuated it.

The repercussions of this moment, when art meets life on its own terms by breaking its bounds, literally gaining another dimension, are visible throughout Beaton's career. The disguise, which was no disguise at all because only by penetrating it was it possible to experience the full impact of the pose, retained all its attraction for an artist who, it was said, could remember 'a period when for eight or ten days at a stretch he did not ever confront the world in ordinary costume but having removed his fancy dress to go to bed stepped straight into a new disguise as soon as he emerged from slumber'.[5] Eventually all dress became fancy dress for Beaton, an extension of that flair for mimicry he so admired in Pavel Tchelitchew or Frederick Ashton, natural Brechtians who 'acted' without ever surrendering their individuality.[6] In psychological terms, disguise may have reflected a need to be present when the 'aesthetic moment' took place and he, like all other participants in the tableau, would be transformed, not least in status. What did he have to lose? As a self-confessed snob and social climber, he just wanted to be accepted as an equal by those in whose circles he tried to move. The objection to this theory is obvious. It is that, far from simply being a bit actor, Beaton had it in his power to bring about the rearrangement he so desired. Of course, he had to do both. When he had achieved his aim, when he had become a 'society photographer' who was himself a member of Society, he continued to act out both sides of the predicament at once. In new guises those two views of selfhood were taken to logical extremes: on the one hand Beaton was playing God (the secret motive of any photographer who employs the 'directorial mode') and on the other he was submitting to permanent metamorphosis, making himself a walking reminder of some fault in the system. A single example of the simultaneous use of both approaches will suffice. In 1933, at rue de la Boëtie in Paris, Beaton photographed Pablo Picasso. He faces us, his back to a mirror in which Beaton's head is reflected, a reminder that our audience with the great man has been granted only at the intercession of someone he respects. Hanging, apparently, on the very wall at which Picasso is gazing, Beaton's framed face resembles a portrait exchanged in an act of gratitude.

The management of a public persona had now become a complicated matter. Beaton's diaries were edited to give an account of his life as 'Cecil Beaton', no longer merely a photographer but a gentleman artist, modelled on Noël Coward, who lectured him on his attire early in his career, and Beverley Nichols, who opened his eyes to sex. For Beaton the edited version of the diaries and his other publications, which often repeated the same anecdotes, supplied a running subtext for a body of photographs that, like tableaux vivants, seemed to incline towards narrative. Their personal use was as a record of social cultivation. And the qualities Beaton most wanted to cultivate were those of an actor. (As if to prove a point, to himself most of all, he eventually played on Broadway.) 'Great acting', he wrote as late as 1957, 'is always the highest artificiality.'[7]

'Artificiality', the maintenance of what Coward called a façade in both personal and professional spheres, was a preoccupation of male homosexuals from the 1890s onwards. The continued distaste for sincerity and the middle-class concept of 'nature' persisted long after the pronouncements of the Aesthetic Movement had ceased. Indeed, the very persistence of a set of cultural habits, a private vocabulary, an emotional range and particular ways of expressing it, demonstrated how little the lot of this particular minority had improved in the course of a century that had been prefaced by the trial of Oscar Wilde. Within the terms of this subculture, Cecil Beaton's behaviour and artistic preferences followed a well-worn path. Like Beaton, Aubrey Beardsley preferred to be known as a man of letters rather than an artist.[8] Like Beaton, the young Wilde entertained actresses, including Lillie Langtry, while Ronald Firbank, whose favourite word was 'artificial', kept an album filled with picture postcards of musical comedy beauties during his school years. Biographical coincidences between Beaton and this set of contemporaries could be expanded indefinitely. Particularly in the earlier part of the century, the cultivation of a style that was too eroticized or too satirical, too opulent or too clipped, indicated the flouting of norms: Wilde's overloaded descriptions in his stories and epigrams in his plays; Firbank's exotic, languid sentences and abstract precision, as in Chapter

XX of *Inclinations*, which in its entirety reads 'Mabel! Mabel! Mabel! Mabel! Mabel! Mabel! Mabel! Mabel!' or Beardsley's rococo flounces and economic line. The use of cosmetics; a tone of voice pitched either too high or too low, confusing people wherever possible; and the use of theatrical behaviour as a protection against vulnerability, all constituted a defence from, and an attack on, those bourgeois values which homosexuals did surprisingly little to try to disrupt. A common denominator exists in Beaton's taste for travesty; his deliberate avoidance of cliché and sentimentality in the choice of the most ugly shot from a Judy Garland contact sheet; his deliberate use of the same qualities in his 1947 portrait of Her Majesty the Queen, posed in front of a Christmas card setting; the flagrant grotesque of Elsa Maxwell's total baldness in 1960; and his purely artistic employment of religious iconography in the portrait of Lady Diana Cooper of 1930. The sexual glances implied in his photographs of servicemen during wartime and his documentary photographs of London in ruins, many resembling theatre sets, show an unusually effete and perverse approach to the wartime situation that faced him. As so many of his travel pictures and royal portraits show, Beaton was happiest when not confronting his own time and place. Armed with a limited number of themes, contexts and approaches, he often played at jumbling them up, so that a European spire looks like a Hollywood set, or a savage tribesman resembles one of the chorus line in a bad musical.[9] Perhaps Beaton's most characteristically homosexual act was the urge to modify his 'image', to try to show a 'front' to the world while, oddly, giving himself away at every turn. Perhaps he thought that the English were hypocrites who would find him acceptable if only he went through the motions of trying to conform. It is possible. But it is more possible still that he was falling into a pattern of events that had been repeated so often during his formative years that it constituted an identifiable stance. André Gide regarded Oscar Wilde's entire body of work as the product of a simultaneous desire for advertisement and secrecy. In his *Journals* Gide wrote: '1st October 1927: I believe . . . that this affected aestheticism was for him merely an ingenious cloak to hide, while half-revealing, what he could not let be seen openly; to excuse, to provide a text, and even apparently motivate, but that very motivation is a pretence . . . Always he managed in such a way that the uninformed reader could raise the mask and glimpse under it the true usage (which Wilde had good reason to hide).'[10]

If the strategy of concurrent revelation and concealment pervaded every aspect of Cecil Beaton's life, the reason may have been that it represented the only possible compromise between his incompatible views of his own selfhood. An 'actor' in the sense of having rejected a life of contemplation, he lived as if on a stage. Yet he changed his parts at will in an attempt to handle the materials of his existence as an artist manipulates his medium. So while he admired figures such as Cocteau for having taken control of the 'design' of their lives, by which he meant that they never allowed themselves to be seen except as they wanted, he himself may have craved a 'grand design' which would determine all his choices. He ended as a moral relativist and as a split personality, wavering between the avant-garde and the academy, between revolution and revivalism. Never really part of Society, however much he dreamed of it, he was not antagonistic to it either. Of all fictional characters, he most resembles Thomas Mann's Felix Krull, who, when asked whether he was a socialist, replied 'Certainly not, Herr Generaldirektor! I find society charming just the way it is and I am burning to win its favour.' Perhaps Beaton always expected more of both art and life than they could really offer. His distress can best be seen in his view of disorganization, the jumble of his hotel bedroom, the back lots in Hollywood, the confusion of the masked ball. His own reaction to these was touchingly indecisive, reminiscent of that total estrangement which Beerbohm sensed in Beardsley. He wished only to be close to it all, to those focal points of glamour, High Society and Hollywood, which he felt poetically fertile. There and only there play could arise, personae could be lost and found, stars could be born. If for him photography became an agent of transformation, clothes represented the harsh facts of survival, a capitulation to the world outside him. Nudity has no place in Beaton's scheme of things. His pictures of Dolores del Rio wearing oceanic garlands or Johnnie Weismuller, relaxing under a tree, might equally well be Sanderesque studies of people at work or remakings of the myth of Adam and Eve, with little sympathy for their predicament. There is no escape from the role-playing mankind is forced to accept. In the words of Felix Krull, 'He who truly loves the world shapes himself to be pleasing to it.' Beaton would have nodded vigorously.

Who knows what Paul Tanqueray thought of Beaton that day in his studio. A pleasing young man, but one who had picked his brains. No shortage of talent. Too much for his own good, perhaps. The embarrassment of one photographer photographing another who he knew in time would pre-empt him. But what to do about it? Praise him to the skies? See him in hell? Suddenly it all became clear. He would turn him into something like a playing card or a chess-piece. Only Beaton would have properly understood the allegory. As he sat there under the hot lights, his mind a blank, he became Fashion. Or Photography. Or maybe both at once.

1. Cecil Beaton, *Diaries 1922–1939: The Wandering Years* (London: Weidenfeld & Nicolson, 1961), p.30.
2. Cecil Beaton, *It Gives Me Great Pleasure* (London: Weidenfeld & Nicolson, 1955), p.4.
3. *The Wandering Years*, p.59.
4. Ibid., p.214.
5. Peter Quennell, *Time Exposure* (London: Batsford, 1941), p.43.
6. See Cecil Beaton, *Diaries 1939–44: The Years Between* (London: Weidenfeld & Nicolson, 1965), p.78.
7. Cecil Beaton, *The Face of the World* (London: Weidenfeld & Nicolson, 1957), p.150.
8. Stanley Weintraub, *Beardsley: A Biography* (London: W.H. Allen, 1967), p.159.
9. Cecil Beaton, *Far East* (London: Batsford, 1945).
10. Philippe Jullian, *Oscar Wilde* (London: Paladin, 1971), p.229.

Pablo Picasso

Review of exhibitions at Pace and Pace/McGill galleries, New York, published in Artforum *XXV, 2, October 1986.*

'Later he used to say quite often, paper lasts quite as well as paint and after all if it ages together why not, and he said, further, after all, later, no one will see the picture, they will see the legend the picture has created, then it makes no difference if the picture lasts or does not last. Later they will restore it, a picture lives by its legend and not by anything else.' The discovery of so many 'lost' sketchbooks by Pablo Picasso only confirms that what he told Gertrude Stein about masterpieces applies equally well to the reputations of the people who make them. How many Giorgione paintings are by Giorgione is a question of interest only to academics. By the same token, these more or less 'new' Picassos will make neither more nor less difference to a legend that will, of course, be refurbished periodically but which remains a legend despite everything.

When Picasso succeeded Auguste Rodin as the epitome of artistic creativity he proved to be last in the line of succession. 'Genius' is not a twentieth-century ideal. The increasing embarrassment we feel about the deployment of strengths of, say, Charlie Chaplin is a mark of our own distance from the entire idea of his career. The urge for change without development, the desire to entertain, the equation of predatory heterosexual behaviour and artistic prowess . . . these and other characteristics separate Picasso from us, as they separate us from Honoré de Balzac or Victor Hugo. In the age of Andy Warhol, of Michel Foucault's 'death of the author', changing concepts of originality have affected the kind of homage we feel is due to the figure of the endlessly fertile male artist.

Monsieur Picasso's sketchbooks show how early he was imbued with the need to be an artist, with all the habits that eventually came to overwhelm him: the urge to sketch places, to draw the women he was attracted to, to hoard the raw materials of his daily life, such as visiting cards or pencils. They also show that he worked out ideas exhaustively, page by page, with a talent for being able to redraw perfectly those parts that satisfied him while experimenting with the others. To Picasso an idea was not an idea unless it could be thoroughly rehearsed, a physical involvement that militates against Roger Fry's description of him as an 'intellectual'. It was his rehearsal of it, and his initial decision to involve it in his life, that mattered most, and the almost animal capacity for ingestion and expulsion, each expulsion marked with the same signature.

Is it any surprise, then, that these sketchbooks give away so little of his life, his thoughts, his secrets? Instead, they offer one more opportunity to see the great man put himself through his paces, with one virtuoso performance after another – a view of a garden, a leg in armour, a harlequin with a wand, a mother and child – like the excuse for a private life. Picasso's popular success needs no explanation. The general public demands that art exist as autobiography. Picasso never stopped promising this yet never really made the connection. Instead, his life was a life manufactured as a device to render him impervious.

Perhaps Picasso's notebooks existed as proof to himself that he could produce masterpieces even without the benefit of an audience. Since he managed to do so, it is time to suspend definitions that never really applied, and to regard these and other sketchbooks as art works in their own right, with their own characteristics and integrity. In no way are they marginalia to the paintings or the sculptures or the theatre designs. Indeed, they are proof that in the case of certain artists anything they make is interesting and relevant. Perhaps we are too fully enmeshed in the legend to ask why.

In the affiliated Pace/McGill Gallery Picasso photographs were on show – pictures of his studio, with maquettes and canvases, or, later, of himself with friends garlanded with scribbles by the maestro. As unassailable as a Franz Kafka letter, even these tiny, utterly seductive objects cannot be relegated to the status of memorabilia. They constitute works of art in their own right, the true demonstration that 'genius' is only one more word for something no one is able to understand, much less review.

Martin Ramirez

Review of an exhibition at Phyllis Kind Gallery, New York, published in Artscribe *59, September/October 1986.*

Martin Ramirez (1885–1960) was a mute paranoid schizophrenic who spent much of his life in psychiatric hospitals in California. Much of his time was spent drawing. A report written in 1954 described his working method as follows:

> When good paper is not available, he glues together scraps of paper, old envelopes, paper bags, paper cups, wrappers – anything that might have a clear drawing area. He often makes many small background studies, seashell and nature forms, which he stores in his shirt, in a paper shopping bag, in tied rolls, or behind a radiator, suddenly to be taken out and glued to an evolving picture. He fashions his own glue out of mashed potatoes and water – sometimes bread and saliva. He squats on his haunches, moving about the floor between two cots, using stubs of coloured pencils and Crayolas, drawing a little here, a little there. His drawing is kept rolled up and usually only a portion of it is exposed at any one time.

As well as partially unrolling them, Ramirez liked to guide viewers to one spot from which each of his pictures could be seen to best advantage. If he considered them as either scrolls or icons, with no sense of disparity between partial or entire viewing, he had good reason to think that way. Bold general outlines, incorporating complex perspectives and extreme fluctuations of scale, are enlivened by rhythmic patterns which challenge or oppose each other, giving a sense of continual movement. But the daring with which initial divisions are made within the picture space – largely dependent on the scale and shape of the paper available – is where Ramirez shows his great talent. Horizontal rows of shapes are often subsumed by some greater pattern of repeated curves, for example, sometimes like a bed of feathers, at others like the articulations on an insect's back or simply camouflage suggesting quite other spaces. The relation of part to whole proves so satisfying because more than one visual approach is in play at once. The emotional tenor of the finished work is extraordinary. Extreme theatricality of setting prevails, with proscenium arches or undulant body-like landscapes. Gestures of individual figures vary between high spirits – like the devil-may-care banditos and cowgirls – and self-effacement, as in one drawing of lines of tiny horsemen plodding into an obviously vaginal tunnel. This divided feeling gives Ramirez's religious works a requisite degree of awe; humility and splendour combine perfectly.

Ramirez is the ideal artist. His forty-five years of silence ensured his anonymity. His sources are a matter of conjecture; for parallels to his talent it is necessary to look outside the Western tradition altogether, to bark painting or Indian miniatures. Though nothing is known of his thoughts, we can guess that the trains rushing out of tunnels or the sheer sense of freedom in the pictures he cut out of magazines both exhilarated and frightened him, and that he could still his fears only by incorporating them into his own designs, which so often form shrines for worshipping the humble: an animal, a person writing, a few men making music and a woman dancing, the infant Jesus at play. But these are only suppositions. Art is always therapy and always far more than therapy. And Martin Ramirez was a very considerable artist indeed.

Richard Wentworth

Review of an exhibition at Lisson Gallery, London, published in Artforum *XXV, 1, September 1986.*

Richard Wentworth's work depends on two positions about our relationship to objects. First, that it is governed by an acknowledged grammar of small moves performed unconsciously with things near to hand; second, that it is constantly modified by words. Each of his sculptures exists at an intersection of modes of communication, distinguished for convenience but mingled constantly in daily life. Though Wentworth may draw on it, he is not trying to imitate the vernacular. Indeed, one of his recurring scenes is the rift between high and low, art and life, function and use. These may be contrasted, but neither appears alone. Inflection of found elements is balanced by craftsmanship, which brings about slight but irrevocable alterations.

In *Store* (1986) a galvanized steel tank of what appears to be water but is in fact a false surface also made of galvanized steel is supported at one end by an upturned glass covering a pack of Camel cigarettes, a fact that causes the liquid to seem to tip. The combination of the two approaches – casual and deliberate – yields two quite different readings. 'Someone has invented a way to guard cigarettes,' runs the casual alternative, 'but this miserly approach is self-defeating. They are in danger of getting wet.' The deliberate reading is associative. 'Camel suggests "ship" suggests hump. Hump suggests wave suggests tilt suggests danger. But hump also suggests storage suggests safety.' One may sound facile, the other too elaborate, yet neither works without the other.

Something is being explained, it seems. But what, exactly? Wentworth's use of French derivatives for his titles suggest that if a word resists translation by straddling languages, an object may define it instead. So the 1984 *Queue*, which in English is a line of waiting people, in French a tail, consists of a long bent pipe winding over and through a row of tubular chairs, making a connection between them. The trouble is that both literally and metaphorically the bond is too obvious, too clumsy. Queues need no commandeering; despite an unbreakable etiquette that governs their behaviour, participants strive to look as if they are there by accident. Something that seems as casual as a tail is ruled with a rod of iron. Though often far-fetched, Wentworth's explanations are persuasive because he is so very aware of the very oddness of the titling process. Held with tweezers as if for scientific investigation, a quoted word is matched with some unlikely solid. That is one way of looking at it. The other would be to argue, as William Empson did, that having now become an integral part of a poem, the word means all of its dictionary definitions simultaneously.

These works generate conversation. A concrete lump sitting on a gutted tyre in *Logo* (1986) turns out to be a letter rack with the spaces filled in. But why? An answer might involve drowning and defeat, teeth and gripping, laps and clutching, and much more. Image, gesture and attitude are reduced to a three-dimensional haiku. In Britain avant-garde developments are tempered and humanized; only here is anecdotal Minimalism conceivable as a serious option. But given that Wentworth's sculpture amounts to more than a teatime chat, each of his works is a collision, a misunderstanding, a trick, a knot, a joke. The argument against complexity is self-evident. What is gained by splitting hairs again and again instead of pursuing linear, detachable argumentation? The answer is pleasure, sensitivity, wit, the exercise of the mind for its own sake. What is to be 'gained' by art at all? Søren Kierkegaard said that philosophy was like a man who brought his clothes to a shop where he saw the sign 'Clothes Pressed Here'; but when he went in, they said they didn't press clothes, they only made the sign.

Rose English

Publication not traced. An account of The Beloved, *by Rose English, performed at the Drill Hall and at the Tate Gallery, London, in 1985 and 1986.*

Dr Marten's soles and the old black dress beneath the velvet robe denote grandeur subdued by practicality. Yet hope springs eternal. After the intermission English is discovered in diamante ear-rings, a tiara and a shabby tutu, her rustic bridge replaced by a more upmarket, wrought-iron version. Was this the answer to some unspoken prayer? Or an inevitable part of that permanent subjunctive the dramatic experience implies? 'How wonderful it would be', she muses, 'if suddenly I were enclosed in a pool of light.' And the pool appears when summoned, as if by magic – proof that dreams can come true, however tatty their manifestation.

This metamorphosis is one of several structural principles, all of which English herself is helpful enough to elucidate. Another is mild suspense. At the outset she announces that under no circumstance whatsoever will she let the audience know the identity of her 'Beloved' until the very end of the evening. Yet another, acted out in the constant crossing and recrossing of the bridge, is 'a journey on which I recover my memory'. By stages she recalls that moment when the audience walked into the theatre to find 'a vision of loveliness' who awoke, conscious of not having dreamed a single dream but also of having forgotten 'something tremendously important'. Gradually she recalls what it was – 'the true meaning of the word "abstract".' 'I sometimes pause to see how the theme word of the evening has gone down. Sometimes I feel it's written in granite above the audience's head. At other times I feel it is ether and they breathe it in and out with every breath.' Increasingly English's 'journeys' from a spot on the stage, over her bridge and back, assume epic status. 'When I return it will seem as if I have been away for a thousand years. You may not even recognize me.' By linking these odysseys with the recovery of her Golden Fleece, the true meaning of the word 'abstraction', she brings together three of the four abiding issues of *The Beloved* – a dream, a journey and a memory. The fourth – a problem – will be resolved quite naturally; like a good Aristotelian, English punctuates the latter half with reminders of how everything is falling into place.

It is. After a few hints that her body is growing lighter, she prepares for the climax. 'A performer's body is a sacred vessel, at the same time completely empty and completely full.' And because sacred vessels clothe themselves in 'sacred shrouds' she puts on hers, in the form of an old flannelette night-dress, then, with the help of an elementary machine, 'nearly' flies. When the shroud takes off without her it seems that her big finish has collapsed into bathos. In fact this is the big finish. A hoary theatrical device, the forgotten dream, was adapted so that what was forgotten was only 'abstraction', defined and redefined in the course of her rambling monologue until it resembled a black hole, meaningful only between sets of parentheses, because it can only be referred to, not represented. The search for the true meaning of the word, accounted as 'archaic' as it is 'unfashionable', must result in a wild goose chase, a condition of stasis, or both. Finally, English employs another Baroque image to situate that void she has been struggling to define. Current British commentators seem divided on the future of performance, contending that it must move towards cabaret or back towards being a by-product of high art. English intervenes by recalling an older, more significant squabble: Ben Jonson's argument with Inigo Jones about the correct terminology for the court masque. Jonson held that the 'body' of masque consisted of stage mechanics but the 'soul', the true invention, lay in the words and the entire concept. English may be an empty vessel, but when the apotheosis of the shroud leaves what should be a dead body on stage, it marks only the end of a single repetition of a ritual in which neither origins nor endings are of any account and in which soul may depart from body with no ill effects. Performance, strictly defined, means enactment, initiated by the performer but outside her too.

But her search – and it is the same search – was for abstraction, presented throughout as emptiness, the spot that a body has just vacated or where a garment is still warm. In visual terms nothing is there, but that particular 'nothing' has an intimate connection with English herself, what she calls her 'enormous body'. Abstraction is neither granite nor ether, body nor soul. Instead, its definition involved the promise of apparent change, defying sense – the willing shift from the substantial to the insubstantial and back. Unconscious, inanimate, she forgot abstraction. Awake, alive, she rediscovers it by practising it. Yet her behaviour is only half the story, important only to the extent that a bond is created between herself and her audience. Created? Celebrated, rather. Simply as a rhetorician, English would be forced to rely on some principle of attraction to link the two poles of her definition. When her performance ends with a tender full-scale parody of stock show business clichés, an irony is stated, then transcended. Finally there can be no doubt about the identity of her Beloved.

Max Ophüls' *Lola Montès*

Notebook entry, mid-1980s.

Saddled with Cinerama against his will, Ophüls confided to the co-star Peter Ustinov that he had found a way of getting around the horizontality he so disliked: two pieces of black velvet which move from each side towards the centre at various points in the action, to make a square frame around a picture he wants to dramatize. Indeed, square frames occur throughout: Lola (Martine Carol) is seen through windows of her carriage or glimpses her mother dancing through a window as if it is a TV screen. Her imprisonment, looking out, persists, as do carriages (later to become a circus caravan) and cages. But her real shape is a circle, or more particularly a spiral, like the staircases in her own private palace bought for her by Ludwig of Bavaria. She revolves, finally trapped in the middle of circles in an American circus, re-enacting her life story in a totally theatrical way (midgets draw a curtain at the end). As a courtesan, she is advertised like a wild animal. Yet it is she who is caged, pent, from the first, and the midgets in the circus carry models of her head, reversing the Salomé/John the Baptist motif often reserved for 'man-eaters'. Ustinov, the ringmaster, tells her she can't dance, and we almost never see the Spanish dances that make her famous, though we see a little of her tightrope-walking. The entire story is told in a sequence of flashbacks on a night when she is suffering from high blood pressure – her doctor has told her not to smoke or drink – and says that her life is revolving before her eyes.

Lola becomes a courtesan because her mother's ambition is to marry her to a rich old man. She rebels, elopes with her mother's boyfriend, and after leaving him pursues a reckless course around Europe as an acrobat and ballet dancer, courting sensation wherever she goes and having affairs with Liszt, whom we see leaving her, and Ludwig of Bavaria, in whose country she causes a revolution. Why? We never know. Survival, simply? She seems incapable of being happy for long with one man. Or is it that the initial cruelty she sees in her life scars her for good and makes her act cruelly towards men. Only the Bavarian affair promises happiness, though it is not devoid of longueurs, as when the king reads *Hamlet* to her in the evenings. In effect she wants to be alone, though what inner resources she has to support this are unclear.

The film begins in a circus, which with great spectacle and a good deal of poetic licence, is presenting the life of Lola Montès, starring Lola herself. Quite why we work out only later when the ringmaster who is carrying her through her performance – this is a bad night – appears in a flashback, offering her a contract to appear in Barnum and Bailey's circus in the US. He makes a play for her, certainly. Only later, at the very end of the film, does he make it clear with a single line that he cannot live without her. Are they man and wife? We never know. And the constant glitter and limelight make it even more difficult to know what motivates her. Could it be danger, as her last death-defying jump seems to suggest? Lola makes a bid for freedom but does so by flouting convention, and having once done so, may realise that there is no turning back.

Ophüls' film does not tell all but it never skids carelessly across subtleties of characterization. The problem is that in life, as in the circus ring, Lola remains in the centre of the action, which whirls around her. Her enacted life is a series of vignettes, of course. The odd thing is that her actual life (as seen in the flashbacks) emerges as the same series of vignettes. The net result is a film about star quality itself, not beauty merely but the ingredient that turns her from a *femme* to a *femme fatale*. And she, of course, is the last to know what it could be. That she is not a fake or simply naive is obvious from the leave-taking with Liszt, partly carnal, partly intellectual, with sensitivity and wisdom where real clichés might have been expected. She is no fool, nor does she fall for toyboys. (She tells Oskar Werner, the cocky student, that she really did love Ludwig, despite his age.) Finally, we are reduced to the level of the Barnum crowds, who pay a dollar just to see her, and file past in their hundreds as the film closes.

It is an extraordinary work, quite out of its time, nearer to von Sternberg or Lubitsch in its passion for frivolity and decoration. And beneath the thrills, what? A good woman? That perhaps, takes us far beyond the love and death of Viennese culture, or the capers of Dietrich. This could be a feminist film – not in any doctrinaire way, though. There is a quality of strange authenticity about the dialogue: true (not assumed) sophistication, especially in extra-marital affairs. Yet to argue that Lola even ranks as a heroine would be overstating: revelations about her never come. She remains trapped in an artificial universe of animals and midgets, with a clown as the proprietor and every decision, even about her own life or death, taken out of her hands, not (as von Sternberg would have treated it) because of some sadist revenge of the jilted ringmaster because life is like that. For finally, it could be argued this is a great FRENCH film, comparable in its tact and wisdom to *Les Enfants du Paradis*.

Anne and Patrick Poirier: Journey Without Maps

Published in Anne and Patrick Poirier: Lost Archetypes, *published by Artsite, Bath, 1986.*

> From landscape to landscape, from ruins to gardens, our work is a collection of wanderings, from landscapes of experience to landscapes of desire, from physical wanderings to mental ones, from exile to exile – real landscapes and dream landscapes become confused.
> – Anne and Patrick Poirier

The metaphor of a journey is an apt description of the art of Anne and Patrick Poirier. Yet theirs is not a trip from A to B; *errances*, the term they use, can mean mistakes as well as wanderings. Regard their travels as a series of divagations, the motives for which have changed as time has passed; as an increasingly complex meditation on time and place, matter and thought; as an investigation not only of the conscious but also of the unconscious, where no mistake is possible, or as a prolonged act of research, where imagination runs to the aid of scholarship and desire, not scientific truth, is the ideal.

As artists beginning their joint career in the late 1960s, the Poiriers were party to the innovations of that time, when sculpture expanded to cover two-dimensional image-making, photography, prose, music, even film or dance, but most typically more than one of these forms at once. Critics debated the 'disappearance of the object' in art. More accurately, it could be claimed that artists lost faith in aesthetic theory based on certainties about reality. One practical result was the possibility of suspending meaning between different forms, of letting it ricochet between visual and verbal, the tactile and the intangible. For the Poiriers the image of the archaeological site provided a point of departure. Both building and ruin simultaneously, both plan and the outcome of that plan, architecture half destroyed by time permits the viewer to see its interior and exterior at once to ponder its creation and its destruction in the same moment. In postmodern architecture, the ruin inspired a characteristic space; 'fragmented, rich with symbols, ambiguous, layered with cut-out screens and ordered for the experience of surprise much like an English landscape garden'.[1] And indeed the formal garden has provided an alternative site for the Poiriers, who have returned to it at important moments in their career. In 1969–71 paper casts made from statues in the gardens at the Villa Medici in Rome were displayed in boxes together with samples of leaves and photographs of the original sculptures in situ. Like an obsessional secret between themselves, the idea of possessing surrogates, at least, for the works they so admired led the Poiriers to a process of careful reproduction. The moulds transfer public experience to private. (Significantly, the narrative that accompanies these works is that of the Poiriers themselves, appropriating.) Life-size souvenirs of entire objects and the act of purloining them, these boxed busts, made by touch, celebrate the performance of an act of looking and the perpetuation of that performance. All the Poiriers' subsequent moves can be seen either as a continuation of the act of making these moulds, or as reactions to it.

The paper moulds continued at Ostia Antica and Isola Sacra (1971–3), but now the project of commemorating an entire town was uppermost in the artists' minds. The futility of the ambition also became clear. 'The inexactitude of our construction is not an obstacle', reads a poem in a diary entry from 13 August 1972, 'given the idea to which we have dedicated ourselves from the start: to know that the whole of this town is only a pretext – a pretext, a story which we can live'. They go on to describe 'our absurd revolution of making this great image of a surface 72 metres square which has no more reality than a vague memory, tangible, transparent'.[2] For a second time they were acting out the removal of the 'object' from the art work, that dream of Conceptual artists. Yet already it seemed that rather than the recovery of a 'vague memory' of each site, the model of Ostia Antica and the plan of Isola Sacra in marble were attempts to formulate an ideal that already existed in their minds.

Suddenly they were scaling down their reproductions. Looking out over a miniaturized version of a ruined town, the viewer sees it fully but at a distance, a perfect, self-contained world. The *Domus Aurea Project* (1975–8) retained the connotations that reduction of scale implies, while abandoning the urge to trace the origins of an experience in their own personal history. Purporting to be based on the remains of Nero's Palace buried beneath the Colosseum in Rome, *Domus Aurea* became a vehicle for the exploration of new metaphors: of completeness, taxonomy, an entire civilization. There were reports of vast underground chambers, of confusion in darkness, yet the wonders of the Golden House – an immense subterranean lagoon, the remains of a library, a young girl in a black garden – were all of their own invention. From them, they wrote, *Domus Aurea* was a metaphor of the brain itself. The prevailing image was darkness; and some of the models were shown in near darkness, indicating a descent into the unconscious.

The first of the *Domus Aurea* geographies was *Ausée*. Symmetrical in relation to a north–south axis, reflected perfectly in the black water from which it rises, *Ausée* is a conundrum: a perfectly planned city destroyed by some mysterious catastrophe. Tentatively, its designers took responsibility for its destruction. In a fictionalized note they proposed two theories, both relevant to known facts about Nero. Was the destruction of the city only part of an elaborate suicide planned by the sick mind of an artist? Or was it the fault of an unknown monarch whose androgyny had driven him to put a torch to his life's work? The complicated attempts to conceal authorship, yet to do so by devising clues which lead back to the Poiriers, those androgynous arsonists, recall devices employed in metafictions such as Vladimir Nabokov's *Pale Fire*. Other aspects of *Domus Aurea* parallel the thinking of Jorge Luis Borges. *The Burning of the Great Library*, a charred model of pillared space, involved a classification system on which the plan was based. The Room of Devastated Landscapes, the Room of Doctrines of Fear, the Room of the Bestiary . . . each one relates to the Poiriers' own concerns, yet the combination of the library and the universe, the ideas of classification and totality, have a distinctly Borgesian ring. So does another authorship fantasy about the mausoleum of the architect of *Domus Aurea*, built to a plan that categorizes his entire architectural output. Leading from a central room are six doors bearing the names Room of Symbolic Architecture, Room of Symmetrical Architecture, Room of Anarchic Architecture, Room of Feint Architecture and Room of Black Architecture. As a deviser of fantasies such as an encyclopaedia that is the complete representation of all knowledge (*Tlön, Uqbar, Orbis Tertius*), a divine word which 'cannot be inferior to the Universe or less than the sum of time' (*The Writing of God*) or an ultimate library which contains every book which ever existed, does exist or could exist (*The Library of Babel*), Borges takes as a major theme 'representational totalization'.[3] That this is a fiction has serious implications for our daily life. Museum collections, for instance, involve synchronicity, classification, decontextualization and autonomy. Items in a collection relate to a social, not a personal, sense of time; they are historical. And they form part of a whole. But why is that whole brought about so laboriously in the first place? One explanation and the critique of that explanation is provided by Eugenio Donato:

> The set of objects the Museum displays is sustained only by the fiction that they somehow constitute a coherent representational universe. The fiction is that a repeated metonymic displacement of fragment for totality, object to label, series of objects to series of labels, can still produce a representation which is adequate to a non-linguistic universe. Such a fiction is the result of an uncritical belief in the notion that ordering and classifying, that is to say, the spatial juxtaposition of fragments, can produce a representational understanding of the world.[4]

Not surprisingly, the Poiriers took this fiction to the limit. Their *Circular Utopia* (1979–80) – physically circular and also circular in description, since the last word of the description naturally led back to the first – was planned on encyclopaedic principles. Based on the number of planets, the weeks in a month and other basic human knowledge, it contains concentric rings of differently proportioned ziggurats. Essentially it is the illustration of a conceit; the verbal element far outstrips the visual. At last, the reader discovers that it contains a library of books on Utopia. As well as texts, there are plans and models, classified according to geometry, and appropriate spaces to house them: the Room of Circular Architecture, the Room of Cubic Architecture, the Room of Pyramid Architecture and so on. If they could be their own best critics, providing a running commentary on their own work by means of diaries and books, why shouldn't the Poiriers categorize it or imagine architecture to contain it? The *Circular Utopia* proved more than a simple distancing or encapsulation of their own private museum, however; it was an all-out attack on ideas of order. Heavenly, anaesthetic, it toppled into other identities – from paradise to hell – as it took shape in the mind. Like *The Library of Babel* described by Borges, it was ultimately a prison in disguise. The idea that by pushing an idea to its furthest extreme one is automatically transforming it into its opposite has a distinguished pedigree. Perhaps it applies in this case; from now on the Poiriers were to shift from images of stasis to images of movement, from captivity to freedom.

First came a detour in the form of an apparent return to their starting-point. In the Boboli Gardens in Florence they became interested in the gigantic statues of Giambologna, all of which turned out to depict Jupiter. Paper casts ushered in a body of work that continues even now: an obsessive treatment of incidents from the Gigantomachia, the battle between the Gods and the Giants, which they themselves explained as follows:

> What do the texts say, so often confused and contradictory? The Giants were born of Gaia, the Earth, fertilized by the blood which ran from the genitals of Uranus, severed by the Titan Cronos, his rebel son. When Zeus, in his turn, rose up against his father, Cronos, and imprisoned the Titans in Tartarus, Gaia forced her other monstrous sons, the Giants, to declare war on the Gods of Olympus. The Giants were armed with rocks, picks, and burning trunks of oak trees. The Gods were led by Zeus, armed with his lightning bolts, forged by the Cyclops, divine arms of the best kind; Hercules fought on the Gods' side armed with arrows dipped in the blood of Hydra. The Giant Porphyrion tried to rape Hera, but Zeus let fly his bolt and Heracles finished him off with an arrow. Another Giant, Ephialtes, was killed with an arrow in each eye, one shot by Heracles, the other by Apollo. At another Giant Athena cast the island of Sicily, beneath which he lies, imprisoned for ever, and his fiery breath sometimes escapes from Etna. Hephiastos buried Mimas beneath the volcano Etna, with a mass of molten metal. Athena killed and flayed him and covered her breastplate with the monster's skin . . .[5]

At least one great art work is devoted to these incidents: Giulio Romano's *Room of the Giants* at the Palazzo Te in Mantua, where (deliberately) poor lighting enhances the impression that the masonry is tumbling about the heads of the unfortunate Giants as the Gods launch their attack. Flames burst from the rocks, bodies seem to spill forth into the room, and there are even teams of apes running about. Theatrical, sophisticated, decorative and emotionally distant, the Poiriers' works on the subject of the epic struggle preserve some of the stylistic traits of Mannerism while establishing continuity with their previous work. *Blasted Landscape* (1982–3), for example, built in charcoal around a black pond, with a temple and an amphitheatre, is based on a site in Asia Minor which was supposed to be the battleground itself. In other works piles of broken columns and statuary suggest the scale of the defeat, hinting that when the Giants fell, entire civilizations were toppled.

Frequently regarded as the last of their race, giants are victimized for violating standards of physical propriety and presenting an affront to morals. They rebel even against credibility; in English the lie, an example of verbal gigantism, is called a 'whopper' or a 'tall tale'. While miniaturization is connected with preserving, the giant seems too much of a human outrage to last. Hence this urge for self-destruction. The idea that the giant becomes a landscape or that outlandish natural formations date from a time when giants roamed the earth reinforces a perception that the Poiriers share: that while miniaturism deals in fixed, knowable terrain, gigantism occurs at an interface between the human and the natural. The Giants were not gods but men. Perhaps it was only this fact which brought about their downfall.

In science fiction, Susan Sontag once wrote, matter is subject to two modalities, intact and destroyed. The fate of the Giants is an odd conflation of the two. Entire bodies breathe underground in an eternity of punishment, while for exceptions such as Ephialtes retribution followed swiftly. One motif that underlies the Poiriers' interest in the legend is that of sculpture itself – perfect craftsmanship by the Cyclops, the transformation of giant into breastplate, and the epic fascination with armour, body parts moulded to fit separate limbs – but another is the raw, untrained power of beings who were half beast. Yet the Gods too have links with bestiality. As the themes are reworked, in sculptures about the petrification of Medusa on seeing her own reflection or the birth of Pegasus from the blood that fell from her neck when Perseus killed her, the grotesque is celebrated alongside the beautiful.

From utopia to dystopia; from miniaturism to gigantism; from fragmentation to totality; from beauty to the beast. The Poiriers have veered from one extreme to another. More importantly, they have kept these extremes in motion. What possibility can there be of stasis in an investigation founded on ontological scepticism? Seen spatially, their career would resemble a palimpsest, of which no part was complete or secure, in which the relation between the signified and signifier was inconstant. Their own terms for their investigation – confusion, exile and wandering – are metaphors of unhousing. But what does it mean to be homeless? It means lacking 'a roof over one's head'. What does it mean to be a traveller? It means voluntarily accepting that no single box can contain the self, that routine or system is of no consequence. Little wonder, then, that the Poiriers celebrate their travels – to India, to the jungles of Guatemala, to Egypt, to Burma – almost as art works in their own right, or that their career began while living as temporary exiles in Italy. Nor is it surprising that they have played so many variations on the theme of representation and the body – so many, indeed, that the very urge to play has become compulsive.

That deceptively simple act of making paper moulds and examining their validity as replacements for existing statues is a projection of what is invisible to the solitary artist, more frustratingly invisible to the artist who is also two people: a head, face and neck. Returning to the mould of superficies of a loved but fugitive object, then using it as a device to explore the unknown territory of one's own body, using it also as an extension of the problem of the displaced (invisible) object in Conceptual art, the Poiriers approached problems of the relationship between interior and exterior with reference to the body. The body is our way of understanding scale and content; we are inside it but also looking out at it, and it is the only housing proper to us. Containment, the capacity of objects to serve as traces of experience that has escaped, provided the starting-point for a definition of the problematic self as it relates to containment: in artistic terms, the idea of representation. Wavering between the 'closed' body of the Greeks and the Renaissance and the 'open' body of the medieval world – what Mikhail Bakhtin called the 'grotesque body', 'the body in the act of becoming' – has played a part. So has fragmentation, with all the implications of fetishism, of that substitution of part for whole which Freud dwelt on. At the opposite extreme from the fragment is the order of things considered as a manipulable unit, with its connotations of miniaturization. Espousing theories of the library, the museum, the work of art as repository of universal knowledge, is symptomatic of an urge to obey authority. There is an equal and opposite urge for rebellion but that too has its dangers: uncontained passion, liberty with anarchy as an inescapable concomitant.

From a heightened awareness of the issues of status, stature and statue, those very issues which Lacan suggested were of pivotal importance in the formation of the child's view of a self, the Poiriers expanded their dialectical debate. Incapable of not quoting for a Western tradition, their 'body' of work has succeeded in touching on unresolved issues which present the most dangerous challenges to that tradition. It has become an act of collective psychoanalysis.

The seriousness of this undertaking is at stake in the latest of the Poiriers' exercises on the theme of containment and the body. Their theatrical siting of sculpture acknowledges a difficult truth: that, just as science fiction offers its audience images of catastrophe to be enjoyed at their leisure, in an attempt at catharsis, so their work must incorporate paradoxes of warning while giving pleasure. But it must do so without compromising artistically. Here the increased influence of Mannerism has been important. Obeying one urge of his time, to depict a confusion of human and material fragments, Giulio Romano enclosed the entirety in a model house, never meant for living in. Like Mannerist design, which clarifies the inescapable degree of collusion between criticism of society and the governing forces of that society, the Poiriers' recent works have occupied a middle territory between collaboration and disruption. Their wish to make works specific to gardens or architectural spaces or public piazzas involves one of the most difficult suppositions of Western art: the distinction between design and art, between 'deep', polyvalent, 'meaning-full' art and shallow surface decoration with no transmissible 'content'. This is a prejudice none of the greatest civilizations of the past would ever have entertained. The high ideal of restoring the validity of decoration, with all its concomitants of 'emptiness', is one of the most difficult an artist can undertake in our time.

'I cannot rest from travel', says Ulysses in Tennyson's poem. The apparent casualness with which Anne and Patrick Poirier have happened upon aesthetic moments that have yielded insight is their joke. For them intellectual vagabondage, and its accompanying openness to new experience, has resulted in a continuing project of great subtlety, a project that has gradually embraced and related vast and serious issues. Each stage provides a commentary on the others, and takes the discussion and the possible terms for the discussion a stage further. The image of life as a journey must be one of the oldest known to man. That initial reaction against putting faith in objects led to a quite different paradigm – of moving through and past them, of journeying in time and space at once. Their decision to travel was a wise one. There is no reason why they should stop now.

1. Charles Jencks, 'Towards Radical Eclecticism', in P. Portoghesi, V. Scully, C. Jencks, C. Norberg-Schulz, *The Presence of the Past* (London: Academy, 1980), p.31.

2. Anne and Patrick Poirier, *Voyages . . . et caetera, 1969–1983* (Milan: Electa, 1983), p.26.

3. Walter Moser, 'Fragments and Encyclopedia: From Borges to Novalis', in L.D. Kritzman ed. *Fragments: Incompletion and Discontinuation* (New York: New York Literary Forum, 1981), p. 113.

4. Eugenio Donato, 'The Museum's Furnace: Notes toward a Contextual Reading of Flaubert's *Bouvard et Pécuchet*', in T. Harari, ed., *Textual Strategies: Perspectives in Post-Structuralist Criticism* (Ithaca: Cornell, 1979), p.223.

5. Poirier and Poirier, op. cit., pp.92, 94.

An interview with Louise Bourgeois

Recorded on 21 December 1986. Unpublished.

Louise Bourgeois: [*Nature Study: Pink Fountain*] This is one of my favourite pieces. It is really a human bathtub for the unborn. I know people say it is erotic. Well, it's a free world. Everybody has a right to their own interpretation. The intention was *not* to express eroticism. It was to express the total safety and happiness of the child which is not there. The thing is ready for him or for her. Nothing erotic about that. It has to do with life itself. It doesn't have to do with eroticism or sex, which is only a part of life, not all of it. But this is a different subject. All these things have very, very precise subjects and I love to talk about it. It's no mystery.

This is different. This is called *The Cliff* and it represents danger, not safety. It's the opposite of the previous subject. So this is a person on the edge of a cliff. And you'd better watch out.

These are either optimistic or pessimistic statements. This one is obviously optimistic. It means that when you are together you don't have much to fear. It is a very friendly piece, like the others. They keep me warm and I have enough strength to give them something to them and keep *them* warm when it is my time to assume responsibility. So it is a 50/50 arrangement: you keep me warm, I keep you warm.

I don't feel like talking about this. This is the 'Janus' series. The others are suspended. It has to do with the double aspect of our personality. Obviously it is aggressive against the inquiescent, the passive and that means that it is hard to put yourself together. In this case the piece does hold together in spite of the inner contradiction and tension.

Let's talk about anxiety, which is really the crux of the matter, as far as the motivation is concerned, The reason I flipped when I saw the photograph of the Albright Museum was that a mistake was made. A mistake for me is a freak accident. It makes me afraid and I am afraid because I don't understand what happened, which is the definition of a freak accident. What happened, nobody knows, except that there is a victim or many victims and there is obviously a culprit. It throws me into a spiral of anxiety. Not to understand makes me anxious and as a result makes me aggressive.

I cannot stand not understanding the problem. Now how does that apply to that piece at the Albright-Knox? It applies because in a Kafka way a freak accident occurred – a ridiculous, idiotic one, and it obviously betrays the work. How are you going to repair it? I don't know the photographer. In the maze of a museum organization, who can you talk to? Nobody knows. This amounts to such an impotence that obviously you freak out and become aggressive. This is the origin of the terrific aggression found in my work sometimes. Impossibility to understand what is going on. Obviously it goes way back to when as a child I simply could not understand what people were about – I suspect very specially when they fucked. I must have witnessed something that was so overwhelming and so ridiculous ugly and impossible to understand that I'm still there. I never moved on. Today it is the intensity of the reaction.

The latest problem was when I proposed a subject that interests me terribly much, which is the relation of redemption to insanity. This is my subject, my latest one. The relation of redemption to insanity. Of course some people are going to put their two cents in and declare it is a religious subject. It is not a religious subject in the least; it is *my* subject. Nothing superstitious about that. It is just a rational problem. You have to understand the mechanism. And if I do not understand mechanisms I go wild, like any animal which goes wild when they cannot make out something. They cannot make out whether you like them or you don't like them. This is an eternal *point d'interrogation*, because it makes you look into yourself. Somebody said the other day, 'Do you like me?' They asked me if I like them. So I said, 'Look in your own heart. Do *you* like me? I feel towards you exactly what you feel towards me.' The situation was peaceful enough for the child to be able to go back and say, '*Do* I like Louise?' I'm not certain about that. But what I am certain about is that if you don't like me I am going to smell it and I *know* it. This is my privilege. No I shouldn't say that. I should say that I *think* I know it. In effect I am just projecting. I usually like people so I assume they like me, which is highly irrational. So I return to my subject, the relation of redemption to insanity. You ask me what I'm interested in, and that's what I am interested in, for better or for worse.

Stuart Morgan: *What is the reason for insanity?*
Not understanding. Not understanding the mechanism of behaviour. Let's keep it at a very close range. I'm talking about two people; and when a lot of people are in the room you drown the fish and it's completely safe. However when another person is in the room and you are face to face with another

human being, anxiety is as solid as a rock, let me tell you. I really have to make an effort to control my anxiety. I don't say I can do it but I try to. It doesn't frighten me. It can be talked about. The notion 'I am not afraid of it' brings to mind the fact that I am absolutely terrified by the thing I want most. So you can see the predicament.

What are the things you want most?

Now you are getting personal. I am not ready to say that because it is obvious. Right? I am not ready to say that. Stuart, if we wanted to explore *this* subject, out of the window goes the Cincinnati show. Because this is really very different from talking about slides. In fact I wouldn't mind exploring this taboo and Gert Schiff *has* talked about this. Thus, by a circular turn of the conversation we are going back to the relation of redemption to insanity. Or – let's not get dramatic now – or the relation of redemption to sanity. Or the relation of redemption to rationality. And since I am both agnostic and rationalist – it goes together – there is a very simple mechanism that I cannot get. As I said before, when I cannot understand the mechanics of a thing I go wild. So this is why the problem represents such an intensity for me, such anxiety.

I'm puzzled. You keep talking about redemption, but I only understand that as a religious term. If you're agnostic, how can you say 'redemption'?

This is the crux of the problem. Redemption, in my vocabulary, does not have a relation to religion at all. It has to do with the price you have to pay to be an artist. And the art is produced only if there is an exchange, a bargaining between the need for redemption and the price you are willing to pay to get it. So it has to do with the redemptive value of art. Are we getting there?

Well, redemption means being saved.

So this is it. For instance cleaning. I hate cleaning. I was fortunate not to have to do too much of it first of all, because my standards are very low. And second because I had people to do it. Right. So, however, as I became older, and I could not stand people fidgeting around me, I preferred to do my own cleaning than put up with the cleaner. All right. So I came to that territory which was cleaning. And I do it now because of the redemptive quality of cleaning. You might say that it takes a way from my work as an artist. It's absolutely true because art has a redemptive quality, which is almost its only *raison d'être*. It is a useful thing. It keeps people from getting killed. It keeps people level. It keeps them . . . I don't know if it keeps them happy, really, but it does. It keeps them happy, it keeps them worthwhile . . .

But cleaning is just toil, isn't it, simply hard work for its own sake?
But it has a redemptive quality. After you have cleaned you feel better, at least at my age now I do feel that I have a great pleasure in looking, for instance, at the light through a perfectly cleaned glass. I really do. I enjoy that.
The Greeks had religious ceremonies that only involved women, and these involved carrying water on the head or performing a single task for a long time. It was felt to make you a better person or bring about some kind of catharsis.
Catharsis may be another way of talking about the redemptive quality of an activity.
Art is more than just physical work, isn't it?
Work is work. If you have a high IQ your work is to make calculations. If you have a low IQ your work is to clean up the slop. Work is work. It depends who you are.
But cleaning up is not going to change you.
Non. I agree with that. But since we have to clean, I can clean only if I give it the dignity and the value of a redemptive need. Otherwise I don't clean! But it has to do also with the self-defeatism of the artist and the redemptive value of suffering.
When you were going through the slides, you said there was a very strict chronological sequence to the way your themes recur.
Yes, I will accept the fact that the chronological order, which is so simple, explains the evolution of the forms. The forms of the eighties are not the forms of the forties and you can follow this evolution through the work.
But some of the forms are things that you've been talking about for a long time – the Femme Maison *theme . . .*
But the *Femme Maison* is a *subject*. I was talking about the formal aspect of the work.
You have forms in the 1980s that you haven't used before.
Yes. This is my pride. My pride is not in being a psychologically grown person. It is to achieve a perfect formal aspect in any subject.
Take the subject of eyes, which you had never touched on before. You have eyes that are hollow and movable.
They are not *my* eyes; they are the other one's eyes. I am not interested in my eyes. I am interested basically in eyes of somebody I love, because they eyes of somebody I am not interested in do not carry much weight. But the eyes of somebody I want . . . that's something else. In erotic subjects I am

the chooser. I am not interested in the chosen, but in being the chooser. Or is that an illusion?

So when you deal with eyes, you are talking about intimate communication.

Yes. I am talking about *Velvet Eyes*, which is to do with communication. *Pink Eyes* is a bad title. These are eyes made of pink marble. Why do I get so riled about this? Because *Pink Eyes* has an association; it is the title of a play by Pinero. His subjects are not my subjects. I do not want the association with a work that has different overtones. These are the eyes of the other, made, accidentally, of pink marble. The theme of eyes is recurrent, and it has stopped. So the pieces I am doing now, about the, you might say, 'computers', in the sense that they concern mechanism, where there is an input and an output, it really means that the input is what you want, it is so enormous that it would fill the sky. Then there is the mechanism. The mechanism of reality which reduces what you want to get, it is a trickle of nothing. You'd better understand that. So what you'd call the result, being the trickle, total dissatisfaction, revulsion, is the subject. This is what I'm doing in 1986. I don't know what I'll be doing in 1987, maybe I won't be there, but it is the subject of 1986.

So when, in the eye sculptures, you have two sets of eyes engaging . . .

It is not the look of the eye; it is the language of the eye.

And what is that language?

As usual it is the language of the 'I love you' versus 'You are nothing. You don't exist. It's not that I don't love you: you don't exist. To repeat what I said before, I have a tendency not to be too interested in people who are interested in me.

Lair

Published in Louise Bourgeois, *Taft Museum Cincinnati, 1987, together with the earlier essay 'Nature Study'.*

A heavy black form hangs from the ceiling. Bulbous below, narrowing towards the top, with incisions, partially flattened planes and a rectangular tunnel all the way through, it looks like a number of things, but not too much like any of them. And though in physical terms it recalls phenomena we may have seen – pendulous paper cities made by termites, for example, like entire dangling labyrinths – in terms of reverie it conjures up many more. An epigraph to T.S. Eliot's *The Waste Land* quotes one of the guests at Trimalchio's banquet in Petronius's *Satyricon*: 'I saw the Sibyl at Cumae with my own eyes, hanging in a basket . . .' Doomed to exist apart from the populace yet unable to escape her crowd of enquirers, the Sibyl must have meant a lot to Petronius, whose existence at Nero's court was one of mingled threat and profit: independence at a fatal price.

Pendulous, pendant, independent – watch a drop of water as it forms and falls. Its change from a convexity to an ellipsoid could be described as increase in sheer surface or as yearning for separation. At the moment when it is nearly free, when its skin is at its most strained and bloated, the metaphor it seems to demand hovers midway between connectedness and partition. How easily these terms slip from an account of physical properties to one of human relations. This suspended home is for a self that is isolated yet still in touch with a world framed as an object of contemplation. *Lair*, it is called, and though its shape alone relates to the title it has been given, it also gains meaning by taking its place alongside other items from within the same body of work.

Louise Bourgeois's paintings from the 1940s introduced one dialogue that would loom large in her later career. In a painting, *Untitled*, from 1944, six lines of bare trees reappear, stretching into the distance. The rest of the picture takes place underground, where earth strata give way to panels of uninflected colour, refractions are suggested by removal of paint and areas of pattern intervene before roots fan out and finally stop altogether. 'Underground' turns out to be a region of free play, totally distinct from the regimentation of the upper world. And since this is a painted image, all of the freedom, beauty, celebration and sheer *painterliness* occur below ground. One danger exists: that an unharnessed, aestheticizing abstraction is being proposed as a means of escaping an unbearable reality. Beyond the canvas a similar opposition had been established when Clement Greenberg encouraged New York artists to adopt a new bohemian stance after their more direct attempts during the previous decade to ally both production and subject matter with their political beliefs. Accustomed to the European model of an avant-garde that Greenberg had in mind, Bourgeois, who came to the United States in 1938, may have had reservations about any attempt to transplant it to New York. Certainly, subsequent paintings took archetypes of freedom and transformed them into images of secrecy, closure, even death: like the caravan bier in *1932* (1947), so much more precisely rendered than everything around it that it looks like a collaged element; or, as in plate vii of *She Disappeared into Complete Silence*, her book of etchings and stories, also from 1947, the single balloon, trapped in a closed room, is unable to escape through a door too small to let it out. Yet there are also compromises. Scarves or leaves or furry tails blow as if in a high wind in an untitled painting from 1946–48. Although the structure they are attached to stands on bare blue floorboards in its red room, part temple, part radio tower, with an observatory halfway up which doubles as a cage.

More cage than observatory, the house planted on the woman's head in the *Femme-Maison* series disables her, and sadly, she does not seem to realize it. The richness of the theme was such that Bourgeois returned to it for forty years, regarding it as a question of balance between enclosure and escape, happiness and desolation. Before the series began around 1940–42, there had been paintings of houses – inhabited, with suggestions of figures, or distant on hills. Similarly, in its latest manifestation in 1982, the *Femme-Maison* conjunction has resolved itself into its component elements once more. Seen as a tiny edifice on top of a cloud of billowing drapery, carved in marble to resemble smoke or water as much as fabric, the house has become a dream – hermetic, transcendent, unattainable. Perhaps this dissolution of a lengthy preoccupation marks the end of the entire series. Yet this is unlikely, since within it sub-genres have sprung up, like the *Lair* sculptures, flat on the ground like nests in the 1950s, then hanging, with suggestions of nesting (*Fée Couturière*, 1963) or dwelling parasitically within rotting flesh (*The Quartered One*, 1964). One recent revision was *Articulated Lair* (1986), an environment built out of metal shutters. Inside the space, sitting on a small stool, the participant could exist in a state of semi-retirement, ready to escape through the rear door if an unwelcome visitor should enter at the front. This is no place to be disturbed; instead the occupant sits quietly, content to look at a selection of moulded black rubber forms, hung around the room like trophies or playthings.

To begin with a problem and confront it by carrying on a discussion which grows progressively more complex sounds like no solution at all. But what if the discussion and the solution cannot be separated in this way? If the theme is power and survival – one theme, not two, as Elias Canetti has pointed out[1] – then simply framing the question becomes part of that question, not merely its context. The shift from the paintings to the *Femme-Maison* drawings marked a difference in who was being addressed as well as a different awareness of talking about privacy, of demanding it as an essential right, and of asking uncomfortable questions about the barter which is assumed in one age-old pattern of human relationships. From that point to *Articulated Lair* marks as great a shift; this is a place for plotting strategy. And, despite its reference to animals, the space itself reveals two main human references, characteristically, for Bourgeois, one low and two high: first, to the temporary battle rooms traditionally erected for army commanders during wartime and second, to an idealized version of the smallest room in the house, where one squats contentedly, taking stock – 'on the throne' as one English expression puts it. Altogether, it suggest that the shape one's life assumes is far from accidental, that it can be controlled, and that the state of being in control is worth celebrating. Let us be certain of the nature of this strategy: to bring about a shift from the personal to the political.

Context has been a touchy subject among Bourgeois's critics. The bravest have recorded their feelings that the sculpture and the zone it is made to inhabit are forced out of alignment. One describes 'an atmosphere of figuration' surrounding undeniably abstract work.[2] Another coins the phrase 'field of emotion' to try to describe how Bourgeois turns formal relationships into symbols for human relationships.[3] Given this felt disparity, one obvious conclusion would be to blame her for attempting the impossible, for her apparent inability to grasp the limitations, that is to say the conventions, of sculptural modes. Not an inability but a dogged refusal is really the case. Bourgeois's tactical adjustments could be thought of as part of her fundamental artistic gesture: her own transgressive variant of Shklovsky's *acmpattettue* ('making strange') or Brecht's *Verfremdungseffekt* ('distantiation'). A better comparison might be the process of translation; bilingual for most of her life, Bourgeois deliberately espouses that state of mind George Steiner has called 'extraterritorial', a deliberate choice available to late modernists to maintain a condition of exile by artificial means, if necessary, not for themselves but for their work, instigating complex, paradoxical projects like retranslating translations of their own books, for example. The effects are obvious: to redefine the text as the sum of the ways it communicates, to recreate the state of linguistic experiment which prevailed in the international modernism of their youth, to cause an endless ricochet effect which may result from a loss of certainty of national consciousness. Never certain whether the phenomenon he describes is symptomatic of a more general state or just a game played by bored geniuses, Steiner more or less contents himself with description.[4] Apply his findings to the work of Louise Bourgeois and a more pointed argument emerges of its own accord.

Progressively more disengaged, Bourgeois's use of modernist tactics has recently been punctuated with references to that monumental statuary which was current in her youth; one of a recent series of giant carved eyeballs, boxed in the case of *Nature Study (Pink Eyes)* of 1984 or movable, like giant toys, with chambered spaces in the pupils in *Nature Study (Eyes)*, made two years later, *Eyes* (1982) – essentially, perhaps, a Mannerist ornament on a grand scale – was transferred to an outdoor location in an experiment that resulted in a parody of the whole idea of monument as architectural adjunct. Sculpture, it has recently been suggested, is a modern invention[5] that on principle disengages itself from the past. So looking back through modernism to nineteenth-century statuary and playing between the two smacks of rule-breaking for its own sake, like the surface of *The She-Fox* (1985) which has been attacked repeatedly with a chisel in deliberate stabbing fashion. But more than that, it represents a conscious attempt to engage with disengagement, to confront the problem of working with an outworn language by ignoring the very possibility that sculptural 'language' *can* become outworn, and setting to work adjusting the *context* of an avant-garde which has turned into official currency. Prepared to concede that her position is one of displacement, Bourgeois capitalizes on her 'unhoused' position by accepting its inevitable concomitant: translation, in German *Übersetzung*, a bringing from one point to another. Essentially, this is a critical enterprise; Edward Said has described the contemporary critic as someone 'between homes'.[6]

Not surprisingly, loss plays a large part in the generation of this work. Bourgeois once told Lucy Lippard that in the 1940s she made pole-shaped sculptures in order 'to summon all the people I miss'.[7] In another interview she made what might be a mock Freudian slip: 'My memories', she begins, then quickly adds 'which is to say my sculpture'.[8] There is no need to interpret this urge as nostalgia; on the contrary, it offers a clue to the state of reverie which the sculpture demands, a state celebrated in *Partial Recall* of 1979. Reverie is not incompatible with the gradual nature of the processes Bourgeois has known for so long: processes of casting and carving, therapeutic acts of work by which an idea changes, too slowly even to notice. Remembering can occur on this even, near-somnolent plane, subject to infinitesimal alteration, that 'healing' which time is said to bring about. More often, it is punctuated by refusals to recall what *really* happened, stabs of embarrassment, hatred that turns to self-hatred and back, above all a desire to defeat the linearity of time by folding it into patterns, as in origami – wishing we had known then what we know now in order to alter the course of events. In Louise Bourgeois's creation, a wavering between past and present results in a style of disjuncture that becomes more marked as her career continues. It would be easy to misconstrue this as feminist theory put into practice or as postmodern historical collage. But the worst offence by far would be one that the artist herself invites: a reading of her work based on biography.

In 1982, in a photo-essay for *Artforum* magazine, she focused more fully than ever on a single formative 'family plot' involving her father, mother and governess, a situation that left her threatened and defenceless. Though fascinating, this kind of confession conceals a curious rhetorical strategy which may prove all the stronger for being an unconscious repetition of her mentors' predicament: the need to sprinkle false trails, as in a paper-chase, in order to divert potential detectives. A biographical reading would ignore the long-term planning by which the problems are set and solved. Now, as then, the issue is control, a wish to set matters to rights single-handedly. It is particularly evident in some of the *Nature Study* works of 1986, one of a number of subspecies polemically grouped under the same bland traditional title, tangles of limbs or entrails with protruding tails and hands, sometimes strained, sometimes relaxed. It would be hard to imagine closures more resistant. And, as if to seal off the entire situation, to present it as a dead weight with no hope of resolution or intervention, they are carved out of solid stone with the 'sculpture' inseparable from the 'base'. Somehow these correlate with how we feel, how we exist and go on existing.

Quite separate from her personal life, the unfolding of Bourgeois's career has involved a high degree of reflexivity. At this stage, when titles, subjects and visual moves permutate almost of their own accord, she may seem far away from her early statements. Consider the drawing, for example – little more than a doodle – showing herself and her children nestling in a restricted space like animals in a burrow, with no room to move. In such situations what can be done but to force a space to exist, by embracing isolation, courting it as one component of the psyche, deliberately making oneself an alien in time and space? And there are indications that as an artist Bourgeois has done exactly this. Yet that will not explain her strategy fully. Bourgeois achieved her aim by forming one space within another, admitting adjacencies to other artists, perhaps, but absolving herself of dynastic relationships. She made herself small and her issues particular and extreme, as a natural extension of that prime move, making 'space' within her own output for disruptions and repetitions, rhythms and counter-rhythms. (So *Woman-House* contains the subsection *Lair*, which cross-references with other forms and concerns unrelated by title. In turn, *Lair*, a woman-as-animal-house, expands into real, architectural space, a repository for those dangling bones and limb-like forms that feature in her work from the beginning. In *Lair*, another heavy black moulded-rubber form, entrances are made, as they are in the solid marble block *Curved House* of 1983). Each form can become a basic unit for a lengthy exploration of one concern, pursued continuously for many years or exhausted in a sudden burst. In time the career fans out like a delta. But as it does, the possible inter-relations multiply, so that even a single move can alter the drift of an existing unit of meaning. Above all, one simple gesture is obvious: the gesture of occupying space.[9]

In their study of Kafka, subtitled 'Toward a Minor Literature', Gilles Deleuze and Félix Guattari define the term 'minor literature' as one which displays three characteristics. Firstly, it is written in a language which a minority constructs within a major language, it is the choice of a 'deterritorialized' language like those used by black writers working in English today. Secondly, everything in a minor literature is political. Whereas major literatures occupy a large space in which concerns are joined to other individual concerns, with the social milieu serving as no more than a backdrop, in minor literature 'cramped space' forces each individual intrigue to connect immediately to politics. And, they add, 'the individual concern thus becomes all the more necessary, indispensable, magnified, because a whole other story is vibrating within it.' And they quote Kafka's diaries for 25 December 1911: 'Even though something is thought through calmly, one still does not reach the boundary where it connects with similar things, one reaches the boundary soonest in politics, indeed, one even strives to see it before it is there, and often takes this limiting boundary everywhere . . .' Thirdly, minor literature takes on a collective value; it allows the author to move quickly from speaking as an individual to making 'collective assemblages of enunciation.'[10] Kafka's solitude opens all doors to him because he disconnects his message from 'an enunciating subject'. Deleuze and Guattari's conditions apply to Bourgeois precisely because in her art every separate work serves to sustain the kind of lengthy exploration as *Lair*, and, because of some deep-seated conviction or confusion of Bourgeois herself – between strategy as a tactic of both art and life simultaneously – each of her works provides a model for a possible future art. Not women's art, specifically. In her case another quotation from Deleuze and Guattari is relevant: 'There is nothing that is major or revolutionary except the minor'.

1. Elias Canetti, 'Power and Survival' in *The Conscience of Words*, trans. Joachim Neugroschel (London: André Deutsch, 1986), pp.14–28.
2. Jean-Patrice Marandel, 'Louise Bourgeois', *Art International* (December 1971), p.46.
3. Carter Ratcliff, 'Louise Bourgeois', *Art International* (November 1978), p.26.
4. George Steiner, 'Extraterritorial' in *Extraterritorial* (Harmondsworth: Penguin, 1972).
5. Margit Rowell, 'Avant-propos', *Qu'est-ce que la sculpture moderne?* (Paris: Centre Georges Pompidou, 1986), pp.11–14)
6. Edward Said, *Beginnings: Intention and Method* (New York: Basic Books, 1975), p.8.
7. Lucy Lippard, 'Louise Bourgeois From the Inside Out', *Artforum* (March 1975), p.28.
8. Paul Gardner, 'The Discreet Charm of Louise Bourgeois', *Art News* (February 1980), p.82.
9. See Nicole Dubreuil-Blondin, 'Feminism and Modernism', in B. Buchloh, S. Guilbaut and D.Solkin eds., *Modernism and Modernity: Proceedings of the Vancouver Conference* (Halifax, N.S., 1983), p.194.
10. Gilles Deleuze and Félix Guattari, *Kafka: Toward a Minor Literature*, trans. D. Polan (Minneapolis: University of Minnesota Press, 1986), pp.16-18 and passim.

Donald Baechler: Run Over by a Truck

Introduction to Donald Baechler, *published by Mayor Rowan Gallery, London 1987, © Mayor Gallery*

'The secret is to do a thing badly', Jean Dubuffet told an interviewer. 'If you serve spinach the way it should be, no one notices or remembers it. Whereas if you *burn* it . . .'[1] Commentators with sensitive nostrils have sometimes been overcome by the smell of burnt spinach that emanates from Donald Baechler's art. They complain that it is not 'adult'.[2] They write about its regressive qualities and its infantilism, or they decide it is 'catatonic'. And in their way they may all be perfectly correct. Another response is to comment on its 'inaccessibility' and to leave it at that.[3] Baechler never disagrees. 'I'm interested in a sort of suppression of meaning in the pictures', he told Joseph Kosuth in an interview in 1985.

Secrecy and scandal are involved in any reading of the paintings. There are the concealments and delays: that patching, the sense that cracks have been papered over, that wounds have been dressed, that the canvas comes laden with its own private history. Yet these delays are obliterated by a rightness of perception. Barthes used the word *éclat*, a flash or explosion.[4] Canetti isolated the moment of 'discharge' when a crowd took shape.[5] The simultaneous joy and violence that both terms suggest have been described by Baechler himself in a statement from 1983. 'A really good painting is sort of like a guy who's wandering on the highway by mistake and gets run over by a truck. What was that guy doing out there with twelve dollars in his pocket and no wallet? There's the mystery, the vague recollection of body parts and the head rolling down the centre lane like a bowling ball. As with all great art, the mystery involves sex and religion.'[6] It is exactly that rightness he is trying to capture. The parallel between a sudden, unexplained event and the effect of a great painting is couched in the language of the grotesque: a mixture of horror and laughter. Why not? After all, in a Baechler painting a severed head and a bowling ball might bear a striking resemblance. But by far the most significant aspect of his description is that as it proceeds, an image of violence is equated with one of play. To understand what this might mean involves an analysis of the historical choices he made and the way he implemented them.

Baechler's career reads like a little case history in post-Conceptual practice. While studying under Hans Haacke at Cooper Union, New York, in 1977 he encountered Gerhard Naschberger and Jiri Georg Dokoupil. Encouraged by them, he continued his studies in Frankfurt for a year. Back in New York, he worked for the DIA Foundation, organizing the papers of Blinky Palermo, who had died in 1977 under mysterious circumstances. So his prentice-years provided experience of hard-line, politicized Conceptualism, the rumblings of Mülheimer Freiheit and an example of non-doctrinaire, anti-symbolic abstraction. By the end of the 1970s the Conceptual assumptions that had dominated the avant-garde for a decade were applied at last to painting. The result was an art of signs in which Expressionism was courted and debunked, elements of differing ontological status were offset and universal themes were broached. This approach to post-Conceptual painting was evident in Europe before it extended to America. In New York in the late 1970s three approaches offered painters a way forward; Douglas Crimp's 'Pictures', Richard Marshall's 'New Image Painting' and Marcia Tucker's '"Bad" Painting'", all exhibitions being more significant for their catalogues than for the work they included. Appropriation, reconciliation of abstraction and figuration or anti-aestheticism all had their appeal for Baechler, while the graffiti phenomenon provided a direction he chose not to follow. His strategy became as combative as it was hermetic.

Early paintings such as *Balcony* (1981) were attempts to marry image and field, a black line and an indefinite Twombly-esque background. As Warhol had done when he became a painter, Baechler looked at cheap monochrome commercial printing, finding some of the best designs in the pages of the New York telephone book. Furniture advertising intrigued him in particular. In *Untitled (Horsehide)* from 1981, a Le Corbusier *chaise-longue* outlined in flat black against an 'abstract' pink and blue striped background recalls Sigmar Polke's experiments from the 1960s. But Baechler had decided that he needed 'subject matter' and set to work painting ancient history. In the Yellow Pages he discovered a drawing of a man drinking from a stream. Combining this with the image from a set of busts, he made *Hadrian in America* (1981). At school history had bored him. Reading Hadrian's memoirs at the insistence of Cy Twombly changed his mind. From then on it seemed appropriate to paint the Cycladic heads, the Colosseum and the Seven Wonders of the World in a borrowed style that reflected a different kind of historical change: the process of decomposition that Peter Nagy called 'the cancer of images'.

Baechler's *Sphinx* (1981) dated from this period: a ruin, a grotesque, above all a mystery.

Drawing on paper day after day, Baechler developed a style based on that of uneducated artists. Schizophrenic art appealed to him, as did the drawing of teenagers old enough to know what they wanted to draw but lacking the artistic means to do it. (The best art was not in museums but on toilet walls, he announced, naming a later series *W.C. Drawings*). At nights he would go to bars, ask customers to draw for him, study their work, then incorporate elements of their style into a final version which was projected on to canvas and copied. A twofold process had begun. On the one hand he was experimenting with loss and the accidental rediscovery of subjectivity. Needing something to draw, the drunks in bars drew Baechler himself. Put through the usual process, with the addition of the artist's painted signature, the result became an elaborate study of interaction not between people but between subject, object and identity. On the other hand, Baechler was working to cultivate his own line, an identifiable 'signature' style. The paradoxes of an art in which identity would constantly be lost, rediscovered and put through a succession of changes may have been the purest of Baechler's debts to Conceptualism. Gradually, the idea of history had been reflected in the history of images themselves, then in the process of change by which they were turned into a work of art. From this point on the enterprise would take less account of other people's values and histories, and turn to the development of more private fictions.

The turning-point came with the Oum Kalsoum paintings, named after a dead Egyptian singing star who had achieved near godlike status with her fans, notably a group of restaurant workers Baechler had encountered in Rome in 1979. Distance, in historical terms, had been replaced by cultural distance. In Frankfurt Baechler had met Peter Kubelka, the film-maker whose *Unsere Afrikareise* influenced a series of his paintings around 1984-5. Kubelka showed tourists descending from their jeeps to poke around in huts and interfere in village life. Baechler painted what they expected to find: woolly-headed tribesmen with bones through their hair dancing around cannibal pots. Oum Kalsoum involved another attempt to revive the past, which in so doing overshot the mark and ended as a primitive fantasy. With one difference. The tourist idea of golliwogs is false and pernicious, while the version of Kalsoum as goddess figure may have been the only possible response to her greatness during her lifetime. Whether Baechler was drawing on the Egyptians' own image of her or merely on his own is irrelevant. We call images into being because they satisfy certain needs. The tourist Africa is toothless, knowable and comforting, a toytown in which murder, albeit ritualized murder, cannot take place. Summoned up by a cultural tourist, Oum Kalsoum emerges as a less than reassuring presence, dangerous and exciting, though worn away by time. While New York colleagues had been focusing on appropriation, Baechler never stopped practising what he has called 'anecdotal formalism', painting as painting, with the power to illuminate charisma if not to criticize it.

Reading a Donald Baechler painting would become an exercise in measuring distances. In a literal sense scale became a source of confusion; since the source was lost in the lengthy process of transcription, its correct size was abandoned early in the painting procedure, with the result that the viewer never managed to measure the number of removes from reality. Things became simplified too, more manageable and fluent. Doodling has its own streamlining as well as its own awkwardness. Surface became another source of confusion. Before painting, pieces of fabric were applied in order to break up the line. First attempts at an image were whitewashed over, leaving barely readable shadows of forms, the historical record of the making. Drips were not concealed, so that the first and last moves were commemorated equally. And the motives of the painter, the tone of voice of the painting, were confused too. When Baechler began including more than one element on a canvas, the relation between them provided a final source of bafflement. The line of trudging men in *Schwarzwald* serves as an opportunity to rehearse similar marks over and over again rather than to explain anything or tell a story. Despite this, the emphasis on display and looking within the pictures themselves has grown steadily, from the outlined figure of a man waving at a spaceship to a boy pointing to his paper boat. Figures rarely look directly towards the viewer in Baechler's painting; they are intent on an existence that is halfway between their inner reality and their external experience. In terms of communication, a blockage has taken place. Yet there is no evidence to suggest that direct communication was ever intended.

Between inner reality and external experience lies a zone in which the child first encounters objects, the last in a sequence of events that began with thumb-sucking. The objects in question are likely to be toys, and it is interesting that Baechler both collects and paints toys, as well as incorporating into his painting pieces of cloth, with weave and seams that remain visible, almost graspable, despite the layers of paint that cover them. If the initiation of an affectionate object relationship constitutes the final stage of the child's recognition of 'not-me' reality, one preliminary to this is a stage at which the baby holds and sucks pieces of sheet or blanket. D.W. Winnicott's theory of 'transitional objects' and phenomena,[7] which deals with an intermediate period between a baby's inability to recognize and accept reality and the growth of the ability to do so, copes also with grown-ups. It deals with 'the substance of illusion, that which is allowed to the infant, and which in adult life is inherent in art or religion, and yet becomes the hallmark of madness when an adult puts too powerful a claim on the credulity of others, forcing them to acknowledge a sharing of illusion that is not their own'.

Winnicott's theory is of the utmost interest in thinking about Baechler's art. Following interpretation to the very limit, it would make it possible to argue that what Baechler terms the 'archaeology' of his canvas, with the image as the final, most superficial addition, corresponds to a natural process of differentiating self from other, subject from object, what is possible from what is desired. Baechler's dedication to painting as opposed to fully three-dimensional objects or ideas in themselves is comprehensible; painting alone deals with signs that relate to reality yet can be regarded formally as coloured shapes in their own right. (That this view of abstraction as an end in itself is of no use to the viewer of his works is suggested by *Abstract Painting with Spaceship* of 1985, in which a figure rides happily along, insulated from late modernism by a black and white doodle craft.) It also accounts for the careful, instinctive juggling with distances. By entering the zone his paintings occupy, the spectator must share an experience where relief is offered from the strain of relating inner and outer reality – an area akin to that of a child 'lost in play – while never releasing his or her grasp on the fact of the art as public art'. In play reality-acceptance is both tested and suspended, and it is play which Baechler's procedure most fully resembles.

The style is marked by gestures, repeated with small but apparently significant details, such as the tripartite mark that serves to indicate both the bird's wings and feet in *Composition with Birds* (1987). Motifs are taken from one painting to the next, and repeated just as they were before, but in a different context, then combined and recombined with two or three others to the point of absurdity. In paintings from 1985, for example, the globe, the cauldron, the fedora, the monk, the coloured balls and the disembodied head – Baechler's own head, from a collage made in the same year – interact until they seem to mimic each other, with the globes and balls forming a man, or the globe replacing a hat. The indication may be that he is trying to start a language, or at least playing a language game. Yet 'game' is too fixed a term to cover what he is attempting. He is indulging in undirected play, in which causes and effects have been separated, either artificially or not. And in the public arena – that is, in the context of a figuratively based art – the result is ostensibly destructive. As Gregory Bateson has argued, in play the messages or signals exchanged are either untrue or unintended, and whatever is denoted by those signals is non-existent.[8]

Faced with the prospect of an art that professes to deal with universals in universal terms, Baechler decided to confuse the debate. The 'constant juxtaposition of images'[9] – a phrase of Walter Dahn's to describe the tactics of the new painting – becomes more playful and more sinister as time goes on. In the coloured paintings from 1987 the dichotomy is particularly clear. Alongside the Fun-with-Dick-and-Jane compositions is a flat, chilling, head-on study of a girl with no nose or mouth, and slits for eyes, in a pointed hat with birds circling around her. After such a confrontation, the set grins of the other children no longer seem guiltless. Think again of Baechler's passion for intermixture, its motives and results.

Instead of picking away at one debate like the birds in *Realists Playing Together* – in effect, a collection of early modernist abstract marks – Baechler skirts the entire issue by using tactics of contamination. The juvenility of his approach is a crucial factor. In *Fountainhead* (1984), for example, a sacred symbol of Persian and Byzantine culture is reduced to profane contemporary terms. Pushed to logical extremes Baechler's play can result in the debasement of objects of veneration, not necessarily by direct means but simply by juxtaposition and equalization. Perhaps purity and impurity were once indissolubly linked. Their separation, if indeed it is a separation, leads to contagious defilement. Though play and the sacred resemble each other in certain respects, Roger Caillois has pointed out, there is still a major difference between them.[10] Whereas before the sacred man is a supplicant, in play he is master of his own destiny. Confuse them and the result is the same. If their shared purpose is the transcendence of day-to-day existence, the act of profanation produces one of two effects. Either the agent of sacrilege himself becomes holy or he is damned completely. And in the process unique characteristics are lost, a primordial state of licence is restored and the resultant shock or ecstasy is violent to the point of death. 'My operation', wrote Jean Dubuffet, 'is to erase all categories and regress toward an undifferentiated continuum.'[11] Little wonder that Baechler's explanation of a great work of art is a severed head on a roadway, the voluptuousness of panic unleashed on the lucid mind.

1. Jean Dubuffet in conversation with Margit Rowell, 31 January 1973, quoted in Margit Rowell, *Jean Dubuffet: A Retrospective* (New York: Solomon R. Guggenheim Museum, 1973), p.23.
2. Donald Kuspit, 'Donald Baechler' (*Artforum*, June 1983), p.80.
3. Robert Pincus-Witten, *Increments of Inaccessibility* (New York: Tony Shafrazi Gallery, 1983), n.p.
4. Roland Barthes, 'Textual Analysis of Poe's *Valdemar*' in Robert Young, ed., *Untying the Text* (London: RKP 1981), p.157.
5. Elias Canetti, *Crowds and Power*, trans. C. Stewart (London: Victor Gollancz Ltd, 1962), p.17.
6. Quoted in Alan Jones, 'Donald Baechler', *Arts Magazine* (March 1983).
7. D.W. Winnicott, *Playing and Reality* (London: Tavistock, 1971).
8. Gregory Bateson, 'A Theory of Play and Fantasy', in J.S. Bruner, A. Jolly and K. Sylva, eds., *Play; Its Role in Development and Evolution* (Harmondsworth: Penguin, 1976), p.123.
9. Walter Dahn, quoted in Wolfgang Max Faust and Gerd de Vries, *Hunger nach Bildern*, 1982, p.139.
10. Roger Caillois, in two books: *Man and the Sacred*, trans. M. Barasch, 1980, and *Man, Play and Games*, trans. M. Barasch, 1961.
11. Jean Dubuffet in a letter to Arnold Glimcher, 15 September 1969, in Margit Rowell, op. cit., p.26.

Anne-Marie Watkins

From Under the Sign of Saturn, *catalogue of an exhibition curated by Stuart Morgan at Nigel Greenwood Gallery, London, 1987. The other artists included were Tony Carter, Marc Camille Chaimowicz, Hannah Collins, David Dye, David Godbold and John Wood, Flora Natapoff and John Virtue.*

The sculptures of Anne-Marie Watkins begin as white elephants or irritants. Made in one-inch thick board with no special tactile qualities, painted black (a cancellation of colour) and assembled to be too high for any viewer less than eight feet tall, *Lullaby* is a figure of authority, undermined partly by humour, partly by its ability to defy the viewer and therefore provoke curiosity, rage or involvement. Its appointed task is one of denial; painted gold, its interior can barely be glimpsed and never possessed. Yet this lumbering bully has a weakness: it can be rocked very slightly from side to side. Petty though that concession may seem, it comes to stand for a triumph. The bully has a weakness; he (it is undoubtedly a 'he') has feet of clay. Read it another way. The need to be rocked is part of the nature of the beast itself, and craving affection is too normal a circumstance to be construed as a chink in the armour, a frailty to be turned to one's ends. Rocked too much, it will topple and destroy the kindly soul who does the rocking. It can happen – the mad composer Gesualdo rocked his child to death, but this is exceptional. When *Lullaby* rocks, two battles have been won. It gets what it wants; we get what we want. Authority is proved childish, yet is strengthened, not punished, for this. The weak are encouraged to believe that they can defeat the forces that keep them weak. Or is this a delusion? *Lullaby* begins as an annoyance and ends as a presence, with that mixture of demands and contradictions that defines every human relationship.

Warhol's Piss Paintings

Account of exhibitions at Larry Gagosian and the DIA Art Foundation, New York, published in Artscribe *62, March/April 1987.*

In the 1960s, on the principle that anyone who works in a laundry knows more about dripping and staining than a mere artist, Warhol decided not to wash his dirty linen in public. Opting for chance methods, he placed unsized canvas on the floor of the factory and let people urinate over it. Doubt exists about whether the first 'piss paintings' survived. When he returned to the same idea in 1978, working with what catalogues describe as 'copper metallic pigment mixed with acrylic medium and urine on canvas', he had found a way to stabilize colours and alter their range from pale yellow on white to a coppery ground, with various shades of green, brown or black, depending on the depth of the puddles and the length of time they were left standing there. These 'Oxidations' are on show at Larry Gagosian. Results differ widely. Delicate all-over sprinkling or long trailing movements with periodic splashes produce a latter-day equivalent of chinoiserie. Large pools of wee result in blackened areas, no longer a celebration but a grim reminder of its role as superfluous waste. In vintage Warhol fashion, half of the oxidations belong in the drawing-room while the other half relate to the streets. At this point, just when inklings are beginning to develop into interpretations, the viewer becomes unsettled. There is nothing wrong with the works themselves, but there is something peculiar about their context.

In an ideal textbook world art drops from spaces and critics catch it. In other words, they supply a context. In a world as fallible and messy as ours, this rarely happens. Galleries, magazines and an entire support system try to provide a ready-made context which our fictional ideal critic will politely ignore. In Warhol's case the danger of slipping from talk about work to talk about its context is very great; more than anyone else he has altered his context and that of others. A one-room display of 'hand-painted' pieces at the DIA Art Foundation, mostly from 1960, recalls the early days of that paradigm shift. Although 'hand-painted' is simply a term meant to distinguish these from mechanically produced images, which began in 1962, when Warhol started to work in series, they have many of the 'made by hand' qualities of amateur art. A headline copied from a newspaper ends in mid-air. A photograph of Hedy Lamarr is traced, then filled in 'artistically' in pencil. The front page of a newspaper is drawn in ballpoint pen, with empty boxes where the pictures ought to be and some but not all of the words copied. This is the handiwork of a man filling time, embarking on elliptical experiments, which confuse nonchalance and misplaced labour. The Hedy Lamarr sketch could be interpreted as a corrective to de Kooning, just as the use of words could be seen as an extension of Rivers. But the idea of art history as a set of blockages, and blockages of these blockages, would not help in this case. Warhol was not disagreeing with someone else's answer to a question or even quibbling about the way it was asked. He was thinking of another question completely.

The 1978 piss paintings and the 1960–62 handmade works serve as epilogue and prologue to an entirely separate phase of his career which began with his shooting, a phase of proto-conceptual and conceptual propositions that culminated, as it had to, with the stylized Warhol signature serving merely as imprimatur for *Interview* or the films. After that he returned to work as a hobbyist. It was his proud boast that *A*, transcribed from tapes, had been the first novel never to have been read by its author. It belonged to the robotic, conceptual phase. *From A to B*, from the subsequent period, was personal, quirky and old-fashioned. It would be possible to continue listing instances of the distinct phases. One thing is certain. The post-shooting Warhol showed little taste for the social criticism that marked his 1960s work; Warhol as exemplary Marxist, the figure discussed by Rainer Crone in his early monograph, had disappeared for good. His capitulation to dollars, ease of consumption, the expectations of a vast audience unconcerned about his talent or lack of it, seems complete. Refusing to conceive of any redemption whatever for a man who spends his time making screenprints of Donald Duck and idolizing the rich, taking photos of parties and offering to make portraits of anyone at all for ready money is probably fair.

So is it feasible to suggest that the lost piss paintings of the early 1960s were masterpieces whereas the glamorized 1978 remakes were rendered harmless by their altered context? They are all piss paintings. Can a self-induced contextual shift alter even the contents of one's own urinary tract? If only the matter were that simple. 'Andy Warhol' now consists of a set of selves, with careers to match, connected and yet independent, like the panels on a folding screen, so that at any time one panel can be obscured while the others are brought into play. (Such explanation verges on an apology. But it is an apology for an amorality Warhol openly admits.) The piss paintings of both decades, like the odd works of the early 1960s, may be idle tamperings or fragments from the most gifted nay-sayer since Marcel Duchamp. The work and the context are one. Elitism and democracy merge. In terms of piss paintings we are all peers.

Things That Go Bump

Published in Artforum *XXVI, 2, October 1987, as one of five responses by art critics to Documenta 8.*

Discarding the idea of an exhibition on a single theme, the organizers of Documenta 8 seemed to have decided on an event that would touch bases, would circle round problem areas rather than exploring them fully. And the argument that emerged looked like a string of separate problems, lined up in linear fashion, as if solving one would solve them all. If only things were that easy. The result was like the content of the most popular work in the show, a film by Peter Fischli and David Weiss.

A lighted fuse ignites a rocket tied to a tiny wooden cart. The cart shoots along a rail, and a brick it is carrying hits a valve on a balloon of gas. The balloon deflates, which tilts a see-saw, which causes a chemical to fall into a pan of water with a candle in it, which reacts to make a fire, which eventually results in the melting of a plastic tape, which sends a tyre rolling along a sloping ladder to hit another tyre, which crosses a ladder to knock over a plank, which diverts the tyre into a semicircle of paper now flaming from the fire, which sets off fireworks tied to the tyre, which propel it forward, slowly at first then with gathering speed, and the process continues. The ultimate in child's play, featuring items of makeshift equipment, Fischli/Weiss's film is a chapter of accidents, of objects taking matters into their own hands. They enact a Scheherezade scenario – a prolonged digression that, like hers, might encompass the whole world if sufficiently prolonged, yet which is so limited by its occasion, by its manic urge to solve an immediate problem, that artistically it risks everything. As a metaphor for Documenta 8 the film was perfect.

The organizers of Documenta 8 seemed to be calling for a recovery of modernism proper, before its petrifaction. Modernism went wrong, the consensus opinion suggests, when it played safe and declined into academicism, when the art object, immured and autonomous, was no longer called upon to take risks. Postmodern art, the argument might run, abandoned the ideal of communicating with a single clique and tried to function on more than one level simultaneously, charting its course, where necessary, outside conventional institutions and channels. Somewhere between these ideas lies the critical issue of art's 'job'. It should be remembered that the question of audience was in some ways no less vexed in classic modernism than it is today. The shift from a modernism engaged with its social context to a solipsistic and élitist one followed a series of disasters – the rise of fascism in the thirties, the war, the McCarthyist period in America – that art had been powerless to prevent; there were reasons for its turning away from the world. Today, what the earlier modernism wanted for a while is actually here. (In 1984, for example, 33 million viewers saw a video by Nam June Paik.)

The risk is that of reduction in potency, of all art aspiring to the condition of journalism, abandoning not only its ivory towers but also its undergrounds, to operate instead on some permanent middle ground. Many of the new media outside the traditional territory of visual art – records, television and so on – have established themselves in a centrist position in culture. And though it is possible to work in those media and to remain on the margins, if that is what one wants, there is more than a suggestion that these forms are being drawn towards the centre too, by some independent need of their own. How much of a difference will be retained between work in video as a medium pursued in its own right and work on television practised as a business, between the music on experimental small-money record labels and chart-busting, overpromoted rock? By working in these media artists are necessarily addressing the question of the mass audience, no matter how 'marginal' their work may seem. Art's attempt to break out of its late-modernist cage entails a dangerous proximity to entertainment and the fashionable. These are real conditions, states to explore, not avoid.

Art is what a society believes it to be at any given time; the signs are that the complexity of our beliefs about art has been pushing art into an undefined arena. Instead of exploration of these realms, talk of the late-modernist autonomy of the art object as the great enemy to be defeated once and for all ran throughout the dialogue about and within Documenta 8. (We've heard that even at this moment psychoanalysts are working on a name for this anti-formalist phobia.) The result is that sculptors make ice cream kiosks or benches in parks, while installation – that reinstated medium – relies on spectacle for its own sake. Some sufferers from the phobia, including those among the Documenta curators, insist on design as the cross to be brandished in the face of belated Greenbergians, either in the belief that design in the future will move forward in unison with 'fine' art or on the more plausible theory that the two exist in a state of reciprocity, so that the more 'useful' art becomes, the more 'beautiful' radical designers will make their work. One exhibition within the exhibition – of imaginary museums – did not suffer from the same phobia. In the fashion of Mallarméan aestheticism, it was comfortable with the idea that art ends up in a museum, and therefore that the museum is the proper space for contextual manipulation.

There was a time when no sculptor would have used a word such as 'object', but twenty years after the 'dematerialization of the art object', objects are getting restless. And as Fischli/Weiss's film loop at Documenta shows us, as the objects keep up their cause-and-effect sequence the audience keeps on laughing, and unfortunately, with this curatorial perspective, the conditional tense never leans towards the present.

Neil Bartlett: A Vision of Love Revealed in Sleep

Review of performance at Battersea Arts Centre, London, by Neil Bartlett, designed by Robin Whitmore, Artforum, *XXVI, 1, September 1987.*

'Poor little devil, what will become of him?' asked Dante Gabriel Rossetti about Simeon Solomon, in his youth a celebrated painter and socialite, later the forgotten man of Pre-Raphaelitism, an alcoholic who sold matches, worked as a sidewalk artist, and died in a London workhouse. After the police caught him having intercourse with a man twice his age in a public urinal, Solomon's circumstances grew steadily worse until his death 32 years later, in 1905. 'My behaviour has been perfectly disgraceful', he admitted cheerfully when he was sentenced. Yet nothing resembling an apology ever passed his lips. Instead, he continued to base his art on fantasies woven around his affairs with teenage boys and decided to reject the society that had already rejected him. Interviewed late in life by reporters who could see the wretchedness of the workhouse, Solomon, lice-ridden and half-starved, refused to tell them what they wanted. 'I like it here', he said. 'It's so central.'

On three staircases and the colonnaded marble terrace of a Victorian building filled with garbage, scrap metal, fake paintings, church candles and smoke – an environment designed by Robin Whitmore for the performance piece *A Vision of Love Revealed in Sleep* – a nude figure resembling both Solomon and the swooning youths he painted undertook the dramatized equivalent of a poststructuralist analysis. His text was one that few in the audience were likely to have read: Solomon's prose poem 'A Vision of Love Revealed in Sleep' (1871). This solo performance by Neil Bartlett (a work in progress, the first phase of his theatre piece for five performers) involved a complex rhetorical strategy consisting of equal parts lecture, recitation, comedy routine, mime and drag act. By varying his tone of voice, demeanour, and even his persona – assuming the identities of other historical and literary characters such as Marie Lloyd, the smuttiest and most popular of British music-hall comediennes, and Miss Wade, the desolate but uncompromising lesbian from Charles Dickens's *Little Dorrit*, or acting out vignettes of present-day gay life under the threat of AIDS – he gradually comes to terms with Solomon's ecstatic idealism, flamboyant eroticism and obsession with brave young warriors.

Although AIDS is not the real subtext for Bartlett's interpretation of Solomon's poem, it provides the stimulus for recognizing both the significance of the text and the lifestyle of a forgotten, disreputable, unrepentant, flagrantly happy painter who made himself immune to starvation, condescension, neglect and brutality for more than thirty years. So far, most gay men in Britain have felt unable to acknowledge the seriousness of the crisis that faces them and to engage in full-scale revision of their culture and attitudes. *A Vision* begins to confront the mixture of sadness, anger and confusion they are feeling. All of these are reflected in Bartlett's shifting mode of address, inside and outside characters and issues at the same time, ranging from apology to denunciation, from camp exchanges with the audience to a calm report by a single man of returning home in the early morning, listening to the messages on his answering-machine and cooking a meal for one. Not only are conventional acting techniques rejected, but the performer's very ability to transcend traditional modes of persuasion becomes a measure of his veracity and the truth of the evidence he presents. What we are left with at the end is no longer a palimpsest but a lone, naked man facing a problematic future in a Britain where homosexuals are reviled as never before in his lifetime. He is not asking for help; he is demanding respect.

Thomas Locher: The World in Pieces

Published in Artscribe 65, *Sept/Oct 1987, reprinted in* Art from Köln, *Tate Gallery, Liverpool, 1989.*

Not long ago Thomas Locher was invited to take part in a photography exhibition. Not ever having been a photographer, he surprised even himself by participating. A bigger surprise was the photograph he submitted. With simple elements made of cardboard, illuminated in colours as lurid as those of a 1950s Hollywood B-movie, he made an abstracted mock-up of the plan of the laboratory in which the atom was split. At first it seems irrelevant to his other concerns. But perhaps it serves as a commentary on them after all.

Part of a Cologne-based reappraisal of classic American Conceptualism, Locher's work recalls both the spirit and the focus of Douglas Huebler's crowd studies, Robert Barry's inert gases released into the atmosphere, Lawrence Weiner's public announcements or Joseph Kosuth's first ontological demonstrations. They take the form of lucid proclamations: lightboxes bearing messages, books, paintings on (or rather, behind) glass. In one way the work is simplicity itself. Locher's method is to use the chop logic we use every day. His material is the entire universe as we perceive it. And he, the artist, uses the one to deal with the other as precisely as his means permit, making his own decisions, adjusting those of others, then watching to see what happens. And what happens can be very strange indeed.

'Dog. Amazon. Dilemma. Cement. Spoon. Banana. Future. Discus. Electricity. Groove. Urn. Jubilation. Anvil.' Translation proves difficult; the nouns he chooses all sound a little off-key. And since each is singular, in the sense of not being a compound word, they assume the role of particles.

'Anode. Compulsion. Nozzle. Cedar. Glacier. Marriage. Filling.' Their slight oddness ensures that they will be regarded not as things but as words for things, in an order so wild that it becomes natural to invent a tidier one as the reading process is continued: 'Basalt. Tender. Orient. Plankton. Grill. Diver. Guidance. Boomerang. Altar. Wool. Jam. Poverty. Sausage. Jewels.'

If words form constellations, apparently of their own volition – wool/jam/poverty/sausage/jewels – then that process must result from an inner need to organize information that comes to hand. For Locher that gesture dates back to his childhood, when, as an avid model-railway fan, he collected pieces from complete sets, arranging them differently with each new part he was given. The mental disposition of component parts and their constant reshuffling is the way perception verges on knowledge. 'The World', as the list of nouns is called, suggest that what we register is a tangle of self-created Symbolist poems, each so tenuously related to the next that, the moment comprehension seems imminent, it dissolves altogether. In *Zen and the Art of Motorcycle Maintenance* Robert Pirsig describes the invisible knife we all employ to make divisions between the complex of components which confronts us. The process of reducing a complex whole into constituent parts, then (perhaps) arranging those parts so as to make some reconstruction of wholeness, is Locher's theme. And it provides him with a running problem: how to do justice to wholeness and fragmentation alike. Sixties precedents hinted at inner taxonomic faculties that differed from one person to another. Lamonte Young composed music on a single note from a siren, so unyielding in volume that listeners' ears would register not one note but different ones, with silences separating them. Incapable of tolerating such strain for too long, the ear automatically created such rests in order to avoid damage, and the result was that each of them heard a quite different sound. If cerebration proper can be separated from what looks like naked perception, Locher might be thought to deal with the former.

Yet his project, which is bound to fall foul of the forces that block either cerebration or raw perception, is so involved with those barriers that every line he draws around something, every word or title he uses, represents some heroic capitulation to enemy powers. Received knowledge forms the basis of works in which (for example) the headings and subheadings of a thesaurus are grouped diagrammatically in order to demonstrate that they mean to embrace all human experience. In one sense such works pay homage to the concept of wholeness, of grand theory; Locher reveres such thinkers as Humboldt or Alfred North Whitehead, who straddled science and art. In another sense they expose the fragility of such attempts to be complete, alerting viewers to the semi-fictional nature of the task at hand but, more urgently, of the unreliability of available materials. Trapped in a web of words, philosophizing comes to a halt.

But if an urge for clarity underlies Locher's art, so, in equal measure, does the need to avoid nitpicking. At any time we choose, we can start again, defining the world anew. As lyrical and fluid as the thesaurus experiments are daunting, his number paintings adhere to no set pattern, but match number, colour and space at will. After making seven of these Locher stopped, having made it clear that they could go on for ever. But he must have been aware that he could make his point in an opposite way, as Flaubert did with his *Dictionary of Received Ideas*, a celebration of the apparent illimitability of poetic language by means of a presentation of the artificial limitations placed on language in everyday life. In his book *The One The Same The Identical* Locher recites what is known, as if by rote, exposing language for what it is. 'I have observed,' the text begins, 'I have seen, I examined, I have looked closely. I have watched. I have not closed my eyes.' Later 'Nothing escapes me. I recognize everything. It has become clear to me.' Later still, 'I have regarded myself as an exception. I am like no one else. I am more than everything else. I am the first. I am unique.' And at this point footnotes begin their chant. 'One-off, incomparable, undivided, special, predetermined, liberated, free, single-sexed, alone'. When the text repeats 'I alone', 'alone' is footnoted. 'Single, divided, unaccompanied, lonely . . .' the footnote runs. And suddenly, once more, the text is suffused with emotion. If ordering is motivated by a will to power, that has its own particular penalties. 'I have established boundaries', the speaker states. Yet with each successive footnote, the number of permutations of the text increases alarmingly and the title of the book becomes easier to understand. *The One The Same The Identical* so disturbs the reader's sense of the unitary, the identical, or the comparable, each footnote adding permutations of meaning to an already complex text, that it could be regarded as self-detonating. And finally, the text is about power defused, language floating free of its vehicle, to be given its head for good and all.

Gradually it becomes easier to see why Locher made that photograph of the laboratory where the atom was split. No apples dropping on periwigged heads or naked Greeks jumping out of baths . . . simply a room, an apparatus with nothing visible at all. The significance of the experiment for Locher's work could hardly be overestimated. Since his practice consists of dividing the world into parts, he is bound to run head first against a basic assumption of twentieth-century physics, of the world as a continuum, with the observer raised to the god-like level of creator with each new glance. The footnotes in his book hint at the downfall of the speaker. Yet it conjures up the undifferentiated, unfragmentable whole which the splitting of the atom inaugurated. It is a problem he will touch on more than once in the future.

Strange Days: an interview with Ross Bleckner

Published in Artscribe *68, March/April 1988.*

Stuart Morgan: *How does art relate to the present?*

Ross Bleckner: We live in a strange time and my paintings are intended to be about this time. They are less about a language, more about the world of that language, and it is a social world. Works being made now are tinged with the idea of failure and death. The whole idea of abstraction has altered in the same way. So for works of art to exist they must take into account a sense of impossibility, of rupture, of the breakdown of what we thought abstraction could have done in a more idealized world where the discourse of abstract painting was connected to some essentialist view of social relations, where iconic abstraction – which is what modernist abstraction really was – could somehow stand for a universal. I find that reductive, and believe that abstraction now must be expansive. Paintings have to be about how we are here now. But *how* we define ourselves now, through all our cultural productions, is *so* different from what abstract painting could have done before. We no longer have the sense of things being infinite or real and natural, and it is certainly not an artist's job to reinforce those cultural clichés, to let people image some immutable reality. Our job is to make what we thought of as natural become unnatural, so that ideas of the self are inscribed in language symbolically, not organically. The artist picks the ideas that are difficult to say. Describing the difficulty of saying them is the most expressive I can be.

So you are dramatizing a failure.

We are living in a time that is about failure – of the governmental process, of artistic ideologies, of health and care – and we are concerned with images that fail or images that succeed. Most interesting are those that fail, because those that succeed have to comply with what comes to us, what locates things but doesn't think things. (The difference between locating thought and thinking thought is very great. People who use cultural critique or the mirror of culture to criticize culture might just be locating the thought with which that critique complies.)

If your images court failure, they must be deliberately vulnerable.

I do see it as vulnerability. That's the first point. The second is that I'm interested in the position of an artist who does not necessarily focus on patriarchy or egocentricity. One myth of modernism is that we are centred creatures who find strong images to propel vision. Painting is a search for the consciousness of the artist's relationships to images in the culture. Admitting a sense of vulnerability in relation to the question of what could exist in a painting or how painting could continue and still speak about the social world means a closer relationship to its search for thinking, for consciousness. I am trying to talk from a point outside myself to say, 'How do you exist? How do you live your life? How do you get through a painting?' And that, to me, is how you get through a day and still preserve those fantasies you need to continue, how you disentangle yourself from that historical baggage which is so oppressive, how you use those elements which already exist. I try to allow a painting to be as complex as living and thinking.

But that would lead to extremely complex paintings. In fact, your painting changes from work to work.

I don't want everything to exist in the same painting because I don't want the viewer or myself to have to make choices between things and end up talking about how everything is meaningless. The paintings can be different, as long as each one is clear.

Do you believe in painting?

Through my paintings I'm trying to find how to define why I'm painting. So a lot of it has to do with flirtation between different belief systems.

Does this mean you're not actually painting? That you're faking painting? Or avoiding painting in order to fall into painting?

You make paintings to stay alive. Any painter will tell you that. Yet although that's true, it's not conceptually interesting. I paint my way into a place where I have to make paintings. And I feel that my work can somehow open itself up to the fact that I feel fractured and confused about the different ways of organizing relationships between internal, psychic reality and material reality. An artist does exactly what Freud did: to describe a phenomenon, a mechanism, the inability of our conscious mind to contain and control unconscious desires. What painters do is also to describe. By describing everything they also describe what is not seen. And by describing the way thought is thought by making paintings, suddenly you have a proposition that is broader and more fragile than you expected. If artists allow their work to reflect on the libidinal processes that instruct desire, if they reflect on loss, on our sense of history and of the future, their work becomes a passageway that throbs with possibility but speaks of failure. It maps the trajectory of the workings of the mind. But the mind constantly tricks you, and can make proposals about what those tricks are and mean.

So the meaning arises from the distances between intention and significance.

A place is opened up in painting by means of the light in it, which manipulates pictorial space and allows you to enter a world that fascinates you, a world unlike this world. By means of the disparity between the two worlds I want to express repressed or latent communal feelings.

Political feelings?

In a sense. In the work of every painter who interests me there are things that aspire to political change, to a deeper spirituality than art can admit to, to a pre-capitalist reconciliation with that sense of wholeness and completion that doesn't get found in life ever again. I would like the paintings to reunite, to speak of a perpetual loss, which I see as melancholy, which painting can develop into a belief about how it can be used.

Are you saying that formal resolution aspires to social resolution?

Formal terms depend on history and a psychological scenario. But it is important that painting should connect to ideas and that ultimately these ideas connect to people. To paraphrase Barnett Newman, you can't wait for the self-appointed guardians of culture to decide which ideas are correct. It is not cynical to undermine people's assumptions about what constitutes their relationship to the world, to disturb their polite submission to social norms. One aspect of that submission is the monolithic way abstraction has been constructed. Dismantling that is another aspect of that vulnerability I am trying to capture.

Tell me more about that capture.

It's almost like taking a deep breath. Your body expands. You bring in air and let it out. So these paintings are about breathing and looking. Their blinding or hypnotic effect creates the possibility of a break in how you look at things, so that while nothing's really happening everything is happening at the same time. Which is another answer to the question about 'faking' painting. I'm saying that I'm trying to make things happen.

How do images fit into this plan to make things happen?

Iconography is a ruse to describe something I don't know how to paint because it's not an image and it's not abstract; it's somewhere in the world outside, outside of representation and outside of theory. I'm looking for an air between all the different feelings and stages in our lives. I think this air is thick now. I'm not interested in the pictureness of painting, I'm much more interested in the paintingness of painting. I want to address the idea of making paintings and to keep inventing new reasons to want to address it. I have to say I'm looking for something I haven't found yet. That's part of being a painter. Since we're constructed socially, what we're looking for will always shift. We'll always have that air surrounding it. If you live in the world and have a sense of that world, your consciousness is always responding to the way the world works. Or the way it isn't working now and the great changes this failure has made.

What changes? What failures?

In our time we are saddled with an inability to deflect our thinking about death. Art and death are closely aligned, of course. But the fact of AIDS has brought us close to certain truths: to meaningfulness in imagery, to the change in the ideal of being a producer in life. People have always had an ideal of a life cycle as a natural development process. Because of AIDS this has been completely suppressed. In other words, there's a greater sense of urgency. Imagine a pane of glass. We contain ourselves by means of formal procedures that keep us just this side of the glass from those procedures that have decayed. The process of making art has to do with being very close to that pane of glass, with destruction on the other side. We used to be very separate from mortality. Now we're not.

Are we powerless?

Absolutely not.

Is painting a means of grasping power?

It is. But grasping power is futile unless you know what to do with it. Any artist with a modicum of intelligence can grasp a certain amount of power by coming up with a body of work that has novelty appeal. But art is really a place to stand and speak from. Just to say 'I'm here' is not enough. Aside from the immediate fact that people are sick and dying, it is not yet clear what effect our changed view of mortality and sexuality are going to have on our culture. Art must comment on more than art; it must encounter mortality, change, desire, the fact that nothing is certain and nothing is unalterable.

So you don't agree that art is exhausted.

I started making striped paintings because I was looking for an economical image that was also exhausted. I was curious to see if it could or couldn't yield the emotional range I was interested in. My idea of abstract painting had to do with testing the limitations it assumed, limitations in the idea of what it means to be an artist. I wanted to use a way of working that seemed idealistic but which I knew to be exhausted.

So you are *interested in exhaustion.*

I'm interested in *aggressive* exhaustion.

Richard Artschwager: Permanently Ajar

Published in *Richard Artschwager, Selected Works 1964–1988*, Nicola Jacobs Gallery, London, 1988.

'The most striking property of doors (although not unique to doors) is RESONANCE between two different states, which can be conveniently labelled as "open" or "closed"', wrote Richard Artschwager in 1967. Historically speaking, he was continuing the train of thought that led Marcel Duchamp to make a door that remained neither open nor shut but permanently ajar. Artschwager is not Duchamp, however: his approach has a less dandyish, more downhome quality. Above all, he is a craftsman. The things he makes resemble things we know, but not quite. A sense of didactic comedy is never far away. He is trying to teach us a lesson. But what? Despite an entire generation of New York sculptors who profess their indebtedness to his work, no consensus of opinion exists on what Artschwager has been doing for the last thirty years. At this stage, it seems simply analysing what is there will no longer do. The alternative is to analyse the way it is looked at.

When his furniture factory was destroyed by fire in 1958, Richard Artschwager kept thinking about furniture. At the same time, in reaction, perhaps, to the vast, tragic paintings of the Abstract Expressionists, he was thinking about abstraction. Characteristically, he turned to everyday life, its routines and points of stability, then subjected them to a perverse revision. In daily life handles can be grasped, chairs can be drawn up to tables, drawers can be filled with clothes. Artschwager changed all that. *Handle* (1962) could indeed be grasped, but it led nowhere; like the frame, one of Artschwager's preferred forms, it had no beginning or end. The table in *Table and Chair* (1963) consisted of a single block and the drawers in his *Chest of Drawers* (1964) turned out to be solid. The aim, it seemed, was not discomfort but disequilibrium, which for Artschwager seems inseparable from abstraction.

Materials helped. Retrieving a photograph from a pile of rubbish in the street in 1961, he had gridded it up and transferred it to canvas, square by square. Replacing canvas with Celotex a year later only accentuated the oddness of the result. The eye refused to settle on familiar outlines, detail was lost or assumed a ghostly presence (like the chandelier in *Staircase*,

1971) and the collision of the patterned surface with any imposed pattern, as in the paintings of fragments of weaving, resulted in abstraction more complex than its source. If in drawing on Celotex he had taken photography, a medium with no tangible presence, and tried to make it sculptural, in using Formica in his sculptures from 1960 onwards he had done the opposite. Wood-grain was present but only in pictorial form – like a 'memory' of wood, as Artschwager described it. Works where Formica met Celotex, such as *Diptych II* (1967) emphasized the visual difficulties of both, difficulties that lay not in the material but in the focus on large or small patterns which may or may not correspond to touch. If, as he once claimed, sculpture for him means 'felt space', by the same token painting should be described as 'seen matter'. Determined to confuse the ways two or three dimensions were represented, he leaves the two to battle it out. The result is a profound disparity which leaves the viewer with the sense that the combined evidence of touch and sight by no means add up to the truth about the world, and the ways that feeling and seeing are registered in art are similar, exhaustive in their own terms but finally faulty. Artschwager indicates what we know but choose not to dwell on: that perception deals in images of things and not the things themselves. Who we are, the angle from which we look, the sheer partiality of understanding, is a besetting theme in nineteenth-century American culture. Properly, wrote Henry James, summarizing the entire debate in one of his prefaces, 'reality ends nowhere'. Mistrust of perception was particularly pronounced in the case of Nathaniel Hawthorne, who lived a life of self-imposed hermithood and developed the habit of leaving a room, then rushing back in to see if the furniture had moved in the split-second he had been away. It is not coincidental, perhaps, that through the years 1974–5 Artschwager made a series of 53 drawings under the collective title *Basket Table Door Window Mirror Rug*, in which the same domestic motifs were subjected to seemingly endless permutation without disappearing or losing their identity or being distorted in a way that ignored the context of the entire drawing.

If Artschwager has thought long and hard about perspective, he has annihilated it with the invention of the blp. On radar scanners the eye is made to follow the track of a line moving around 360 degrees. Suppressing a vowel, making the 'blip' more dramatic by its single appearance, he began making blps – flat, pill-shaped marks that can be placed anywhere: on pictures in magazines, on the sides of buildings, in any size or scale, executed by anyone.

This extension of graffiti alters the balance of what is seen; the blp functions as a black hole, sucking everything in from around it. In Artschwager's private lexicon of forms, the blp most resembles those question marks, exclamation marks and brackets, three-dimensional punctuation included in his sculptures as if to make the size of the identifiable objects relative to it and to stress their role as elements in an artistic language. Just as the punctuation casts doubt on the stress placed on a singular statement, the blp brings into question which is dominant – text or context. Size is important. In a letter to Coosje van Bruggen, Artschwager wrote: 'They are given a size which will first of all make them visible in the field and will, secondly, permit them to (resonate?) flux between a dominating and subordinate condition.' And in the same letter he describes the effect when blps are categorized as being the same: 'On-going memory which is busy all the time, finds the blps, collates them under the 'same' and stores them together. Dragged away with the blps are their context, stored as 'different' but together like the scenarios in photos that make up a family album . . . The *summa* blps, whatever that may be, is a fact of my life, a sort of fixture such as my cousin Hans or that there is such a thing as a triangle . . .' Again the thinking is about visual registration, and Artschwager's work comes to resemble a collection of tests to which neither he nor we know the answer, on the subject of perception and its limitations. And more and more he comes to resemble an eccentric inventor, operating everywhere at once, asking more questions than he can answer.

Within the body of work itself certain poles can be located. The use of rubberized hair as a material indicates one; the entire question of focusing and whether it is possible to 'centre' peripheral vision. Traditionally sculptures have been looked 'at' and paintings looked 'into'. Artschwager addresses the problem by making sculptures that are assemblies of paintings, or using surfaces that are pictures of other surfaces. Especially in recent works, the problem of reflection has occupied his attention, and the mirroring effects he produces never leave the viewer in doubt of the image's potential for deliquescence and desuetude, a fate that casts doubt on the terrifying technological newness he has aimed at in the past. His procedure seems to be to locate extremes, then amalgamate them in a single work. Yet the works escape, talk to each other, and exist in an ever-changing climate of meaning. Bad news for a man that claims that stasis, silence and separation were the most powerful conventions in art, and who seems to want to work under laboratory conditions? Perhaps not.

Too often regarded an artist's artist, particularly now, when an entire generation of New York sculptors admits to being in his debt, Artschwager should sometimes be discussed for what he so obviously attempts to be: the model of a democratic artist, operating with objects and situations people know, with materials they see without even thinking about them, and aiming to return those people to an appreciation of simple things when those things seem to be under threat. 'Celebration' was a word he used in early interviews about his work, when he had recently gravitated from making portable altars to making artworks. There is reason to suppose that the word would not apply today. Yet it is not easily won. The pessimism that has been sensed in his work is real enough – an object submitted to an AIDS auction was titled *Chest of Hope: Block of Wood* – and critics such as Donald Kuspit, who sees in the work 'one relentless purge of meaning in the name of objectness' are not wrong; that objectness can be read as a critique of technology or the emptiness of the materialist ideals of American life. His aim seems to be to alert his viewers to the strengths and weaknesses of their perceptual apparatus, not to make them feel they know less but to reveal how they know. The playful aspect of his art is not easily ignored.

The 'resonance' he describes in discussing doors or blps assumed tangible form in his *Sliding Door* (1964), which did nothing more than that, revealing nothing, achieving nothing; but the fact of the slide recalls how sound travels. As a musician, Artschwager recognizes art as an 'organ of cause and effect' and the quick bounce from one wall to another, from one extreme to another, as the way meaning is engendered. Early on, when he looked first at the work of Jasper Johns, he wrote about how good art transmitted sound. Somewhere between the walls, between fixed ideas, is where Artschwager's thought is located. His *Yes/No Balls*, designed to be rolled to provide answers to all one's problems, sum it up well. So does the detail Robert Pirsig gives in his *Zen and the Art of Motorcycle Maintenance*. In Japan he tells us, there are three possible answers to a question. One is yes, the second is no and the third is *mu*, meaning that the question as phrased does not permit an answer that is either yes or no. It would be hard to find a better description of the position Artschwager adopts.

Degree Zero: Grenville Davey

Published in Artscribe 67, *January/February 1988.*

When, after a decade of Conceptual revision, sculpture re-emerged in the 1980s as a presentation of discrete entities, it returned willing to open negotiations with its surroundings, to engage in dialogues about public and private, function and decoration, imposed or embodied meaning. Suddenly, those dated *New Yorker* cartoons of old ladies in museums adjusting their pince-nez in order to examine the air vents or the heating systems became relevant all over again.

But the best recent sculpture moves far beyond easy jokes about design objects. Grenville Davey's work, for instance, fairly bristles with references to 'anonymous' British street artefacts: the assembled metal handrails to stop pedestrians from crossing in dangerous places, or those convex mirrors of polished metal placed at corners of underpasses, things that admittedly serve a physical purpose while functioning clearly as interpretable signs. If a single art-historical reference prevails, it is to British New Generation sculpture of the 1960s, based as it was on one reading of David Smith, as a set of signals from which meanings seemed to have drained away. Like Caro, Scott, King and others, Davey has adopted the strange habit of painting a coloured skin on his metal surfaces. Pristine, cool, two such blue discs protrude from the wall, each in its own adjustable socket, each slanting obliquely, their broad, flat surfaces facing each other like an oriental hand movement. Meanwhile, a pair of identical, adjacent, flattened hemispheres in the corner of the room seem happy to be overlooked, like lamps before they are turned on. Like the two blue discs, they give the impression of having been around forever.

A second type of Davey sculpture seems to have sprung up overnight. These perform some apparent impossibility with a maximum of effect, as a conjurer performs tricks. In the middle of the wooden floor lies a rusted steel lid, its nuts tightened as if it had been screwed into place, presenting the unlikely proposition that a tunnel has been sunk into the gallery floor. This is gallery art with a vengeance, as much to do with the space around objects as the objects themselves. When Oldenburg wrote about an art that would do something other than 'sit on its ass' in a gallery he overlooked the possibility that both art and its place of display might alter at the same time.

Mediating between the two, Davey's works resemble punctuation marks: blips or dashes that separate and connect at the same time. As in his earlier sculptures, consisting of metal rings at equal distances along a single strap, or a sheet of rubber, pierced all over, standing in a cone shape, without any artificial support, curling round, totally visible, air circulates freely and as little is concealed as possible. Yet other pieces deny this freedom of approach: the lids or covers which seem to be flat on the floor but, by resting on an outer rim, form a dome over circular space on the gallery floor. Bruce Nauman attempted something similar in a homage to Ornette Coleman, with a mirror face down on the floor. Yet Davey plays on that moment of doubt when a tunnel or even an airtight chamber might be expected below. The model for the rusty cover, he admitted, was an old cartoon in which Bugs Bunny took one look at his rabbit-hole, represented by a black ellipse, then picked it up, tucked it under his arm and walked away with it. Again the issue is the divorce of gesture from meaning: theatricality for its own sake. But it is also one of vacancy. That circle which perspective transforms into an ellipse, the white zero framed by a metal handrail and placed on the wall, the nought as two eyes, of the same person or of two different people, the O that both states and consists of an actual absence covered and therefore (foolishly) unseen on the floor: all roads lead to nothing in particular, it seems.

As he zeroes in on his theme, a theme that may exist only to inspire those variations he can play on it, its significance becomes less, not more, obvious. When is a hole not a hole? When it is represented, one answer would run. But how, then, does depicted vacancy differ from common or garden emptiness? Perhaps it never does – not one jot. Look all the way round the O in *Rail* and it turns into a straight line, into its own frame. elsewhere, the circle becomes elliptical, in the fullest sense of the word. What can it mean to have these different slants on absence conjured up time and time again? And where does it lead, this comic activity of stating and restating some positive nihilism, transforming the process of registering nothingness into a gesture of approval. (Think of the European hand signal in which the tip of the thumb and forefinger are brought together, ideally accompanied by a knowing wink, as the eye loses and regains its roundness for a second.) Tough though they are, Davey's ideal art works may be paper-thin, like shells or fans, and hollow, like inverted cups. Combining this formal preoccupation with a passion for signalling – though finally all they are signalling is that they are, indeed, signalling – Davey hits on a weak historical moment, late British formalism. How chic those Caroesque confections could seem, with their designer colours and insulated surfaces. Just as Ross Bleckner employs sixties stripes or Philip Taaffe redeploys the optical kick of Bridget Riley, Davey picks a moment that ensures the vacuity of his art, employs a fabrication process so elaborate that it seems almost perverse, and by announcing that there is nothing up his sleeve when he really *has* nothing up his sleeve, brings his sculpture to a point where it plays on its positioning and its potential to signify nothing at all.

Could the result be no more than an academic adjustment, an attempt to reassert Minimalist premises? Davey's approach is too quirky for that argument to stick. In his first solo exhibition in London, at the Lisson Gallery in October 1987, every piece seemed goofy and oversized, and the sensitive treatment of privacy and impingement were too personal to be mistaken for generalities. The principles of Davey's earlier sculpture, movable with no alteration to the principle of the work or fixed like indicators, left viewers in an ambivalent position. Their ambivalence has psychological overtones, linked with modes of reality and represented reality but also with embarrassment. Negotiating with objects which proclaim something hermetic or irrelevant or avoid investigation is an uneasy experience. When rhetoric is denied and reinstated, free will seems on trial in the subtlest possible way. As Rosalind Krauss demonstrated in *Terminal Iron Works*, David Smith resisted tactility at all costs. Borrowing Smith's habit of coating metal, and treating it industrially, Davey elaborates on this theme. Where does the viewer stand? Does the freedom afforded the viewer relate to his or her thraldom, real or imagined? And does that thraldom relate to value and use, the street or the gallery, the fixed or the unfixed? Bugs Bunny remains the hero of the piece, neatly denying gravity, convention and materiality. One's natural respect, even for manhole covers when shown in galleries, is a different matter. We leave well alone, feeling vaguely threatened and manipulated, as unfree as in the street.

Was it the installation we were looking at, or the work itself? Was the work entering into the spirit of things or lying down and playing dead? Somewhere along the line, it seems, something was on offer, but was quickly withdrawn. If Davey tells lies as a conjuror tells lies, he offers the same truths: wit, disbelief and an infinite number of ways of showing us that there is nothing up his sleeve.

No Warts, No Fanny: Panza's Minimalism

Published in Artscribe *74, March/April 1989.*

In Chapter 8 of Raymond Chandler's *Farewell, My Lovely* Philip Marlowe is forced to discuss money with an aesthete he detests.

> I lit a Camel, blew smoke through my nose and looked at a piece of shiny metal on a stand. It showed a full, smooth curve with a shallow fold on it and two protuberances on the curve . . .
> 'An interesting bit,' he said negligently. 'I picked it up the other day. Asta Dial's *Spirit of Dawn*.'
> 'I though it was Klopstein's *Two Warts on a Fanny*,' I said.
> 'You have a somewhat peculiar sense of humour,' he said.
> 'Not peculiar,' I said. 'Just uninhibited.'

For a hundred years abstract sculpture has been an object of derision. The more extreme the form, the funnier the jokes. Brancusi was tried for obscenity, cartoonists depicted small children with their heads caught in a Henry Moore. Minimalism was the point at which the laughter stopped. Admittedly, it was ideal for *New Yorker* cartoonists, who were guaranteed to show gallery-goers discussing the merits of air vents or heating grilles. And, not surprisingly, they did just that. But from the start, it seems, at least one person took the new direction seriously. Count Panza di Biumo bought Minimalist sculpture so promptly and sensitively that he almost deserves to be ranked as a Minimalist in his own right. He had begun collecting in the late 1950s, buying Rothko and Klein. By the 1970s he had become the prototype of what the late Willi Bongard called the 'Supercollector'. What Panza bought was on display at his home at Varese, but for years he had been trying to place it elsewhere. The early section has been sold to Los Angeles Museum of Contemporary Art. Perhaps the era of the Supercollector is on the wane. But not before what may turn out to be his greatest achievement of all: an exhibition in Madrid staged by the Count himself, in which some of his greatest Minimalist acquisitions went on show.

Madrid has first-rate spaces for art: The Fundaciòn Caixa de Pensiones, with its white marbled rooms, or the Palacio Velázquez, two late nineteenth-century conservatories in the park behind the Prado. But the Centro Reina Sofia, near the Atocha station, has the largest, longest rooms, built around a garden, and corridors so wide that they themselves can be used as galleries if necessary. Limited almost completely to works by Robert Morris, Donald Judd, Bruce Nauman and Dan Flavin, sometimes only one per room, the result could have looked like a set of mini-retrospectives lumped together. Instead, as so rarely happens, it provided a total visual resource: the period at a glance, without curatorial intervention, without ideas, without any educative import.

They still looked shocking, those early Morrises, such as the blank grey cornerpiece from 1963. The sheer resistance of the grey material made these works 'blocks' in every way, fit successors to his previous Duchampian nonsense. Space inside or outside was cordoned off, set aside for examination by lumps of neutrality. A single, early, fibreglass 'frame', placed in the middle of a room of its own, reinforced the satire. But was it satire? Working more and more with elementary forms, Morris embraced a kind of giganticism – the vast steel slab resting on a cylinder of solid granite, for instance – but also a methodical rehearsal of sculpture's formal moves, performed with no sense that any meaning might inhere in the result, beyond setting the seal on a move made by the artist. Morris had opened up a line of enquiry that would extend his career while closing off one avenue after another: the artist as hero, the artist as narcissist, the artist as sexist . . . but the labelling came later. During Morris's Minimalist phase the object was put through its paces so thoroughly that intention was bound to be the next subject for inquisition. Then that, in turn, would be inquisitioned. Jokes demonstrated the brilliant coherence of the course he steered – a vast untitled steel piece from 1969 reads as an I-beam, but also as a monumental version of his earlier *I Box*. But these signs are along the way. The career would move in a straight line, heartlessly followed as if deriding early modern avant-garde tactics. The inquisition is about what it feels to be an artist in America, and his argument is peculiarly American and peculiarly tragic. See him as the Daisy Miller of modern sculpture.

Bruce Nauman has fared badly; recent works only confirmed weaknesses that were present from the start. Robert Pincus-Witten once argued that the moment he ceased to be an acolyte of Duchamp, the work would fall apart. He was right; the essence of Nauman's thinking had been revealed by the early 1970s. The last phase seems especially empty: ideas for shaped rooms into which participants would be locked or corridors of light were posited long ago, but was it ever clear enough what they meant? Glamorous dabbling plays a large part in Nauman's career, yet in this collection it is played down in favour of large-scale solidity. *Lighted Centerpiece* (1970) seemed to sum up the entire career: four lamps attached to the sides of a thick metal tray, to draw attention to a surface buffed and worked. The lamps were powerful, with hoods to ensure that no light spilt anywhere else. But why? Finding a set of concentric circles incised on the metal does not help: this really is the Derridean *parergon* enshrined.

Perhaps Judd was best served by the long, high Spanish rooms with their arched ceilings, all the better to watch his pieces change as you walked past, as passengers in cars watch rows of houses. Judd's recent furniture works have confused the issue. The direct approach, the unfussy handling and a style nearer Shaker furniture than hi-tech are basic Judd, an artist who stated issues and worked things through, an artist in whose work even the slightest alteration became dramatic and interesting. And the corridors meant that Nauman could show a long work with neon tubes stretching into the distance, in alternate pink and yellow. Two Carl Andre floor pieces were set in corridors too, but with light coming in, hitting the polished metal surfaces. He too looked uncompromising and direct, a plain speaker. But that, perhaps, was predictable.

The real surprise was Flavin, whose habit of selling works with a slip of paper telling owners that anything they wished to do with their own property is their own business presumably means he did not turn up to see the results of his labours. He should have tried. From *Untitled (To Henri Matisse)* of 1964 onwards, Flavin's art has revealed an odd combination of subtlety and directness: clear, celebratory and unashamedly decorative. His large installations are less well known than the wall works. *Untitled (To Jan and Ron Greenberg)* was mounted perfectly, across the middle of a large room with two doors, inviting viewers to gaze first at a wall of yellow tubes, then to leave, re-enter by the other door and look at an equal-sized row of green ones, the glow of one colour seen like the aura around the other in each case. It is not neon, of course, but fluorescent light, to be purchased in containers of ready-made length. (Could this have explained Marcel Duchamp's interest in an artist whose views on difficulty could hardly have been more different from his own?) 'There is no hidden psychology, no overwhelming spirituality you are supposed to come into contact with', Flavin confessed in an interview in 1987. 'I like my use of light to be openly situational in the sense that there's no invitation to meditate, to contemplate . . . it is . . . as plain and open and direct an art as you will ever find.' *Ultra-Violet Fluorescent Light Room* from 1968 proves him wrong, perhaps. Visitors stayed there for hours, not in a mood of worship certainly, but because of the strange spatial distortions his L-shaped patterns of light brought about. And, despite his remarks, a high proportion of the works on show could rank as barriers rather than wall-bound icons. *Artificial Barrier of Blue, Red and Blue*, also from 1968, is an obvious example, a room that could not be negotiated because of a double ladder structure of light. *Green Crossing Green (To Piet Mondrian, Who Lacked Green)*, from 1966, two sets of illuminated fibreglass elements crossing in mid-air like flirtatious aqueducts, was also closed off. Whether or not he was doing what he thought he was doing, Flavin was undoubtedly the discovery of the entire exhibition, the dark horse of light sculpture.

Minimalism was a misnomer, experts will tell you. The Madrid show proved them right: one self-regarding object-maker, one dyed in the wool Duchampian, one frustrated cabinetmaker and a decorative painter in fluorescent tubing don't seem to have much in common, except a single problem: what happens when abstraction no longer looks like *Spirit of Dawn*, what to do when the shiny curve and even the two balls on top have disappeared. When the artists came up with their solutions, one man didn't laugh. His own mounting of his own collection showed why. Only he, perhaps, recognized immediately how gallery-bound sculpture had become. For him each work he bought involved dramas of space and scale, light and darkness, above all questions of access, resisted or denied. How close his interpretation was to that of the artists themselves no longer seems relevant, particularly on this occasion, when the hero was the Count himself, who had bought the work, preserved it and cared for it enough to perfect a virtuoso presentation of each separate piece. When history books are written a long chapter should be devoted to Panza's Minimalism, as persuasive an interpretation as we will ever get, and to his masterpiece of stage management: the display in Madrid.

An interview with Count Giuseppe Panza di Biumo

Published in Artscribe *76, Summer 1989.*

Stuart Morgan: *When did you stop collecting?*

Count Giuseppe Panza di Biumo: In 1976, but in the last few years it has started again. Some of the work is by artists we collected before – Dan Flavin, Eric Orr – others are new figures, like Robert Therrien.

Therrien looks traditional in the light of previous acquisitions like Robert Irwin or Don Judd.

He deals with forms like a painter, paying attention not only to the shape but also to the surface of the shape, and how this could be arrived at by using colour and different materials imposed on the basic sculptural form. This is not entirely new; up to the Middle Ages they used to paint sculpture. But it shows a new sensibility. A form develops in different sizes, with various materials – wood, steel, bronze – and colours are applied. Minimal sculpture showed how elements are different however similar they may appear, because of the relationship to the light and the space. Here the changes are of size, form and colour.

Do you take an interest in Simulationism?

This is an interesting way of continuing the research of Conceptual art. My favourite in this group is Peter Halley. Peter Halley is economical; he uses simple shapes and opposing colours to make complex works where every party interacts with every other. That is his great talent.

Do you see Halley's writings as a key to the paintings?

It is rewarding to read what artists write. But to understand the meaning of the art we have to look at the works themselves.

How did you react to the return to painting in the late 1970s and early 1980s?

This was a kind of art that was very far from my experience or interest. I never became involved in neo-Expressionism in Germany or the Transavantgarde in Italy. Art is important because it is the right expression of a period. At this time no one knew where to go, so they moved back instead of forward.

What about Cucchi?

Too easy, too clear. Not interesting.

Clemente?
He is the worst because he deals with sexuality, a human being's lowest instinct. Art should help people understand themselves, and live better.
How do you explain the popularity of some of the eighties art you so dislike?
Bad artists are often recognized immediately, because they are easily understood, whereas good art takes thirty years to be understood. The English radical paintings I collected, by Bob Law and Alan Charlton and Peter Joseph, are still not understood because they need thought. Joseph, for instance, deals not with colour and shape but with daylight; as the weather changes, the paintings change.
How do you react to Kiefer?
For me Kiefer is only a negative political statement about a people whose goal was power but who were defeated. His art is always about worldly power. This is why it is so sad. People who believe that in losing power they are losing strength are impossible to like. Admirers of Kiefer do not understand this. The same people who destroyed the values of Western civilization in the last world war are still alive, as the last general elections in Germany demonstrate. People are impressed by Kiefer because it is something they understand immediately. And it is not against Nazism but for it.

This art which deals with politics or the body reveals the situation of a society which has lost its direction. When we don't know what to do we don't try to understand what is new or look to the future. This art is just a documentation of a place where so many new generations lost their souls.
Don't you see Warhol and Beuys as political?
No. Both of them took a critical view of society because they believed in something important that society was unable to achieve: Warhol was strongly critical of the American way of life, of people who believed only in goods. Beuys made a powerful attempt to reveal a new society very far from a present which is intent on productivity.
You once spoke of Beuys as a medieval artist.
Yes, he is an artist who reveals the soul of Europe in a faraway past of strong mystical experience with strong oppositions between terrestrial will and heavenly power, between self and sex, between the present and a better life to come.
Did Warhol feel this tension between good and evil too?
Very strongly. Warhol was dominated by the vision of death because he realized that the kind of life we are living brings death; we have deadly goals,

not good ones. He was willing to show how success is the only real goal, a success that happens for no reason. By using this system of mythical success we can show how wrong it is.

Do you still look at the work of Robert Morris?

Yes, but I believe the best were made twenty years ago.

Yet you have found younger artists who oppose or modify Minimalist tenets.

Certainly. Peter Shelton uses organic forms for making sculpture. Minimalism uses geometric shapes – squares, pyramids, circles – which are strictly intellectual; perfect circles and rectilinear lines do not exist in nature. Behind rational form Shelton deals with the possibility of organic form with a content that is rational but has that richness of the originality of form that nature makes. Another artist I like is Martin Puryear, who started to make sculpture at the end of the 1970s. His forms relate to animals, something alive, a deeper relation to nature. In New York there's Ford Beckman, a young painter who deals with Minimal shapes in a way not as intellectual as Ryman or Marden, with strong blacks and dirty whites that seem to have been consumed by time.

Over the last few years you have been involved in large projects which have long time spans. James Turrell's Roden Crater, *for example.*

Yes, making the crater into a work of art has been a long process. My first visit was in 1974, and I've been back many times since then. It is one of the most beautiful places. The crater needs special attention; it deals with the relation of man to nature. We are destroying our environment; man is getting too powerful and is unable to control that power.

When will the work be finished?

That's anybody's guess, because it is such a costly operation. The work of making the shape of the crater nearly perfect is almost over. Some earth still needs to be moved, but that can be done very soon. After that we have to build a tunnel from the foothills of the volcano to the centre in order to be able to see the sky. Inside the volcano we have to build entire rooms from which the stars, moon and sun can be seen. Each room costs $200,000 to make, but the interest in this project is increasing so we hope Turrell will find a sponsor. It is important for our society to realize that nature is a great mother and that we have to love her. Visiting the crater we feel we feel we are living between the earth and the sky. As we walk on the top of the crater we feel the horizon around us, we see mountains 200 miles away, we feel clouds coming out of the horizon, we fell that the earth is round, that the moon is large and the stars are very close. The light is clear; it is in an area where there are many astronomical observatories. You need to go and stay there, detached from daily life.

With Walter de Maria, as with Turrell, we are dealing less with works of art than with events.

I was also very interested to see the *Lightning Field* made by Walter de Maria with the DIA Foundation. One evening, one morning and one night in that place was a great experience. When we arrived, we could not see the work because the stainless steel poles, six metres high and very thin, are invisible at first, then closer not at all like stainless steel but like light coming out of the ground. At sunset and sunrise this is unique and beautiful. When the sun is gone there is still light because the earth is not completely dark but the poles reflect the light in the sky. The moment when the poles became a range of lights was unbelievably beautiful. De Maria's art always made a relation between the rational and the natural, the earth and mind of man.

You have said on more than one occasion that the future lies in huge large-scale programmes like this.

This is the result of the vision of Los Angeles artists. Especially in the 1960s and 1970s Los Angeles had a culture quite separate from that of New York, with a strong influence from the Far East and artists able to use the products of technology for making art. LA is a new city. Eighty years ago it was a small town. Now it is one of the most densely concentrated populations in the world. The emphasis on instability results in a contemplative tendency, a need to feel that individuality belongs to an entity which is above personal concerns.

Robert Irwin would be an exemplary Los Angeles artist.

Yes. He explored the relationship between the nature of perception and reality, from the point of view of a man with a strong philosophical background who spent time in Japan. In his work perception drifted from the object to the space, then to the light, and so that it became less and less material and more and more intellectual, a process which shows that knowledge of reality comes from our memory, not from facts in front of us. Western man is so involved with his relation to things that he loses contact with the real world, which is the inner world. Irwin reveals that knowledge is not in things but inside ourselves.

What is he doing at present?

Making a work for a public space. He is making a study of how to use the space at Miami airport.

May I ask you about the future of your collection?

The goal has always been to make the work available to public institutions for permanent installation. The first part of the collection, from the 1950s and 1960s, is on show at the Museum of Contemporary Art in Los Angeles. Now there is the possibility of a large space at MassMoCA in Massachusetts and part of the collection of Minimal art could be installed there. It is being built now, and I am confident that Tom Krens, the director, will find a solution to all the problems the museum has thrown up. This is the right moment to consider the problem of a space for the art of the last twenty years, because in future the art will be more difficult to find. Existing collections are being dispersed, and the cost of the works will increase in a big way. That would dispose of a large number of the Minimal works, but other parts of the collection are still available: the Minimal paintings, the Conceptual art and the environmental art from Los Angeles still need a space. The collection would fill several large museums. We need buildings with 800 to 10,000 square metres. At the Centro Reina Sofia in Madrid we were offered 6,000 square metres, with the result that all the works of Flavin in the collection could be exhibited, in spaces separate from other works.

I know that you own many plans for unrealized works.

Well, next summer there will be an exhibition at St Etienne of works by Richard Long and Bruce Nauman, and the plan is to make works by Nauman bought in 1971. And discussions are taking place about a big Los Angeles exhibition next year, showing Irwin, Turrell, Doug Wheeler, Maria Nordman and others.

Meanwhile you continue to look at younger artists. Do you find enough to satisfy you?

Certainly. There's Michael Brewster and Meg Webster, in Germany beautiful sculpture by a whole new generation like Schütte, Klingelhöller and Förg, and technological pieces by young Italians. Then there's Roni Horn, and Hap Tivey – there's plenty going on.

Future Perfect: Khlebnikov Revived

Published in Artscribe *68, March/April 1988.*

The stage is almost completely dark. Below a high wooden platform broken windows and naked light bulbs suggest the poorest part of a modern city. On a vast back wall of white plaster fragments of geometry are distinguishable, and, nearer the ceiling, icons. To the right, on the platform itself, the audience sees a wooden tower with a metal cage at the top and on their left a giant telegraph pole. From high wires stretched across the space between them a ragged figure is suspended, his face obscured, garbage bags tied to his arms and legs. He is declaiming poetry. And as he babbles about alphabets and numbers, the fall of civilizations and the destiny of mankind, old black-and-white movies of cityscapes are projected behind him. At the same time a soundtrack, played live on stage from the wooden tower, superimposes Tibetan chanting and pygmy voices, the Saharan wind and Russian bird calls, controlled like colours from a keyboard 'palette'. New York theatre critics called *Zangezi* 'undramatic'. Perhaps it was never meant to be drama at all. Its author called it a 'supersaga', 'a new kind of operation in the realm of verbal art', and composed it in twenty independent 'planes', each with his own rules and style, intersecting like elements of a geometric sculpture. In essence it is a poem with interruptions, recited by Zangezi, the hero, a thinly disguised mouthpiece for Khlebnikov himself.

After claiming to have discovered the laws of chronicity he crowned himself Velimir I, King of Time. He also elected himself President of Planet Earth. Eager to be distinguished from the Futurists, particularly the Italian variety, he voted himself onto a Martian Council and invited H.G. Wells and Marinetti to join him. His entire behaviour was directed toward a future described in detail in his writings. He envisaged a time when people with the power of flight would hover over lofty cities; when tastes and smells could be transmitted globally; when weather would be transformed into universal music; when news would be available 24 hours a day on vast Book Walls; when standardized living capsules would be transported anywhere by train or steamer, with their inhabitants inside, then slotted into skeleton structures based on natural forms. The beehive houses, poplar houses and flower houses Khlebnikov drew were to be set in environments where man and nature met on equal terms. In this stone-age future animals would be released from servitude, nudism would be the norm, earth and even smoke would have been made edible and mankind would adopt a universal language to ensure world peace.

'Words die, but the world stays young for ever', wrote Kruchenykh and Mayakovsky. Khlebnikov thought the reverse. His *zaum*, transrational poetry, handles words in two opposing ways at once: as found in dictionaries, with meanings and historical changes emphasized, and in peasant speech, with all its implicit music and magic. History was at work in language, Khlebnikov believed; changes of sound and of government were mysteriously aligned. Numbers provided another key; his *Tables of Destiny*, referred to in Plane 4 of *Zangezi,* offered equations that prophesied the eclipse of empires. With planes consisting solely of birdsong or pure colour, speeches in which sounds become letters and characters of the alphabet ride into battle, *Zangezi* is not only a hymn to its author's inklings of underlying order; it dramatizes his entire self-presentation. Zangezi makes converts but enemies too. In the epilogue two people read of his death and the destruction of his manuscripts by fiendish villains 'with big broad chins / And lips that went smack smack chomp chomp'. They so closely resemble the supermen in *Victory over the Sun*, who sing 'We get stronger like pigs', that Khlebnikov might be offering a deliberate alternative: a poetic titan as the driving force of the revolutionary apocalypse to come. Yelling 'Zangezi lives! It was all just a stupid joke!' the hero re-emerges to dispel rumours, as if to suggest that Zangezi represents not the lowest but the highest aspirations of mankind, at the farthest extreme from that revolutionary brutishness advocated elsewhere.

References to the Russian church are apposite. Not only is Zangezi a Promethean figure – at one point the collective shout of a thousand-strong crowd startles the gods, who take flight audibly – but one theory has it that transrational language was influenced by the glossalalia of Russian mystic sects. Such hints are necessary in any contemporary production of *Zangezi,* such as the one by Peter Sellars at the Brooklyn Academy of Music late in 1987, shown first at the Los Angeles County Museum of Art; after all, Tatlin accompanied his presentation with lectures and even an exhibition. In the 64 years between the two productions little has changed; Tatlin's reviewers agreed that his version was lifeless and amateurish. The DIA Foundation's major plan of translating the whole of Khlebnikov into English promises more unsuccessful productions of works by one of the most inspiring and visionary of modern failures.

Rem Koolhaas on Ivan Leonidov

Published in Artscribe *68, March/April 1988.*

Stuart Morgan: *Why are you interested in Ivan Leonidov?*
Rem Koolhaas: He was the first architect in Russia to be a pure product of communism because he was a pupil of Vesnin at Vkhutemas. In the mid-twenties he was a big star at the school and made great experiments like the Lenin Institute. When Social Realism was introduced it was inevitable that modern architects would feel the pressure to relate to history in a non-classical way. In the early 1930s a competition was held to put the Ministry of Heavy Industry next to the Kremlin, which was a loaded problem in terms of both modernism and anti-modernism. Melnikov's plan was for a building in the form of a colossal W shape. The idea of putting the entire ministry into a single building and putting that next to the Kremlin and St Basil's Cathedral was crucial in terms of both symbolism and politics. Leonidov's project was sited in a park like Central Park. The three offices, between two low buildings, were in the shape of a rectangle, a circle and a triangle, and the columns supporting them were all set at different angles, defining courtyards. The colours were the same as those of St Basil's. The problem was how to anchor the project in a historical way. Since Leonidov felt that the rectangle shape was old-fashioned and that the circle was modern, and that stone is antique while glass is up-to-date, he made a dialectic between classicism and modernism by means of a planned gradation. So the plan of one tower is rectangular and in stone, one is curved and in stone and glass and another is circular and all glass. But, because the stone faces the glass, when the visitor stands with his or her back to the Kremlin the reflections of the other buildings are caught in the glass one, which enfolds them, involves them and outdoes them. So the vision is of a future unfolding.
The black tower has little platforms outside.
They are gold and in the shape of toadstools, and since they coincide with lobbies or voids inside the building I guess that they were espresso bars or lunch rooms where the workers could dine on gold platforms and survey the city.
And the top of the highest building?
The lozenge shapes are just decorative, a response to the cupolas of St Basil's, but probably the roof would have been used for physical culture

demonstrations or for sending signals in semaphore.

What happened to the project?

The entire competition was cancelled because collectivism and other developments made it impossible. So both the project and the entire competition exist only as a daydream from start to finish.

What happened to Leonidov?

Because he was such a star in the 1920s it was easy to attack 'Leonidovism' in the uninformed way Prince Charles is attacking current architecture in Britain, as wholly bad. Leonidov had a very hard time. He lost his job and his apartment in Moscow. But when you can't stand the heat in Moscow it is always possible to escape to the provinces. At some point he was working in the Crimea on sanatoria and children's hotels. It is there that his only existing work stands: an outdoor staircase.

Can you explain why there was so much pressure to silence him?

He was a kind of genius. His extremism consisted of pushing one kind of abstract architectural language as far as it could go.

What interested you about him when you began work on him in 1972?

Well, my office is called the Office of Metropolitan Architecture. My book *Delirious New York* employed no single formal criterion for architecture; I was interested only in *programmes*, the way architecture can be used to trigger problems. Russian architecture of the 1920s and 1930s interests me for obvious reasons. For example, Melnikov planned Laboratories of Sleep, a chain of motel structures circling Moscow, where people could sleep at given angles, listening to the sound of nightingales and the sound of waves – most Russians have never seen the sea, remember – and gases would be released into the atmosphere to help them relax. Oddly, the architects of Radio City Music Hall in New York saw this when they visited Russia. So they released ozone into the air-conditioning and advertised that a visit to Radio City was 'as good as a month in the country'. My new book *The Contemporary City*, a deliberately downbeat title, concerns cities like Atlanta, Tokyo and the peripheries of Paris.

Why the periphery?

Out of the 8 million inhabitants, 6.5 million live in new towns on the outskirts in huge apartment blocks. Some architects have applied themselves to the problem, like Manolo Núñez, Kevin Roche or Ricardo Bofill, whose gigantic complexes stand in the middle of nowhere looking like marooned spaceships.

It's light-years from Le Corbusier.
It doesn't relate at all. The whole discipline of planning is about control. As the century wore on control was discredited; every attempt at coherence backfired. The entire issue becomes one of living with certain developments. All those things have an immutability. It is important to stop looking at them as disadvantages.
What a pity that Leonidov's buildings are lost.
'Lost' is the wrong word. None of them was ever built.

Miroslav Krleža: The Return of Philip Latinowicz

Introduction to the edition published by Quartet Books Ltd, London, 1989; the novel was first published in 1932.

Early in Miroslav Krleža's *The Return of Philip Latinowicz* we catch sight of the hero as he looks at himself in a mirror: a pale, tired man with greying hair, wearing a French shirt and an English suit and carrying in his pocket an X-ray photograph of one of his lungs. Perhaps the reason for returning to his home town is mere nostalgia, as he supposes. Yet gradually other motives come to light: confronting his national identity, gaining a firmer hold on reality and discovering the truth about his parentage.

One premise is that all this has a bearing on Philip's painting, for Krleža's novel outlines not only a mid-life crisis, but also, perhaps, the maturing of an artist's talent. Traditionally, heroes are tested. In the case of artist heroes, their sensibility, not their valour, is on trial. Compare *The Return of Philip Latinowicz* with Thomas Mann's *Death in Venice* and common features emerge: journeys and breakdowns, the confrontation with an object of desire who transcends logic and beckons the artist to his death; the use of characters who serve only to highlight the hero's predicament; above all, the uncertainty of the dividing lines between dream and reality, factual author and fictional protagonist. No amount of distancing, no degree of irony can conceal the use of fiction as surrogate autobiography. It can be no accident that the author was Philip's age – almost forty years old – when he wrote *The Return*, and that the book addresses what must have been major problems for Krleža himself.

Decline is uppermost in Philip's mind on his return; confronted by decadent local aristocracy, he experiences both a heightened sense of his European identity and a feeling of acute parochialism. Konstanjevec, on the Danubian plain of Croatia, was once Pannonia, part of the Roman Empire. So, he concludes, it must retain some of its former grandeur. He may be mistaken. Balocanski, the man he could have become, compares his own fate with that of the Romans: 'That was Rome, what I am now, a heap of trampled, flyblown meat.' Images of decay recur throughout the book, as well as misshapen figures, more frequent as the plot progresses, who may be regarded either as part of the landscape or as delusions of Philip's. By the time of the feast of St Rock, the undercurrent of violence can no longer be subdued; savagery seems unavoidable, as the omens suggest. The tension that gathers in the course of the novel, like a storm about to break, needs little explanation. In the early 1930s Germany was drawing ever closer to full-scale regression designed to unite high and low, old Liepach as well as Joe Podravec. Perhaps the only mode that does justice to such events is the grotesque, with its suggestion that brute matter may take on a life of its own. 'The flesh waits for the awakening of its pulse', Philip explains to Bobocka. That he is describing the conception of a work of art seems doubly frightening; a human lightning conductor capable of attracting all the violence that surrounds him, he may also be guilty of misunderstanding it, or turning it to his own uses. And that, perhaps, is the most decadent act of all.

Surely one of the saddest protagonists in twentieth-century fiction, Philip seems dangerously passive, exiled from even his own experience, as if someone else were leading a life for him. Krleža records his sensitivity to vision and sound in one long stream after another, as stimuli overwhelm him, breaking barriers between past and future and making the present as poignant as it is deceptive, as if his masochism is so intense that he refuses to focus on it for fear of umediated emotion. Instead, some internal censor intervenes, allowing him to feel what he needs when he needs it. A morose state of mind is suitable for the realization of his ideas, we are told, as if this could be willed. It can, of course; as an unusually gifted artist – a point that is never in question – Philip Latinowicz is equipped with a brain and senses but also an apparatus for managing his own talents. Is it really surprising that he moves among people less creative than he and that he so overvalues them that he even falls in love with one of them? His creative machinery has taken over, that is all. To accuse him of aestheticization, of using other people or refusing to acknowledge that, in Balocanski's words, 'Art is beautiful but life is serious', means ignoring the kind of stimulation artists need: a perverse, even masochistic stimulation that demands a passive role, a position from which the eye can be encouraged to outrun the brain. 'Man really sees only what he notices for the first time', Philip believes, and uses all his skill to make paintings that bypass intellect, release him from introspection and echo his original sensation. In such a project passivity is all-important, knowledge is subordinated to feeling – 'stupid as a painter', in Duchamp's taunting phrase – and morality becomes irrelevant. Philip aspires to a state of childlike wonder. In the eyes of the world, however, he is simply out of control.

Krleža traces the limits of Philip's control, drawing ambiguous conclusions. In his work a painter can force metaphors to seem real, to turn three dimensions into two, to suggest skin without the intervention of touch, to give merely aesthetic coherence to sensations that lack real unity. Considered this way, the artist's vocation smacks of unhealthy tampering, wholesale confusion of art and life, as when Philip admits to himself that his homecoming resembles the return to an old picture he never mastered. Krleža's narrative technique, with its mobile point of view, capable of overhearing Philip's thoughts only to pause and remind readers what a strange person he is, subjects his hero to the same kind of treatment he gives his subjects. It introduces an anarchic element into the novel, not exactly a comic but certainly a parodic note. Perhaps Philip's real punishment lies in his inability to construe images or wrest power from them, even though he might have played a major part in their generation. By the time he succeeds in witnessing a version of the primal scene he never interrupted as a child, the climax of a melodramatic plot with unbelievable characters which he may have fabricated simply as a distraction from a dull holiday in the country, he has become hopelessly embroiled in his own dramatic masterpiece, a succession of tableaux vivants of which he is the sole spectator.

Part Fauve, part Expressionist, Philip serves as focus for the familiar accusations of fragmentation and incoherence that accompanied modernist experiment. His exile, rootlessness and loss of a defined audience – he can deal with the problem of a church window in New Orleans by letter – are the point of departure for Krleža's book. By the end various resolutions have been proposed: that Philip's return may have reconciled the divisions his modernist beliefs served to enforce, that a stronger faith in national identity has improved his artistic vision or that really after violent catharsis healing is bound to take place. But what really happened? Does the ending leave Philip and his mother locked in permanent combat, while strangers have drifted in and out of his life, strengthening his painting in the process? Or has he found that instead of lying in artificial, stylized tatters, his world is really ruined, along with his sanity?

Kabakov's Albums

Published in Artscribe 75, May 1989. A second essay on Kabakov, 'Empty Rooms', was published in Forum International *(Antwerp) 14, 1992.*

Between 1970 and 1980 the Russian artist Ilya Kabakov made 50 'albums', which have gradually come to be known in the West. Kabakov's own description of them is the simplest:

> The 'albums' are a stack of solid sheets of white (or grey) cardboard consistently of the same size (72.5 x 35cm). Drawings, cuttings, documents, texts and other works, painted by the author or ready printed, are stuck to their front side. These stacks of sheets (their number varies between 35 and 100) are contained in boxes 75 x 38 x 15cm in size, which are placed on a small plinth in a vertical position. The spectators sit in front of the opened box. One of them turns the pages one after the other, from left to right. They look at the drawings and read the text.[1]

It is no accident that the albums invariably end with a white page. One result is a heightened sense of passage, and of the brevity of a single life history. Another is the feeling that the amount of possible interpretation of events is severely limited. Perhaps it is not the whiteness, then, but the black lines by which it is defined that must be considered the fundamental gesture in his art, not simply in the albums but also elsewhere. (Recent sculptures, more like installations, shown in Paris early this year, consisted of furniture, purportedly from home, placed on cardboard and other materials to dissuade visitors from closer investigation.) Since anything is possible within the demarcated territory of the albums' 'white' pages, whiteness becomes a symbol of perfect ambiguity.

Above all, Kabakov is a storyteller; his decision to abandon a form of Abstract Expressionism for an elaborate kind of fiction, no doubt influenced by his profession as an illustrator of children's books, must be counted as the biggest step in his career. Robert Rauschenberg's famous statement about wishing to operate between 'art' and 'life', a logical development from one type of Abstract Expressionism, led to a confusion of the real and the depicted, or alternatively of different levels of depiction. Instead of teasing viewers into supposing that 'picturing' might not be taking place, Kabakov decided to emphasize it all the more. The degree of interaction both men desired reached its zenith with monochrome surfaces: Rauschenberg's 'white' paintings, which acted as screens for the shadows of their viewers, and Kabakov's uninflected white rectangle, neatly signed and elegantly displayed, as if to announce that now a problem has been posed, discussion can begin, based (perhaps) on the commentaries provided.

And in the period between the late 1960s and the mid-1970s, Kabakov recalls, discussion was concerned with 'sublime, absolute, definite questions', part of the unusually metaphysical climate which prevailed at that time. One of the stories in his 'Ten Characters' series[2] is about a man who develops a theory that energy moves in sheets about the universe. Since the movement of these vectors is predictable, it is possible to calculate when one will come close enough to the earth to permit him to reach it and escape to some other zone. Secretly he begins work on a giant catapult. That occupies half his time. The other half is devoted to split-second calculation. When he disappears, the reader has only the accounts of neighbours to rely on. Flying is a recurrent theme for Kabakov; *Komarov, Who Flew Away* (1972–5) involves a man who jumps from his balcony to his death but who in the passage from life to death discovers that the apparent order of things has changed and that it is possible to escape gravity and float at will. Seeing these stories as ironic comments on the Russian space programme or, indeed, the cosmic pretensions of the early twentieth-century Russian avant-garde is insufficient; the fairy-tale aspects of flight are stated and celebrated, but they remain in the realm of fairy tale. Having said that, they reveal the potential of fairy tale and dream, wish-fulfilment and popular mythology for stating unconscious needs. Flying occurs in a more indirect way in an album called *Archipov Who Looks through the Window*, in which the proximity of death is measured by what a sick man can see out of his bedroom window. This is a familiar pragmatic nightmare in Kabakov: point-of-view becomes character. But in Archipov's case it veers into theological debate, as fullness of perception gives way to the sight of angels' wings, which exclude everything else from vision. Finally, the image of a circular hole, which first appeared in the story as a way of drawing an apple, that familiar focus of meditation, now appears as a way of registering Archipov's diminishing hold on the visible. When it appears, the image of total whiteness doubles as transfiguration and annihilation – the opposite, perhaps, of the blackness that Primakov chose to confront in another of

Kabakov's albums, by sitting in a cupboard all day. Angels' wings can be a topic for discussion, but essentially they are not open to questioning in a fiction of the type Kabakov is constructing.

Another topic for discussion is aesthetics. In the series 'Ten Characters' everyone in the communal apartment block Kabakov describes has his or her own perception of art. One resident has spent years arranging displays of garbage in a boiler- room everyone assumed was locked. A very short man has made art tacked to screens for residents to walk around and read. (This involves closing the communal kitchen for an entire day. When his neighbours are allowed in, they are disappointed that he has not spent his time cooking food for them and inadvertently kick the display over. And on finally discovering that he has a supporter, he is upset to discover the man is as short as he.) The interest in rubbish and movable signs refers to aspects of Kabakov's art that would emerge more powerfully after the decade of thinking and planning that the albums represent. (In the early 1980s, for example, he was displaying labelled garbage.) But his characterization of himself as 'The Person Who Describes his Life through Characters' diminishes Kabakov's achievement: to have established a kind of private academy in which aesthetic possibilities could be explored, regardless of the actual art being made at any given time. Critics have made much of his struggle to achieve impersonality, to create the 'polyphonic' novel Mikhail Bakhtin proposed earlier in the century. Kabakov's own view of his albums, with their permanent rectangle in which the action takes place, is slightly different: an attempt to bring the consciousness of his 'actors' in line with that of his 'spectators', all of whom are locked into consciousness itself. His final white pages could signify the abandonment not only of a particular character but of the entire project of presenting that character, a renunciation by Kabakov of his own vision. Boris Groys has argued that this renunciation can be regarded as a way for the author to keep a possibility of 'personal Utopia'.[3] That conclusion need not be so optimistic. The bright light that shines so strongly that it dissolves edges and, finally, images – a description of his own white pages by Kabakov himself – may be destructive, after all, or at least an acknowledgement of frailty. Like the character whose philosophical views consist of noting the opinions of others, Kabakov (like any artist) veers dangerously towards solipsism without discussion of his art. As in any Elizabethan epilogue, the white page indicates that his and his characters' very existence as fictitious actors depends on the applause of an audience.

Yet, finally, the repetition of the image of whiteness is bound to assume greater and greater importance for the reader of the albums, partly as a reminder that plots, like lives, give out: in other words that the idea of the artist as male genius, like Rodin's Balzac, endlessly producing art, is no longer viable or reasonable. Partly, the whiteness serves to indicate the meditative effect of turning the pages of the albums. But partly it seems to promote a mingled feeling of frustration and calm. 'The blankness of the white paper is almost the total equivalent of silence', Kabakov has written, 'which does not mean total negation but rather the converse – total fullness that surpasses any message!'[4] One of his best critics, Claudia Jolles, has interpreted this as a theory aligned with those of Malevich in his *Non-objective World*.[5] The truth that emerges from the albums may be a little harsher – that life is more petty, more tiresome, more circumstantial than we would like; that our limitations far outweigh our capacity to fulfil our dreams; that the individual self is lost in a babble of voices, that there is no single truth; that the utopians among us are destroyed gradually but automatically, and that artists' lives are short. The most they can hope for is to make not a work but a method, as Kabakov has.

1. Ilya Kabakov, *Description of the Albums* (Frankfurt: Portikus, 1988).

2. Published as Ilya Kabakov, *Ten Characters* (London: ICA, 1989).

3. Boris Groys, *The Artist and his League of Personages* (New York: Ronald Feldman Gallery, 1988), n.p.

4. Ilya Kabakov, *Okno* (Bern: Benteli, 1985), p.26.

5. Claudia Jolles, *Okno*, p.26.

Stuart Morgan interviewed on Conceptual art by Juan Vicente Aliaga and José Miguel G. Cortés

Published in Arte Conceptual Revisado/Conceptual Art Revisited, *ed. Juan Vicente Aliaga and José Miguel G. Cortés, Universidad Politécnica de Valencia, Departamento de Escultura, 1989.*

J.V. Aliaga/J.M.G. Cortés: *To begin with, could you define Conceptual art, taking into account Henry Flynt's definition, which goes 'Conceptual art is the art whose material is the concept'? Could you also make a comparison between late sixties/early seventies Conceptual art and so-called neo-Conceptualism?*
Stuart Morgan: The basis of the late sixties Conceptualism was a set of experiments in which an object was either excluded or replaced with a definition of an object. This resulted in a tendency to make either linguistic works or examinations of what an 'objectless' artwork would be. The unspoken motive of neo-Conceptualism may be to repeat those earlier experiments because the significance of the vanishing object still has not been taken to heart. This is one way of looking at it, though it must be added that the implicit political meanings of an art of concepts have not been perpetuated in neo-Conceptualism, which speaks of a fall back into the acceptance of art as object, object as commodity and commodities as an integral part of the very gallery system that had been interrogated in the late sixties.
Do you think there is a double notion of Conceptual art which could be separated into a linguistic and tautological approach on the one hand and on the other the dematerialization of the art object? Could both aspects be amalgamated into a superior definition?
There is no duality here: just two directions taken by the same impulse, which was also referred to, for example, as 'conceptual poetry' in some of its first manifestations (and, since the impulse is also critical, particularly of formalism, it might be best to regard Conceptualism as an implosion of traditional distinctions between separate fields). The lack of allegiance to any single definition, the uncertainty of any audience beyond a clique and the antagonism towards the gallery system gave sixties Conceptualism the air of a traditional modernist movement at a time when modernism had become

refined and clubby, needlessly aestheticized by Greenbergian disciples.

Like (for example) Russian Constructivism, Conceptualism was a utopian art; the future was implicit in the methods of the art itself. In the future there would be time for group activity, play of the most intellectual kind, and an art community which would embrace and be embraced by the rest of society. That was the implication, and the sudden surge of international recognition demonstrated how precisely these ideals corresponded with those of an entire generation.

Do you think that in Britain there was a kind of inflation of the Conceptual art epitomized by the experiences of Art & Language and the analytical art backed by a magazine like Studio International*?*

Studio helped by working its way through the excesses of Greenbergian criticism, preparing the way for closely argued argumentation like that of the Art & Language group. History writers thrive on definitions and large generalizations. How 'British' the Art & Language group were and are is open to debate. A month ago one of their maps was included in the Situationist survey at the Centre Pompidou in Paris, for instance.[1] Maybe that came as a surprise to some people who had forgotten that the psychogeographical branch of Situationist thinking was British-based. It is important to stress the Britishness of Art & Language – the art school aspect, the constant use of humour to attack opponents, the self-conscious pilfering from British linguistic philosophers, indicating a tradition no one seemed willing to acknowledge. Yet the way their combination of hectoring and amateur scholarship has been taken up by another generation – the group around *Durch* magazine, for example, confirms the political usefulness of making a problematic context for argument. The very basis of what historians might choose to call 'Conceptual art' may lie in this suspension of context, which the late sixties generation viewed as a legacy of Marcel Duchamp. Earlier in the decade Duchamp would have been regarded as the forerunner of Pop – the man who displayed garbage, and somehow changed low into high art. In the late sixties this changed and the urinal and the bicycle wheel were regarded as models for the floating context. After criticizing the reductive aspect of art history, I seem to be replacing one reduction with another. Nevertheless, it is crucial to any reconstruction of the late sixties to see what was jettisoned and what was common to the discussion taking place. Briefly, in Britain and elsewhere, the idea of 'dematerialization' proved so potent that making was subordinated to a rethinking of the relevance of art. The importance of exhibitions like

'When Attitudes Become Form' lay in the shared basis of the experimentation it revealed. One early essay by Victor Burgin, 'A Very Abstract Context' (*Studio International,* November 1970), shows what I mean. The 'floating context' was that which annihilated the political hopes of the 68 generation, of course: an overestimation of the humanity or sensitivity or idealism of their opponents, or perhaps a refusal to be complicit in the workings of a world that they despised. In artistic terms, the idea of a 'moment' when no one knew anything and went back to basics was invaluable. Yet, of course, there never was a 'moment'; we will never be able to grasp it, except as a convenience of our own. In his book on post-Minimalism and elsewhere Robert Pincus-Witten argued against the entire idea of 'Conceptual art'. Without agreeing with his arguments, I think the idea of absence instead of presence – the idea of what didn't happen in the late sixties instead of what did – may be a more useful metaphor for a 'period' that is no period at all.

Joseph Kosuth was American editor of Art-Language. *Do you think that there is an American way of dealing with Conceptual art that differs from the British way?*

After a brief period during which he was writing *Art after Philosophy*, Kosuth left Art & Language, and there have been disagreements between him and the group in subsequent years. That is one question. Yes, there is an American Conceptual art, that's the other. It would not be too difficult to trace fundamental concepts of nineteenth-century American intellectual history through to art of the 1960s.

For instance?

There is an implicit connection between the non-hierarchical ideals of American Minimalism and the ideals of Jacksonian democracy, for example, which passes into Conceptualism in the work of Douglas Huebler. And Transcendentalism is characterized by a lurch from detail to entirety, from Brahma to the beanfield, which resurfaces in Robert Barry.

Recently a lot has been said about 'Eccentric Abstraction', a term of Lucy Lippard's to describe the work of Eva Hesse, Bruce Nauman, Keith Sonnier and others. Do you think this movement, assuming it was one, intersected with the rest of Conceptual art?

The 'Eccentric Abstraction' exhibition at the Fischbach Gallery was a moment, not a movement. Pincus-Witten, who found the term 'Conceptualism' useless, tried instead to deflect attention from it to a kind of neo-Constructivism, the mathematics of Mel Bochner and Dorothea Rockburne. Mainstream opinions have run counter to his. (I have always been baffled by Pincus-Witten's unwillingness to cope with Dennis Oppenheim, Robert Smithson, Alice Aycock. There's a little generation unaccountably omitted in his writing, though to be fair he admitted that he had overlooked John Baldessari and rectified this later.) An argument for process has to be based on a series of snapshots rather than solid achievements – Richard Serra's lead splashes, Bruce Nauman's early works and so on – and Pincus-Witten's method is completely suited to his argument. But this is the drawback; he is so keen to pounce on art-historical moments as they happen that the project becomes one of misapplied art historical method. The momentary quality of 'process art' – which, I may be suggesting, veers off into sheer transience – represents an emotive, sexual aspect of art which seemed under threat. Morris, above all, tried to bring the two together in a series of unjustifiably ignored experiments. Judd has said in a very recent interview that Morris has always been an unoriginal artist with no ideas of his own. It is high time he and we acknowledged that, or at least decided that originality is not what we go to Morris's work to find. But my hunch is that for years he was on the verge of making grand reconciliations between the strands we are sitting here and picking over. The early seventies provided a variety of basic moves for artists. 'Process' was one, but to elevate that to the status of a movement seems too pompous. That's all.

So the recent resurgence of interest in Eva Hesse doesn't strike you as a revaluation of her approach, or a revaluation of 'Eccentric Abstraction' in general?

Eva Hesse's reputation has reached a strange crisis. To many people of my age, who saw the work first hand, she seems self-evidently one of the great lyric talents of the century. But – and here we are still talking about the relation of 'Process art' to Conceptualism – built into her decision-making was transience of the result. How much did she take into account of the fact that her pieces would fall apart? Even when they were in good condition after her death their installation was problematic. Only Donald Droll could hang the complex, dangling works, for example, partly from photographs, partly from memory. He needed unlimited time and sometimes gave up and admitted he could not get it right. (The problem of Beuys installations after Beuys's death will throw up some of the same problems.) Now a generation of people half as old as I am need persuading all over again, and rightly; neither the sentimental worship of her sickness nor the first-hand accounts of contemporaries will satisfy them. As a model of feminist strategy or as a study in artistic masochism, Hesse will survive. As an example, and perhaps a victim, of the intersection of concept and process, she may prove to be a historical oddity, bearing in mind any artist great enough can prosper under the most inopportune historical circumstances. At least the problem of impermanence must be approached directly. Consider the case of Morris Louis, whose canvases are being restored already and are bound to perish, but whose approach to this problem of impermanence can't be justified so easily.

Douglas Huebler said that there were too many objects in the world so he didn't want to add more, and Lawrence Weiner said that it was up to the collectors to have his sentences printed or built. Don't you think that in some way his writings have left a kind of presence that could perfectly be revitalized at any time by his collectors simply by putting the texts back on the walls? Is there an intersection between mental and physical space?

You could say that the act of concentrating on nothing, which constitutes a (sarcastic) definition of religious meditation as well as artistic creation, gave modernist abstraction a new twist. Just when the status of painting was becoming ever more certain and restricted, the prospect of an art in which a single ontological status would offset others provided one point of view about perception, and served as an intervention in a longer debate about creativity, regarded in a Romantic way. The tone of the intervention was democratic and common-sensical. The simple point that reality is registered in ways that have nothing in common, by languages that do not intersect logically but constantly battle for dominance, is stated by Joseph Kosuth's works incorporating dictionary definitions. Variations on this theme continued to provide the stuff of interesting art for a generation. Consider Richard Long, whose work concentrates on the impossibility of ever recording reality. Far from being 'about walking', as many commentators have concluded, it states the impossibility of gauging the interplay of mind, body and time in the cause of automotive activity by means of charts, monuments and allusions. Robert Smithson used a different trio of materials – mud, mirrors and mapping – to explore similar territory at one point in his career. Both men found a way of qualifying the thingness of sculpture while restating it. Many other examples could be given. Briefly, the entire Conceptual turn that art has taken in the last twenty years always involves intersections between mental and physical. Huebler's and Weiner's remarks about a surplus of objects recalls the subtitle of the exhibition 'When Attitudes Become Form', which was 'Live in Your

Head'. The concept became the art. But it was also necessary to find a solution to the problem of how artists could live by marketing such quicksilver items as ideas, without compromising their ideals too much.

Is there any connection between Conceptualism and Situationism?

A connection based on general similarities of approach, perhaps. Ideas of spectacle, détournement, the way texts were couched and promulgated, and their shared tone of revolutionary utopianism could be cited as proof. There may be another connection. The recent exhibition by Peter Wollen and Mark Francis for the ICA, London and the Centre Pompidou, Paris, and other places demonstrated conclusively that no exhibition could really be made of Situationism: that it was an impulse, not a set of works. Could it be that Conceptualism is best approached by assuming it never existed? Or, to be more logical, as if its impulse has still not been fully exhausted. The seventies, as art historians chronicle it – and 'art historians' in this case are usually journalistic hacks who take secondary sources and boil them down into easy generalisations and 'movements' – consists of an interminable series of dull '-isms': Process Art, Air Art, Earth Art, Performance Art, *ad nauseam*. Lucy Lippard's *Six Years* demonstrated that they were all the same thing, made by all the same artists.

Artists nowadays seem less interested in ideologies and in discussing social attitudes about art than they were in the sixties and seventies. Are the eighties particularly trivial and formalistic? Why?

The political temperature is different, modes of protest are different, the role of the galleries is different, the role of criticism is different and the part played by magazines is different. Doublethink and cynicism have escalated. No one assumes that writing a letter or marching through the streets with banners will achieve anything. Galleries protect their artists as Hollywood studios once protected their stars; they vet statements and generate or refuse to generate publicity about them. Since it is possible to manufacture a successful artist despite negative reviews and lack of critical interest, negative reviews have become meaningless and magazines have abandoned them. (That's one theory. The other is that magazines are controlled by advertising to such a degree that reviewing is a charade.) The question assumes that the role of the intellectual, which in most cases changed little between 1960 and 1980, has not changed now. It also proposes an equation between triviality and formalism which is not necessarily the case. What I'm saying about magazines seems less scandalous or biased if you stop to consider the quick and steady decline in the quality of newspaper journalism over the last decade, by the way.

Do you think of Simulationism as a puritanical development?

It's WASP (White Anglo-Saxon Protestant) art and there is bound to be repression in a making process that aims at the same degree of perfection as objects of industrial design. So perhaps the critical aspect of the making – Holzer's lightboxes, Alan McCollum's multiple objects, and so on – accounts for the preoccupation with the grotesque which has become all too evident as a reaction against technical purity. Meyer Vaisman's preoccupation with money, faeces and sex; Richard Prince's *Spiritual America*; Jeff Koons's undertones of bestiality and Cindy Sherman's increasingly hideous deformed identities could all be construed in this way.

The real question is where this leads. In the 1970s Joseph Beuys and Robert Smithson, to name two main examples, construct a dialectic between idea and matter (fat in Beuys, mud in Smithson), artificially – even comically – heightening a tension unresolved by Abstract Expressionism. It was perceived and dealt with by Barnett Newman, if we accept both Thomas Hess's estimate of Newman as a Kabbalist commentator and Harold Rosenberg's verdict that a Newman painting was either a transcendental statement or a piece of junk only good for throwing into the dustbin, but that *only those two choices existed*. Now, the emphasis in the recent work that I have mentioned seems thoroughly despiritualized, at first sight. Look again and it becomes plain that, in the work of Jeff Koons, for instance, the potential for spiritual meaning is remarkably strong. How it came to be this way is as mysterious as the question of any artist's maturation process. But it's obvious that the way forward has been through the examination of social ritual, and that applies to all the other artists I've mentioned.

Do you think there is something stylish in showing piles and piles of books and impenetrable texts, all sorts of writing and lists of words, both in the sixties and now?

As books become increasingly redundant, the experience of reading and the sculptural qualities of books will become evident. Conceptual artists have used both books and photography in a sculptural sense, as objects; consider Christian Boltanski's output of bookworks, for example. And the relationship between reading and looking in other ways (as one looks at pure abstraction) has been taken further in Conceptualism. (A working procedure like that of Lothar Baumgarten is not created without a generation of precedents.) Just as

Abstract Expressionism could easily have been named 'Abstract Surrealism', Conceptual art could easily have been referred to as 'conceptual poetry' in the early days. The fact that artists experiment with words in space, however insignificant in literary terms their experimentation may be – I'm thinking of Carl Andre's poetry as an example – can be related to concrete poetry, the world-wide, international movement that just preceded Conceptual art. But there are other powerful sources: sixties gurus like Cage or McLuhan wrote texts which moved increasingly further away from traditional linearity, in their format and in the kind of thinking they encouraged. McLuhan, of course, was a professor of literature who had researched the works of Thomas Nashe, an Elizabethan pamphleteer who straddled two distinct modes of rhetoric, those of the street and of the study, and bounced one off the other in his writings. By the time of *The Gutenberg Galaxy* (1962), with chapters on Don Quixote and Lear which stand as models of traditional literary criticism, he was already moving away from logical presentation of his arguments. *The Mechanical Bride* (1959) used techniques from Sigfried Giedion to organize arguments spatially. The fact that McLuhan was Canadian is not accidental. Northrop Frye was proposing a spatial model for thinking about literature in an ahistorical way, and Wyndham Lewis spent his last, blind years in Canada. Anthropology and religion had their oddballs too, Father Walter Ong and Edmund Carpenter, the latter a difficult figure to estimate because his papers are still being edited and the large proportion of his work remains unknown. The cusp between read and spoken, the idea of reading a book without moving your lips, or a newspaper without moving your head from side to side. Basic questions are repeated throughout McLuhan's writing, and he spent longer thinking what a book was than almost anyone, synthesizing insights from major modernists (Joyce, Lewis, Pound) and perpetuating an anti-Eliot, anti-Symbolist stance. The same kind of approach could be applied to John Cage, another sixties guru whose texts and music and notation supported the same general notions: that the meaning of a thing resides in what it is, not somewhere else. Essentially it is an argument against traditional thinking of composition as parts that support other parts, and historical thinking, and goal-orientation in general.

There is a downhome quality about Jasper Johns's refusal of Symbolism or what Charles Olson chooses to make of Pound that marks the thinking of Black Mountain College, and that too becomes an important sixties strand. The upshot is this. Everything they were saying and the way they chose to say it took a strong and knowing approach to space and time, and reminded us that a confluence of Western and Eastern thinking would become the highest and most urgent cultural priority in years to come, that progress was a redundant notion, that sexuality must detach itself from any needs beyond its own satisfaction (the hardest of all lessons in the age of AIDS) and that experiment in art should be sacrificed to wisdom (for what are Cage, McLuhan, Buckminster Fuller, Norman O. Brown, Timothy Leary and others but born-again Victorian sages of the kind of Emerson or Ruskin?) and that a politics of the body should prevail in art as well as in the outside world. To return to your question, if you are asking whether books and texts are some kind of fad in Conceptualism, my answer is no. The reasons they are there have to do with a cultural moment, in which type and typesetting and reading (as opposed to speech) became the matters of importance they remain. Henry Flynt, whose definition of Conceptual art you began by quoting, could certainly be categorized as 'impenetrable'. A figure like Arakawa I find impenetrable. Consider their ways of thinking as alternative to the accepted norm, simply. Or consider their texts in other ways, as sculpture or poetry. The question is whether Conceptual art would have meant the same if it had been beamed free of charge from one computer to another. The answer is no. It speaks of the studio which has become a study, the pleasures of thought and its freedoms, and a kind of public that it wants – precisely the people who subscribe to small magazines or run them. This is the world of Conceptualism in the late sixties and early seventies, of course, not today.

Are you thinking of Simulationism?

Both newer artists and the continuing work of older practitioners. On paper, the contexts of (say) Barbara Kruger and Sol LeWitt seem different enough. In context, the two strains of Conceptual activity have helped each other in a critical and a market sense, and the younger generation has helped to direct attention back to the older. In critical terms, the claims made for Cindy Sherman, Jenny Holzer and the rest are quite different and their public may also be different. And very recently, their careers have turned a corner. As they move into mid-career, figures such as Sherrie Levine, Richard Prince and others are interpreted in the light of their previous work and their choice to break free or to continue in the paths on which they have begun. Suddenly, now, Sherman's art speaks of our deepest collective fears, of exile, madness and death; Vaisman resembles a bad comedian going through his offensive routines; McCollum looks like a magician bringing out one great spectacle after another. And in each case our readings of their new works are conducted in the light of their previous careers – a Conceptual approach, but escalated now, so that each new development or entrenchment is awaited and analysed in detail. This means, of course, that the art world has penetrated Conceptualism through and through. The image of the studio/library in a little apartment has given way to a venture with assistants, perfect manufacture and a minimum of the friendly amateurism that characterised the late sixties. The entire business is clean, business-like, knowing to the point of cynicism.

And self-absorbed, it seems. Are there any New York artists of that generation who embrace social problems?

All of them, in an art sense, but not in any other, in most cases. And that leads to problems, as it always has done. The achievement of New York Conceptualism is to have made a platform for visual debate that is so vivid it flouts accusations of cynicism or financial complicity. The challenge for these artists is to understand how to control a medium which involves an unorthodox attitude to social research as well as expressing the obsessions of the researcher. In a general way the work tells us about the time. Koons's dustless vacuum cleaners or Ashley Bickerton's snatches of erotic fantasy inscribed on his armoured paintings could have been produced only in the era of AIDS, for example, when the practical principles of what is physically safe or not are often disguised as the return of a Manichean morality, and where solitariness is a given. (The techniques of closure employed by neo-Conceptualists have an air of loneliness and yearning that recall yet another Duchampian prototype: the 'Sad Young Man' motif of the early work, with its implied equation of solipsism, masturbation and creativity.) Problems arise when a figure like Koons makes statements, because, due to the nature of his work, those statements are about money and power and it becomes difficult to pass them off as little poems or alternative, supplementary artworks. The debates in Europe over the degree of play that is advisable with political ideas in art – attacks on Gilbert & George for joking about right-wing politics or Martin Kippenberger for toying with what appears to some like neo-Nazism – throw up a score of questions: about controlled meaning, which is wiry and electric; about avoiding a dandyish, uncommitted attitude to one's own output, and so on. The answer to your question is, 'Yes, there are New York artists of a post-Conceptual cast of mind who embrace social problems, like Krzysztof Wodiczko, but directness is not in the nature of the statement made by the artists we've been discussing'.

Walking around the third floor of the Centre Georges Pompidou it is possible to see plenty of Conceptual work on display. But however hermetic, cold and distant it was meant to appear, it now looks almost decorative.

The answer could lie in the nature of museums. Or it could have something to do with the difficulty of recreating installations, which may be one reason for that retreat from installation in recent art, highlighting older figures like Buren or LeWitt who continue to work in their old ways. Installation is primarily a European issue, perhaps, since the influence of Arte Povera has been so strong here. Artists like Rebecca Horn, Christian Boltanski, Lothar Baumgarten, Niek Kemps and many others need to make their own space. And spaces for their own work will be beyond their control after their deaths. A third answer could be that the works are too locked into their own time, too concerned with smaller and now irrelevant debates, to persuade us now. I don't believe this. Far from being hermetic, it seems to me that the best Conceptual works have a claim to be considered as great public art. But, like all public art, they need sensitive installation. In the Pompidou Centre's exhibition 'Les Magiciens de la Terre' a single work by On Kawara was shown in a large room on the third floor which uncharacteristically – given the rest of the exhibition – was not blocked off but looked out into the city of Paris. The piece was called *One Million Years* and consisted of twelve books placed open on a large table in the middle of the room, with twelve chairs, one for each volume. The books contained figures, the notations of years BC up to the year zero. After looking at them, as one looks at a text which cannot be read but can only be thought about, the viewer might turn back to the opening page, with its author, title and dedication – to all the people who were alive and are now dead – then walk to the window, look out to the city of Paris, seeing no figures at all, only roof-tops. Anyone from any country can understand a work like that, and with a little help from the installation, can see the universality and nobility of the way the theme of time has been dealt with. Having said this, the work in question would not leap to mind as a good example of gallery art as it is usually understood. Instead it demonstrates the continuing contribution of classic Conceptualism: to free our thinking by encouraging us to see things at a slight angle.

1. The exhibition referred to was 'Sur le passage de quelques personnes à travers une assez courte unité de temps: à propos de l'Internationale Situationniste 1957-1972', Centre Georges Pompidou, 1989.

Jeff Koons

Published in Artscribe *74, March/April 1989*

Even people can make themselves into playthings. Bunny girls know it, toyboys learn it. Jeff Koons has made it a subtext for his art. One publicity shot for his latest tour shows the artist grinning. The tan and the flawless texture of his skin make it look as though his face is carved out of solid Formica, while his hair, flicked casually in post-punk style, heightens an allure that is threatened by a pig's head nuzzling in alongside his and by a smaller piglet Koons is clutching. Other shots are set at cocktail time beside the pool, when leggy lovelies vie for his attention and stuffed animals stand guard like heraldic beasts. Are the animals there to ruin the illusion? If so, they fail. The tone of expectancy is maintained – heightened, even – by the perfection of figures, sets and scenario. Koons's mode combines dignity, clownage and a childlike sense of beauty, only to rise beyond this to a vivid sense of wonder.

In musicals everything is wrong until the actors start singing. They may burst into song as ordinary people do, or allow their voices to modulate and become more rhythmic until, by easy stages, they have begun to make music. Our relief is overwhelming. The atmosphere summoned up by Jeff Koons is something like that. We could say he is serious about not being serious, or that the 'him' and the 'us' distinction in his work has been reduced to the level where, instead of prescribing or preaching, he simply provides his viewers with what he knows they need. More specifically, it could be argued that as a real figure, just emerging from the advertising medium in which he is embroiled, he succeeds in both ratifying and outdoing it. Do we really believe that Elizabeth Taylor uses the perfume she advertises? Does the firm that makes the perfume believe it or think that *we* believe it? Who has the power over whom is the ultimate, and most delicate, question in advertising now, as it was in film during the days of the classic Hollywood star system, which also depended on perfect control of distances between audience and product. Koons is beyond the stage of commenting on some art world star system. Instead he luxuriates in it, baby-fashion, continuing to perfect his pose as the overgrown trinket any star must agree to become. It is a fragile position at best, and he realises it. Another publicity shot shows him flanked by sea-lions with garlands of flowers around their necks. Relaxing in his beach robe, he sits triumphant before a pom-pommed circus-style pavilion, serenely confronting the incoming tide, a quietly confident Canute.

A carnivalesque undercurrent unifies Koons's recent work: a parade of cherubs, cartoon characters, children and animals that brings fascination and repulsion into close alignment. Scale is everything. The sculpted vignette of a brown bear grabbing a policeman's whistle depends on the fact that the bear is taller than the policeman, so the figure of authority is viewed as a child. Yet however docile, a gigantic bear carved out of solid wood becomes increasingly sinister the closer one gets. And two of his relatives, waving and smiling, present an image of madness that is even harder to dispel. Again and again the breaking of boundaries verges on taboo, chaos and loss of control. And contemporary references indicate that the threat of confusion is nearer than it seems.

Made from white china, Michael Jackson can be seen for what he is: a white black man, a 'freak' of the type our ancestors might have put on display for quite different reasons. Is he an inspiration to the black community or an insult to his heritage? By the same token La Cicciolina, also featured in Koons's latest shows, combines the professions of politician and striptease artiste, lawmaker and buffoon, flaunting her power over men while revealing a desire to prostrate herself before them. The woman is a walking contradiction. When a journalist from *The Face* magazine asked her about reports that her act now includes urinating on men from a catwalk above their heads, she answered, 'I am La Cicciolina. Men pay to drink my wee-wee.' Yet her refusal to take precautions during filmed scenes of multiple intercourse undercuts this pose of vaunted dominance, turning her into a quite different figure, as sad as she is vulnerable. Little wonder, then, that the Pink Panther (another unlikely breed) looks apprehensive in her embrace.

An urge to domesticate the grotesque, to turn animals into human beings, to subdue sexual fantasies of violent death by revealing them in throwaway, ornamental guise as if they can be dismissed that easily: all this is implicit in confections made by craftsmen of the world, whose expertise has been geared to Koons's own specifications. A strong reading of each would emphasize usurpation of authority, gynaecological irregularities, bestiality and the invasion of privacy. Yet these themes are never, and could never be, explicit given the type of presentation Koons offers – not only of objects but also of their context as objects. Somewhere between a *frisson* (a presentiment that all is not well) and the expansion or solidification of that feeling into a modern-day antique to love and cherish, lies the real threat of these creepy, oversized ornaments, detained for a while on their way from one context to another. The distance preventing direct negotiation between us and them is evidenced as sheer, stretched skin: the glaze on china, a swelling breast, the Disneyesque streamlining of a bulbous cartoon animal. Most of all it is there in the mirrors, which propose a rupture between viewer and wish, viewer and nature, viewer and body, showing a figure trapped, blown to pieces, and (in one case) floating gently up and away. How difficult it is to face the truth. How doubly hard amid the current enthusiasm for the mercantile, for the half-truth that is almost self-confessedly hollow. Koons supplies what he thinks we need, and even leads us to expect more. That heightened sense of surface tension finds its counterpart in a particular tone of voice that has moved from business to everyday social life, a tone in which 'Yes' no longer even means 'Perhaps' while 'No' lacks any finality. We exist in a conditional tense, on a promise that is always made but never kept. It protects us from threats of change and disintegration. It keeps us from what we want. Koons senses this and makes it visible. That's all.

English Drag

Published in Artforum *XXVIII, 9, May 1990.*

When Alastair Sim was approached to play two roles instead of one in the 1955 Ealing comedy *The Belles of St Trinian's*, he hesitated. One of the roles was Clarence Fritton, an unscrupulous racehorse owner. The other was his sister Millicent, the headmistress of a boarding-school for girls. Thankfully, the hesitation was short-lived. Heavy-busted, broad-shouldered, Sim minced his way through the movie wearing an elaborately marcelled wig, *pince-nez*, buckled shoes, drop ear-rings, any amount of pearl and jet chokers, fur everywhere, and a skirt that looked like a converted hammock. 'I suppose I'm just a foolish, weak woman', Millicent tells Clarence, stuffing a ten-pound note into her ample bosom. It is near the start of the film, yet the illusion is complete. 'Sometimes I think it's just the frustrated mother instinct in me that urges me on', she later admits, musing over why she runs a school at all. The whole thing is very English.

It is English, of course, because of its sense of normality or, to be precise, the way viewers are expected to find it unremarkable. Urgent and disruptive, sexual needs are rightly described as 'demands'. But the act of demanding does not square with good manners and the constant attempt not to stick out from a crowd. So demands are simply worked into the fabric of daily life in the hope that they will not bother other people too much. On the surface of it, this works. There is an antique shop in Brighton whose owner, a man of simian bulk, dresses in a floor-length red gown and a mantilla and never lets his double life as a saucy Spanish señorita prevent him from lifting furniture above his head. In England, you see, customers would never be impolite enough to ask him why. Perhaps, for the English, not satisfying one's curiosity is another type of pleasure.

I remember, as a small boy, being fascinated by a figure I knew to be a man, despite the high heels and pencil skirt. I watched him wait alongside the housewives who were trying to cross the street. As the light changed, he reached out one hand and grabbed the buttocks of the woman next to him. Though he did it quite hard, the poor woman was too busy crossing the road to do more than shriek. I was with Gloria, my aunt, but neither of us has ever mentioned it. It is this ability not to mention things that is the really kinky part. It permits the continued ordinariness of a clandestine, heterosexual buttock-fancier, willing to go to any lengths to satisfy his craving, or a Hispanophile eager to understand the real spirit of flamenco. Or, of course, the magnificent Sim. To my knowledge, Sim never wore skirts again. Perhaps no one told him he could make a full-time occupation of it.

Every night at the Vauxhall Tavern the same thing happens. As a sign that the show is about to begin the lights in the bar are dimmed, all eyes turn to the stage, and for a minute spotlights illuminate the designs on the red plush curtains. The glitter has dropped off, but you can still pick out the shapes. On the left is something that looks like a giant tomato on wheels, while on the right a girl with a dented hat, no nose, and a forearm like Popeye's engages in single combat with a pinheaded hussar. Regulars know what it is: Cinderella's coach awaiting her as she waltzes with the man of her dreams, her rags magically transformed, for one evening, to an elegant gown. No better allegory could be found for that stage, that pub, and its nightly entertainment. On Thursdays they are all Cinderellas. The 'Stars of the Future' are amateurs with too much make-up, miming to records. For them, being seen in other clothes is an end in itself. Since the audience has become one more element in a private scenario of their own devising, entertainment is in short supply. The unemployed plumber from Lambeth makes Liza Minelli seem painfully shy, while the Greek waiter from Streatham who packs four costume changes into twelve minutes makes Connie Francis look very like a Greek waiter from Streatham. Drag like this is a procession of no-hopers dreaming of metamorphosis, though it thrives twice nightly at Madame Jo-Jo's over the river. But state-of-the-art drag is a different kettle of fish.

Tall, flirtatious, and undoubtedly vain, Adrella walks on and greets the audience. 'Good evening, Adrella,' they reply in singsong unison. 'My, don't you look stunning tonight.' What follows is more like sado-masochism than entertainment. Victims from the audience are subjected to merciless interrogation, forced to show everyone the labels from their clothes, or are rounded up in a corner. They are asked to speak, then interrupted by a telephone that rings sporadically. It is Captain Mark Phillips, Adrella explains, Princess Anne's estranged husband, tired of a horsy wife and on the loose at last. Royalty is invoked more reverentially by Regina Fong, billed as the last of the Romanovs, resplendent in floor-length, backless velvet, embroidered with the regal insignia RF. If Fong will never be able to claim the Russian throne, there is the consolation that no other living pretender can boast such a devoted entourage. Where Regina Fong goes, so do the Fong-ettes, a tidal wave of devotees who study the act religiously and sing, dance, shout and gesture it in unison, yelling instructions that are declined or acceded to by Fong, haughty and coquettish by turns. What they shout are the titles of film clips, television advertisements, parts of quiz shows, documentary soundtracks, interviews and other more obscure material, which is then mimed by the would-be Empress of All the Russias, buck-toothed, equine, and looking like a print Toulouse-Lautrec forgot to make. The working-class counterpart would be Lily Savage, white-faced, in cheap wigs, dressed, perhaps, in a floor-length artificial leopard skin with handbag to match. The relics of an act are still there: Lily is married, with a husband ('our Vincent') and children ('our Vera and our Bunty'). But these collapse as the flow of talk continues, a conversation with the audience punctuated by torrential, inspired impromptus compounded equally of nonsense and filth. Politically speaking, Lily Savage resembles a revolutionary Marxist moving at high speed towards anarchism. But, of course, the act uses no political terminology; it is just talk. There are points when the free association is so inspired that the words tumble together, and for minutes you lose your way as the meaning roars ahead of you and you think of Antonin Artaud, possessed and screaming, somewhere on a council estate in Peckham. It is the naïvety that is subversive: speaking truth and not straining to be liked.

This characteristic unites all three. Though drag cannot but help draw on the British pantomime tradition, in which the part of Dame is played by a man and the Principal Boy by a pretty girl, Fong, Savage, Adrella and others like them never bother to ingratiate themselves. Nor do they opt for easy laughs by that constant play on sexual oppositions that makes old-fashioned drag unpalatable. In the sixties Danny La Rue would drop his voice to demonstrate that he was a man. More recent drag stars relate to other sixties figures, like April Ashley, the notorious transsexual who married into the aristocracy. Bette Bourne, who formed the company Bloolips after a deliberate attempt to bring drag into line with left-wing politics, accepts neither gender. 'Bloolips', a nonsense word, is his sex, and the occupation stated on a Bloolips passport is simply 'Clown'. But such blunt refusal to be categorized should not be confused with escapism or double values. It indicates a choice, and a relevant one.

Forget the ideal of double-sexing and the hermaphrodites who overpopulate the new American 'bisexual' pornography. Forget the complex that motivates clandestine transvestites in Catholic Europe, where mother knows best, at church and at home. Forget clothes fetishism and the manipulation of fashion – the point at which *The Face* recommended skirts for men, to take one example. Forget arrangements of sexual parts, random or otherwise. Most importantly, forget what happens between the sheets. (This orgy of absent-mindedness could only happen in Britain, where politeness forbids interrogations on bedroom routine.) Recall the period we have just entered – a combination of *fin de siècle* and end of millennium, and its inevitable mood of decadent apocalypse. Imagine its most sacred texts, most cherished of all Pierre Klossowski's *The Baphomet* (1965), with its marriage of sacred and profane and its endless conundrums. Bear in mind what the masses want but cannot achieve: on the one hand, a life of irresponsible, tawdry luxury in which talentless participants flout law, taste and protocol only to be rewarded with notoriety, the fool's version of fame; on the other, a born-again sense of sixties selfhood, a dissolution of individual self into the group identity offered by acid house parties, currently suppressed by both police and state, which are intent on passing an act to ban them as soon as possible. (In other words, read your daily papers.) Take into account the bankruptcy of the ideals of heroism, respect, leadership and morality. Remember two major stereotypes of European decadence of a century ago: the androgyne (half man, half woman) and the sphinx (half woman, half monster). And it can be seen that, like Aubrey Beardsley's version of Pierrot, invariably construed as a self-portrait, Bourne's term 'Clown' smacks of determined innocence, untethered sexuality, skewed religiosity, a compulsive return to legends of temptation and promises of instant transcendence, and a wary approach to the ins and outs of the sexual act. All these are ammunition for that worse which is yet to come.

Resisting labels is essential in Britain at the end of the Thatcher regime. Right-on, left-wing stand-up comedians should be reminded that the situation is one of utter moral crisis, not simply a procession of day-to-day events that demand revision. In times of crisis taking sides becomes irrelevant. All you can hope to do is be yourself and speak the truth. As T.S. Eliot realized in his sad, envious essay on the music-hall star Marie Lloyd, the Victorian music-hall was all about its audiences. And, if the building blocks of history were properly defined, the music-hall audiences might prove to be the most significant crowd in European history since the French Revolution. Subversion is not revolution, of course. Alastair Sim played teachers, criminals and Millicent Fritton. The stars of the Vauxhall Tavern are a combination of all three, and their audiences adopt their own shifting identities – courtiers, henchmen and confidantes. No uprising will follow. The English detest uprisings. The result of the new drag may be to strengthen and prolong the mood of dissension, of refusal to be bought off or taken in by easy truths, that precedes some major change. Or perhaps that is just wishful thinking.

Martin Kippenberger

Published in Martin Kippenberger: Heavy Mädel, *Pace/MacGill Gallery, New York, 1991.*

A smoked cigarette is the humblest relic of all, a measure of time wasted or employed, above all forgotten. 'The burnt-out ends of smoky days', wrote T.S. Eliot. Our names for these small finales change from one language to another. *Kippen*, they are called in German. A mountain of them would be a Kippenberg. The pun is not wasted on the artist Martin Kippenberger. Dismantling a pile, he takes the butts and sinks them into moulded acrylic souvenirs, silly toy dogs which he attaches to the surface of his new batch of paintings, a trick he first used in 1987. Using exhausted cigarettes may not qualify as recycling in any real sense of the word. Rather, it constitutes a kind of personal archaeology, which others can investigate. For his own part, it may be the simplest step towards a complex variation on a diary, a way of examining time as it passes, lending a further, more consciously self-reflexive layer of meaning to that significance his work already conveys. Like a second, more private signature, they lie buried until we notice them. In a more intimate way than the paint and canvas, they have been touched by the artist. And, identical though they seemed in the packet, they all turn out differently. Kippenberger creates his own memorabilia as he goes, letting his work relate to his travels, his friends, his enthusiasms, above all his own persona. Eager – dangerously eager perhaps – to expose his entire existence to the public gaze, he creates his own posters, catalogues, records and performances with a speed that is nothing short of alarming. Drawing from an image bank of his own creation, work is made by plundering other work. But to take him for an autobiographer or self-publicist would be wrong-headed; Kippenberger is a less focused artist than mere narcissism would allow, an artist whose attitude to his own process of creation involves an entire politics and aesthetics, a regimen and a code of decision-making that draws on his daily practice while feeding it at the same time. Throughout the twentieth century artists have refused to dismantle the Ivory Tower, struggling to preserve an autonomous, artificial environment that may be no more than a figment of their own imaginations. This is a struggle from which Kippenberger is proud to abstain. For him the everyday provides a basic material for an art with no set distance between it and himself. Critical methods will almost certainly fail to make terms with an enterprise so headlong, so amorphous. Only his irony allows him room to manoeuvre. Yet to begin to lay stress on that irony might make Kippenberger seem a satirist, content to deal with the universe only from above, correcting what he supposes to be its mistakes. In fact he is present, engaged, biased, above all inconstant in his chosen distance. His tactics must change constantly. Life does not stand still, nor does it proceed in a straight line. Kippenberger's image bank allows for an intricate process of doubling back: to places (Los Angeles – 'Mein Angeles'; Madrid, where he lived for a time; Rio where he took a vacation; Cologne, where a room is permanently ready for him at the Hotel Chelsea); people (fellow artists Albert Oehlen, Werner Büttner, Georg Herold, Hubert Kiecol members of the Lord Jim *Loge*); his own works (his model gondola, shown last year in California, where they have their own Venice; a single, glittery, glam rock stacked-heel boot on a pedestal in a New York Gallery; *Negative Bathtub*, complete with an arm rising vertically into the tub itself, fist clenched in angry salute); corporate identity logos (BMW, Chanel); names of bands (AC/DC, Status Quo) and self-created slogans ('Don't Cry – Work', 'Cool It Dig It Do It', 'I Love Jeans', and 'Smoking'); but mainly self-images, illustrating not only Kippenberger's physical state (putting on weight, with his naked stomach poking out of his shirt in a poster for an exhibition in 1987, then the slogan 'A THINNER KIPPENBERGER' some time later) but also his willingness to think in public about what he is doing. 'We don't have problems with experiences if they're not still alive', reads the text on a photographic collage of 1986. '*Vorsprung durch Kippenberger*', one of his own slogans announces. 'Humour is round', a title informs the viewer. And the question of repetition, change and permanence is broached, periodically but persistently. The spent cigarettes in their canine, resinous mausoleums are attached to Kippenberger's new works: paintings of collages of posters, catalogues and invitation cards. The next stage is to make photographs of the paintings and then to print these in the sizes that have become standard for all of Kippenberger's work: in centimetres, 60 x 50, 75 x 90, 120 x 100, 150 x 180, and 200 x 200. When drawings have been made from the photographs, the paintings are destroyed. Meanwhile, the drawings, made not by looking directly at the paintings but at a mirror image of them, are themselves re-photographed. Reversing the usual course of events, Kippenberger's plan shifts from painting to photography, from photography to drawing. It comes as no surprise when an iconoclast overturns traditional hierarchies, nor that after more than a decade of battling against painting and photography he should opt for drawing as a final stage, capable of summarizing the past while giving into the future as projection (*Entwurf*) in the fullest sense. Yet there is no guarantee that the images are going to stop their constant process of change. For the sequence of stages also contradicts the order of events in the traditional scientific experiments. What was to have been proved remains unproven; as the process of assimilation takes place, the overlay of memories with which the entire work began is simply maintained. After all, perhaps we do have problems with experiences because of some inexplicable need to keep them alive. 'Upside down [you're] and turning me.' This phrase from a Diana Ross song has become part of Kippenberger's repertoire of slogans. Upside-down is how the photographic process works, of course; upside-down and night for day. Then, when the negative is printed, the reversal is reversed once more. No one really believes that anything is restored by the second part of the process. Indeed, when negative becomes positive and the process moves to completion, the usual reaction is one of surprise at something seen differently, or seen for what seems to be a first time, as if a slot in time has suddenly opened up, and in it an event that may never have taken place at all. Even what passes for 'copying', Kippenberger seems to suggest, constitutes a series of mistakes. Or perhaps the word is 'interpretations'. Is it the case that with each of these stages the 'original' moves further away? Not really, since the 'original' itself consisted of a collection of Kippenberger motifs, in no particular order, indecipherable at certain stages of the process but not at all at others. Misdrawn, it gains in conviction and definition, no matter where the process ends, like a phrase in the English game Chinese Whispers. So the process Kippenberger arranges, carefully separating the exhibition into its constituent stages, begins in memory and returns to it again, with changes along the way. And those changes mean that the model of the workings of the memory that he has constructed has as its major characteristic the property of creativity itself. At the heart of Kippenberger's current project is the aim of concentrating on that time when the image remains in transit, without physical concomitant, or at least any we can trust. Confronted by a stick in water, one's reaction tends to be doubly sceptical; though the apparently bent section may be no more than a trick of the light, it cannot help but cast doubt on the reality of the straight part. For Kippenberger, who seems to be aiming to keep the image between physical manifestations for as long as possible, the result may be to loosen his own grasp on reality, fixity, even on the image itself, in an attempt to preserve and cultivate what are simply the reflections that occur at each stage of the necessary transfer from one medium to another: subtle forgettings and changes of focus that have less to do with him than with the impetus his career has achieved. The idea is the machine that makes the work, Sol LeWitt wrote. And though Kippenberger could only ever be described as a renegade Conceptualist, this is also true of him. His 'idea' is himself as a reputation, an enterprise, a going concern, a business venture. One of his recent publications, *Input-Output*, consisted of a set of drawings, all made on receipts from hotels. On each was a drawing of the architectural kind Kippenberger favours: plans of spaces, based on the rooms he himself has occupied. Just as such a plan exists beyond time or location, as no more than readable intention with perhaps no particular translation into more concrete terms, his new project hovers between settled, tangible manifestations. Examining the stages through which any visual idea has to pass before it emerges as one of his own works, he embarks on an experiment that any factory owner should try. To ensure that the business is in working order, he absents himself for a time. Then, from a distance great enough to ensure that he will not be tempted to interfere, he simply watches what happens. And what does happen, of course, is that business not only continues as usual; it talks to itself. In other words it 'creates', with minimal interference from the boss. Such behaviour demands an unusual willingness to surrender, a willingness to allow decisions to be made behind his back. But Kippenberger has a long history of experimenting with his own identity as an artist. Playing in bands, collaborating with friends whenever possible, he allowed a man who painted hoardings to make his own first exhibition, has shown alongside another Kippenberger (his father, who is also an artist), and has raised the use of assistants to an imaginative art form in its own right. In short, Kippenberger has researched the idea of the 'death of the author' for himself, not only relinquishing but satirizing the ideal of belligerent male genius by a studied blurring of edges. People are the most complex entities we are forced to deal with, and the problem of where a 'person' starts and stops is highly debatable. Kippenberger makes it more problematic still. Only Beuys, with his fanciful claims to have held exhibitions when still a child, has used the biographical sections of his own catalogues to such great effect. It is as if for Kippenberger mere recitation of facts and dates can constitute a creative activity in its own right. Unlike other artists, who establish a permanent format for the histories of their careers, Kippenberger arranges and rearranges facts about his own life in order to highlight the tiniest detail, intent on playing games with the evidence. To believe that mistakes creep into any closed system or that mere recitation of detail necessarily bestows importance on it is more characteristic of oral than literate cultures. What Kippenberger realizes is that to anthologize and catechize – in other words, to order and recite available information from the past – is also to mythologize. A recitation of the details of education, retrospectives, one-man and group exhibitions in the back of every catalogue for every artist in the world only confirms those artists' heroic status. Simply in terms of power play, Kippenberger cannot lose by tampering with the apparatus available for conferring renown; just as the mock-epic mode retains all the trappings of epic. But in opting to become a comic hero, he preserves a sense of amplitude and activity that establishment figures lack but are in position to alter or to want to alter. If individuality, as Kippenberger sees it, is to be kept at arm's length, the stereotype of what an artist does needs circumvention. Since art, like humour, is round, little more is needed than to adopt the title ARTIST and repetition will confirm your claim. Recycling one's own work may seem indefensible, yet the result may not differ from the work of any tired, middle-aged, middle-of-the-road artist who is provided with a cage to live in. Kippenberger cannot fully escape this set of affairs. Collectors who want 'a Kippenberger' will be rewarded with the imprint of his personality on everything he makes. Yet his irony remains unscathed; turning his old work into new work by mechanical means makes him part of the audience all of a sudden, almost as surprised as they by the result. Kippenberger's open response to the question of how to define himself as an individual is related to the problem of how to define himself as an artist. One answer is to conform, then use the security this brings in order to subvert the system. If every Kippenberger exhibition is just another Kippenberger exhibition, then the art can be made well beyond the artist's reach while the artist becomes one of his own audience, scanning his own work for subtleties of variation. And since every work of art has to be photographed in order to be successfully publicized, then a plan must be hatched to make photography more than simply a means of registering, poorly, what already exists, just another stage through which art moves in its progress from studio to magazine or book, from privacy to publicity. This is one way an interpretation could proceed. There are others. Make collages from existing art, paint the collages, photograph the paintings, draw the photographs and rephotograph the drawings. The collage takes various works, various memories, and puts them together. With its different order of events, painting makes a parallel image in its quite different way, while photography does the job in less time, in dark rooms. By the time a drawing is made, the collage seems miles away and the paintings are destroyed. What was meant to be preserved? Detail, immediacy of perception or simply information? Perhaps the idea was that nothing should be left, and the entire process was a kind of divorce, a permanent distancing of things that did not mean enough or that meant too much. Destroy art and more springs up, looking unfamiliar, like a relative you have never met. The machine made the art, no doubt. But an artist invented the machine. No medium is preferable to any other. No memory can properly be erased. No artist can ever give up art. No artist can delegate authority. There are conclusions to be drawn; like these, perhaps. Yet the moment of the work, the idea of the refractions and continual, creative misreading, is untypical of the old, Rabelaisian Kippenberger. More human, perhaps, and more ordinary. Seized with a sudden panic, he does anything to his art to change. The result is unexpected. The art refuses to lie down and play dead. It begins a life of its own, for which the artist grumblingly, then proudly, feels responsible. Laying his work to rest turns out to be a recycling process. And not only the 'art' is recycled; the artist is, too. It will not happen again. What's past is past. Only an idiot would think of emptying his ashtray as a work of art.

Life and Death: an interview with Damien Hirst

Published in *frieze*, pilot issue, 1991.

Stuart Morgan: *The fly piece was a complete break for you, wasn't it?*
Damien Hirst: I wanted it to be about something particular and I wanted to say something worth saying. Life and death as a sculpture is a surprise. And the acceptable look of it is a bigger surprise. It's like a society of some sort. The flies could be people, as the bottles in the drugs cabinets could. Formally, I wanted an empty space with moving points in it, moving like stars, a solution to the problem of how to suspend things without strings or wires and have them constantly change pattern in space.
The first was called One Hundred Years. *Why?*
There's a weight to it. First, it sounds like a lot. Then it sounds like a little. But it's longer than you live. It's relative. Flies don't live as long as you. It's important that there's another called *One Thousand Years* and that it's the same.
Not Quite.
Well, there's no cow's heads in it.
Let's pass to the pieces you've conceived but haven't yet made. The butterflies don't live long either and are more acceptable in aesthetic terms than flies.
Sometimes you're negative, sometimes you're positive. If you see people as flies, you can see them as butterflies, small and disgusting or fragile and beautiful. Something that intrigues me in all the work is the action of the world on things.
In the butterfly work the butterflies are encouraged to settle on the monochrome paintings.
Yes. On the floor there's a white Formica table top eight feet by four laid on wooden trestles, then in the four corners, large bowls maybe with a splashy abstract painting inside each, as well as sugar and water solution and cotton wool. That's all in one space.
Weren't you going to have cubes with holes in them?
Not any more. I don't want the idea that the live butterflies came from somewhere. Then there are five white paintings with pupae stuck on to them, sprayed with sugar and water. And it's called *In and Out of Love*

– *White Paintings and Butterflies* – a constantly ongoing thing, and the idea of a mini-universe with a title like this suggests that you are or you aren't. If you are, you're experiencing something delicious. If you're not, then you're out of love with somebody. I like the word 'relationship': relationships with objects, with people, relationships in a composition. That you can talk about anything in terms of relationships is quite funny. And relationships change all the time. It will look like an abstract 3D painting, moving. You want to make paintings more alive. I hope there will be moments of calm and moments of movement. If they all settle at once, it may be hard to see any butterflies at all. Then they will come to life in a way I would like art to come to life. So that's in one space. In the other are four boxes with holes in them, a hole in every face, darkness inside, then there are seven butterfly paintings on the walls with dead butterflies in the paint and I was thinking of having a table and on it either four empty bowls or big white circular ashtrays. Both spaces are called In and Out of Love. There's no 'in love' or 'out of love'. One's the romantic view of it, the other is the harsh reality. I'm not sure which is which. There may be stubbed-out cigarettes or half-full wine glasses. Then in the other space are two cabinets filled with drinking glasses, painted white, made of MDF and with doors that open. I may call them *I Want You Because I Can't Have You* and *I'll Love You Forever Until I Don't*. They will be really bland glasses. Nothing fancy. And there will be too many for it to be a household object, but that's the idea. An idea of nothingness or different uses for the same substance: looking through and looking at. So you'll look through one glass to see another. Again they're related to people, to the idea that people are transparent, empty.

Are *people transparent?*

Sometimes you think they are.

Does that relate to the title?

There's something ungraspable about certain things. Because it's glass you want to look at something that's not there or see something that's see-through. Or it seems different. Or you can have it because it's in your home. It's an ephemeral substance, but there are things like Cinderella's glass slipper. Glass seems as if it shouldn't really be there. Or like magic. And to do with drinking.

After art about death and love, what is left for you to do?

Art about life. I've been reading Kafka, which is helpful. You can see the end and know it but along the way you get caught up in infinite possibilities. And

it's personal and universal at the same time.
Can your work encompass religion?
With difficulty. But if you believe in love you must believe in God, in the fact that there's more in something than what it's made up of.
Can't the love come from some super-human agency?
I can't see it anywhere but in people.
Coming after the fly piece doesn't the love theme seem flippant and frail?
I hope so. That would be quite refreshing.
But I know you want to shift from that to work with a dead shark . . .
I think all these things exist simultaneously anyway. I see it as constant life. I don't think I'm moving forwards. I'm just moving. The more you know the more there is to know. Each new piece makes the other pieces make sense. I like to think of it all together, or in terms of group shows, if possible. I don't think the spot paintings go with the butterfly works. That would be visually confusing.
Do your drug cabinets go with the butterfly paintings?
They could.
Why do you want everything to go with everything?
In any individual work the elements go together. So why not entire works? It's carrying on that arranging. But if you have two pieces that don't go, you have two options: you either change them or you change the way you look at them.
Perhaps this applies to the exhibitions you curate? You tend to show the same artists over and over again.
I don't look far. I'm interested in what goes on around me, in the immediate vicinity. The group of artists I know is what interests me.
What have you decided to call the shark piece?
'The Physical Impossibility of Death in the Mind of Someone Living'.
In other words, the way we think we'll never die.
The fact that we know we're going to die but we can't know anything about death while we're still living. It can't be experienced.
Why a shark?
I like the idea of a thing to describe a feeling. A shark is frightening, bigger than you are, in an environment unknown to you. It looks alive when it's dead and dead when it's alive. And it can kill you and eat you, so there's a morbid curiosity in looking at them. I like ideas of trying to understand the world by taking things out of the world. You kill things to look at them. You have to

preserve a shark in liquid, which looks very similar to its natural habitat. It has to be that size. You expect it to look back at you. I hope at first glance it will look alive. It could have to do with the obsession with trying to make the dead live or the living live for ever.

And does this work also belong to a set?

A set in the way my collages were a set. It's called 'Internal Affairs' and there's about ten pieces in it. Another is called *The Acquired Inability to Escape*. The title came from a conversation with Ulrich Loock. He wrongly translated a Bruce Nauman title and when I found out it was wrong, I used it for myself. It's a glass case, like the fly piece, in two halves with a table in one side and a six-inch gap all round, so there is no room for a person to sit at the table. On the table is an ashtray and a cigarette lighter and perhaps a wine glass and bottle. It's so obviously in the real world but then there's that gap inside, leading to the empty half. Another is two cows' heads in liquid. I'm not sure of the title. *Two Heads*, maybe, or something about Noah's Ark. Then there's a huge cabinet with bottles and jars.

Stop. Tell me first what the cows' heads are about.

It has a lot to do with placing: one that way, one the other. But what's being placed doesn't warrant that kind of arrangement. They're food, preserved food. It could be your head. The two heads piece is so obvious. It has to do with relationships between two people. Are people linked because of their similarity?

Go on.

Another consists of sixty or ninety fish, all in different jars or bottles, all facing the same way, called *Isolated Elements, Swimming the Same Way for the Purpose of Understanding*. I really like these long, clumsy titles which try to explain something but end up making matters worse, leaving huge holes for interpretation. And isolation is a scientific technique. But isolation is such a complicated thing. In personal terms, I mean, if you're an outsider. They all face the same way yet they can't make contact as they do in the sea. In life we're separated by flesh and bones, and you can't really move beyond that.

Why do you say they're swimming?

Because they're not.

A number of your works in the past have been doubles, like the cows' heads.

The cows' heads are twins, with their heads turned away from each other.

And of course one idea for the two pairs of spot paintings, John John *and* David David, *was to have twins standing in front of them.*

I'd like to be a twin.

Surely if you get married you can pick your own twin.

That's only what you think.

Why do you think people get married?

They wouldn't if they were twins. No, I take that back; twins get married.

Which leads us to the pieces that contain two entire cows.

Four cabinets with bottles and jars in each, containing the entrails and brains of two cows: two sets of lungs in one jar, two sets of kidneys and so on. *The Compromising Lovers*, it's called.

Compromising?

They have become one. You make compromises when you live together. They're dead.

Isn't that a rather cynical view of relationships?

Not at all. There are perfect relationships based on compromise. Take Jack Sprat and his wife.

But surely 'compromise' means each partner makes sacrifices.

You can give something up without losing anything. It's about changing your mind. An element of an art work can be surrendered without damaging the whole perhaps. Ideally all problems can be solved by giving something up.

Then it's The Compromised Lovers.

No. It must be as if they're alive. Art tries to resurrect the dead. The compromise is that they are together. What they've surrendered to get that is their life. Compromise makes people unhappy, because it makes them happy but it's not the happiness they expected. Something is lost. With lovers there's no way to get anything through compromise. People want everything. The acceptance of an impossible situation is what it's about. And in physics, if they don't get the answers they want, they change their way of looking at them.

I suppose you'd see modern physics, where the observer is included in the observation, as a 'relationship'.

What is a relationship, after all? I'm having a relationship with everyone I've ever thought about or communicated with, and every object I've ever seen. I feel that life can be a composition; things relate to other things.

Life means live things, though. Lately you seem preoccupied with dead animals.

Well they're almost human.

What I call human is alive.

One day I had a horrifying thought. It changed everything. I was looking at my collages: all these rotten little bits of wood, these decaying, discarded bits of rubbish on the floor, very close to death (I felt) in the formal arrangements I'd made, with bits of plastic and dirty tissues almost breaking apart. 'This is happening to me,' I thought. It changed everything. So you see, they are about life and death together.

An interview with Ashley Bickerton

Unpublished; recorded in 1991.

Stuart Morgan: What did you learn at Cal Arts?
Ashley Bickerton: Permission, I guess. John Baldessari taught me that. His influence permeated the walls. John was always mumbling little gems. He said 'I don't care what people have in common; I care about what you yourselves have to say.' So I learned to be loose.
When you got to New York you showed with artists you are still associated with.
That was the group show at Sonnabend which consisted of Jeff Koons, Peter Halley, Meyer Vaisman and myself.
Do you feel you have a lot in common with these people?
Yes and no. There seems to be something afoot now that is very interesting, with artists like Jeff, Bob Gober, Mike Kelley and Cady Noland. Instead of discussing the conditions that are art, pushing out into its own sort of perverse poetry, which so much of the early eighties was obsessed with, they seem to be using a range of strategies including Pop, Conceptualism and Minimalism to discuss the formal qualities that make up art or culture. Bob's work has a certain romantic flair, a certain sentiment. Cady's has a sort of trashy rock-and-roll poetry . . . I think what is going on is really healthy.
So instead that's the group you've adopted for yourself?
Yes. Things were very turbulent in that first period, and the media created a lot of sensationalist packaging.
You were blamed for a lot of things.
Yes. One article comes to mind immediately: 'Masters of Hype', which saw four of us at the Sonnabend Gallery as reflecting a coked-up, sensation-seeking society. The media fed on itself as it often does and it snowballed. There were all these stories about sitting around with gallery dealers at board meetings constructing images. As far as I can remember, several of the artists involved didn't even speak to each other at that point.
The name Susie turns up in your early work. Who was *Susie?*
Susie is an embalmed transsexual. I thought of her as the ultimate transgression of the natural order by the cultural: to change sex and then, in death, to create life. I once said I wanted my art to operate in the interface between Robert Smithson's unfinished project and Michael Jackson's face. Recently I've become interested in cargo-cultism, which I see as a form of cultural

transvestism. The movie *Paris is Burning* made it evident that there is a similarity between cargo-cultism and cross-dressing. Dressing up, building airstrips in the New Guinea highlands and building airplane hangars out of vines and wood and brush; building look-out towers and even false airplanes, waiting to intercept the cargo that was really destined for the people of New Guinea: it's an elaborate form of belief and spiritualism. There's an adoption of an absolute role with complete conviction. Nobody works harder than a transvestite. I think it's a 24-hour-a-day obsession or lifestyle choice.

Susie has a friend called Bob. Who's Bob?

I was trying to make paintings, and a painting is just form and content. So Susie was a first piece I did and it came out of Sherrie Levine's head pieces, where she had a photograph of a model doing some housework cut out in the shape of Lincoln's head, which I thought was like Frank Stella, the form defining the content and the content defining the form. I liked the idea of being a painter but doing everything except painting. The reason I picked Susie was phonetically casual; it became a sort of object name to key up the plastic quality and drive a wedge between form and content.

This plastic quality comes to the fore in the great walls which you make again and again. You have a set of pieces called Wall Wall *and another set called* Floor Floor.

I just wanted to make an obvious relationship between artist and viewer.

So you're not saying that when there are words in the paintings you're using a set of permutable counters which in this case have simply spelt a word. A lot of the titles in the early works are words that are not words.

Yes. 'Gug, Ook' . . . I call them coital blurts. I wanted to take it even further from *Bob and Susie* and bring them down to a sort of phonetic belch while keying up the plastic armature again even more absurdly and layering it with information. I guess I got lost in intellectual dandyism. I really wanted to try to make an expressionist painting and I knew it was easy; you really just had to load up the signifiers. So I stuck a lot of skulls and knives on it.

Another interesting thing is the titles, such as Abstract Painting for People. *Do we take it that what you were doing was abstract?*

I always thought I was a painter up to a point, and that the work was always addressing traditional painting but in a way that made it everything that a painting was. That's why they project off the wall, because I like the idea that a painting has an aura and projects into the viewer's space. I made them gold because art is valuable; I put corner brackets and covers on them because art is an object of cultural significance and has to be protected. I put jokes on the back for the art movers, handles on them, levels to lift them on. In fact, I wanted them to operate with equal significance in all their states of existence. For instance, storage, shipping, transportation and, at the point of aesthetic reckoning, on the gallery wall.

What do you have when you've finished all of that? Do you have a perfect work of art?

I don't know.

Or do you have something that fulfils everyone's requirements without being anything at all?

Yeah.

What about Le Art?

That was the end of my obsession with Frank Stella. I guess I had a love–hate relationship with the absolute banality of the black paintings, they were just so mute. Again, I wanted to do a piece where the form defined the content and the content defined the form, so I just used the product logos of all the materials that went into its construction.

Your work is also about you; all the time you come back to yourself. There's even one called The Me Portrait.

Yes, I liked the idea of doing a self-portrait and really trying to be a painter. I'd just come from the Metropolitan show with all those van Gogh self-portraits and I remember staring into the cavernous angst of his eyes, and I thought I'd like to do this too. But you can't really do that so I decided to make myself like a discotheque in Nevada. There was another one that said 'SIX GUN'. I liked the idea that the piece projected so far into the viewer's space that it had to be held up by this ridiculous contraption; it was taking literalness to its perverse and ultimate limit.

So far we've got a sense of endless permutations of elements, an idea of simultaneous announcement and concealment, a sense of science fiction, in a way of technology, of naming, of being confronted by something that doesn't give much back. But it doesn't go much further than that. So the work is beautiful and funny and seductive. The statements up to 1987 have a decidedly bleak ring. But despite the fact that they are about the end of everything, the works are funny. All your work is funny.

How could you not laugh at the utter bankruptcy of possibility? I mean, what is left to do? People sometimes say my work looks sort of sci-fi and I'm somewhat aghast because I loathe science fiction. I wanted to make paintings. *About the Artist* is a sort of questionnaire I made up combining a Dewar's Profile interview and the *Playboy* centrefold interview. So I have 'last book read', measurements, turn-ons, turn-offs, and on the back you see instructions on how to hang the piece. It's funny, but they end up looking science-fictional when I really wanted to make something that discussed what a painting is without actually being a painting.

By this time whole swatches of fiction appear in the work. 'The smell of sex lingers on our sweating bodies', one of them begins, a long piece of prose let into the picture.

That goes back to the *Wall, Wall* pieces. I got the idea on a bus in Mexico. We were just outside Acapulco and I looked out the window and saw this gaudy pink and purple wall and the idea just clicked. I made these allegorical walls but then thought 'That's a bit banal; art has to have a transcendent quality, which is usually a desire.' So I put these little snippets of romantic, sexy prose on them because it has to have content and a sort of romance.

Is that where these foreign countries come in?

Yeah, I thought that package tours were like an art experience; both of these live in your memory as a brilliant vignette against the grey morass of your everyday life. So I put words on the sides of pieces, because I thought the gallery experience of seeing art popping off the wall was like a package tour of something, like *Four Nights and Five Days in the Yucatan.*

And you had ships' wheels and dolphins . . .

They're hideously ugly but I really still like the idea. I wanted to design the first paintings that you stand with your back to. I had this idea of Ivana Trump with a Martini glass getting photographed in front of it and you clip these walls on to your house, so suddenly you have a John Huston set from a movie in Mexico filling up your New York apartment wall.

Is the viewer Ivana Trump or are you Ivana Trump?

Technically, the viewer is the viewed; you stand in front of it and you're looked at and you're exoticized by the background.

By 1988 there was a big change in the work, a different way of thinking.

I think I got tired of addressing culture in all the early pieces, which I refer to as culture-scapes. I began to see art discussing art as a sort of ingrown hair follicle, a tiresome ellipse. I wanted to break out of that circle and do romantic landscapes.

The word 'ark' appears. An ark is something that takes everything we have that is precious to another place when something goes wrong.

They're covered with all this hardware, which I saw as the medium by which we equilibrate our cultural and biological selves in what amounts to an unfriendly, natural macrocosm. These are covered with tent-ropes, ropes we place up the side of a mountain, devices to float on the ocean, shipping hardware, all the tools by which we remove ourselves from the cultural matrix and put ourselves in the natural order. We need to protect our biology, so I made the constructions using all these tools. In a way I was trying to do the inverse of what earth artists did by making pieces out in the desert and taking photographs which they then brought back into the sphere of art. I wanted to take a chunk of the natural world and put it into the context of art in a way that meant one couldn't extricate the natural from the cultural.

Does it change the natural when you put it into a gallery?

I think we can only recognize the natural through the cultural and wanted to take that to an extreme.

From this point onwards, you turn to agriculture, the sea, the biosphere. Jeff Koons used the term 'equilibrium', which seems to be a good description of what you're looking for.

I had all this trash in the studio. And I thought, what do you want to *do* with all this trash – just put it into Mount Koch, which is a big pile of garbage out on Staten Island? And I thought, 'What better place to put it than in a collector's home. If we reified and spiritualized this garbage, and made it into something of cultural vitality . . .' So I just dumped it all inside the floating pieces. So that it would float. I had the idea of its being a Flying Dutchman, going around and around the globe for ever in a current called the Screaming Fifties, right above the Roaring Forties. I guess this is where it does relate to Conceptual art because it's really the idea that matters.

In a work like Minimalism's Evil Orthodoxy in Monoculture's Totalitarian Aesthetic Number One*, are you doubling back to the art of van Gogh?*

Yes, it's a definite response to Donald Judd and Carl Andre. I began at one point to see their aesthetic as operating in a way very similar to both monoculture agriculture and saturation bombing in Vietnam. It was totally insistent and reliant on technology and repetition. Like monoculture agriculture and saturation bombing, it had limited effects and it created a lot of problems. I wanted to use agriculture as a sort of metaphor to address problems I saw in Minimalism.

What kind of problems?

In monoculture agriculture you get miles and miles of undifferentiated wheat fields. It's very pesticide-reliant and very fertilizer-reliant, as opposed to a jungle garden, in which you'll have legumes putting certain chemicals into the soil that another plant takes out, and that plant will offer shade for another plant that needs shade and you get a symbiosis. I wanted to draw a parallel with Minimalism with its drastic repetition and absolute reliance on technology and its value-soaked hymns to industrial order.

What about Big Screwed Up Cycle of Wood, Shit and Human Tinkering, Number Two*?*

There are so many magazines and they're all made out of wood, and we eat so much crap. And I thought there's something wrong with the whole cycle: the crap goes down the rivers and out into the ocean and the wood is in these magazines, so I thought of making a silly piece that tried in some vain way to be dragged into the woods, filled with magazines and night soil, which is fertilizer, to sit there and rot.

Is it odd that these are in a gallery and that a gallery audience is seeing them?

No, in a sense it is Conceptual art in that it's really about the idea – short of taking a bus out into the wilderness.

In your show at Sonnabend, a theme show about love, Bob and Susie return. The work, you explained to me, is not as well made as usual. Could you tell me why?

When Karen Kilimnik and Cady Noland emerged, it looked like some sort of epistemological rupture because it was unslick, which seemed to me very silly because it was really just a stylistic difference. I wanted to say that the ideas were much more at issue than the style, that in fact things didn't change just by going from shiny to rusty.

How do you feel now?

In the corniest way, I often think of my studio as the *Calypso* and I'm Jacques Cousteau. If I look at it that way it seems very open. I get bored easily and so the last body of work was about landscape and the next show is about people. I like to leave the studio open so that you can use the work to carry you where you want to go instead of being slaves to precision, which is the problem that I had with the Minimalists. I'd like to create an open-ended equation where art is purely geared to your ongoing interests. If you have to go to live with a tribe in the highlands of New Guinea then that's what you have to do. If you want to talk about love or last night's escapades, art is able to do this. To be limited to talking about how paint butts up against paint or how something attaches to the wall seems desperately banal. What I really want right now is to open it all up and make it discursive and make available as many tools as possible to say as many things as possible.

Boyfriends, Girlfriends: Richard Prince's Alternative Bondings

Published in Artscribe *86, March/April 1991.*

In Richard Prince's new paintings nothing remains stable, singular or whole. Images occur sporadically on the white canvas, then suddenly give out. Paint may be applied over them, as unsuccessful camouflage, an attempt at making a surface on which more print can be added. So images and words can be seen through others, while interpretation remains uncertain, postponed. If a visual equivalent of stammering existed, it would look like this. But speech impediments simply distract from some underlying logic. Here information is dispensed in no particular order. Handwritten passages, printed like the other images – attempts to remember the correct spelling of a name or snatches of some private singsong – give the impression of a mind only half-focused. And barely recognizable photographs are included: old source material, perhaps, or even the mainstay of Prince criticism, that studio table on which he held the exhibition on which his claims to historical precedence are based. Yet the drift can hardly be described as autobiographical. The work seems to have broken free of Prince altogether. Mumbling half-intelligibly behind the artist's back, it is a confusion of at least three of his major series: hoods, gangs and jokes.

With the hoods a heraldic device is returned to its function as a shield, a means of deflecting certain interpretations and cultivating others. The perfect insignia of a corporate, commodity-oriented culture, they also double as nods towards acceptable current artworks: those half-hearted variations on late-Minimalist strategy which change hands daily in SoHo galleries. Above all, they look as if they have something to hide. A similar, disturbing doubleness underlies the jokes. In other circumstances they may reveal hidden truths about American society. Prince's jokes do nothing of the sort. Apparently selected for their ability to resist analysis, Prince's masterpieces of lame comedy are constructed according to an easy principle: if it sounds like a joke, it must be a joke, and if it is a joke it must be funny. Grotesque and faintly obscene, Prince's comic repertoire returns compulsively to cross-breeding and even cross-dressing. 'I met my first girl, her name was Sally. Was that a girl, was that a girl. That's what people kept asking.' Acknowledging the doubts of others (Was that a *girl*?) would place the speaker in one of two positions: of dating a woman who looks either like a man or an implausible transvestite. Suddenly the humour backfires and the speaker is caught with his Freudian slip showing. If the hoods serve as advertisements for a culture that puts on a false front, the jokes indicate cracks in the mask, sudden indications of unrest, and the gangs explore alternative, if obscure, bondings, part of a hidden agenda that can accept or cope with anomalies. Perhaps any subculture is based on Freudian slips. 'Here comes Dick he's wearing a skirt here comes Jane she's sportin' a chain', a handwritten jingle runs.

Prince's new series of prints on paper do not invite analysis in the manner of the jokes, however. 'Skirt' is no longer readable as 'shirt' subjected to some obscure mistake. Now everything is surface, everything is believable, however wretched it may be, and what were previously names for collective groupings of Prince's works – *Boyfriends, Girlfriends* – have burgeoned into reality. So the Tom of Finland muscleboy who featured in previous gangs has been supplanted by boxers from the front pages of cult magazines and by all-too-solid, chap-wearing, groin-groping leathermen sizing each other up in a bar; while the 'girlfriends' from earlier years are now seen enjoying the horizontal embraces of their biker sweethearts. The self-referentiality of Prince's paintings, with their quotations from *New Yorker* cartoons or the imagery he has used before turns into ostensible sincerity in the prints. 'My boyfriends', the handwriting reads, 'my girlfriends', even 'my wife'. And the alternative bondings which hinted at some hidden agenda for a society and an art with nothing to hide dissolves into metaphor, as a man in his studio, playing with his chosen counters, fantasizes about low-life, using his imagery to make the imagined connections between him and black boxing champions, or the people who read boxing magazines and experience a sense of community in doing so. Whiffs of Whitmanesque transcendence are rendered ironic by harsh facts. (Aren't all artists bad comedians, unthinkingly delivering their patter, hoping to be able to make mistakes but, more importantly, to notice and act on them?) And the fact that structures change and the level of fictionality remains unresolved, that the artist's motives as a man and as a non-artist are acknowledged but that no deep motives can ever be openly admitted, ensures a lack of resolution that both appeals and discourages. What 'self' means, what 'society' means, what 'culture' means are among the questions broached and left frustratingly unresolved in a career that, like the structures of thought and imagery it presents, remains unresolved for good if not completely defensible reasons.

Paul Stone

Review of exhibitions at Riverside Studios and West London Hospital, published in Artscribe *87, Summer 1991.*

'This is an unsupervised play area. Children who play here do so under their parents' supervision', the poster reads. Riverside Hospital's Maternity Services Department is there to supervise the parents. At least fifty posters on its waiting-room walls advise on everything from drug abuse to arthritis, yoga to toxoplasmosis, smoking to immunization. Mothers-to-be must read them all. What else is there to do in this dingy place, with its deep ochres and dirty greens, powder pinks and bright yellows. There may be toys for the youngsters. For adults there is only a wooden sculpture of a stork swooping, beak clamped together. The disturbing part is that a basket it must once have carried has vanished, and the baby with it.

To coincide with his exhibition at Riverside Studios Paul Stone was invited to make a work for this space. In the form of a simple grid he quoted a fifties advertising photograph of a girl at a birthday party and a pattern with the letters A, B, C. While the card is all simpering cuteness, the leer on the face of the child, who resembles a wizened, toothless crone, hints at unfathomable depths of evil. Children are not lovable moppets, Stone reminds us. Nor are learning experiences restricted to play areas. Barbara Windsor reeling back in amazement, wearing next to nothing, the artist as a child in *Running Free,* and older in *Y Viva España* all seem innocents poised on the brink of knowledge, particularly worldly knowledge, while wisdom and innocence are combined in foetus and E.T. images. Youth and age combine strangely, as if life is cyclical by nature. At Riverside, his familiar cibachromes were augmented by wall-size, photocopied paper works, their repetitive images emphasizing the considerable decorative potential of his work and the far-ranging nature of the interpretations it invites. Increasingly his style becomes more Mannerist: ludic, recondite, witty and erotic. Thumb-prints, a map and a left and right dance diagram meet in *Under*, while *The Bakers is Closed* juxtaposes a palm print, a kneeling woman and a caricatured baker and disturbingly shaped loaf. Stone's themes are as always: life and death, religion, sexuality, separation and attachment. But gradually he nears his early ambition, implicit in *Richard of York Gave Battle in Vain*, of working towards the encyclopaedic. It becomes clear that his scope is wide and funny enough to reach a larger public than the art world can offer, and that it could do so without diluting the enterprise.

Beyond the reading-room lies an antechamber with photos of midwife teams, leaflets about vaccination, whooping cough and post-natal depression, leading to an inner sanctum marked MIDWIVES REMEMBER TO LEAVE THIS PLACE AS YOU WOULD WISH TO FIND IT. Here are the charts of cervical dilation and uterine contraction, the floppy models of wombs, diagrams exhorting pregnant women to lie on tennis balls and another frieze-like photocopied work by Stone, with a grinning, wavy-haired lad, a sketch of a teddy bear on its back and an intricately shaped key. Teddy doubles as baby and mother, while the inane lad smiles, innocently or not, at the 'combination' that produces life. What does sex have to do with children, Stone asks mothers-to-be, as if they do not have enough problems already. Returning to the waiting room, I find that someone has finally stuck something into the stork's beak. It is a condom.

James Casebere: Broken Home

Introduction to James Casebere, *published by the James Hockey Gallery, West Surrey College of Art and Design, 1991.*

An impressive moonlit edifice combines turrets, chimneys, steps and columns in a collage of Hollywood medieval, Victorian domestic and Italian postmodern. Somehow it also gives the impression that a second structure is inside, struggling to get out. A high, sheer building features row upon row of windows in the same curvilinear style. For a while we are taken in. Eventually, it occurs to us that something is wrong: surfaces are uniformly bright, the moonlight is too seductive by half. And the medium itself combines aspects of television and advertising, media offering a high degree of wish-fulfilment, capable of luring viewers from rational thought. James Casebere uses lightboxes to present carefully planned pictures of table-top sculptures which he makes from styrofoam, cardboard and plaster, and photographs himself. Persuasive and inconceivable by turns, the result is as fascinating and corny as film noir. Or dream. Or photography, accurate in its reproduction of surfaces but deficient in underlying reality.

Of course, if you believe that the 'reality' around you is deficient or inessential, Casebere's work will be seen as registering that lack. If a single gesture characterizes his work, it is one of dramatizing a vacuity, demonstrating how emptiness has been concealed beneath a shell. And he identifies this state as being typically American by setting some tableaux not only in the present but also in a formative period of American history, the Civil War, and in the landscape of the Wild West. The search for relevant experience has made Casebere a mental transient, a state conveyed well by a recent lightbox showing an empty space like a gallery, a shop or some other place of display. In this case it presented nothing but itself, its steps and ramps and ghostly walls. Surprisingly, in the context of Casebere's work it could also be seen as a house.

Casebere grew up in the Midwest. 'Mundane, middle-class and midwestern', he called his youth, mentioning the 'absence of an ideal of home'. 'In the second half of the twentieth century', he wrote in a book of the same name, 'American children often had toys they played with and learned from. They went to school, did chores, left home to prove themselves and sometimes made homes of their own.' And, he added forlornly, '(These things try to go on forever.)' The emphasis is on the word 'try'; for Casebere the permanence of temporariness becomes a private preoccupation as well as a metaphor for the American experience. The sense of profound distrust conveyed by his light-boxes may result from an emotional battle between wanting something to exist and realizing the impossibility of that desire. Presenting his viewers with a condition that is half right may be one way to examine imperfection. And if Casebere focuses on architecture, housing and the idea of the home, this must relate to motives for building a place, a set of relationships, a country, a life, a family: to do it right, once and for all, and avoid the errors of the past.

In a circle in the middle of the floor useless objects are strewn. There are wheels, but they cannot work. There is a fence, but it lies useless. A bucket appears, half embedded, while a second, with no bottom, perches atop a pole like a signal. A building has come adrift: one half stands higher than the other. And signs of disaster abound: a small propeller is perched on one roof, while from another a soiled flag dangles. Only tornadoes leave such desolation in their wake. Thirties overtones are unmistakable; the Dustbowl region, its droughts and desolation, came to symbolize the futility not only of sharecropping, but of a whole generation.

If agriculture is shown as unproductive, industry suffers a similar fate in Casebere's more recent work. A single forlorn chimney nudges a conveyor belt along which round black excreta are meant to run along rollers and drop into a string bag. Through a circular hole in a bent sheet of corrugated metal a flag mounted on a gramophone turntable may or may not be about to wave. A lone black ball runs nowhere, while another has dropped free. Near by a plug has been pulled and a flap swings aimlessly. The abandoned factory was another staple of regionalist art in America during the Depression, a sad footnote to the Machine Age hopes of the previous decade. In Casebere's adaptation of the theme, the white flag says it all; it is hardly even possible to summon enough energy to surrender. Belief in permanence implies an equally stable political stance. In Casebere's thinking the process of striving for perfection and the fate of such striving is presented in purely visual terms. But the wish to make parts whole, hollow things solid and imagined space real has social, even mythic overtones. Solidity is in short supply in Casebere's sculpture. Walk around it in a circle and parts seem to adhere and become detached, to relate now to one, now to another. Identities become confused: the tall chimney becomes a tower at one moment, a cone the next.

And, as was the case with the light-boxes, the mind is attracted to perfection while the senses mistrust it.

At one stage a picture of a synthetic version of stereotypes was Casebere's nearest approach to reality. Building life-size environments based on models failed to dispel feelings of distance and disorientation. Perhaps the most recent turn to a medium that hovers somewhere between sculpture and drawing while continuing to deal with clichéd versions of history gains full significance only when it is seen alongside the light-boxes. In physical and mental terms both evade our grasp; the object remains fugitive, not yet made or still to be constructed in the mind. Either ruined or planned, the buildings exist half-way between past and projected time, in a present that seems all disappointment or potential, but which shares its sense of eerie immanence with Casebere's light-boxes. That the United States was in a state of constant flux was a familiar feeling in its early years. (Jefferson even considered changing the laws every seven years.) Casebere's sense of ruin and loss is counterbalanced by an urge for construction, though what is made is a model that basks in its own unreality. Seen as a country, a place, or a state of mind, a stable existence between past and future, plan and rubble, 'home' seems harder and harder to set up, a more hopeless ideal than ever.

Vice-Versa

Published in Blocnotes: Stratégies d'exposition, *(Paris), 1, 1992.*

ENOUGH OF EXHIBITION. WE KNOW ITS VAIN DISPLAY, ITS ENCYCLOPAEDIC ASPIRATIONS, ITS TENDENCY TO TURN, SHOWING OFF. CONSIDER INHIBITION INSTEAD.

1. The participant acts as interloper, discovering and desecrating that space in which secrets seem to abide. Night suits these sweet violations. Gates are best unlocked by moonlight. Then they are doors to be prised open, locks picked until, with an imperceptible click, their intricate guts engage. There will be loneliness and frustration; this is solitary work and no one must know of your presence. Naturally, it is dangerous. (One slip and you're dead, but who's to know?) Focus instead on your own reactions. Burglars know those cold sweats, that sudden realization of the self and its impotence. Forget that ferocious pummelling, like a fist on a table. (The heart my dear, simply the heart.) Ignore the tattoo it is beating. Retreat is out of the question, for retreating is a matter of to and fro, but always as the role of the visible diminishes, directions are lost. Perhaps your eyes have failed. (Hard to tell, it has been dark for so long.) Perhaps you are back where you began. (That is more than possible.) It may resemble a direct path, as rooms give way to others, one door to the next. But after a few years the trajectory will be clear: always in the same space, of course, that space now utterly dark, but inwards rather than forwards, inwards towards a centre. 'The journey, not the arrival, matters.' That's a true saying. Here it does not apply. By now your goal has become plain: towards some final gesture in which you too must be enfolded. Too late for tears; your own destruction was always part of the deal. Dedicate yourself to secrets and you finally become one, you must have known that. No one knows what happens next. A final revelation of concealment? A last manifestation of secrecy? Permission after a lifetime of denial? Or has the quest been its own justification, its constant inhibition a sort of release?

2. We will not understand black holes until we encounter one. And since their eccentricities come into play so gradually, we may not realize what is happening when we do. Entering the penetralia of the universe, where, in the guise of an insane housemaid, God turns reality outside in, inside out, time

and time again, as if folding a sock, we are held in some steady state, in which secrecy and openness are neither identical nor opposite but components of a single, complex movement.

Will this be visible? Or will everything seem the way it was before? Perhaps looking will no longer qualify as an instrument of knowledge. In a black hole, visible and invisible will meet, the moment of meeting will be prolonged and in one simultaneous expansion and contraction will translate into a new mode of visibility, present though perceptible only as absence.

3. At openings he would tell people that his art was about non-meaning, or, to be precise, how to mean nothing. And he'd screw up his eyes in that cute way of his, so he knew people would like him and he'd be sure to make a few sales. Critics fell for it. So did customers – some customers, at least. Oddly, they never knew each other. So when strange things began happening no-one could think what to do or whom to contact. Finding his painting gone when he came down to breakfast, A contacted the police. While waiting for them, he checked to see if anything else was missing. The police did not stay long. They found him hesitant and vague, unable to remember why he had summoned them. While moving house, B saw to it that her paintings were put into the lorry last and lashed down with ropes to prevent damage. She followed in her car. As she watched the lorry doors open again and saw the men lifting the furniture, it seemed for a moment that something was amiss. What could it be? When she arrived home one evening C was told by her maid that the framers had come to take the painting away. It never came back, but after two or three days they had both forgotten all about it.

MORAL: If it doesn't mean anything, it isn't worth worrying about.

Peter Joseph: On Tonality

Published in Art Press, *Paris, May 1992; reprinted in* Peter Joseph, *ed. Matthew Higgs, Lisson Gallery, London/Galerie Meert Rihoux, Brussels, 1998.*

Criticism does Peter Joseph a disservice. Not only is his work meant to be looked at in daylight, but the effect of his simple design – one rectangle of colour inside another – alters constantly. At one moment the inner area of the painting might resemble a window, the next a shape set against a background. Since it is impossible to focus on either the edge or the centre, the only alternative is to concentrate on the composition as a problematic whole. Is it true that the format began in 1971, after Joseph went to the cinema and caught sight of a screen with no picture, a blank area of light amid darkness? That throbbing edge remains, as well as the singular impression of tone. 'Tone,' he wrote in 1980, 'the sensitivity of light and dark, is missing from modern life. It has been superseded by shape, the crude definition of personality.' His paintings frequently lead to confusion: colours refuse to stay still or be what we expect them to be. To borrow Joseph's own terms, they refuse a fixed 'personality'. Ceaseless fluctuation is their main effect, that striving toward wholeness which Joseph has described as 'the experience when the eye and mind unfocus and are at one with what is physically outside'. For Joseph empathy and the concomitant absence of self-consciousness form one aspect of human wholeness, it seems. He talks about bringing together nearness and distance in a way that makes the two 'marry and hold'.

Joseph's working method is taxing in the extreme. First, he studies swatches of construction paper, chosen because no sheet is ever dyed the same twice, in search for the two colours to be offset. Having made a sketch, he has to mix acrylic paint to exactly those hues, then apply it to the canvas in washes. This is less a process of making than of remaking; the artist is fond of pointing out that his working method resembles that of a Renaissance artist, operating according to 'design' or *disegno*. With the exception of a few twentieth-century artists – Newman, Rothko, John McLaughlin – Joseph's visual research is confined to Old Masters such as Claude Lorrain, Veronese, Boucher, Guido Reni and Fragonard. In limiting himself to a deceptively simple conception of painting in two colours and a single shape Joseph is a willing classicist. Yet the effect of the work denies this time and time again.

The complexity and contemporaneity of his colours is notable. And the quality of change matters to Joseph, who speaks with passion of the modulation of emotion and melody in Schubert's songs, the shift from one to the next as the parallel to a set of emotions in a state of flux. Though he has rarely chosen to show his paintings in sets, the comparison is clear. Joseph's formal vehicle for his painting succeeds in suggesting a single mind in process, a range of perceptions and emotions that, in terms of reaction, pleasure, balance, feeling, even morals, suggests what human life could, or perhaps should, be.

A major influence on British artists of Joseph's generation was the exhibition at the Tate Gallery of masters of American Abstract Expressionism. The results were visible in the 'Situation' shows in 1960s and 1961, where artists such as Richard Smith, Robyn Denny and John Hoyland revealed the influence of the Americans. Only Newman and Rothko held any lasting interest for Joseph. In this installation he was aiming for an effect similar to that of an 'all-over' painting, by making a work that functioned like a frieze. He often employs musical analogies to illuminate his ideas. In this case, he speaks of his preoccupation with Debussy during the period in question, his discovery of the 'strangeness and lightness of the sound, almost like a perfume arising from the notes rather than the notes themselves'. The mobility of the viewer's body was matched by a decentring of the gaze. So an open, harmonic texture, corresponding to the effects of both physical and optical change, never came to rest. (Another work from this time, aptly called *Passage*, was over nine metres long.) However hard viewers tried, it proved impossible to locate any principle of formal unity; moving past it and having their movements registered in the process of sensing, rather than of perceiving any underlying pattern, heightened their perception of their own mobility. In many ways Joseph was clarifying what his art was not about. It had nothing to do with Josef Albers, for example, whose book *The Interaction of Colour* was published in 1962. Nor did it have any bearing on Constructivism in any of its peculiarly British, systematic guises. It was, however, 'modernist' in a general way – an American reviewer once wrote that Joseph's work could have been made 'any time during the last four decades'.

Debates over painting as object formed a backdrop to Joseph's early experiments. Shown in 1992 at the Royal Festival Hall, London, in a selection of classic sixties paintings, *Yellow Painting* (1969) is a prime example of shape and colour combined. By this time Joseph's influences may have altered. (Ellsworth Kelly, in particular, springs to mind.) Poised on one point, the triangular structure is painted yellow, the colour Joseph used for *Passageway* as well as for the three discs he placed against trees in the park at Kenwood. Taller than people, these unexpected circular interruptions altered the environment. In contrast, the unframed triangle, with its implacable surface, stood precariously against a wall, rebuffing interrogation, demanding attention as a solid, singular form.

The rectangle-within-a-rectangle composition, a synthesis of the 'hole in the canvas' and 'the protruding interior' alternatives, prompted a far higher degree of introspection from the viewer. Now the ambiguity between the two points of view existed in the mind and not in the definition of the paint. In passing from the sculptural works to the painting, the issue of proportion was interiorized. Asked about human proportion, Joseph agrees that this is what he intends, 'but human proportion not just in terms of geometric, mathematical ideas but also of an attitude to the quality of thought or an investment in it: something of care and sensibility that cannot be paraphrased'. Hardly surprisingly, Joseph regards himself as a classicist. From this time onwards his works offered possibilities of visual adjustment and reconciliation that may have moral concomitants in terms of everyday behaviour. What cannot be grasped and held in visual terms, existing in a state of constant potentiality, is interpreted as something of value to which we can only aspire. It must be construed in human terms, if only because people are the most complex entities we know. And the persistent condition of trying to grasp something that evades us not only engages our capacity for aspiration but may convince us that is a crucial factor in the interpretation of the work.

Joseph's triumph is to have invented a vehicle so sensitive that it can register infinitely subtle changes, changes that can alter the effect of the paintings. Paradoxically, the apparent rigidity of structure is exactly what permits continual alteration, as accurate a gauge of mood as the human face. Though the aesthetic that underlies Joseph's experiments involves mimesis only in the most general way and despite the fact that the particularity of effects produced by the paintings is remarkable, no single viewing can exhaust the range and potential of one of his works. Critics have written of the sense of 'vulnerability' that they feel when looking at Joseph's work. Instead, perhaps, they should say that by concentrating on making a visual situation that remains permanently unresolved, Joseph locates a plenitude of potential feeling in his observer.

Joseph's position in current painting is debatable. Self-taught – he worked in advertising before becoming a painter – he has never fallen back on current schools of thought to define what he does. With reference to his work, the old term 'Minimal painting' means very little, for example. Besides, from year to year the aspect of his paintings differs, driven by the kind of emotional weather that may or may not have a bearing on his daily life. (Dark works from 1982 and just after were born out of despair, he admits, made simply 'in order to keep myself alive'.) It is a given of his entire project that in choosing to operate as he does, he relinquishes control over entire areas of his enterprise. 'The risk I know only too well –' he wrote in 1983, 'I have felt compelled to discard innovation of form in order to express mood and sentiment.'

Behaviour: an interview with Nayland Blake

Published in frieze *5, 1992.*

Stuart Morgan: *How did your first sculptures look?*

Nayland Blake: Mundane, small-scale. By 1986, when I began showing, they simply juxtaposed a found object and a plaque, for example, or a text and an object. A pair of bongos with 'Vanity of Vanities' written on the drumskins. A pair of men's black shoes chained together, and on the toes plaques that read LAP and DOG. What interested me was how objects could contain narrative.

And the theme?

Unspoken power relationships in everyday life.

Why did you begin using puppets?

As the next stage of that control metaphor. But they also have to do with the space between the prop and the actor; they are clearly characters but they are not active.

In your work, control always includes sexual control, and sex is constantly reduced to S&M.

Not S&M as much as bondage. S&M involves two people enacting scenes for each other's sexual gratification, scenes of domination or submission. It is a game they agree to play by certain rules which are successfully fulfilled, with variations introduced as sources of pleasure. Bondage is about the sexual satisfaction of being maintained physically in a position and the sexual attraction of seeing someone in such a position. For the person in that position the satisfaction is that of being immobilized, not of being in pain.

For years now you have been making imaginary instruments of restraint – leather or cloth harnesses and stainless steel paraphernalia – and including these in displays of your work as a constant undertone. I'm beginning to see how this engages with the puppet motif. Except that puppets don't have a sex.

You mean they don't have sex. Mr Punch is very phallic; he has a phallic nose, a phallic chin, a phallic pot belly and a phallic back. In a catalogue for my *Punch Agonistes* in Los Angeles in 1990, Richard Hawkins described how putting your hand up a glove-puppet's butt is the only way it can get an erection. Perhaps we do know how puppets have sex!

For viewers your work involves less physical methods of activating the props you provide. Three historically based installations, for example – The Trotsky Suite, The Schreber Suite *and* The Philosopher's Suite – *have prompted revisions of historical reputations.*

The most recent, which is ongoing, was *The Philosopher's Suite*, displaying materials for a marionette production of Philosophy in the Bedroom, by the Marquis de Sade. You came from the back to find a large, free-standing marionette stage made out of scaffolding, and by the time you'd walked to the front you'd registered what it was. Puppets hung around the room. So there was no other option: the viewer had to decide either to be audience or puppeteer. There's a certain frustration about everything in the performance being there. So the piece started to be about our desire to see that text acted out, to watch that writing happen, which returns to the idea of what a revolutionary or utopian language might be. Years before, I'd made pieces burning de Sade or using photography (the actual pages), about the difference between the mental image of de Sade and the actuality; ink on paper. In fact, *The Philosopher's Suite* was first shown in Orange County, California, a place so conservative that visitors to the gallery couldn't buy or even order books by de Sade.

Why did you choose Schreber?

Because his case contained the most overt references to homosexuality in the whole of Freud, and I wanted to produce what was almost a commentary on the text.

How did you disagree with Freud?

With where he claimed Schreber's delusions were coming from. In fact, there were places closer to home. Schreber's father was an early champion of physical culture. He also had theories of child-rearing and developed metal armatures to correct children's posture. Schreber developed delusions about his body being manipulated and organs replaced, removed or switched. But Freud never discusses the possible impact of the father on his son's delusions. And Schreber's paranoia centred on the fear that his doctor was engaged in an attempt to turn him into a woman in order to bear the child of God. In fact, that doctor had prescribed castration for manic depression, and this was common knowledge among his patients. Freud knew this. So Freud's reading of Schreber's book is tortured and circuitous, if not exactly invalid. My aim was to return to the text and offer a reading which was more indicative of the circumstances and which tried to situate it historically, repositioning Schreber's writing in the flow of late decadent/ early modernist/ proto-Surrealist figures like Raymond Roussel or Félicien Rops. When the installation was shown at the museum in Berkeley, part of it consisted of works from their collection by artists who were Schreber's contemporaries – a Puvis de Chavannes, for example, and a Schiele drawing – with their labels replaced by paragraphs from Schreber.

Here and elsewhere you see your role as critical, revisionary.

That was evident first in 1988 with *The Trotsky Suite*, which consisted of records of myself reading Trotsky's autobiography, divided into six sections, with the tapes subjected to editing systems derived from the manipulation of Richard Nixon's memoirs. So positions would be omitted or overlapped. The whole piece was about the process of erasure or editing of history.

What do Trotsky, Schreber and de Sade have in common?

All three had systems, visions of the world, utopian projects that were flawed . . .

And all three have a potentially saintly side. But you followed them with Punch Agonistes, *and Punch lacks this totally. Was this a wild card, meant to undo any conclusions derived from your previous, historically based thinking?*

The way Punch appeared was as a kind of phallic aggression, so it's not Punch but Punch's head, without the body and without the stick. That image of a severed head has cropped up any number of times since then.

Punch is a kind of psychopath, isn't he? He attacks everyone and everything.

And without provocation. He's pure ego. He's very much like a Sadean hero: a libertine. There's no reasoning with him because all the things you would have recourse to, like the church or the family or any kind of social contract, are just disregarded. I think that's why he is a hero. He appears in my work in castrated form because I don't think that position is possible. *Punch Agonistes* wasn't about Punch; it used Punch. Because it is so easily encapsulated, the Punch figure became a key to how, say, de Sade functions. And because a series of miniature puppet stages gave viewers the option to be in front of or behind them, people were given a way of addressing the notion of theatricality. Punch takes us by storm, demanding rather than asking politely: works that involve him deal with pleasure. Punch is not about 'desire', as in commedia dell'arte, where Harlequin moons after Columbine; it's about immediate, infantile pleasure-taking. This serves as an almost talismanic background to the way the work is looked at, always reappearing as a reminder. After *The Philosopher's Suite* I realized that much of what I'd been doing had been a type of theatre, like Camillo's memory theatre. A motif would keep appearing in the work or there would be a body of text or imagery that would intrigue me. My pieces would be stabs at that idea, attempts to explain my fascination with it.

Do you regard the Punch work as a reply to the de Sade piece?

A variant, perhaps. One thing to do now is to decide what it would mean if it was a reply. Much of the experience of the de Sade suite involved the desire to see that revolutionary text acted. You could argue that Punch is the way to do that, after a time when it has been safely bracketed in order not to disturb our idea of what the world is.

Not all of the works in Punch Agonistes *featured Punch.*

That's true. There were restraint pieces that referred to the armature of puppetry. Others used texts from horror novels about people being menaced by various forces – a grand piano, a herd of swine . . . These are all castration stories in the hyper-hysterical style of horror novels. One thing about Punch is that his universe is not sublimated; what we work so diligently to decode in other texts becomes the baseline narrative.

You made a horror video.

I re-edited a sequence from John Carpenter's version of *The Thing*, in which a person's head pulls itself off a body, uses its tongue to pull itself across the floor, sprouts legs and scuttles off, only to be burned up by a flame-thrower. The sequence continues endlessly. Perhaps television is the severed head par excellence; it's in your home, talking to you, keeping you company. In a way, the Brian Masters book on Dennis Nilsen, *Killing for Company*, is about that: having a relationship to the outside world where the only way you can feel safe to interact with an emotion, is to keep it acquiescent by killing it.

Presumably the Nilsen and Jeffrey Dahmer cases relate to the edible heads you're making for the London installation.

The chocolate heads – for the fourteen victims of Nilsen and of Dahmer – are cast from a bust of Wagner I found in a music store. Then a group of bronze heads of Wagner will be made, with mallets attached. Then there will be an amended poster of a photograph by Herb Ritts, a series of three paintings and a large poster to go up around London and also be available from the gallery. The aim is to figure out what these severed heads mean to me and why they keep surfacing in my work. The poster is the same one that Dahmer had in his apartment: of a worker holding two tyres, a very phallic image which cropping will emphasize. Probably a CD will be fixed to it, by The Pixies, who made an album to do with decapitation. And there may be something from horror movies.

What relation did the two murderers have to the world around them?

Unlike Nilsen, Dahmer continually denied his homosexuality. But both men seem to have had one thing in common; at the moment when they needed some emotional connection with another person, it became a problem if that person was either conscious or living. Some argue that this was a fear of rejection. Dahmer's men were mostly black or Asian. He would bore holes in their skulls in an attempt to lobotomize them and turn them into emotional slaves, just to have around. Nilsen kept their skulls as shrines. Sometimes he decorated them.

So you are dealing with a set of parallels between loving and killing, eating and 'consumption' in life as well as art.

Plus a self-portrait. I identify with the image of a detached, wandering intellect, the Odilon Redon eyeball-as-balloon idea. Then there are the images of racial difference.

For the first time you use an image of black people. Why? And why now?

Because my father is black. And because I never found a way to address that.

How does Wagner fit in?

He's the artist as proponent of racial purity, the millennial figure who is going to reorganize and somehow escape history by returning us to a state of myth, something I disagree with.

Wagner becomes hollow.

There is a dichotomy between marble and bronze in the history of sculpture, between what it means to carve something instead of moulding it. To me, carving is about mastering something from nature, while moulding is playing with your own shit.

He also turns black.

Our notion of transcendent sculpture is based on the idea of white Greek sculpture which, as we know, was not white. Posited as a white, ultimate form, it was divorced – in history's reading of it – from the physicality of the people who made it: people who were dark. Another art-historical anomaly is the divorce of public sculpture from domestic, interior sculpture: votive bronzes in darkened places. One of my influences for this was a series of small, seventeenth-century bronze lamps in the Victoria & Albert Museum, combinations of a human head and, at the base, a bird's foot with entwined entrails. The labels say 'grotesque'. In fact, the features are completely negroid. The idea of the decorative blackamoor slave returns us to Dahmer's skulls.

Are you punishing Wagner?

He's beyond punishment. But I like the idea of turning him into shit. Supremely edible shit. Or resonant shit, in the case of the gongs.

Beheading, Punch, The Thing, *cannibalism, slavery, chocolate . . . you keep moving sideways, rather than forwards.*

Proceeding horizontally rather than vertically; tending to move in a number of directions at once, so that particular tropes stop for a while then begin again, reinforced by what has happened; the use of different media in the same show form part of a larger project in which my work is engaged: making the case for a different definition of a gay sensibility.

I can see that specific readings seek to alter preconceptions about homosexuality – to divorce it from a clinical notion of paranoia in the Schreber piece, for example – but what is a 'new gay sensibility' moving from and to?

Traditional views of gay male sensibility propose a standard idea of male gaze and male object. Politically and ideologically, this is regressive. At this point a greater number of possibilities exist for what a gay reading could be: a blurring of gender, the idea of the pathetic or decadent, a formal preference for the fragment over the masterpiece, working against the grain of accepted readings. There is a way in which my methodology is about asserting the pleasure of the anus. To me, talking about chocolate means something different if it is approached from a gay position. But we should be past the point of asking 'Is it gay or not?' That is a question which continually privileges the mainstream, ghettoizes gay people and trivializes what they do. It means much more to ask 'What do black people think about this?' It's really about interrogating material rather than about measuring the degree of gayness in any particular case.

So it's not a culture within a culture.

It's a position among positions.

And essentially it opposes the unitary.

In the eighties a lot of art demanded an understanding of the entirety of the project every time you saw a piece. I see my own work as the snail trail of the journey. Objects are residue. Their meaning tends to grow and become richer as more objects are made. But making is an experience that's not an end in itself; it's about thinking out loud how to get to the next idea. I don't know the ultimate point to which it's tending. That's why I keep doing it.

The Pleasure Principle

Talk given for a Wimbledon School of Art symposium at the Tate Gallery, 'The Curriculum for Fine Art in Higher Education', 19 February 1993, transcripts published by Wimbledon School of Art, October 1993.

I taught for some years at the Rijksakademie in Amsterdam, which was made what it is today by an odd sort of route. The Dutch government used to give a lot of money to artists – in fact a great deal of money. A man came to your studio once a year and even if you weren't an artist at all, it was a good idea to keep a studio and to make a work of art once a year and he would say 'You haven't done much work,' but you'd say, 'Ah yes, But I'm so exacting that I've burnt all the rest and this is my masterpiece.' And he'd say, 'Well I have to buy that then because the Rijksdienst has this money for buying art.' The idea was that the man would give you so much money for your work of art that you'd be able to live until next year on that money, until he came again. Finally, everyone in the world thought this was a bad idea, and finally the Dutch thought it was a bad idea too, because everybody told them and they took notice, and they announced that they would cut this down in three easy stages. At the end of the first stage anybody who wasn't earning a certain amount of money from their art would not be able to call themselves an artist. At the end of the second stage, a year later, the amount was put up, and so on. As soon as they announced this there were multiple suicides all over Amsterdam from people who had such a bad drug habit that it couldn't be supported any other way. And finally the thing had been done. Three years had gone by, but now they found they had so much money they didn't know what to do with it and so they put it in a very large academy because they felt that Dutch artists still weren't able to keep up with artists in the rest of the world, and the idea was a European art academy in which this would be possible and Dutch students would study next to other people. I'm not sure that's worked.

If we wanted another sort of model from Europe to hold up to what we have it would be German art schools, where you sign on for master classes with great artists, usually male, but not always male. Frankfurt would be a good example. Based on, I suppose, Harold Bloom's idea of the 'anxiety of influence', the idea that you have an artist you want to be better than and to overthrow. Again in a rather male way, and the driving force behind that idea is, I suppose, greatness rather than simply success. If you want to go for simple success, you hang around the studios of the School of Visual Arts in New York when nobody knows you're there, and you listen to the students talking and what you hear will turn your hair, particularly if you're a critic because what they're talking about is what parties to go to, what gallery owners can be bribed and critics and curators, and what with and how much of it.

One thing – these are just preliminary remarks and they don't add up to anything at all I'm afraid – one thing I sense today is a creeping bias against contemporaneity in art; criticism is deemed as marketing, and so on. Colin Painter's suggestion that journals on current art mislead, for example, is surely based on the misapprehension that art stays still. Students know it doesn't. The staff don't always know that. It is in the interests of the staff to prove that it doesn't. I would also like to say that we're here to produce great artists and not great students. How many marks would van Gogh have earned for team skills? What percentage would Leni Riefenstahl have been given for effective judgement? Where are the great artist of the future and this concludes my opening remarks, which I've said don't make sense – I suspect that they are young. Why do we leave it so late to expose people to the full panoply of what art can do, and take them instead to see sickly pretty dolly paintings? I suspect that they're criminals and that jails are full of potential artists, all of whom have something to say and are dying to say it. I suspect that they are fast learners. I think that three years is too long and that if you took people younger you could give them a quick hit and that would be enough for the whole of their lives. And I suspect they are unemployed. Only one woman in Britain has seen all of these things properly and that's Kay Fido, who is not here today, and I am not at all surprised. [Kay Fido set up a foundation course for the unemployed; see Morgan's comments in *frieze* 1, 1991.] My paper comes with the same warning as the old episodes of *Dragnet*. The names have been changed to protect the innocent. Well, I'm not so sure about that.

'The pleasure principle.' History can change overnight. You wake up in the morning and everything is different. I was studying for a doctorate when suddenly there were no jobs. To be exact, there was no longer a guarantee that once your doctorate was complete a university job would await you. The scramble was immediate and embarrassing. Traumatized by it, I stood my ground. That was my first mistake. Then I drifted into a major depression;

that was my second. It had never occurred to me that I would ever leave university. I took to reading at random and wandering in the same way. One day began to feel the same as the next. If I'd had a diary it would have been completely empty. Gradually I developed new methods of passing time. For example, on my walks I used to pass a large anonymous-looking building with a glass front and every time I did I would strain to look into a room where different paintings went on show month by month. One day, a day of particular desperation, I took the bull by the horns, striding up the stairs and through the front door. I asked the man sitting there if I could go and look at the pictures. Of course, he replied, it's a public gallery. I didn't know that, I went in. What happened then took less than ten minutes. They were the ten minutes that changed my life. Paintings meant nothing to me; it had been like that for years, although I had never stopped wanting to know what people saw in them. On this particular day the paintings said no more than usual; I was more interested in the place itself. What could this building be, with its view of the trees outside, and its evident connection with art? Then as I looked through the glass door through which I'd passed to the entrance hall outside, I saw the front door burst open to admit a group of young people. They were the most attractive people I had ever seen. They were only a little younger than I was but everything else about them was light years away. My head spun. One idea after another occurred to me. What had happened to me? I was nothing more than a morose, long-haired – that's not a joke – hippie with no future. What was going to happen? It was up to me. What did I want? To be like these people, to be with them, to be one of them, here. I'd realized where I was. This was the famous local art college with an ethos every university student envied, but few could break into. By all accounts it was one of the best art schools in Britain. Suddenly it all became clear. I would leave university, I would forget about my doctorate, I would get a job. I would get a job here and I would stay here forever. As I opened the door of the gallery, a sign caught my eye: 'General Office'. I knocked and entered. My head was spinning even more now. This was an adventure. This was life as it should be lived. The room was a typing pool with a wooden counter. I rang the bell and one of the girls got up. 'Can I help you?' I paused. 'Have you got any jobs going?' She looked me up and down. 'We have enough models for the moment,' she said. I said I was not a model, thinking quickly, realizing what the next question would be. 'Well, what are you then?' 'I'm a lecturer.' She was struggling to conceal her disbelief and I could see her point. 'A lecturer in what?' 'Literature,' I said. She said, 'English?', I said 'No, literature.' I said it so casually that it shut her up. It might have been this tiny victory that swung it. The girls at the typewriters tried even harder to pretend they weren't listening. I was handed a telephone. A telephone with a voice at the other end. 'Mr Morgan?', 'Yes.' 'My name is Brady. I'm the Head of Complementary Studies. I understand you teach literature.' I said I did. How interesting. Well, I'm in a meeting at the moment, perhaps we could arrange a time to talk.' My heart leapt. 'Would Wednesday be all right?' I said I was almost sure it would. She said, what about 3 o'clock. I said, better make it 3.15. '3.15 it is Mr Morgan, I'll see you then.'

The typists were impressed and so was I. In the street I actually laughed out loud for the first time in six months. Mrs Brady was a woman of a certain age. She wore sailor suits and had risen from being a primary school teacher to become head of one of the largest departments of its kind in England. At my interview she asked me what must be the silliest question in the world, for someone who says they know all about literature. She leaned forward and looked serious and said 'Have you read any good books lately?' I said I had. She said, tell me about it. I said, 'What do you want to know?', she said 'Anything, tell me about it.' I could even tell you the name of the novel. It was quite saucy in a way. I got to the high point in the plot, where the hero is lying naked under a sun lamp when his lover comes in and asks him if he's murdered his wife. At this point I realized she had the palms of her hands flat on her desk and she was rising from her seat. 'Stop,' she said. 'I see it all rising before me.' She was that kind of woman. She then proceeded to offer me an extremely small job. The day of my first class she summoned me into her office. 'You're a clever sort of person,' she said, 'with a university education, but you have to forget all that here. No one seems to know facts or pass exams. These are artists, Mr Morgan, their brains are in their fingers. They may not look as though they are listening but it all goes in and it all comes out again in their work. Their job is to make art, your job is to inspire them. Now go out there and do it.' It would have been like *The Dam Busters* if she hadn't been dressed like a sailor.

After the class her second-in-command showed me around the college. It began with the canteen. The janitors had found some whisky and were drunk at one end. At the other the students had taken their clothes off and were throwing custard at each other. It seemed as if I'd walked into another universe, but no one seemed to think there was anything odd about it at all.

I asked my colleague what he taught, he said Chinese. I asked if there was much call for that, he said yes, and Japanese too. Gradually I found that my poetry class was going on alongside classes in Ancient Egyptian culture, Italian language, Scandinavian culture, mime, extra-sensory perception, economic history . . . perhaps not economic history. On a Monday morning Mrs Brady had a habit of coming and calling a meeting to ruin all our plans. 'Russia is in the news,' she would bellow. 'This will be Russian week. You will all teach Russian studies.' 'But I teach music!' 'Then teach Russian music!' 'I teach theatre.' 'Well, do Chekhov.' One of her most annoying habits was to include herself in other people's courses, uninvited, usually to give one of her two classic lectures, the one on African masks, which she felt was applicable under practically any circumstances, or the one on Rembrandt, in the course of which she would burst into tears because he'd had such a bad life. But it didn't stop there. The drama teacher was delighted when Mrs Brady arranged for her students to do a public performance of their improvised mimes. Unfortunately, Mrs Brady had omitted to mention one fact: that she herself would be joining in dressed in a leotard. No one could say Mrs Brady did not invite visitors; we would have everything from Sir John Summerson on classical architecture to a man who happened to have been to Tibet and thought we'd like to see slides of his journey.

Lectures like this were full, but so were those of some of the resident teachers. One of them sticks in my mind particularly; his name was George. His name really was George, I'm not altering his name. He was a charming older man who'd been born in Russia. When he was a boy his family left and settled in Paris, where he became interested in architecture, and he trained for years as an architect and the day that he qualified he gave it up. He was really more interested in art and he knew it. His friends were Picasso, Chagall – in fact he knew everyone. Women adored George, who was surrounded by girls – secretaries particularly, as he would hold their coats for them. Isn't that pathetic? And as he took them to lunch he would sing little snatches from Russian opera. His classes worshipped him just because he was interesting. One day I saw a notice. '4pm', it said, 'George Simonech on Surrealism'. I'd read a book about Surrealism and so I thought I knew all about it and I went. It was full. George stood there for what seemed like an eternity, rolling and lighting a cigarette. Finally he drew on it, puff, and began. 'The last time I saw André Breton he said "George, if I were to write the Second Surrealist Manifesto again this is what I'd put in it".' It was and remains the best opening to any lecture ever. This was not learning, this was life. Staff would spend all their time at the college, whether they were meant to or not. Domains were not at all circumscribed, Op art was fashionable and the Chinese lecturer was good at wiring, for example, so he spent all day helping to make the flashing machines run. When he wasn't in foreign parts, that is: he'd left his wife and was having an affair with an oriental air hostess who gave him free tickets. I had difficulty knowing whether he told the truth or not and suspected him of being a bullshitter. The trouble is I could never pin him down. He claimed to have negotiated the sale of a battleship to the Japanese, for example. I think he was actually telling the truth there. But he would always open conversations with remarks that could not be left unchallenged. One day we were sitting in the canteen and he said 'To think that this time two days ago I was having a massage in Bangkok, and what a massage it was.' That was my cue to say 'Why?' and I did. He said, 'Those girls even massage your eyeballs.' I said, 'Probably if you paid enough you could do that in England.' He looked me straight in the eye and he said, 'Not half so cheaply or so well.'

I left university of course and moved nearer to the college. I abandoned my PhD too after a while. The students had become my friends and my heroes. There was only one problem, they'd talk to each other about art and I couldn't join in, so I'd sneak off to the library and read articles. How different the art magazines seemed from what I'd been reading before. To write about art, what a strange thing. They threw Mrs Brady out in the end of course. Not sufficiently academic, they said. The place became a polytechnic and extended into other turns. People like George were laid off, gradually or given so few hours that they disappeared. This was academic. I stayed. I'd been invited to teach at my old university but, oddly, they wanted me to teach art. Out of shame more than enthusiasm my employers let me do the same at the polytechnic. We taught together, sometimes in the same room. The academic challenge could be met and incorporated with the older ideas of an art college, we thought, and it worked for a while. But gradually the number of students increased. The classes became so large you never got to know them. Heads of department would complain that courses were not immediately relevant to the jobs the students would be doing when they left college. Contact with students was positively discouraged in some ways. A letter was stuck under my college door one day, for example, which said that from now on no member of staff should spend time discussing students' problems with students because there was a social worker/counsellor upstairs to do that in Room 437. So if a student you barely know, who needs an abortion, comes to you in tears – not that she even knows you but she's picked you out and thinks you in particular might be able to provide a sympathetic ear, and she's been working up her courage for days, even weeks, to tell someone about her problem – you shut the door in her face and send her off to Room 437 to someone she's never met. Then there was the other letter stuffed under my door, which said that from now on under no circumstances should we mark spelling or punctuation errors in student essays. I took it immediately to my boss and pointed out that I'd never let one go and I never would. By this time I was writing a lot in magazines. Instead of increasing my desirability at work it lessened it greatly. New art historians were appointed, a new word. Always from the Courtauld Institute, always wanting to teach nineteenth-century French painting, never able to give a decent lecture. Term after term the number of students who signed on for their courses was minimal for these people. I was doing their work but they got paid more than I was. My boss was a man who sat in his office all day doing sums. Students didn't even know who he was, the ones who did know laughed at him. He lied to me and told me my opinions were being heard and acted on. I knew they weren't. Design had taken over at this time, art historians were on their way out and the rest were already out. By the rest, of course, I mean complementary studies. Those great swear words that represent to me everything that was best in art college training. They tried to force me into other mixed courses, a bit of this, a bit of that. I refused. I wanted to teach artists. I wanted to teach them literature. There was no place for such frippery. My old friends had been broken. The Dean had nobbled the drama teacher by refusing to let her do public performances and forcing her into an awful performance course. George had gone long before. He had very little teaching by the time he died and he died playing snooker, as I'm sure he would have wanted. He was still living with the student he'd lived with for so long. When he died the college didn't send her a card because they weren't married. Finally, they offered me a readership with my own students to teach up to degree level. I could work half the time and write the other half. It was coming soon and I would get it but I mustn't tell the rest of the staff. I didn't like that idea at all and I did a bad thing, I kept my mouth shut. The entire business turned out to be a lie. I waited years and it never came. Finally, I left the polytechnic altogether. Now of course it's a university.

There's a footnote to that story about the readership. A few years later my old boss announced that he was standing down from his job, in order to take a readership. Everyone was amazed. 'There is no readership in the department,' they said. There was, of course. He stood down, took it. A few months later it was taken off him again, showing I suppose that there is a God.

The skills that I learned were not useless to me, I think I still spend all my time with artists and help them in a different way now by responding to their work. I persist in thinking that they are reckless and attractive and gifted human beings, and I suppose I've become a professional groupie of some odd variety. I hang around artists and I'm proud to know them. None of that should prevent me from saying that I do feel like the last man in the tribe. Complementary studies, my friends, have died and there is no place for me any more. Complementary studies is what I taught and it was based on a range of skills, topics not studied for their own sake but, well, to inspire, as Mrs Brady said. 'What is Matisse "about"' doesn't seem a bad exam question to me. Matisse is about pleasure, he's about communicated pleasure. In order to communicate pleasure you have to feel it first, you have to feel it through, you have to reproduce it physically somehow in your play on the canvas.

'They are artists, Mr Morgan, their brains are in their fingers.' Some days I feel as if my brains are in my backside for having stayed at that place so long. The art school tradition is in tatters. The marketing of art schools has taken over. Meanness of spirit is rife. Teaching of the kind we were encouraged to do has been suppressed. What fun it was, how creative fun can be. Art is not a game but no art is possible without creative play and a lot of it. That's really all I have to say.

Jeffrey Dennis: Something in the Air

Introduction to Jeffrey Dennis, *published by The Orchard Gallery, Derry, 1993.*

Traffic moves so quickly through Leytonstone on its way into or out of London that visitors scarcely register it as a place at all. Perhaps they are right. Off the main roads lie mile upon mile of terraced houses. Not much happens. Perhaps nothing ever did. Yet the area has boasted famous residents: Alfred Hitchcock and William Morris, one as intent on the machinery of evil as the other was on banishing machinery altogether. A more recent Leytonstone resident, Jeffrey Dennis, put them together in a painting called *Unnatural Growth.* As Hitchcock's jowl contrasted with a distorted frond from a Morris wallpaper design, the viewer sensed their shared taste for concealment, eroticism and pattern-making, features that combine in Dennis's newest paintings, where iridescent surfaces threaten to overwhelm everything else. Distance becomes confused in a mass of detail which resembles soap bubbles, bodiless counterparts of the baked beans in Dennis's earlier work. The surface makes it hard to register other features: motifs resembling pipes, for example, with smaller pipes inside, parts of what seems a permanently fractured whole. Or perhaps not, since they resemble bones or foldaway sticks that blind people use. In one painting the larger pipes are arranged in the shape of a bicycle.

Unable to recognize this, tiny figures looking lost and dwarfed like true city dwellers, occupy territory of their own, no longer artificially inset as before, but added like items on a notice board. Baffled though they are, they retain a modicum of heroic potential, explorers in an urban jungle. And, as in wilderness, measurement fails. Equivalents for the viewer, simultaneously awestruck and disorientated by the terrain, these alienated individuals may seem less significant than the urban orienteering in which they are forced to indulge. For navigating outlying districts of London, where amenities such as cinemas, shops, stations and banks are either clustered together or widespread, a compass should be compulsory. In Dennis's previous work, figures were alienated from the rest of the composition. These days, though their insertion is less blatant, they continue to be dwarfed by the surrounding space. The effect seems almost oriental rather than occidental, and induces a sense of harmony in which part and whole are resolved, though that resolution muffles a certain disquiet. Above all, the anonymity of the figures and the incongruity of their presence contribute to the prevailing air of Dennis's paintings: a sense of deep unease.

Combine 'unrest' and 'dis-ease' and you begin to define it. The practice of everyday life is featured as before. Yet in Dennis's recent paintings the alienation is emphasized less than the possibility of subsuming the figures in some grander scheme. The walker in the city, that archetypal figure in the modernist period from Baudelaire through Benjamin to *Blade Runner*, seems less like a surrogate viewer trying to solve problems than an element integrated in some larger fabric. Morris made patterns for wallpaper, in which subliminal eroticism informed the effects of wind and waves. The result was to hint at a universe governed by such forces, visible by their effect. For attraction or expansion in Morris's designs become elements of an emotional gamut which have been translated into visual form. But is it logical to suppose that this is possible in that, for example, a pattern could ever be tragic or life-denying rather than life-enhancing? Is unnatural design feasible? Classic Hitchcock – *Vertigo, Psycho, The Birds* – has been compared to the mature tragedies of Shakespeare, since both depict 'a precarious order in constantly imminent danger of being undermined by terrible, destructive upsurgings from an underlying chaos'. How well that describes Dennis's paintings, their disquiet and their world.

Dennis's titles hint at a grand sweep of history (the Kafkaesque *The Covenant* and *Playing the Gatekeeper*), paralysis (*A Journey Postponed*), archaeology (*Digger*), above all the idea of ending (*A Box Not Yet Shut*). The vision of ripe-rottenness that proceeds from a sense that the time is 'out of joint' – a feeling that Morris would have seen as the premise of Arthurian romance as well as Victorian England – is widespread in post-Thatcher Britain. Signs of dissolution, even dissoluteness, are plentiful in Leytonstone: a rough sketch for imminent apocalypse. Not surprisingly, Dennis's dystopian view reveals normality as an elaborate set of disjunctures that promise yet never achieve definition. His paintings consist of stage-managed interruptions that escalate alarmingly. The effect of sad farce is achieved by a style akin to Mannerism. Painting on curved surfaces is nothing new for Dennis; works such as *The Green Cradle* or *Antoine's Curve* seemed to bulge like the surface of a television tube. Another Mannerist variation were composite works in which the flat canvases were arranged like dominoes, each taking up from the last, inheriting unresolved elements then proceeding to reply or to elaborate on them. (Perhaps nothing is gained by this, for parataxis is an anti-structural form of structure, and the interplay resulting from the curves of the depicted tubes served to heighten the intransigence of the entire arrangement.)

The next stage was for the canvas to seem to modify and bend, as in *Cello* or *Six Easy Breathers*, where the pipes, springing from two to three dimensions, became the grounds for painting, with all the spatial play that this implied. A work such as *Paranoid Abacus* combines play with drawing and diagram, miniaturization and actual size, part and whole, real and represented in a way that forces viewers to abandon hope of any permanent system of representation or even of any sense of stability in perception itself. For Dennis's luscious surface only serves to heighten the feeling of unease. Clustered, iridescent globes make the picture plane seem to move forward, locking incident into place as bubble-wrap cushions an object in transit or polystyrene chips prevent breakable items from harm. Sensuous yet off-putting, they represent a deceptive space which seems to bulge or give way at different points and has drifts of colour as illogical in their appearance as a rash, a kind of shrubbery in which recognizable forms are bedded. At other times pipes simply protrude, half in and half out of the deceptive background, either bending convincingly in terms of perspectival convention or painted so naively that no such description could be applied. Similarly, in a work called *Curved Studio*, it is a painted photograph of a studio that becomes convex, for in those pictures reality is placed at one remove, while painting itself is interrogated.

For Dennis, piping has multiple connotations: of looking, as though through a telescope, as a perfect example of curvature, or as tunnels, nozzles, conduits or even bones, for they seem threaded together relatively tightly by some elastic substance. What they have in common is everyday practicality. This is exactly what has broken down in these paintings, or has been broken down for examination, as the need to put elements to painterly use became more pressing. Tensions are possible between the parts, though for the time being these remain in abeyance. Also in abeyance are ideas of size and scale, though there is something inevitably human about both. The same cannot be said for the bubbles, an entire housing in which the other elements can lodge. The slight Surrealist aspect of this, an aspect that permeates Dennis's work, may not be a style but rather a function of the time:

> In 1986 Margaret Geller and her colleagues at the Smithsonian Center for Astrophysics undertook a systematic redshift survey of galaxies at distances much deeper in space than ever performed. Their structures were astonishing. Structures were observable of very large scales, tens of mega-parsecs, which had not been identified previously. Very well-defined filaments were seen, and galaxies seemed to be located on very sharply delineated, relatively spherical 'sheets' surrounding huge voids. Geller and her colleagues described it as resembling a 'slice through the suds in the kitchen sink'.

The anticlimactic aspect of language, recruited for such sublime projects, is paralleled in Dennis's painting by the music hall undertones of the tubing that runs through the paintings like drainage or faulty phallic symbols. Perhaps its pervasive presence is understandable; after all the 'subject' of Dennis's paintings is increasingly their own genesis and the circumstances that surround it. And if these are beginnings, the sense of an ending is equally striking: the sense, at least, that though things were together, they are now apart and will not combine. Instead they remain ingredients, presented with evidence of life in all its amplitude. Yet of course such an argument will not hold water; the 'evidence' in question consists of photographs, mere shadows which the painter brings together, like elements in a still life. They, in turn, refuse to play, yet despite this the picture plane gathers an energy of its own – fertile and expansive, admittedly, but also deceptive, like that foam used by the fire brigade which camouflages and smothers.

For camouflage is what these paintings most resemble. In particular, painting on objects has this effect: calming, as in a Morris wallpaper design, yet establishing an order of events in which recognition plays a major part, as in a Hitchcock film. Hitchcock's recognitions can be complex. In *Marnie*, for example, we watch our heroine experiencing psychological recognitions arranged to generate some parallel and vicarious response in ourselves. Her problems are our problems, not 'out there' but implicit in the texture of our daily life. This is Dennis's premise, and one of which he seems increasingly convinced. Yet while layering emphasis on the intrinsicality of the problem by coaxing it to the surface, even inscribing it on objects of use, he demonstrates a loss of objectivity that is inevitable, since the observer is part of the problem. Going with the flow may be one way of coping, but will it offer the possibility for isolating 'issues' that one mode of behaviour stresses? (An unsatisfactory mode, it must be added, in which arms-length tactics have failed). That technique of isolation applies to ourselves: the increased emphasis on the object nature of what used to be the canvas makes it easier to elide the possibility of framing, even to reduce that to the status of a Hitchcockian McGuffin in the cause of a mode that Morris favoured: the idyll, urban now, instead of pastoral. Morris's ambition, to paper over the cracks between opposing lifestyles by instituting one that retained elements of both, and doing so on the edge of the city, as Leytonstone used to be, has returned as a problem of subject and object.

The problem, as Dennis presents it, parallels game-playing, which may be exactly what art as an institution is. Michel Serres defined the 'quasi-object' as not an object 'but one nevertheless, since it is not a subject, since it is in the world'. He hastened to add that it was also a 'quasi-subject' since 'it marks or designates a subject who, without it, would not be a subject'. His example was a ball, which is only what it is if a subject holds it. 'Over there, on the ground, it is nothing . . . it has no meaning, no function, and no value, for ball isn't played alone, and players who hog the ball are bad players by definition.' Passing the ball means transferring the 'I' to a 'we'. But how can 'I' be taken away? How indeed was the 'I' given? Serres explains: 'There are objects to do so, quasi-objects, quasi-subjects; we don't know if they are beings or relations, tatters of beings or the end of relations.' Like the ball in a game. We lose ourselves in play, in temporary loss of 'I' induced by the quasi-object. 'It is the abandonment of my individuality or my being in the quasi-object that is there only to be in circulation.' The transformation of being into relation, the abdication of 'fine' art signalled in the shift to working on objects, the hints of Dionysiac rapture in the surface pattern-making of Dennis's works, have repercussions for his inset 'photographs' of urban dislocation. The shift from art as the province of aestheticism, of high subjectivity, has immense repercussions. Hitchcock knew that; he made thrillers. Morris knew it too; he made furniture. Jeffrey Dennis knows it too, and is also from Leytonstone. It must be something in the air.

Glenn Brown: Confessions of a Body Snatcher

Published in frieze *12, 1993.*

Glenn Brown remakes and retitles other people's paintings, either whole or in part. Though this practice might be thought to assume study and some degree of respect, he works from photographs and admits that in the case of at least one of his chosen artists he has never seen the paintings he has reproduced. But perhaps the term should be 'produced', since one eighties tendency was to reconsider art as an act of work. (Consider a Sherrie Levine watercolour or a Bridget Riley by Philip Taaffe). Brown's self-appointed task involves an attempt to return discussion to questions of manual labour. Painting laboriously, by night, he uses a secret method designed both to reward and chastise traditional expectations of authorship. What would otherwise be an impasto surface has become sheer, impacted, opaque, sinister and involuted. Directed inwards not out, the paintings seem to rebuff one's gaze, achieving a resilience of their own. It is as if, now that they are translated, they will no longer be the way they were. But to say this is either misleading or irrelevant. The reason Brown sets so little store by the 'genuine article' may be that for him the only truth lies in the eye of the beholder. The problem is that his eye is looking at photography rather than actuality. And what better historical period to choose in order to mount a critique of matter than the fifties, when 'genuine' emotion was equated with thick paint, as if feeling were magically imbricated with clots of pigment?

Brown once made paintings of magnified photographs of the moon's surface. The craters in those works resembled distant relatives of paint strokes, rendered in Superrealist style. Perhaps they reminded him of the covers of fifties science fiction magazines. Throughout this century and before, science fiction has presented a popular, sensationalized account of possible futures. And as the titles of Brown's painted versions of Ben Nicholson constructions reveal, he too senses connections between art and the future, whether utopian, like Nicholson's, or not. Could his critique of materiality paraded for its own sake have to do with its retrograde dependence on matter? Or is the word 'materiality'? Or even 'materialism'?

Two highly priced artists in particular attracted his attention: Frank Auerbach and Karel Appel, who both matured in a period when painters registered time – no time at all in Appel's case, all the time in the world in Auerbach's – by means of thick paint and its sensitive registration of the happy accident. Brown's choice was not based on admiration for their art. ('Third-rate van Gogh', he calls Auerbach, while Appel is dismissed as 'consciously mock-naïve'.) His revisions of their work emphasize both the pretensions involved in their attempt to unlearn, and the folly of their faith in 'direct' expression. Informed, perhaps, by his own reaction against expansive eighties paintwork, Brown's argument seems to be that Appel and Auerbach, themselves only representatives of one approach to painting, are no more than sanctified yobs who scrawl their own equivalents of smiley faces again and again and are even congratulated for it. In some corners of the British art establishment, where an eyebrow raised in relation to Auerbach is regarded as a near criminal act, even the juxtaposition of his work and Appel's would be deemed heretical. Despite this, if Brown were a critic he would not mince words. For him, daft, culturally sanctioned gesturalism is an Augean stable and he the Hercules whose duty it is to disinfect it. At this time, for example, he mounted an attack on the ultimate in post-war expressionism. Unfortunately, his version of a chimpanzee painting remains unfinished.

Disordered, diseased, the faces that confront us from Glenn Brown's Auerbachs and Appels are accompanied by that widespread phenomenon of the Cold War years: fear of invasion, a long-standing phobia in American culture that spawned a British equivalent with *Quatermass*, the Triffids and horror comics. While establishing the idea of the body as an empty shell, ready to be occupied by homeless spirits, Brown's method, evidenced in titles such as *Night of the Living Dead*, as well as his working method, can be compared to the concept of 'imitation' in the eighteenth century. A combination of homage and rivalry, it depended on the assumption that any artwork existed in order to be challenged. Can the uglifications of worked impasto in forties or fifties paintings be justified by references to Belsen or Hiroshima? Can Brown's distancing techniques be regarded as a necessary anaesthetic, administered to help us see clearly? Stifling the thickness of the original brushstrokes without reference to the emotion they generated may approximate some latter-day equivalent of the Brechtian *Verfremdungseffekt*, thwarting emotional impact in order to encourage the play of logical argument and sane, moral judgement. Or does Brown's contribution serve the same purpose as an act of criticism, with the same urge to control, place and interpret? On encountering a title like *The Day the World Turned Auerbach*, it is hard to think otherwise. For the 'body snatcher' referred to in titles is, of course, the artist himself; the emotion has been cauterized, the desired effect circumvented. Moreover, the gesture of criticism is held to be one of total partiality, eerie in its powers of reconstruction but biased in its angle of vision and oblivious to whatever might have informed the original. And of course, criticism stresses another type of contemporaneity: the proof of relevance, the demonstration that an art work cannot be defined merely by historical concomitants.

If Brown pushes his strategies to the point of absurdity – 'I'm never interested in what the real thing is', he has observed – he remains secure in the knowledge that his versions of other people's paintings will prove subversive. While each move in the developing scheme was seen as subversive, the effect of the totality was equally so; his meta-oeuvre was expanding by means of a variation between focus and unfocus. Beginning with Ben Nicholson constructions, all fine edge and sheer surface, he embarked on apeshit figuration, only to follow it with hard-edged Surrealism. Salvador Dalí's hotly debated reputation was for genius (the word by which he described himself in his autobiography); for becoming a sell-out (AVIDA DOLLARS was André Breton's arrangement of the letters of his name); for being a poseur (the moustache, for example). Given the benefit of the doubt, he could even emerge as the master of his own fate, a figure who used publicity and scandal in order to make a larger arena in order to exercise his undoubted talents. In 1992 came Brown's reading of *Soft Construction with Boiled Beans: Premonition of Civil War*. Against a ravaged landscape a vast body appears, in what Dalí called 'a delirium of auto-strangulation'. At war with itself, screaming in pain, stands a figure of both cruelty and suffering. It is a response to the prevailing mood of Spain comparable in its seriousness to Joan Miró's *Man and Woman in Front of a Pile of Excrement* (1935) or Pablo Picasso's *Guernica* (1937). Apparently in order to work on it in a more detached way, Brown turned the original on its side in order to copy it, then turned it back at last, as if the unusual depth of feeling might disturb his sense of strategy. Yet at this point, when for the first time it seems that Brown as critic is at least preparing to enter into the spirit of the work in question, strange reversals occur – for example, in Brown's view of the ordinary and the extraordinary. Despite the extreme pain, both mental and physical, for which this painting is a concomitant, it is here that the artist takes an enormous risk. 'Dreaming participates in history', wrote Walter Benjamin. This repainted work by Dalí could be seen as a sermon on that text. So, indeed, could Brown's entire enterprise.

For as well as asserting that no permanent division exists between dream and history, Benjamin described the fate of dream in the modern world as anticlimactic to the point of ordinariness. 'Dreams no longer open up a blue expanse', he continued. 'They have become grey. The grey layer of dust on things is their best part. Dreams are now a pathway to the banal.' And with that word 'banal' Brown's project is thrown into sharp relief. The presence of death hangs over his body of work, as it must, perhaps, in the art of a society for which mimesis no longer remains the test of artistic truth. Photography, in particular, banalizes works of art: eliminating traces of the hand, it minimizes the role of size or even scale, alters colour (however subtly) and insidiously provides a version that replaces the original. 'Representations are formations but they are also deformations', wrote Roland Barthes. 'Never again will the real have to be produced', replied Jean Baudrillard. Barthes's vision of representation as a game of Chinese whispers seems to assume that truth exists, a claim Baudrillard is keen to question. Dalí pondered both positions. Calling his paintings 'hand-painted photographs' he attempted what no photograph could achieve, apparently practising his expertise in traditional painting methods as a form of sabotage. The leap from impasto to thin paint represented by the shift from Auerbach and Appel to Dalí is a long one. And as Brown's paint surface subdues direct expression by means of a protective layer which seals the work, making it more hermetic and less resonant, the image seems to be held captive, and the argument against fetishizing paint is clinched. Though a painting is made up of brushstrokes, it ends as more than simply a collection of marks. Except, perhaps, according to the most banal definition of an art work; and it is this banality with which Brown does battle.

'Each one is my last painting', Brown has said, meaning that each new work alters the significance of the rest. Or, in other words, that the art lies in the order of the moves he makes, either because, as in a card game, one shift of emphasis alters the entire game, or because, as in chess, strategy is everything. To call it an endgame is to miss the point: there still is play. Indeed, in Brown's *musée imaginaire* every new acquisition modifies the meaning of the last, just as Brown's retitlings alter the interpretation of the original. The rationale behind the moves in Brown's game remains unclear; the same rules may not govern each move. One thing is clear: the role not of taste (goût) but distaste (dégoût), a deeply felt obsession with the grotesque and its possibilities which could be explained by repression alone. For his recent Dalí resembles soft pornography.

Arguably puritanical in response to signs of unbridled physicality, Brown has struggled so hard to make the grotesque banal, and therefore harmless, that it comes as no surprise to learn that he is now working on a version of an Arcimboldo portrait. For in Arcimboldo's painting, as in his own, more than one interpretation could hold sway. And as subdued versions of other painters' works assume the status of exhibits in an imagined collection of his own, meaning may be generated on parallel planes. Could it be that what Brown is painting is the sense of art becoming museal – in other words banal, sacrosanct, kitsch, easily arranged in patterns of our own? If so there is something so heroic and foolhardy about the project that, like Balzac's unknown painter, Brown may achieve fame not by making any single art work but simply by the legend that surrounds him.

Missing Persons: Gary Hill's *Tall Ships*

Published in Gary Hill: In the Light of the Other, *Museum of Modern Art, Oxford/Tate Gallery Liverpool, 1993.*

Drawing back a curtain, the viewer enters a dark space. As the eyes accustom themselves to the darkness, the space turns out to be a long corridor, illuminated only by black-and-white images along its sides, and by a single image at its end. They are people, seen first in the distance, then advancing until they are life-size. And though they are all different – men, women, younger and older people, finally, on the end wall on her own, a young child – they behave the same, approaching us curiously as if we, not they, were the object of attention. The space itself is like a long gallery, it allows us to be inquisitive. It is hard not to be; the images are easy to relate to. Perhaps this explains their apparent interest in us, for as moving portraits they patrol a similar territory to our own, a fairly deep space where they approach and withdraw, examining us in every detail, taking time to reach conclusions or to satisfy their interest. For they want something, as they approach and confront us. And although we never realize what it is, by the end of their inquiry, their curiosity seems to be satisfied. Only as we move on, we feel as if we have not got everything out of them that we might. And when, on occasion, they turn their backs and walk away, it is difficult not to feel rejected. What we sense, without pushing it to the forefront of our minds, is that they are responding to what we are doing. These people have something to do with us.

So distance, both literal and psychological, plays a major part in Gary Hill's *Tall Ships*, a work that depends on the fallacy that two-dimensional pictures can suddenly come to life. Our contemplation of them succeeds in making them do so, of course, whether or not we know how. (This Pygmalion fantasy may be as old as time itself, or at least dating from that hypothetical 'breakdown of the bicameral mind' which signalled or brought about the death of idols.[1]) As in any study of images, the disturbing factor is the ease with which what is accurately perceived as a mute, lifeless object outside oneself undergoes a change. Empathy takes over and when that lapses, the artwork slips back into limbo before another viewer approaches and confronts it anew. The language of art criticism gives too little evidence of this imaginative relationship with a work of art, a process that resembles the state of falling in love; always an exercise in potentiality and loss of definition, however temporary and safe. (Jean Cocteau had a habit of relaxing on a divan with his drugs, next to a large two-way mirror through which he could observe young men enjoying sex in the next room.) Surely the combination of safety and freedom, the pleasure of an imaginative foray and the emotional safeguards necessary to avoid involvement in such a situation reflect the reaction of any gallery-goer, in search of an experience that would, ideally, be unforgettable, but without the power to ruin one's own ability to repeat it at will. The vicariousness of the experience and the immediate exoneration it entails are paralleled in our own actions here. When we are tired of art, we simply walk away. The last thing that we expect is that it will do the same to us.

Tall Ships brings into play the idea that pictures lead a life of their own, that they gaze back at us knowingly and that their apparent awareness sharpens our own awareness of the fictional. That dramatic confrontation with a human image which seems to be taking an interest in us makes *Tall Ships* a Mannerist work, for it not only centres on a conceit of image and reality, presence and absence – like those painted guards with drawn swords that suddenly become apparent on turning a corner at the Palazzo Te in Mantua, or the scene in Shakespeare's *A Winter's Tale* where what has been supposed a statue of Hermione comes to life – but also plays on the idea of the 'life' with which we invest images, hinting that they may be doing something similar to us. In this tussle between art and reality the sides are equally matched. For sometimes the shadowy figures on the screens before us seem as dubious about our identity as we are of theirs – and rightly so, for identity ebbs as the work proceeds. The development and subsequent lapse of their interest in us (and 'vice versa') has something cyclical and pointlessly promiscuous about it. Perhaps what is lacking in the figures who engage mutely with us, one by one, in *Tall Ships*, is a more particular type of recognition: that anagnorisis which so often clinches plots in drama and which in the 'real' world, at least, depends on our mutual realization that we need to be parts of each other's lives. In this case nothing permanent will emerge; we are destined to be no more than 'ships that pass in the night'.

They do not pass without an investigation on our part: a human variation on the way animals prowl around each other. Looking, in this case, might be better described as looking for, making certain that not a single detail remains unexamined. As they change positions, then change again to cope with the object of vision from every possible angle, an opportunity arises to watch someone else watching. Are we the point of the investigation? The result is a growing unease coupled with a certain frisson, for we seem the object of extreme, concentrated scrutiny. The eyes seldom leave us. If a figure walks away, he or she will turn once, twice, three times, apparently to check some detail or to be reassured about an assumption. Moving from one image to another, and finding yet another figure engaged in the same prowl, growing larger as it confronts us and smaller as it departs, is a disconcerting experience. And a disappointing one, for there is a sense in which one's courtship and rejection by complete strangers is a test one seems on the point of winning but which finally fails. Yet of course the word 'finally' does not apply, for no two experiences of the work can ever be the same.

It is possible to distinguish differences between the behaviour of the figures. Their speeds, the directness of their confrontation, the distances they establish, differentiate them from one another. It is even possible to relate to them as types. Or supposed types; for in fact these 'characters' are no more than mute ghosts, images flung on to a screen. 'Screen' is one word for it. What space does dream occupy? A Kleinian might propose the breast – an argument, therefore, in favour of concavity, not convexity, for the baby's face is pressed hard enough against it to be surrounded by flesh. More recent theorists have argued differently; the 'dream screen' has a depth, they maintain, if only a shallow one, like the stage of a toy theatre. *Tall Ships* seems to support this idea of a shallow stage. For the sense of being pulled up short in front of some invisible barrier is sufficiently powerful to suggest that communication may be the unifying theme of the entire installation. These figures have the same relation to us as the traditional idea of a ghost: sometimes a familiar, kindly visitor who has arrived to check that everything is all right, at other times a presence intent on some kind of intervention, however obscure. There is one difference: while traditional ghosts seem knowing, experienced presences who return to places they know well, these people exist in a state of limbo. Unable to go any further, they seem to regard the screen as a frustration, and our world as a curiosity.

Being confronted by these strangers is one thing. Being interrogated by them, even in silence, is quite another. No communication is really possible between image and viewer; they remain alien to each other, despite an understandable mutual attraction. Encounters get us nowhere. Art's purpose is to understand ourselves and society better. That, at least, is the traditional humanist point of view, a view in which motives such as an urge for reconciliation and equality play a major role. This urge is central to the experience of *Tall Ships*, which derives its power from the frustration of this need. Real viewers and images exist on such different and even antipathetic planes, this work suggests, that no reconciliation is possible. Any meeting that might take place is hindered by a feeling of awe and strangeness on both sides, and as the end of the sequence of images is reached, a feeling of stasis sets in. Instead of resembling a person appearing in a doorway, for example, the decrease in mobility makes the effect resemble that of a shallow grave. Gradually, as its occupant becomes that much nearer, more present to us, a sense of the sepulchral permeates the entire work. The links between photographically produced images and death have often been discussed. The disturbing prelude to the final, more static images involve people checking our presence, registering the slightest detail, hovering, looking for something, and the feeling that we the visitors are interrogated only increases. For death is the end of and the reason for our interrogation.

Consider the silence of the darkened space; the ghostly aspect of the figures who choose to examine us in an art gallery instead of our examining them; the increased stasis as the viewer moves through the room. Almost every aspect of *Tall Ships* indicates a dual preoccupation with death and identity, death because a moving image thrown on a screen has only virtual existence, identity because that very problem seems in the forefront of the minds who make their appearances before us and, never quite satisfied, it seems, return time after time to revise their initial conclusion. The regularity of their approach, the growing familiarity of the presences, the choreographic aspect of the movements to and fro, their turns and returns, present a visual demonstration of that postponement which characterizes the work itself as well as our approach to it. When Odysseus sails too far toward the edge of the world, he and his men are forced to make a libation to the dead, who approach them and try to hold conversations. (Their voices, says Homer, sound like dry leaves.) Alarmed, homeless, they are not as we would prefer to imagine them. The result is a postponement; the anagnorisis or 'recognition' that should result from such an encounter is put off, and one master plot, of 'knowledge, its loss and recovery'[2] is avoided. Perhaps the figures we see in *Tall Ships* with their regular approaches and retreats hint at a similar avoidance of the facts of death. And maybe, as its name suggests, the work itself has parallels less with art than with other activities – with our comings and goings, with rituals, with sports and with the games we play, unknowingly, as children.

1. The term is from Julian Jaynes, *The Origin of Consciousness in the Breakdown of the Bicameral Mind* (Boston: Houghton Mifflin, 1990).
2. Terence Cave, *Recognitions: A Study in Poetics* (Oxford: OUP 1990), p.235.

Nicholas May

Essay from Nicholas May, *published by Cornerhouse, Manchester, and South London Gallery, 1994.*

The zeal with which certain critics responded to Nicholas May's large exhibition in 1990 was understandable in emotional terms but also as a rearguard action: as a belated vote in support of what they took to be a call to order, a return to painting pure and simple. This was not only a misreading of the historical situation of current painting but also a misunderstanding of the nature of May's work. Perfected in a period when history, especially the history of painting, seemed to exist for the sole purpose of being revised, his gorgeous coagulations were suspended before the viewer as responses to the prevailing cultural climate, not as attempts to turn the clock back. May's aesthetic was formed in a period of uncertainty, when late Conceptualists continued to spurn the fetishization of the 'art object' long after they had capitulated to market forces, and when late abstractionists finally refused to abide by the supposed elision of worldly thinking – about politics, for example – that constitutes a primary flaw in Greenbergian theory. Suspended in defiance of their obvious weight, May's work did not invoke the ethos of classic Abstract Expressionism, but rather a moment of scepticism about painting *per se*. There had been other moments like this, notably in the United States with the Washington Colorists and the work of Morris Louis. As a Jewish artist whose first works were meditations on the Holocaust, Louis could not have avoided seeing his own strategy in relation to destruction, or at least temporariness – though a better term to describe his work might be 'presentness'. May shares Louis's passion for sheer optical resonance but adds a caveat. Whereas Louis soaked his canvases, as Frankenthaler did, May allows colours to rise from the surface of the canvas, stressing the presence of the paint by scattering metallic powder on its surface to emphasize the history of the facture, the shift from liquid to solid – a process the viewer finds hard to believe. If the references to alchemy mean anything – certainly, they pervade the critical responses to his work – the reason must be their relation to changes of state, not only of matter to thought but of the transformation of the corporeal to the spiritual, with all its overtones of Jungian 'transformation' on the one hand and its connections with idolatry on the other. For so frequently May's tactic is to reject flatness in favour of image as substance, substance that means something in and for itself, as well as making a point in an ongoing discussion.

Image and substance seem to vie for supremacy in these paintings, as May plays 'now you see it, now you don't' games with the forms he has coaxed into being. The paired configuration in *Formless Fold (Yellow)* (1992) reveals one tactic, the description of a form that Jacques Derrida calls 'invaginated', a form with no clear differentiation between outside and inside. The skilled control of flowing paint, not 'formless' but formed by gravity and by manipulation other than brushwork, reached its height in *Guardian* (1993), with its majestic black shape, its glutinous runs, its mountain range glowing like an ember against a lambent blue ground. Such a work has nothing to do with the part-for-whole principle that so often triumphs in talk about classic Abstract Expressionism; rather it employs the same strategy of perfect placing to be found in Pollock's drawings on paper, almost Japanese in their simplicity. A second influence is Surrealist techniques of working with surfaces. Late in 1992 May began experimenting once more, shifting from the idea of a bounded shape to that of a single atmosphere. *Fused Blue Metal* (1992) was an experiment in multiple presences and sheerness of surface, with no evidence of mark-making except its result registered as if it lay below a layer of varnish. The effect was of turning the marks inside out: their physicality had been lost so completely that they looked like wraiths. And the paradox was that after so many removals the space still seemed packed with incident. *Blue Metal* (1993–4) combined every technique at the artist's disposal to create a wraith-like blue shape buckling. And even as it buckled, its presence was challenged: it had less physicality than was at first assumed and even that was in doubt, as it seemed blown by the wind or rent by the very forces that created it.

In Rome in 1994 May reconstituted his painting. With metal sealant, normally used on cars, he made a deep ground, then gouged marks into it before colouring it with metal powder. The result is almost photographic in its effect; it recalls Marcel Duchamp's 'domain' in which dust gathered in order to be trapped for ever in his *Large Glass*. Yet the hyper-realist effect is simply a trick of the light; whereas previously in May's work a surplus or a paucity of matter was evident, the new paintings seemed nothing but matter. Their triumph is that they also have the air of being photographs – not surprisingly, perhaps, considering that photographs consist of dispersed powder fixed and sealed. Two American abstractionists moved into similar territory: Jules Olitski, lighting his paintings from the seventies with lamps above them and, however perverse the argument might seem, Larry Poons, whose gross mounds of pigment on canvas, made by pouring paint down staircases, seemed made purely to play with light. In both cases, however, another issue intervened: that of taste and a need to question a Greenbergian stranglehold based on culinary metaphor. May had already experimented with the sense of distance he could achieve by offsetting weight and weightlessness. And in earlier paintings sheer avoirdupois demanded almost architectural support. Now the effect became more eerie than ever; in *Lamina* (1994) the eye is baffled by a *matière* painting that switches without warning into a visual conundrum, surrendering its objectness to a play of light and shadow. It is as if May has come full circle in his own survey of his territory, and what he claims as his is now complete. The sense of Byzantine splendour he was already prepared to forgo when he stopped experimenting with heavy paint gave way to a feeling of greater refinement. Now that too has been surrendered. Still surface is the preoccupation, but now directionality is of no account and the question of presence in painting has given way to problems of sheer visual identity. And as the fetishism that accompanies his earlier run works is abandoned, or perhaps simply shelved for a while, his position seems increasingly clear. It is an exploration of the optical experience itself, what it includes and excludes, and the conditions that govern that: the paradoxes of perceived beauty, the question of what constitutes a work of art and why, the almost erotic involvement in flesh, warmth and voluptuous colour (in the earlier paintings) together with the sense of the high value placed on these, not abandoned in the later works but achieved with equal sensuality by starker means. There is nothing backward-looking in May's experiments: on the contrary, materiality is being put to the test time and again in his work. In the eighties a new and improbable category was mooted: the conceptual painter. Nicholas May's works make him a candidate for such a definition.

Morris Louis

Review of exhibition at Rooseum, Malmö, published in frieze *9, 1993.*

Success came late to Morris Louis: by 1969, when his first one-person exhibition was held, he had only three more years to live. Lateness became part of the myth: of an underdog determined to make it the hard way; an artist working from daybreak to sunset in a studio so small it could hold only a single canvas; a secretive man who kept neither diaries nor notes, and did not even talk to his wife about his work. He only talked painting to one person: Clement Greenberg, who advised him, wrote about him, planned his début and finally became advisor to the Louis estate – inevitably, for only he had any idea of how the canvases should be stretched. So the case of Morris Louis remains an odd one. In 1985, when Diane Upright introduced her catalogue raisonné by claiming that Louis's reputation was 'securely established', she was telling the truth, but not the whole truth. For despite the fact that significant criticism of Louis had been written by this time, it had all been by Greenberg and his acolytes. Nowadays Louis is history and history goes unquestioned. Yet it is possible to voice misgivings, not necessarily about the excellence of the paintings but about the reasons why they are excellent. (This, perhaps, should be a function of retrospectives, rather than the unthinking hero-worship they encourage.) Enter Lars Nittve, with a series of exhibitions called 'Re-visions', starting with a dozen Louis paintings of different sizes and formats, hung in one of the most beautiful spaces in Europe.

It is almost impossible to see how the artist who made the *Charred Journal Firewritten* series of 1951 could have become a great painter. Taking their title from Nazi book-burnings, a topic Louis and Greenberg discussed, they adapted the style of Louis's drawings (from Picasso through Calder) with equally undistinguished results. Seven years later everything changed. *Dalet Nun* and *Dalet Ayin* (named by Greenberg) were made by directing broad runs of paint down large canvases, which, by means of a process akin to filtration, separated the constituents. Then he turned them upside-down. As it stops short just before the top edge, the flow resembles the mobile tip of a fountain, or a gas jet, for sometimes at the limits of a form unexpected colours appear. At an opposite extreme would be *Happy Friday*, a 'stripe' painting from the following year, in which the almost straight, vertical bands of colour occupy a central position, touching but never mixing, producing an effect that is different in tone from anything else of the period. An earlier title for this painting was *Pillars*, reminiscent of the pillar of smoke by day and fire by night that guided the Children of Israel through the desert. Was this an attempt by Greenberg to situate Louis against that background of Jewish mysticism to which Rothko and Newman had already laid claim? Or was he suggesting a visual emanation in which qualities of manifestation and concealment were combined?

Louis himself may have thought in more practical terms. Already he had banished tactility, shown the weave of the canvas and even the constituent parts of the paint. He had left large areas of canvas primed, but unpainted. In doing so he raised the status of the painting to a kind of miracle, for since nothing was hidden, every mark had to be perfect, resonant and unique. Using acrylic paint, he adapted and flattened the 'gesture' of the fifties, underplaying its calligraphic potential and emphasizing its similarity to kindergarten mark-making. In the *Unfurled* series, with its multiple drips the shape of a dog's hind leg running diagonally down each side, he achieved this. Yet these brackets of mobile colour activated a negative version of that same broad, funnel-shaped space that the 'veils' had formed. (Dated 1961, *Beta Epsilon,* the latest painting at the Rooseum, is a perfect example.) *Unfurleds* was the name Greenberg attached to these, as if flags were being caught by the wind or curtains were being pulled. It is transitive only by association: despite the way they clog, flare or dribble, the distances between each run prevents their acting in unison. The childlike quality of the mark-making is due to an expertise so superb that it is neither primitivistic nor *faux-naïf,* but looks as if it just happened that way. If he had lived longer, Louis's ga-ga play might have acquired an entire cultural setting: Berryman's babble; Roethke's rickety rhythms. There is a cartoon quality in, for example, *Para 1* of 1959, that hints at a parallel to their boozy babytalk.

Yet this exhibition rejects the idea that the formalist critics were eager to promote: of a strategic painter intent on finding ways to prolong the concerns of Abstract Expressionism, making it more open, more Matissean. *Addition III* of 1959, for example, reveals a more episodic picture-maker, with a sense of wholeness more risky that we had suspected, while in a tamer way *Para No. 1* explores the idea of blobby columns that jostle and prod. Robust, even rambunctious, both works steer clear of that radical simplicity we have come to associate with Louis. Yet it is impossible not to look for one's own essential Louis by asking what it is that he did best. *Alpha Zeta* (1961, according to

Nittve, 1960 according to Diane Upright) is what painters of the time called 'mural-sized'; it measures 165.4 x 609.6 cm. Two simple forms appear on the canvas, roughly the same: each consisting of four slanting paint-strokes, angled to nearly touch at the top. This mountain or tent-like structure in rust, dirty pink, lavender and bright yellow on the left, more distant greens and blues on the right, offers one half that seems definite, attention-grabbing, and another more demure, traditionally beautiful, then equalizes their force. The technique never seemed simpler: less like paint strokes than paw prints, elementary daubs. And that effect is again undone by the utter sophistication of the product, meant (it seems) to be hung in the office of an ad agency or a fashion magazine. For there and only there have we seen such artificial colours. Gone is what the *New York Times* critic Stuart Preston called Louis's 'chromatic mysticism'. Perhaps it has been replaced by a certain oriental tinge. For only certain Pollock drawings and the gigantic calligraphs that Clyfford Still made toward the end of his life could be compared with this strange drawing. Yet comparisons do not help. Too late for the scholarly and critical treatment that has been extended to even minor painters of first-generation Abstract Expressionism, Louis has had to wait until now for us to realize how baffled we are by him and how intriguing it is to know the work better.

Spunkflakes

Review of performances at the Vauxhall Tavern and the Royal College of Art, London, published in frieze *19, 1994*

In 1986 the French magazine *Traverses* published an issue called 'Disgust'. Jean Baudrillard's contribution, 'The Power of Disgust', argued that because old-fashioned attraction has declined, we no longer know our own minds, and that as a result taste, desire and free will have also perished. On the other hand, bad faith, repulsion and disgust have increased in strength. 'From here, it seems, a new energy comes, an inverse energy, a power of repulsion which replaces desire, a vital reaction against that which for us represents society, the body, sex, an energetic disinheritance which is no longer the result of willingness to change all that, but of rejection pure and simple. Today only disgust is certain; taste no longer exists.' That is putting it mildly, and metaphorically. Now that the eighties are over and a period of conspicuous consumption has come to an end, ritual purgation is crucial. Whether that involves rejecting sex and the body is another matter.

If Baudrillard lived in London and frequented the Vauxhall Tavern, for instance, he could not have escaped Miss Titti la Camp. Dressed as one great female star after another, she rams food down her throat until she gags and spits all over the stage – over the audience too, if they are foolish enough to stand within range – and then slides about in it on her bottom. This is depressing stuff, but every low at the Tavern has its high. Take Spunkflakes.

The night the three Spunkflakes were banned, they had arrived late. By the time they appeared it was so late that most of the customers had lapsed into a semi-comatose condition. Suddenly, to the blare of apocalyptic music, the curtains opened to reveal a set decorated in colours so bright they made your eyes throb. Three creatures, wearing costumes that extended their limbs, filled the confined space: a frighteningly tall mother, a beer-bellied father and a revolting child, mouthing inanities and moving grotesquely. The father's paunch had a life of its own, the mother's breasts hung around her waist and their child repeated the phrase 'I've got beautiful lips' in a soppy voice that can only be produced by flaring the nostrils as wide as possible and speaking in a bad Mancunian accent. To which, time and again, the mother would reply, 'You've got beautiful lips.' Yelling for food, his massive paunch swinging from side to side, the father crammed so much breakfast into his mouth that before long he was eating, belching and spewing at the same time. Suddenly all hell broke loose. He tried to rape the child, the mother turned religious, a mobile cross was dragged in, and to the deafening sound of heavenly music the daughter was exorcized and simultaneously crucified on stage. (I seem to remember a baby getting stabbed at one point, but one or two atrocities may have slipped my mind.) An orgy of violence ensued. Chainsaws appeared, the effigies tried to murder each other and brightly coloured goo spurted everywhere. It even shot over the heads of the audience, whose attitude had slowly altered from indifference to hysteria. They cheered wildly as the cast took a bow.

To my surprise, their next performance was at the Royal College of Art. This time, the stage resembled a showroom at the Ideal Home exhibition – if your ideal home happens to contain a sofa covered in straw – with a computer that simulated other parts of the house, each room fitted out with its own particular obscenity. Though the context was different, the ritual element persisted. The Greeks had a word for it: *catharsis* or ritual purgation. 'An energetic disinheritance', Baudrillard called it. 'Our actions, our enterprises, our illnesses, have less and less cause of "objective" motivation; more often they result from a violent distaste for our selves . . . which leads us to release our energy in what is a form of exorcism.' Spunkflakes knew that all along, as did Jarry, Rabelais and Bernard Manning. They are all what clowns should be: not lovable, namby-pamby jokesters or bulimic Ronald McDonald milksops who distribute balloons to the kiddies, but an updated equivalent of Shakespearean jesters: bikers in black leather with scars and massive codpieces, ramming spunkburgers down our throats till we vomit.

Anthony Wilson

Review of exhibition at Galerie de l'Ancienne Poste, Calais, published in Art Monthly *180, 1994.*

Accompanied by a tape of a loud drum solo and the clicks and whirrs of a row of three projectors all set to run continuously, the images in Anthony Wilson's slide sequence *Coup d'oeil* are thrown across a single, flat wall. Yet as well as occupying their own discrete territories of flung light, images shift, like text on a word processor, from left to right, right to left, top to bottom and bottom to top of any single screen, while behind the insistent drum beat on a looped tape the sound of the clicking projectors alters alarmingly, from simultaneous whirring to waltz rhythms to a tom-tom alarm to near cacophony. On the walls, image follows image in each of the screens at once. Yet they do not change at the same time, and this simple fact accounts for both the pleasure and the obscurity of this installation: a visual bombshell, as the title suggests, and a smack in the eye at the same time. It matters that the slides are black and white, not because of the incidental play on Russian Constructivist photography and a wistful or even sarcastic comment on its idealistic mission, but because of one interpretation of what black and white means: that something is set down clearly, and that it is comprehensible.

Here it is not. A man is shouting; a pair of spectacles magnifies a text beyond readability; bearing the label LUXURY, a record (presumably of the sound-track) is shown revolving; a young woman wipes her eye; a man's shadow appears behind a flimsy curtain; two almost identical faces confront each other – ambiguous, close, absorbed; clouds block the sun, as if a storm is brewing; a pair of hands performs a simple conjuring trick, separating a handkerchief into two parts then putting them back together; a pair of crossed fingers is shown, and several shots of a woman in a low-cut dress, carrying binoculars; a hand grasps a candle; a roulette wheel spins, someone passes a newspaper to someone else; a man flinches from a blow. Though aggression seems the subject as well as the technique, in a moment it can be transformed into its opposite. Indeed, by virtue of the duck–rabbit effect, perhaps the most tableauesque of all Wilson's components, two profiles facing each other – or is it a single profile repeated and reversed? – also register as the outline of the empty space between them, reminding viewers that attraction and repulsion rely on similar postures of belligerence. If all this is about something, that thing might well be secrecy or evasion.

Wilson's roots lie in early photo pieces with which viewers were invited to construct scenarios from only a few scanty items of evidence. By the time of *Satellite* (1987), however, the degree of disorientation was greater and the social comment more evident. The woozy glamour of the eighties was created in a gallery as Wilson summarized a decade of futures and simulation, when plastic replaced coins and credit created a virtual reality of its own. *Satellite* was a place of shyness and tawdry fascination. But if this was his Prufrock, *Coup d'oeil* is Wilson's Waste Land. Full of winks and secret handshakes, clandestine affairs and sudden changes of weather, it is a film noir collage full of omens and surprises, like a Dick Francis novel rewritten by John Hawkes. Luck is important; indeed horse-racing, weather and the spin of a roulette wheel mean so much in this context that the entire work comes to resemble a fortune-telling device, for as dice only fall similarly by accident, so the viewer's perception of this installation differs with each viewing. The result parallels the ordering processes that govern our lives.

Wilson's work is about itself, its own techniques and ordering system. What if only a given number of situations exist and are repeated slightly as time goes by? The key lies in that word 'slightly', for as we watch for tiny differences, by accident entire sequences of coincidence result. Regard *Coup d'oeil* in one of two ways. 'Luck is the fool's name for fate', said Marcel Duchamp, artist and gambler. The first way, then, is a meditation on art or chance. Eventually, however, even fools win. Wait long enough and know what you want and you are bound to get it. That is the second way. It is a recipe for revolution.

Chris Ofili: The Elephant Man

Published in frieze *15, 1994, with a dedication to Dave Hickey.*

Readers of issue 10 of *frieze* were surprised to find one quarter of a page of advertising that contained only two words: ELEPHANT SHIT. If they lived in London, they might already have noticed stickers with the same two words on fences, buildings and hoardings. And if they happened to walk through Brick Lane at certain times, they might also have noticed that a young artist had opened a stall with something unusual on display. After publicizing it and carrying buckets of it home from Whipsnade Zoo, Chris Ofili had decided to let the jaded citizens of London view the waste products of the lordly elephant.

The African elephant, of course.

Born in Britain, Ofili had always felt African. But despite his black skin and the fact that his parents' first language was Yoruba, how African could he be, living first in Manchester, then in London? For him the question was crucial. He had made a series of paintings of black people – a father, a mother, a child – that touched on the sense of identity. Yet it was his own identity. 'The only person in these paintings was me,' he has admitted. All adolescents have demons to exorcize, and they are always the same demons. But perhaps artists remain adolescent all their lives. Or perhaps they do it because they never fit in. Think of the immigrant Willem de Kooning, drawing an imaginary brother, or Arshile Gorky, tugging at his dead mother's apron strings. Ofili's excuse is that he was inventing a style. And asked for a definition of style, he replies without a moment's hesitation: 'To develop my own ego and get in contact with the beautiful.'

Ofili was to develop a style more quickly than he suspected. In 1992, he was awarded a scholarship to Zimbabwe, to travel and make art. Zimbabwe had been Rhodesia, and for Ofili it still was. He was constantly struck by the remnants of colonialism, in particular the inequality of black and white. What affected him most, however, was the animals. On horseback it was possible to study them from close quarters, for the smell of the horse annihilated that of its rider, allowing humans the opportunity to approach species that might otherwise sense attack: wildebeest, giraffe, elephant, roaming free. Yet perhaps animals are never 'free'; in search of food for most, if not all of their lives, they make tracks wherever they go. And what are these signals in the form of footprints and droppings but art: at once the product of life experience (the development of the ego) and objects of 'beauty', expressed from their bodies? As in the case of human babies, animals might regard their faeces as gifts, since they lay a trail for others and may indicate a place of safety. Perhaps more. Ancient human civilizations told fortunes by examining excreta. Even today, doctors take careful notice of them before making diagnoses. Artists in particular are judged by their droppings. Or drippings, if they happen to be abstractionists. Dots had already appeared on Ofili's canvases, but suddenly these seemed meaningless. In Zimbabwe he was taken to the Matopos Hills, to see cave paintings thousands of years old, at least one of which consisted completely of dots, made with sharpened twigs. Another effect of the African journey was that Ofili began pouring resin on his paintings. Always a late addition, it is difficult to see until a viewer moves his head slightly and a sudden flash of light obscures what was visible only a split second before. And because the flow of the resin works with or against the directionality of the marks on the canvas, the flash may either enhance or temporarily obscure what lies below. Ofili associates it with the dung. 'Elephants shit, then piss on that,' he explains matter-of-factly, 'It gives the shit a moist, new feeling.'

In Berlin in 1992 Ofili held an impromptu sale. Well, 'sale' is the word he uses. The point is that nothing at all was for sale: this was simply a display of hardened elephant droppings, seven pieces in all. Visitors to the flea market were faced with Ofili himself, a small sign saying *Elefantenscheiße* and the lumps lying on the ground. Artspeak was one thing, he had decided; talking to non-experts was another. Yet despite the fact that these were people who did not necessarily regard his activities in aesthetic terms, they were prepared to put simple questions which gallery-goers would not. 'How much do they cost?'

'They aren't for sale.'

'So why are you here?'

'I'm just presenting them.'

'Oh. Thank you.'

One fellow trader moved his pitch to avoid the dung, some of which was still wet. Another moved closer and closer as time went on, because a crowd was gathering. Angered by his refusal to make money, a woman from an adjacent stall took matters into her own hands, sold a piece for him and gave him the money. Odder still, a number of people regarded Ofili himself as the work. ('A witch-doctor,' someone muttered.) When he repeated the sale in Brick Lane in London, reactions were quite different. Striving to connect the strange and the familiar, most people gave up, laughed and fled. Others simply asked if he was selling drugs. (Three sculptures resulted from this experience: two rolled joints containing elephant dung and *Shithead* (1993), with an exotic drum as base, a lump of elephant dung and on top of that, three years' growth of the artist's own hair.) After this came the stickers – small labels saying ELEPHANT SHIT placed all over London. Then the enigmatic advertisement in *frieze* and the graffiti: ELEPHANT SHIT painted by night on a wall in Fulham, for example. Finally, the inevitable happened. In an exhibition in 1993 at Atlantis, London, instead of suspending his paintings from the wall as usual, he rested each one on two lumps of dung. Releasing the literal aspects of his art could be dismissed as mere high spirits. Yet it is more than this. It keeps insisting on the childish element in painting (a synonym for getting dirty and making a mess, at least of people under six years old); the financial aspect of buying and selling what is literally worthless; the obsessional aspect of the artistic endeavour and the importance of constant interpretation and reinterpretation, for meaning is never static.

In contrast, Ofili's painting is aesthetic in the extreme. Conceived during the brief vogue for run paint in British art, his spots and poured resin share some of the jewel-like quality of Nicholas May and a little of the emphasis on routine that provides the structure of an Ian Davenport. Yet the sense of complexity and unmaking that animates Ofili's paintings differs from both. His dots form a haze, if not concealing then certainly confusing the place of the canvas, destabilizing space rather than creating it, drawing attention to the weave. His runs of resin do the same, but more intuitively, as if giving the work a symbolic bath. (In contrast, Ofili's drawings and prints tend toward the linear, like weaving.) Ambiguities of depth are created by this lavish gesture, which gives a substantiality to the painting while apparently doing little more than veiling it, as if to heighten its beauty. And shifting approaches to space hint at a sense of time too: not the real time of making that proved such a red herring in criticism of fifties abstraction (how convenient it is to forget the number of times Pollock called Lee Krasner in from the studio next door, to lift the canvas on to the wall so that he could ponder it before making his next move), nor some fictive time but an overlay, with long-term memory piercing moment-by-moment experience, the deeply rooted and temporarily mislaid bursting unbidden into the quotidian with all the power of a revelation. There is a glamour about Ofili's work which he is not concerned to hide: the gleam of the present, its excitement and danger, above all its aspect of sheer display, what might be regarded as its abiding exoticism.

As words like this spring to mind, however, so do the heresies that they imply. Caught between the Black arts movement in Britain – urging the return to African roots - and the multiculturalism of borderline positions which can deteriorate into sheer visual dilettantism, Ofili has devised his own Dada commentary on his activities in order to explain his anomalous position, to himself as well as to his viewers. In *Open* (1993) something resembling a Blackpool boarding-house table-cloth turns psychedelic. And while bejewelled curlicues serve to make the canvas seem further from the viewer, fake shadows from the lumps of real dung, spaced out like paperweights to stop the canvas blowing away introduce *trompe-l'oeil* where it has no obvious use, as if to stress the literal proximity of the centre of the canvas as opposed to its edges, where colours fade. Similarly, in *Elephantastic* (1993), where the canvas is divided roughly into thirds, trails of red, blue and yellow dots are used, and the same colours appear in another key on the upper part, with larger dots and a darker blue. Here too a pair of smaller lumps of elephant dung below one larger one – 'The biggest turd I ever picked up,' Ofili announces with deep reverence – form a rough approximation of the male genitalia. This apparent degradation of high abstraction – how different an Ofili *Open* is from a Motherwell of the same title – leads in different directions: to the street or the studio; to Ofili's own identity and its divided affiliations; to the matter of formalism and genetic purity and to questions of colour and difference.

Like early modernists Ofili borrows and adapts freely. Hints of Aboriginal design, oriental decoration and perhaps Robert Rauschenberg crop up, as do continuing references to elephants. Recent paintings have been named after elephants from Berlin's Circus Crone: Lala, Rara, Mala. Their repetitive, mellifluous names remind us of the effect of the animal life in Ofili's work. Yet Picasso's visits to the Cirque Medrano differ from Ofili's to the Circus Crone in one respect. For Picasso the circus produced fine paintings one by one. For Ofili it provides a thread, however nonsensical, by which painting can continue, commenting on itself, building a language, offering the development of the ego and contact with the beautiful. In short, style, brought to abstraction in a difficult time.

The Institute of Cultural Anxiety

On an exhibition at the ICA, London, published in frieze *21, 1995.*

Once upon a time London's Institute of Contemporary Art was intended as an alternative to a museum. Decades later a make-believe ICA presented as a Christmas treat by guest curator Jeremy Millar is based on the assumption that this project failed. In Millar's parody institute or *musée imaginaire* the building becomes genuinely alternative: a site of definition and redefinition, recalling the past with references to the Wunderkammer, while envisaging the future with quaint sci-fi videos. The future is not what it used to be, we conclude, confronting a glass case containing a copy of *If* magazine from the early sixties, with gems by Heinlein and Ballard. Meanwhile the present is museal, with more labels than objects and more objects than enough. For the fetish of time has exhausted us, fatigue has set in and, like Alice, we must run our hardest to stay in the same place. Take that darkened room in which Neil Chapman's film loop of dredging is shown. Is this a metaphor of an unsuccessful attempt to recuperate, a struggle to stand firm on shaky ground or of an image of a giant, slavering maw, spitting its food out time after time? Useless work, hopeless reclamation? All these metaphors apply to the exhibition itself, a Noah's Ark filled with what is representative of our culture rather than what is best. In other words, this is civilization as we recognize it. 'THE MOUTH IS INTERESTING BECAUSE IT IS ONE OF THOSE PLACES WHERE THE DRY OUTSIDE MOVES TOWARD THE SLIPPERY INSIDE', announces Jenny Holzer, our equivalent of the Cumaean sibyl. For the anti-museum is a museum after all, the museum a body, the body one big gullet.

Questions of time and space are mooted. Taking the long view, Simon Patterson's *Time Machine* (1994), a sort of clock-cum-slide rule which turns out to be useless, situates us in relation to Very Primitive Fish, while Henry Bond's presentation of documents about the damage caused to the ICA in 1984 by the German band Einstürzende Neubauten reminds us that a place that was nearly demolished once, could be again. In *Beyond the Infinite* (1994) two video monitors high on the walls play eerie shots culled by Graham Gussin from the film *2001*. In Gussin's version a space traveller happens upon a stranger with whom it is impossible to make contact because he seems to exist in a parallel universe, an experience a little like trying to get served in the ICA bar. There are more ways than one to suggest a parallel universe, of course. In a darkened corridor the visitor passes alcove after alcove, each containing one of Catherine Yass's lurid lightboxes depicting what look like hospital interiors, while back in the mausoleum the perverse Peter Fillingham has photographed the ground-floor section of the exhibition and attached the photographs to the door, as if when it shuts, the entire space can be transported elsewhere.

On both sides of a passageway two sets of badly stencilled football shirts hang in preparation for a soccer match between Millar's Institute of Cultural Anxiety team and Ross Sinclair's Passive School of Cultural Inertia. (Anxiety versus inertia sounds like a fairly even contest. The match will never take place, of course; instead, both sides will sit in the dressing-room wondering who stole their shirts.) The shirts themselves belong to another, major aspect of the revised Institute: the cultural oddity or treasure. Some of these are of purely historical interest. Or not, as in the case of Donald Campbell's helmet, suspiciously called Pete, or the drawings upstairs which could (but only could) have been made by Hieronymus Bosch. Why are they there? Discovering useless reminders of the past, our first instinct is to put them into a museum – or, of course, the House of Lords. Whether contemporary examples should be placed in the same category is a moot point. Does the top of a lavatory cistern by Michael Joo deserve a knighthood? Or a hairy pole partly shaved by Claire Barclay? Or a Thomas Ruff portrait? (Although everybody likes a bit of Ruff.) This type of exhibit is the stock-in-trade of group exhibitions. A veteran black and white photograph by David Griffiths, *An Even Stranger Secret (medium)* (1987), for instance, is one of those unassuming works that nag you gently for years. (In itself it is not odd; it is about oddity.) The label of a young man's shirt pokes out so that the word 'MEDIUM' is visible. Or, in fact, 'MOYEN', showing that he shops at Marks and Spencer. A small, black and white photograph has become evidence. But what kind of evidence? Like the label, it never quite fits in.

Another haunting item is Andrew Bannister's *Sleepwalker* (1994), a wax candle in the form of a full-size walking-stick. Attached to a canvas covered with blue fabric, it belongs to a series that began with church candles and leather belts. Then the undercurrent was monastic or sado-masochistic. Now the subtext is more complicated. (Its godfather may be Magritte's painting of a man stuffing his pipe with his humungous nose.) Undercurrents of mortality – of needing that stick rather than using it for rambles – are compensated for by the ultimate freedom that dreams bestow, a wide blue yonder into which we all step nightly, candles at the ready. There is also something surreal about Edward Lipski's elegant white plane, signalling as it flies. And continuing his set of works about objects purporting to have been discovered in or around famous places, Simon Starling's *Cast Aluminium Replica of a Toy Pistol Found on the 18th January 1994 in the Grounds of the Weissenhof Housing Project, Stuttgart* (1994) consists of 300 prints of the gun, piled beneath a plastic cover. Starling's main talent is his command of the shaggy dog story; he makes us so interested in the circumstances of his discoveries that we forget the oddity of the scenario. Why was he there? Whose pistol was it? Why 300 prints? Are there 300 prints? Does it matter? What connects the false teeth and the museum? A relic is a relic is a relic, Starling seems to imply, but does that make it art? Then he goes one step further and suggests that it may not matter.

Memories of Victorian living-rooms haunt Mat Collishaw's *Antique* (1994), an ornate wooden pedestal bearing a bell-jar, and, thanks to state-of-the-art technology, a virtual canary, twittering soundlessly – a large initial outlay, of course, but what a saving on seed, grit and slivers of cuttlefish. Also under glass is Dinos and Jake Chapman's *Little Death Machine (Castrated)* (1993-4), a 3D diagram of the act of ejaculation, almost as messy, automatic and mindless as sex itself. Originally made in an even more obscene, mechanical, 'uncastrated' version, it offered a trip from brain to penis and back again. Amazing what can be done with a hammer, a motor and a pot of squirty goo. This is art at its most museal. It is not alone. Under, and made of, glass are piles of artificial eyes from Dumfries. Even Vincent Shine's superb *Untitled Bilateral Dead Papyrus II* has the air of an exhibit, or part of the background for one. A full-blooded comment on simulation theory – it was made in 1990 – this beautiful work plays a double game. So, perhaps, does Jacob Robson's eerie *International Tropicana* (1994) – not, as you might assume, a Las Vegas cocktail lounge, but a strangely hued painting that seems to belong in *Scientific American*, illustrating plant life during the aeons when rhubarb had conquered the world. Equally nineteenth-century, like parlour games, are Douglas Gordon's shelf of books bought for a patron whose task it is to discover connections between the titles – let's hope he is as fond of S&M as Gordon assumes he is – or Christine Borland's partial skeleton in a box with the price (£65) and a description on a wall near by. These do not quite rank as oddities; instead, they can be explained, like puzzles.

Some puzzles do not lend themselves to explanation, of course. Tom Gidley's *Seeing Things (differently for the first time)* (1994) consists of three photographs taken of himself staring at a psychological puzzle made of dots. I saw a bird in flight on the one side and a butterfly on the other. All I saw in the middle was dots, or it might have been Winston Churchill smoking a cigar. Accompanied by a small picture of a dodo, Keith Tyson's very large *Map of the World Part V: (The University) a generator from a series of 5* (1993–4) had a maze at the centre and hundreds of numbered references to parts of the plan. Two things are wrong. First, spelling; even simple words such as 'plumbing' or 'textiles' are misspelt. (The same applies to Vaughan Matthews, who paints two words and spells one wrong.) Second, though it fits in perfectly with the Institute idea, Tyson's plan tends to be a work of work rather than a work of art. Similarly museal, Philip Riley's *Lake of Dreams* (1993) reveals areas of the brain with beautiful names: Sea of Nectar, Marsh of Mists, Seething Bay, Sea of Crises. Riley could either be a poet conscious of the weight and texture of words, or a didact submerging ideas in an overload of verbiage. Let's hope the poet wins. Fiona Banner also writes, although whether her large canvases covered with stories can be construed as comments on 'reading' paintings or whether they are just another way of making monochrome surfaces is unclear. Whatever. At least she can spell.

Some areas of the exhibition prove baffling. Photographs of facial reconstruction from World War II, a black rubber heart by Fischli and Weiss, a painting of a bulky doctor by Luc Tuymans and the appallingly tasteless video *Look Mummy Has No Hands* (1994) by Karen Eslea seem to belong to a medical section. Roderick Buchanan's stylized *Petrol Bombs* (1994), Martin Boyce's witty *Souvenir Placards (De-Luxe Edition)* (1994) and Jean-Michel Jarre's *Oxygene*, played on tape recorders borrowed at the entrance, belong to the 'historical' section of the Institute, where history is misremembered and battles are simplified and sentimentalized. Philip Lai's *Duty* (1994), a video of a hand covering a land-mine with vaseline, also ranks as history and the history of the ICA in particular; it is the kind of work that gave the avant-garde a bad name. Baffling too are the references to invention and travel – trains and planes, air and land, industry and landscape in the form of Peter Fraser photographs and a miraculous Vija Celmins drawing of a desert. A Godzilla video suggests a battle between the natural and the made-made, a theme that characterizes the room, cutting it off from the previous, less clear-cut discussion. Downstairs, arguments come thick and fast, to the confusion of the visitor. As the top of the building is reached, matters become easier. And here, as in the ICA's fine Situationist exhibition, the viewer becomes a *flâneur*. In Marianne Moore's famous line, 'It is a privilege to see so much confusion.'

For me everything else in the Institute of Cultural Anxiety was put to shame by John Haslam's book *Illustrations of Madness: Exhibiting a Singular Case of Insanity . . . with a description of the tortures experienced by Bomb-Bursting, Lobster-Cracking, & Lengthening of the Brain. Published in 1810 by John Haslam to prove the insanity of James Tilley Matthews*. According to Matthews, gangs of people were placed in important parts of London with a machine called an Air-Loom. And 'if the police were sufficiently vigilant, they might detect a set of wretches at work near the houses of Parliament, Admiralty, Treasury . . . and there is a gang established near St Luke's Hospital. The force of assailment is in proportion to the proximity of the machine; and it appears that the interposition of the walls causes but a trifling difference: perhaps at the distance of 1,000 feet a person might be considered free of its influence.' Those attacked had first to be saturated with 'magnetic fluid' by what sound like an early version of spray cans, while not even Matthews, an innocent bystander, was free from the maleficence of the gangs. As he struggled to report their depravities, members of the gangs did their best to sabotage him at every turn. One in particular, Lord Archy, 'the common liar of the gang', tried to defeat him by cheek and bad language. It is unfair to artists to show them alongside material like this. The old show-business principle applies; never perform with animals and children. Yet that sounds purely competitive. In fact, no competition exists, there is no argument to be had. Adolf Wölffli is a greater artist than Pablo Picasso, every child artist greater than any grown-up, every so-called 'primitive' better than any sophisticate. Why? Perhaps by virtue of some quality of belief. That the print in question is not even by Matthews is of no account. It is there, that's all. And we all have our Air-Looms and Lord Archies.

Cultural anxiety, we conclude, takes various forms. First, the anxiety about what culture could be: here Western, sanctified by culture as we know it – monolithic, white, heterosexual, metropolitan – with a nod to actual objects that are not 'art', the most experimental move in the exhibition. Second, anxiety produces a feeling of overload, tiredness, slow development, the eclipse of the new by the novel. Third, anxiety is dealt with as the norm, so that Paul Virilio's wise words, written around the gallery, are incorporated within the exhibition despite their critical content. Nowadays what used to be called buying up the opposition exists in a different form; depending on the highest bidder, criticality is on sale, willing and eager to be incorporated into the way things are.

Perhaps because the weight of the present is greater than the weight of the past – for it subsumes that past and demands a constant, albeit token reaction to it – forward movement has stopped, retrogression is pointless, a pincer movement is still possible but any meaningful definition has ceased. Like a Victorian entertainment, it puts art in inverted commas of its own. Heavy with irony, overloaded with all the paraphernalia that accompanies it, it has tottered to a standstill. The air is thin, the hour late, the forward movement of culture has reached a standstill, the waters are rising. In a glass container in the last room lies a Jeff Koons snorkel. It is behind glass, it is made of metal, but it may just come in useful . . .

Christine Borland

Review of an exhibition at Tramway, Glasgow, published in frieze *20, 1995*

From the drawings of Vesalius and Leonardo onwards art and anatomical research have had much in common. Yet their shared history has been marked by deep misgivings about the mutilations of God's handiwork. Surgeons at the anatomical theatres of Padua or Leyden had to explain to audiences that their practices involved re-creation rather than destruction: Vesalius even went as far as depicting flayed corpses in the self-absorbed postures of live melancholiacs. In the course of time fears about working with dead bodies grew – 'We murder to dissect,' wrote William Wordsworth, while Mary Shelley's Frankenstein was punished for breaching God's sole copyright on making human beings. Even today our view of anatomy seems no less uneasy, as Christine Borland demonstrates in her current project *From Life*, a title that seems at least ironic, at most deliberately misleading.

For some time in Britain, skeletons used for anatomy lessons have not been made of human bone. Instead, they are plastic reproductions. But Borland located and gained permission to use a rare example of a human bone skeleton and, with the assistance of experts, set about constructing a realistic model of the subject. The simplicity of the resulting bust of an Asian woman contrasted with the complexity of the emotional response it aroused in the viewer, and the difficulty of the moral and other philosophical issues touched on in the process of remaking. Borland had set out in search of a missing person, co-operating with scientists in the same way that she had worked with the police on a previous project. And as before, the process of detection mattered more than the result: a likeness that can never be verified. In one of the three rooms that housed the exhibition, the skeleton itself lay in a small box. In another a slide projector showed stages in the reconstruction of the facial characteristics of the skull, a feat that involved experts such as medical artists Richard Neave and Ray Evans. (A computer-generated image of the head also played its part in the process.) A third space contained the reconstructed bust, together with a terse, moving description.

The result could be described as a model of restoration. But was Borland returning something that had been lost, or was she taking a second look at existing facts with the intention of reaching some new conclusion? Since the 'truth' will never be verifiable in either case, it could be argued that the entire project rests on a relativist approach to facts. If it involved a form of sleuthing, it emphasized that all detection – the process of determining and marshalling evidence – must remain inconclusive. Yet the title of the exhibition prompted another comparison: with portraiture and therefore with art-making, a personal point of view brought into alignment with the head of a single human being. While doing much to establish a link between the unknown woman and her viewers, however, Borland has also identified and categorized her, and in verifying her existence in terms of facts and figures she has condemned all that is left of this human being to an eternity of servitude. Hasn't the unknown figure been numbered and accounted for all over again? Historians may regard the recovery of obscure details of the lives of the oppressed as a triumph. Yet isn't there always a chance that in that act of recovery, the original conditions of slavery are being imposed all over again, that once more a human being is being put on display as an object – now an art object, to be bought and sold like any other, and that once again the right to remain silent and private has been denied?

Of course, there are paradoxes here that cannot be accounted for by the artist, nor altered by a single work of art. They involve the status of items on display in museums and a right to silence that has been denied. (Who owns my skeleton after my death?) This is one pivot of *From Life*. Another is human rights and how to respect them while continuing to be 'scientific'. Returning to neglected areas of Conceptual practice – Nikolaus Lang, the early work of the Poiriers – Borland demonstrates that definition remains an important tool, that issues surrounding anatomy continue to be polemical, and that leaving projects open-ended may be their vindication, not their weakness.

Matthew Barney: Of Goats and Men

Published in frieze *20, 1995.*

Contrary to popular belief, performance art never died. First it expanded and merged with theatre, then it took place behind locked doors, without an audience. Silent and serious, Matthew Barney's early actions seemed to happen in a new space he had invented. Objects made by the artist to be manipulated in videos were defined by the moment of their use. (Instead of 'sculptures', he called them 'docufragments'.) Above all, the artist's employment of more than one video monitor gave his recorded movements a sepulchral quality, tacitly showing actions that continued to exclude the viewer. In 1989, the year Matthew Barney graduated, he made the video *Field Dressing (orifill)*. A figure in a white wedding dress descended two flights of stairs. It was the artist himself, using cross-dressing less as a mode of liberation than as a call to order. (One critic even remarked that watching the figure descending was 'like trying to reconstruct a memory from long ago'.) *Field Dressing* was shown alongside a related installation in a sports centre at Yale. Props for the video were displayed as sculptural objects in their own right. More importantly, the space of video and the space of the building were matched, compared, made strange. Looking from one to the other made both seem odder than ever and while the objects, now relics, evoked time past, the video repeated a succession of activities in which sport and performance merged.

The 'Drawing Restraint' series had begun a year earlier. Described by Barney as 'facilities to defeat the facility of drawing', these were experiments in prohibition or hindrance, turning mark-making into a physical trial. His role models were Harry Houdini, who regularly cheated death by means of physical and mental feats, often involving literal restraint, and Jim Otto, the 'Mean Machine', one of Al Davis's Oakland Raiders, famous because he continued playing even with an artificial knee. In an interview from 1991 Barney explained his favourite moment in a football game: 'The delay of game penalty where there is kind of a suspension of play, a refusal to accept the ball and walk into the arena of competition. This brings up the idea of someone who is able to capture creative potential through some sort of withholding or self-imposed restraint mechanism.'

Clad only in a rubber bathing cap, his head and feet bandaged, laden with what resembled the kind of equipment a fetishistic scaffolder might carry – 'internally lubricated self-threading flight blocks, titanium ice screws' – Barney used these instruments to dangle from walls or move across them like a mountaineer. As a graduate in art and sport with experience of modelling, he already seemed to have perfected his dual role as sportsman/supermodel, as well as deciding on his own particular materials, such as refrigerated petroleum jelly. It was as if he had decided to evade definitions. Indeed, if Barney had a genealogy, the most important family member would not have been a performance artist at all. For the complex mythic substratum of his work most nearly approached that of Marcel Duchamp. Didn't the spiral descent recall the slow motion of *Nude Descending the Staircase*, itself inspired by Mallarmé's aesthete hero who decides at last to relinquish his ivory tower and join the rest of the world? As in Duchamp, the self-sufficiency of the artist's fictive universe was paraded, changes of state were proposed and sexual definitions were blurred. (Barney has described the ideal of a 'roving rectum'.) And like that of Duchamp, Barney's sustaining myth involved sexuality, or the differences between male and female. The novel part of his particular use of the myth was his ability to conjure both sexes at once and hold both at a distance while continuing to maintain the impression of sexual interplay. (The work with the climbing nude of 1991 was christened *MILE HIGH Threshold: FLIGHT with the ANAL SADISTIC WARRIOR*.)

An iconography was developing. By 1991, when Barney's 'New Work' exhibition was presented at the San Francisco Museum of Modern Art, titles were turgid and drawings were obscure – titling had become poetry, cross-referencing had lurched out of control until every work seemed part of every other – but the sense of an evolving private language was unmistakable. The tone was humorous, and the joke was a smutty one. Penetration, masturbation, constipation and lubrication featured in the terminology, as well as obscure puns. (It is relatively easy to guess what a 'mile-high threshold' might be, but what is a 'hemorrhoidal distractor' or a 'blind perineum'?) And if the regalia of the male figure in Barney's performances was sportsmanlike and heroic, with swimming, baseball, rock-climbing and gymnastics merging into one activity, his female counterpart, played by Barney posing in a white robe, toque and fifties swimsuit, seemed the epitome of nimbleness and grace. Not even her white gloves and dark glasses could prevent her bouncing a pearl into an elaborately stretched hole designed to receive it by cutting through a skin-like fabric and holding the incision open with a clamp. Shifts between conventional sexual roles, between states and conditions (hard and soft, frozen and liquid, captivity and freedom); the references to protection by coated surfaces (Pyrex, Teflon, silicon); above all the use of materials such as 'human chorionic gonadotropin', relate to the sex act. But which sex act, exactly? As in Duchamp's work – if the works in drag and the halving of the *Large Glass* are taken into account – the theme was gender itself, the test of gender being desire. For perhaps only desire can resolve the whole idea of sexing and of what 'masculine' or 'feminine' could mean.

What Barney meant by anal sadism was 'the impulse to differentiate the sexuality' of a human being. To him the 00 sign (based on Jim Otto's shirt) which he had elaborated to make an insignia for the poster for his *Ottoshaft* video shown at the 1992 Documenta, proposed (for Otto) a 'twin rectum' which became 'more of a roving orifice'. Its extension into drawing in 1991, presented as usual in a frame 'internally lubricated' with petroleum jelly, showed that symbol as a pair of gonads and the Otto 'shaft' – part of the building in which the action was recorded – as the cross-section of a penis, in this case putatively extended to form what could be vestigial ovaries. The videos would elaborate on sexing, from images like the sewing together of two kilts with the occupants still inside them, in the *Ottoshaft* video, or the appearance of the artist's mother in the same work, playing Al Davis, coach of the Oakland Raiders, to the equivalent of male rape in *Drawing Restraint 7* (1993), when one satyr pulls another's horns off after a struggle. Despite the apparent obviousness of its elaborate costumes, high colour and ludicrous games, *Drawing Restraint 7* contains one puzzle: as the satyrs battle inside a moving limousine, a strange goo seems to be forming on its glass roof, and what resembles a string of pearls can be seen vaguely from inside. Could these relate to a puzzling sequence in Barney's new video, the most elaborate yet?

A drum roll introduces a view of an impossibly long Victorian pier jutting from a rocky, green landscape. To the drone of a bagpipe the familiar *CREMASTER* logo is seen at speed, before Barney himself appears in a white performance space, his face more animal than human, the bright red hair offsetting the whiteness of the room, his suit and the white mistletoe in his buttonhole. As he combs his hair over them, we cannot help but notice the two strange holes in his head where his horns once were. The room is a pavilion at the very end of a mile-long pier, leading to a beach and a road.

For the setting is the Isle of Man, a place where mutations can be expected. For man, on Man, may have become as much of a hybrid as the elaborately horned goats to be seen there or the rambling route of the Tourist Trophy motorcycle races. In this white room in the white pavilion, near the end of the long pier, three naked, muscled, red-haired, epicene figures pander to their master's every need. By the insertion of a large pin, they give his hooves new resonance, for example. And as he starts to tap-dance in front of a mirror, they cluster in anticipation. Meanwhile, on the island, two teams of two men in blue or yellow leather start up their motorcycles and side-cars. Side by side and facing in opposite directions, they wait for the flag to drop. Just before it does, the camera rises above them to show that their conjunction forms the outline of the *CREMASTER* logo, with its vertical capsule intersected midway by a narrow horizontal. And, in an unexpected piece of animation, the logo is surmounted by the three-legged symbol representing the Isle of Man. As we watch, the symbol revolves to indicate the start of the race.

The three attendants – described in the credits as 'faeries' – wait for something to happen. As their master dances, they creep over and slip something in his pockets. Meanwhile, inside the yellow and blue leather suits of the duelling teams, strange things are happening. As their vehicles pick up speed and tension rises, slithery forms emerge from pockets in their jackets and move in one case up, in the other down. When the camera shifts back to the pier, we notice a feature that was not previously visible: two curved, empty ramps on the other side of the rehearsal space. On the racetrack, the yellow team is in trouble: unable to negotiate a large puddle, they are forced to change direction. Meanwhile, on a lonely stretch of road, a pit-stop person who looks suspiciously like one of the 'faeries' waits to change tyres. All is still, when suddenly a spectacular, if predictable event occurs: the tap-dancing goat plummets through a hole he has danced in the floor of the rehearsal room, drops into the sea and continues his activities by walking on the sea bed between the end of the pier and the beach in the distance. On the lonely road where a car has stopped for refuelling the pit-stop person muses for a moment and, instead of changing the tyre immediately, replaces it with a skin-coloured version for a moment or two before reverting to the normal black one. The strange thing about the temporary skin-coloured alternative is that it has two nipple-shaped attachments hanging below it, which ruin its symmetry – and which, of course, would prevent it from running. The elated expression on the face of the pit-stop person as the bike roars off after its strange baptism leaves little doubt that a major event has taken place. Meanwhile, the yellow team encounters more problems. The vehicle crashes into a cliff. Well, not 'crashes', exactly; the driver is held in a state of suspended animation only inches from the cliff. Ice on his visor has frozen him to the spot.

Wearing billowing skirts, like a cross between Tenniel's Alice and a pantomime dame, the three faeries have left the pier to take their ease on the cliffs nearby and await the goat's return. Yet their vigil is disturbed when something is thrown into their midst. Underwater, their master seems to be searching. Finally, he finds an escape route, but a perilous one. Manoeuvring his body through different spaces, in the course of which his direction and orientation are muddled, he wrenches himself through white globules which melt and impede his progress, climbs through tight spaces shaped like one cookie-cutter after another, tunnels his way across the beach, which registers his burrowing as a continuous mole cast; and finally escapes. As he climbs to freedom, the three attendants in their yellow dresses ring tiny bells to encourage him, and the unpleasant mobile pink objects in his pocket begin to move about. Suddenly he is free. Through a crack he spies a road and on it a goat, dyed red, festooned with tartan ribbons and looking like a regimental mascot. On the pier the motorbikes have been put on display on the two white ramps. A pause. An empty road. A drum roll, bagpipe music and what looks like the entrance to a tent, its canvas lashed with thread which is pulled steadily to reveal . . . well, what exactly? A haggis? A goitrous growth waiting to be lanced? A mound of engorged flesh meets our gaze, its colour almost purple, the skin tightly tied. And finally, when a second shot through a pair of open male legs reveals bagpipe drones attached to and dangling from puckered skin, the experience proves too quick for immediate recognition. Nevertheless, we are convinced that we have seen something like this before.

The Isle of Man is an obvious place to make a film about masculinity. Or is it? Inbreeding produces freakish anomalies. Where did the idea of that three-legged man come from? Could it be a sign of rampant masculinity? (Do Manxmen have members the same length as their legs?) Or its opposite? (Three legs leave no room for genitalia.) Or some third alternative? In *Drawing Restraint 7*, flirtation or sport leads to the removal of the satyr's horns, which must be restored, for what would a satyr be without horns? That the creature Barney plays is not a goat is crucial, since the sign that he has successfully achieved his aim is his confrontation with a real regimental goat in tartan, the first thing to be seen as he emerges from his undersea journey. Perhaps a goat is to a satyr what a woman is to a drag queen: an object of envy and pity in equal quantities. Sexually, it is a primitive version of Barney's satyr: suave, fashionable, but lacking animal attraction. You are not born a woman; you become one, Simone de Beauvoir argued. That also applies to heroes. The undersea journey is paralleled in every mythology in the world. And, like this particular baptism, it takes place in tight spots. Crawling with difficulty up a symbolic sphincter is the last stage of the rebirthing process. Or is it a ritual of definition? (Hence the sequence of luminous cookie-cutters.) As the action draws to a close, two separate objects, both elliptical like the two zeroes of the Jim Otto motif, appear and reappear: on the strange, symbolic tyre; on the ramps built to display the motorcycles after the race; above all, in the disturbing, mobile objects placed in the drivers' pockets, organs that take on a life of their own and crawl up the bodies of the duelling drivers.

'My heart is in my mouth', we say when we are frightened. Barney's references to heat and cold result in a different metaphor: of the retraction of the testicles, a sign of fear. And the final shots, in which it seems that two pairs of real testicles are displayed (one tied, bulbous and purple with strain, the others nipped, wrinkled and retracted) not only resolves the question of the relevance of bagpipes – played not on Man but in Scotland by men in skirts – but also of the strange, slippery good luck tokens by which faeries set such store. What they are giving the drivers is 'balls' – in other words, bravery, guts, manhood in its traditional sense. Balls are no more than symbolic, of course. And at the end of the century they are under a lot of strain. But when the artist is Matthew Barney, neither discovery comes as a surprise.

An interview with Pepe Espaliú

Unpublished, recorded in Madrid, 1988.

Stuart Morgan: You once painted a portrait of yourself as a broken pot. A pair of hands seemed to be signalling some indecipherable message, as if they were making shadows on a screen. But on the hands were fractured profiles, opposites that, if combined, would eliminate the message the halves were transmitting. There was a certain desperation about this, as if you were hinting that your fractured personality was forcing you to employ a sign system over which you had no control.

Pepe Espaliú: For me the subject of the picture is the empty space between the hands. You define yourself in relation to what is not inside you. Desire is a form of lack. And it is important to speak of desire.

Is it sign language?

No. As a child, I watched a TV programme about conjuring. Two hands would appear at the beginning and the titles of the programme would be spelt out in the empty space between them.

Early memories seem to play a large part in your work. Images of maternity, for example, like a mother cradling a baby.

Call it an adolescent memory. In Spain in the sixties images of maternity were seen a lot, particularly in Jesuit schools – images of redemption, not debatable in aesthetic terms because they belong on another level.

One photograph of you crops up repeatedly in your catalogues. As a boy on a horse.

That is an adolescent dream of power – a strong theme pictured in a weak way.

An adolescent dream of surrendering power and another of assuming power. How do you choose such images?

If something rings a bell – an image, a word, a saying – I use it. There are things you repeat to yourself because repeating them makes you feel better.

Does this mean your art is a form of invocation?

That would be the wrong metaphor. Freud wrote about babies making the game of *fort/ da*, the cotton reel which the mother has but refuses to give back. So the words *fort* and *da* become a kind of demand.

Perhaps a better metaphor would be one of prayer. But when do *people pray?*

When they are lacking something. When they are unfulfilled.

This may be the motive behind the repetitions in your work. Who could satisfy the lack you speak of?

No one at all. They say it is justifiable for mental patients to talk to themselves because there is no answer to what they are saying.

Surely people who pray are expecting an answer.

They are waiting for something, but it isn't an answer.

Concealment plays a major part in your work. Those leather sculptures, for example: hollow works with mysterious interiors.

Concealment is necessary in order to attract, for attraction is based on emptiness. Because the sculptures are looking for a way of getting something, they go on insisting despite the fact that they are defeated every time. Sometimes they even forget why they began the fight; the aim no longer exists, only the insistence on that aim, which is an emptiness.

Why leather, a material usually reserved for objects of use?

I wanted to give the idea that sometimes these objects could be taken for utensils, to sustain the ambiguity between something symbolic and something used. The leatherworkers were convinced that I was going to use these sculptures for some secret purpose.

They are only just sculpture.

Marcel Duchamp used the phrase 'cowardly sculpture'. They are intentionally cowardly. But leather is a live material which becomes distorted as it grows older, and begins to smell as it disintegrates. To anyone who is not from Córdoba it seems exotic, but there it is the most familiar material of all.

How important is the idea of collapse and deterioration?

Most important, because there is something between life and death, between security and chaos. I want them to establish a polarity between cult objects and objects of use, as a human body does.

Recently you made a set of paintings about Jean Genet, whose approach to the human body resembles yours.

Genet is a kind of shaman; he brought together things that everybody feels but which no one dares to admit. Which is a way of saying that he is forbidden.

Do you believe in the concept of sin?

Yes, but Genet is not about sin; his work is about glory. I feel that glory can be touched, if only tangentially and by haphazard means. In Genet's case it could simply have been through reading Corneille's *Le Cid* at the age of fourteen. For other writers and artists it could be something else. Shapes and forms are rhetorical. (That is not meant to sound pejorative.)

What is the proof of glory?

Even without proof, it is still evident. In theology it is the only support for faith. God is because He is.

That's tautological.

It certainly is. You talk about recurrences in my work. To me they mean nostalgia for something, but we don't know what. I'm speaking about a silence in which echoes and images ring a bell for no apparent reason. In African sculptures, for example, regardless of their use and the function they have in the world, I know what the emotion is about.

Are we talking about glory again?

Glory is not Christian; it is a private conviction that you are moving from one place to another, and that at any moment you'll find yourself in the same place again.

Are we talking about flesh?

Soul is flesh, Genet argued, and I agree.

Haven't we fallen into flesh because of the Fall of Man? (Only Christ triumphed by taking on human form.) So aren't we really discussing a human state, fallen and guilty?

According to Georges Bataille or Michel Tournier, for Gilles de Rais the point of the repetition of the crime was to find the same expression on the face of his murdered victims as Joan of Arc had on hers as she was reaching heaven. An impossible quest and an impossible repetition. But for Gilles that meant a sense of life, of pleasure. It may be just a story, but for me it is something essential.

Pepe Espaliú

Published in Rites of Passage: Art for the End of the Century, *catalogue of the exhibition curated by Stuart Morgan and Frances Morris, Tate Gallery, 1995. (The other artists included were: Miroslaw Balka, Joseph Beuys, Louise Bourgeois, Hamad Butt, John Coplans, Robert Gober, Mona Hatoum, Susan Hiller, Jana Sterbak and Bill Viola.)*

> 'I have long had an *entente cordiale* with death.'
> – Pepe Espaliú[1]

Art, said Pepe Espaliú, moves from the complex to the simple. Not surprisingly, his own works used minimal means to achieve maximum significance. Like parables, they offered a variety of readings and existed to instil wisdom, however indirectly. In addition, the high level of coding in Espaliú's work suggested not only that his art was based on personal experience, but also that it served to examine meaning in general. Underlying this was a subtle intelligence and his view of himself as an avant-gardist with a classical outlook.

In 1987 Espaliú painted a self-portrait. In front of a curtain two hands appeared – one masculine, one feminine – each challenging and challenged by the other, each superimposed with half an image of a broken vase, its adjacent parts bearing positive and negative silhouettes of a single face. Panicked, the female hand remained itself, pallid in comparison with its male counterpart, which had absorbed both the colours and pattern of the curtain behind it and was recoiling in alarm. That the artist's idea that his own self-image depended on a balance between female and male stereotypes was confirmed by ambiguous references in another painting. *Glove-making (for Javier B.),* of 1988, featuring on the right a neat glove like a sewing pattern and on the left that same shape dissolving or bursting into flames. Play of language – signing – and language within language, perhaps a message to a friend, above all the shadowy presence of the artist himself, hovering over his own work instead of inhabiting it, seemed essential to Espaliú's sense of self-definition. A favourite childhood photograph was of himself riding: 'an adolescent dream of power' or a token of aloofness or self-protection.[2] In other ways Espaliú was not a loner, however: even early on his plans involved other people. Exhibitions he organized at La Máquina Española, for example, presented works by artists unfamiliar to Spanish viewers, such as Louise Bourgeois, Meret Oppenheim, the neglected Catalan Joan Brossa or the Belgian Surrealist Marcel Mariën, and collaborations with other artists took place throughout his career.

Self-Portrait was a study in absence. 'For me', Espaliú explained, 'the subject of the picture is the empty space between the two hands. You define yourself according to what is not inside you.' But what could be done about this absence? To the question 'When do people pray?', he replied, 'When they are lacking something. When they are unfulfilled.' Who could satisfy the lack they were feeling? 'No one at all. They say it is justifiable for mental patients to talk to themselves because there is no answer to what they are saying.' Not surprisingly anticipation, prayer and loneliness loom large in Espaliú's work. While studying the Mystic Odes or *Rubaiyats* of the thirteenth-century Sufi poet Jala-ad-Din ar-Rumi, poems mourning the loss of his friend Shams Tabrizim which rely on the belief that moods of vivid longing or lack can be eased only by repetition of the terms of that lack, Espaliú was reminded of a television series about conjuring that he had seen as a child. 'Two hands would appear at the beginning', he recalled, 'and the titles of the programme would be spelt out in the empty space between them', an experience referred to in *Self-Portrait.* Yet Espaliú laid particular stress on the meaning of 'conjure'. For him the sense of trickery was never in doubt. Cards, of course, are used not only for playing games but also as the props for conjurors. Both highly conventionalized, games and conjuring demand such constant repetition that repetition itself acquires ritual significance. Asked whether his art was a form of invocation, Espaliú replied, 'That would be the wrong metaphor. Freud wrote about babies playing the game of *fort/da*, the cotton reel which the mother has but refuses to give back. So the words *fort* and *da* become a kind of demand.'

Secrecy was crucial, and a recurrent idea in his work is that of absence. In 1988, for example, he drew and constructed hollow structures, first made out of cloth, then leather cut and stitched by Córdoban craftsmen. 'Concealment is necessary in order to attract', Espaliú declared, 'for attraction is based on emptiness. Because sculptures are looking for a way of getting something, they go on insisting despite the fact that they are defeated every time. Sometimes they even forget why they began the fight; the aim no longer exists, only the insistence on that aim, which is an emptiness.' One major influence was Jean Genet. 'Genet is a kind of shaman. He brought together things which everybody feels but which no one dares to admit. Which is a way of saying he is forbidden . . . His work is about glory. I feel that glory can be touched, if only tangentially and by haphazard means. In Genet's case it could simply have been by reading Corneille's *Le Cid* at the age of fourteen. For other artists and writers, it could be something else. Shapes and forms are rhetorical. (That is not meant to sound pejorative.)' Invited to demonstrate proof of glory, Espaliú replied that 'even without proof, it is still evident. In theology, it is the only support of faith. God is because He is.' The basis of this theory demanded his espousal of another tradition entirely: one branch of literary modernism in which self-destruction was aligned with success, artistic or otherwise. For Espaliú a fascination with artistic self-destructiveness, the convergence of the production of art and the artist's death wish provided a sign beneath which it was possible to invoke 'the type of psychosis that makes you do only the things you are afraid of'.

His series of *Santos* (Saints) resembled the tribal African objects that Espaliú admired; somehow their purpose had been lost. Asked why he chose leather, he replied, 'I wanted to give the idea that sometimes these objects could be taken for utensils, to sustain the ambiguity between something symbolic and something used.' And, recalling Duchamp's phrase 'cowardly sculpture', he called the *Santos* 'intentionally cowardly', drawing attention either to their potential for deterioration or to their mendacity. (In a suite of drawings they sprouted Pinocchio noses.) Comparison with the human body was inescapable. And for Espaliú body and soul were intrinsic. ('Soul is flesh, Genet argued, and I agree.') The sculptures and drawings from 1990 are deliberately made with minimal means. Frailty and robustness are confused, messages seem all-powerful though they may never be delivered; the clapper of a bell becomes a tongue, a lash, even a head of hair. Adopting Kandinsky's term, Espaliú spoke of 'resonance' and poetic intensity in his work. 'It's a carapace your body embraces', he wrote in a late poem, 'like a death in miniature / looking at which would deny you / the interior from the exterior.'[3] By the time of *Untitled* (1990), a bronze torso made up of a vestigial head with a skipping rope over each shoulder, the religious significance was undeniable. Yet piety was not power. In a deserted church, St Paul's in east London, as part of the exhibition 'Edge 92', Espaliú flooded the altar space and placed cushions above the water like stepping-stones. Yet because these hassocks rested on plaster bases which the water gradually dissolved, they began to float, a reference to Peter, he of little faith, who, seeing Christ walk on water, attempted it himself and sank.[4] For Espaliú, faith in himself had begun to depend on faith in others. Despite his weakened state, *Carrying*, a set of closed, black sculptures resembling sedan chairs used to transport the plague-ridden in eighteenth-century Venice, was followed by a simple action, also called *Carrying*, which involved the artist himself, emaciated now and barefoot, being supported and taken a short distance by two people who in turn would pass him to another pair. In this simple action, designed to draw the attention of the Spanish authorities to the existence and plight of Aids sufferers, the 'carrier' was himself carried.

Militant, angry, the final works focused on movement, impotence and friendship. Crutches and cages had already been used as motifs. In *Rumi* (1993) interlocking cages were displayed as staircases for the spirit, while in *The Nest* crutches stood in a circle to enable them to remain upright. Yet both of these are positive interpretations. The crutches make a closed group, while cages remain cages. Or do they? Espaliú's installation in the Hospital de la Venerable Orden III in Madrid (also part of 'Edge 92') consisted of three cages hanging side by side, all bottomless, with the result that the bars continued to spread across the floor, like roots reaching far and wide, a metaphor for freedom. This circular motif reappeared in the performance *The Nest* (1993), in which the artist, now weakened and emaciated, had an octagonal platform built in a tree next to the Gemeentmuseum in Arnhem, and every day for eight days climbed the ladder and preceded to walk around the trunk, removing one more of his eight garments, timing his final appearance, naked, to coincide with a visit by Queen Beatrix of the Netherlands. In a text published after his death, Espaliú writes: 'Circles in which desire is trapped in a repeated driving movement, desire eroded by the "inability to stop", becoming purer and emptier, as in the movements of the dervishes, the Sufi dancers . . . A constant whirling of prisoners and mystics, paranoiacs and homosexuals . . . all those who live without appropriating anything for themselves but simply in a feverish desire to "rotate" the tautological circularity of "being".'[5]

Espaliú's last works returned to this circularity. At the Gemeentmuseum he had 'adopted' a painting from 1930 by Pyke Koch. Called *Nocturne*, it showed an old-fashioned public urinal by night, a sight made more dramatic by unearthly light streaming from inside the round structure around which men would circulate. This further reference to 'rotation' was taken up by

Espaliú, who discovered the sad fate of such classic meeting-places: only two such buildings remained in the whole of Paris. Choosing one in the Boulevard Arago, next to the de la Santé prison, he invited some male homosexual friends, instructing them, unknown to each other, to arrive there at various times on the same day, and to scrawl messages on the wall, each replying to the previous writer. After visiting the *pissoir* in question – or, more correctly, the *vespasienne* – the participants met and talked.[6] In a collage made in 1993 a circle/halo appeared consisting of the words *CON O SIN TI* (with or without you), and above it a photograph of the building around which men strolled, as he himself had on his solitary platform in *The Nest*. As in the case of the dervishes, repeatedly going round had led to ecstasy, a release from the body. Espaliú recalled the search for the Beloved resulting from the poet Rumi's loss of his friend but also the dematerialization meant to result from the dervishes' act of whirling for God. 'My place is no place, my sign is no sign. I have neither body nor soul, for I belong to the soul of the Beloved.'[7]

Early in Espaliú's career critics had singled out what they regarded as the weakness of his tactics: the preference for rhetoric, for mere play of sign systems instead of a concern for meaning. Yet as his life continued, his work dealt increasingly with that same apparent vacuity – so much so, indeed, that its opposite was invoked: not absence of meaning but the potential for significance. And as they became more demonstrative, more public, his previous tactics began to make sense in a larger, political context. For the *vespasienne*, the hollow vessels, the cupped hands, the fact of going through the motions all recall conjuring in its proper sense: an attempt to invoke spirits, to produce something out of nothing, as comfort for a loss. Like the dervishes, Espaliú used ritual to invoke two states in particular. One was love, the other prayer.

1. Pepe Espaliú, *El Periódico de Catalunya (*20 January 1993), p.31.

2. This and other unfootnoted quotations are from the interview with Espaliú made in Madrid, 1988 [now published in this book].

3. Catalogue for the van Krimpen Gallery, Amsterdam, quoted by Juan Vicente Aliaga, 'Speak to Me, Body', in *Pepe Espaliú 1986–1993* (Seville: 1994), p.164.

4. For a description of this work see Adrian Searle, 'The Loss of Pepe Espaliú' in *Pepe Espaliú* (London: ICA, 1994), n.p.

5. Aliaga, p.148.

6. The resulting conversation is published in Jan Brand, Catelijne de Muynck, Valerie Smith, ed., *Sonsbeek 93* (Ghent: 1993), pp.238–54. [Morgan was one of the participants. See also his account of Sonsbeek, 'Into the Trees', *frieze* 12, September–October 1993.]

7. Aliaga, p.146.

Beyond Control: an interview with Susan Hiller

Published in frieze *23, 1995; reprinted in Barbara Einzig, ed.,* Thinking About Art: conversations with Susan Hiller *published by Manchester University Press, 1996.*

Stuart Morgan: *You are attracted to things beyond your control.*

Susan Hiller: I'm interested in things that are outside or beneath recognition, whether that means cultural invisibility or has to do with the notion of what a person is. I see this as an archaeological investigation, uncovering something to make a different kind of sense of it. That involves setting up a situation which welcomes this perhaps anarchic, non-volitional stage of awareness.

An unedited stage?

Yes, in response to a situation structured to create a heightened or more precise awareness.

Gender has been another concern.

These things go together. Understanding the implications for perception and behaviour of my entry into language as a sexed subject, and understanding how this is definitely not the same thing as being limited to activities that are conventionally defined as feminine, in fact gave me the impetus to explore areas that used to be considered off-limits in art.

Work in Progress *(1979) could be seen exactly as a so-called feminine art work: pulling your paintings apart thread by thread, turning them into something different.*

The idea of simultaneously making and unmaking could be traced to any mystical tradition. To associate it solely with women would be astonishing.

Is it a means of prevention?

That seems contradictory. In remaking my old paintings I wanted change, but everything changes inevitably. I just brought things more quickly to the point they would reach anyway. In contrast, the culture of art in our society involves fixing: putting things in museums and not letting them deteriorate. But in other societies the kind of sculpture that influenced the early modernists – African, Polynesian – is left to rot, raising the question of how continuity of style can exist in places where no visual model exists to be emulated. We're different; we think that if we can't keep a painting perfect, we'll have no more painting in future.

You, in contrast, continue your Conceptual exercise of burning your work.

Every year I transform some works into other formats. The series of burnt relics began in 1972. I placed the ashes of burnt paintings in chemical containers that measure and contain what can't be contained. They are like burial urns too, and since I regard them as just as interesting to look at and experience as paintings, maybe it reflects a wish for everything to be seen as having the same potential for insight. Like traces or remnants, they point forwards and backwards at the same time.

You also cut old paintings into equal-sized rectangles and sewed those together, one on top of the other.

I called them *Painting Blocks* (series begun 1970–71). Each has the scaled-down dimensions of the original painting. The project turns surface into mass, painting becomes sculpture. It's a materials-based comparison. (At present in this country we have an untrue history of Conceptualism which suggests it is totally language-based.)

Other early works, like Dream Mapping *(1974), involved other people.*

That's right. In that piece participants collaborated to develop a system for the graphic notation of dream events. After about a month we decided not to work with words but with diagrams.

Diagrams of what?

Of dreams.

Of what they saw in dreams?

Or of the location of events, or of structures. People evolved their own notational system. For the last three nights we went to a site in the countryside where there was a remarkable occurrence of mushroom circles: fairy rings. In folklore, if you fall asleep in a fairy ring, you'll be carried away to fairyland, like in a state of altered consciousness. So on the last three nights everybody picked a fairy ring and went out and slept in it all night. Next day we collectively mapped our dreams, by which I mean that we first diagrammed or drew our individual dreams, then we superimposed them one on the other and came up with a collective dream map. I was writing a book on dreams with David Coxhead, so I was aware of all sorts of traditions about dream incubation, which means going to a special place to have a heightened dream – a pattern the world over for curing ailments – but also the idea of the collective evolution of a notational system for dreams. In many Native American or Australian Aborigine groups such a system as an art form was not seen as representational: it's not a picture of a dream image but a set of notes in visual diagrammatic form. The two ideas came together in this piece.

But then for me there was a difficulty, which was that work which began as a deeply felt attempt to be non-hierarchical, non-élitist, non-product-oriented, outside the gallery system, getting back to basics, working with friends, remained more elusive and more esoteric than a painting could ever be, because it was an enactment, a performance where no gap exists between audience and participants. They're the same. So on one level what had seemed a perfect solution was not really such a good format, because the experience of the piece could not extend beyond the original participants. What I retained from this series of pieces was the conviction that the other person has to be in the work or it isn't interesting to do.

Is there a rift between your two kinds of practice in this early period?

After several years of work that was on one hand Minimalist and materials-based, like the sewn canvases, and on the other hand immaterial and time-based, like the investigation pieces for groups of people, I really wanted to resolve the dichotomy. First I made a mental equation between materials and ideas. (That's why I've always said I have a materials-based practice.) I made *Dedicated to the Unknown Artists* (1972–6), a rough sea postcard work, and a slide piece called *Enquiries/Inquiries* (1973 and 1975) based on a sort of cultural catechism taken from popular encyclopaedias in Britain and the United States. (Hence the two spellings of the same word.) These works used an approach that has remained important for me and comes out of Minimalism: putting together many similar units with tiny differences. My work was starting to come together from about 1973. The early ideas carried through to later works that require the involvement of viewers in a different way. It goes back to Michael Fried's idea of the theatrical. He meant that invidiously. I took it differently. Because I come from a conjunction of Minimalism and Fluxus, I combined the interactive with the non-theatrical and turned this into another position which insists on the participation of the viewer as essential to the work. In *Monument* (1980–81), for instance, where the entire piece is activated by a person who sits on a bench listening to a sound tape, a person must be prepared to be seen in public performing a private act of listening. Since that person is seen by other viewers against a backdrop of photographic images, the piece exists as a tableau with a living centre, while the person is also part of the audience for the work. That was the kind of solution I arrived at for the problem raised by my earlier very private investigative works, which left behind only traces or pieces of evidence and documents. The thing that unifies everything is the use of cultural artefacts from our society as starting-points. At the time this was a new thing to be doing. If you think the idea through, you realize that every type of format is already an artefact, including stretchers and canvas, the television screen, so how could artists not be working with artefacts? In that sense everybody is working anthropologically.

And politically, too?

Well, it's work in the world, which contributes as much to knowledge and shifts in attitude as any other form of work. At the same time, art has a mirroring function; it can only disclose an image of what is already available to us. Because we are products of our society and culture, artists don't know anything that anybody else doesn't know, but we can show people, ourselves included, what we don't know that we know.

You also made participatory works for hundreds of people.

Yes, *Street Ceremonies* (1973), in the open air in Notting Hill, involved about 200 people. Another much smaller group work made later the same year was called *The Dream Seminar*. Some people from both of those pieces took part in *Dream Mapping*.

Artists' early works prepare for what is to come. In your case it was a total assault on the integrity of the art object and a full-scale attack on the idea of the individual.

I didn't see it as an attack; more, that I was wounded and had to make a response. I'm not saying I consciously felt a sense of damage. Those were confident days. It was wonderful to be in England. People were crossing borders freely. It was part of a mood: a different, more integrated period. We were lucky to be around. My confidence came from having emerged at that period. I had nothing to lose, so why not follow my own predilections? I liked being where I was. There was no pressure to establish an art career. Everyone had abandoned all that; you did whatever you did, and if it turned out to be music or painting or writing, great. Or you didn't have to do anything, you could just grow vegetables. We had shrugged off the need to define ourselves, have a career, get a mortgage, all those things.

One work that emerged from this attitude was Sisters of Menon.

Those scripts emerged on a visit to France, where I was staying in a small village. It was there that the Sisters of Menon events occurred. Admittedly, the stage was set for some altered state of consciousness, but it wasn't anything peculiar; I accepted this as part of the way images and ideas were transmitted, at least among artists, because you find that in art and also in science, unconnected people in different places seem to come up with the same idea at the same time. So it didn't seem freaky. Suddenly, I started to write and write and write . . . That was in 1972, and then I lost the manuscripts or misplaced them or put them away somewhere and forgot about them. When I came across them again a few years later, I decided that if I formalized the material it could become a work. At that point I added four pages of commentary. The cross-shaped formation is simple to arrange: X number of A4 pages. That made sense since a cross appears in the text itself; the four pages of commentary became four ends, four panels at the ends of the arms of the cross. The formal configuration and commentary pages were done in 1979, the year I found the lost scripts.

What did you decide it meant?

I don't know. It convinced me of the reality of the divided self, and that one person is many voices but there is no bounded unit who contains them. They could be seen as possibilities of being. We have ways to tune out most of them and tune in some. I suppose that when they become overwhelming, our society says you're mad or schizophrenic. This experience was not overwhelming in that way, nor was it sought for. Except you could say, 'Of course you sought it by going to France and working on an ESP piece (*Draw Together*, a postal event) in the first place'. There was nothing eerie about the experience. The most interesting part of *Sisters of Menon* was that it seemed to address itself to a kind of female sensibility or entity. When my husband tried to tune in on it, he produced a page that said something like, 'Go away, you are not the sister.' There are so many levels, ironies and little jokes, that you have to recognize something with an amazing sense of humour and a very quirky attitude. 'Menon' is 'no men' but I think it was Lucy Lippard who pointed out that it's also an anagram of nomen, which means 'name': the opposite of not having a name, in other words, siting or situating the voices.

For a while it led me down strange paths; I thought I had to investigate all kinds of historical facts. For instance, one of the Menon scripts says, 'We are your sisters from Thebes'. Thebes is of course the necropolis in Egypt which undoubtedly I had already read about, and one famous precinct there is dedicated to someone called Memnon. I also got involved in reading about the Cathars because the village I was in was in their area of France and a circle with an equal-armed cross or X, which was a Cathar symbol, appears at a certain point in the scripts. Cathars followed a Gnostic tradition, which leads to interesting ideas about religion and gender. It all seemed to tie together.

Then at a certain point I realized that the scripts were a fragment and an irrational production; you could spend your life interpreting it but you wouldn't get anywhere. It was a question of accepting this production as a drawing as well as an utterance. The fact that it was a physical production became really important to me. And just to allow it to exist in whatever ambiguous placement it had – just to let it be – was also important. But it did link me with certain traditions pertaining to gender. I became interested in secret languages, ritual languages, coded languages, artistic languages and in my own problem of finding what was called 'a voice', because the Sisters seemed to have so many voices.

Do you think you lost the manuscript deliberately?

I probably wasn't able to accept it immediately and to say, 'Yes these messages or utterances are as important as any other'. It made me interested in art in a different way; I could see all the trajectories through modernism that had been considered unacceptable. You know, Surrealism was like a dirty word.

Taken seriously, Sisters of Menon *would result in a quite different view of culture.*

I see culture as a series of curtailments. The reason we value art is that, despite this, it can provide occasional glimpses of different ways of perceiving and understanding.

How do you see your own work?

I never know whether it is one work or not. I'm aware there's probably the difficulty that one ends up with fragments as evidence of something.

Or as attempts to reach a single place. That wouldn't be so terrible.

Well, to regard *An Entertainment* (1990), for example, as a totality would be completely misleading. It has been seen as a statement about child abuse or domestic violence. In fact, I'm interested in at least three things: one, the kind of mythic underpinnings; two, the left/right dichotomy; three, the eroticized violence, deeply scary but sexy at the same time. I understand the large works as incomplete and as much part of an ongoing procedure as the small works. Even the way *An Entertainment* is constructed: similar episodes with slight differences repeated and stitched together, different takes on comparable scenes, is like the small works. I would say the content of my work is consistent, although the subject matter of different pieces varies a lot.

The way I see it, in a piece like Magic Lantern *(1987), is that you are suggesting that a mental area exists in which creation happens, whether you are the creator or the audience, that here is a zone in which it is possible to release your imagination or use it in some way, and you're asking 'Can we talk about this?' In other words, can we consider this area within which anything is possible because it's not real? Though to us it's very real within certain boundaries. It's like what happens on a stage or when a storyteller says, 'Once upon a time . . .' then everything after that is modified until the end.*
I like your notion of a zone, but you see, to me that zone is totally real, and *Magic Lantern* is one of the clearest, strictest, most direct statements of this I've ever made. I'm showing you – and showing myself, because it's a machine I can use too – that the perceptions of the body and the effect of light on the eye, the intersection of the body and desire, creates beauty, creates meaning. That piece can't be documented because the colours you're seeing are real but invisible externally. So it's specific to you but it's also collective because it happens to all of us in the audience at the same time. It's not unreal, that's what I want to emphasize. Just like the shapes people see in my video *Belshazzar's Feast* (1980–81) are as real as anything else. I think you mean they're not real if they're not objectively there or not outside us? What do you mean?
The idea of an invisible stage, the reaction that Coleridge called 'the willing suspension of disbelief' and how this can be maintained or cut off. If you suddenly start quoting Shakespeare I can tell if you're quoting even if I've never read Shakespeare.
The only time I've emphasized that is in *An Entertainment*. When the curtain goes down you're really stranded after you've been up in the stars, and it's like asking a question about how we are intersections of these possibilities, consensus reality and these states where we experience other things. In that work the story just ends; the curtain comes down. Pieces like *Belshazzar's Feast* and *Magic Lantern* don't end so abruptly; you can still see after-images for a while. We're usually not aware that everything we perceive is a combination of something externally given and something we bring to it so there is never anything without our subjectivity. What I want to make is situations where people are aware what they're seeing is because of who they are; so they are conscious of the fact that they are part of a mechanism for producing pleasure and pain, that we're not just walking through life as though it were someone else's film. It's like dreaming: you're both inside and

outside and it's important to know you're in both places.
How does that help in An Entertainment*? It's disturbing. It's all around me. The figures of Punch and Judy are bigger than I am. People are being beaten, the change of size is tremendous. For someone who had never seen a Punch and Judy show, I'm not sure what it would mean.*
I don't know either. My work is particular to this culture. All rituals are scary. Part of what art is about now is to find ways of beginning to say things about the darkness of the culture. The piece is not intended to be an admonition; it was meant to be the experience of a child. I was subjecting myself to what I saw children being subjected to with every Punch and Judy show. Yet at the same time adults find these little figures hitting each other strangely jolly. The child is just a little person who has the problem of fearful identification at the same time as being told it's enjoyable. The child is being taught something through the terror of ritual, and the hope of the male child is that he will become Mr Punch. Girls see it differently. After seeing my piece, I think everyone's views about those puppets change.
Are we meant to identify with Punch because he is the protagonist?
It's a way to avoid being killed.
What kind of ritual is it? What does it mean? There's a man, wife and child. He murders them all, is sentenced and then kills his judges too.
You can't explain it in those terms: it's not a story about a man who does good or evil. He's not a man, he's Mr Punch and he's not human. He's monstrous, even his voice is distorted through that funny little thing . . .
A swazzle.
To deform voice as well as body. The curious thing is how this character came to stand for Britain.
Presumably Punch and Judy was not English originally.
Commedia dell'arte characters were brought to England by Italian showmen, who produced marionette plays, and eventually glove puppets, which improved the fights: you can pit your right hand against the left so well. That's where English Punch and Judy differs from other versions which are played by marionettes. In the eighteenth century one Italian showman in London reduced it to a series of simple stick fights.
You think a lot about this left/right dichotomy.
It's a universal distinction. (Of course, the left hand refers to the right part of the brain and the right hand to the left part.) The right hand is seen as good, dominant, clean, and worthy, the left as sinister, gauche, dirty. As society

becomes increasingly rational we've tended to downgrade the intuitive. Punch and Judy puts Punch on the puppeteer's dominant right hand and all the other characters – women, children, animals – on the intuitive, denigrated left. As in ancient myth it reduces to a dualism, which may refer as much to these opposed parts of our brain as to anything socio-historical. I find that pretty interesting.

Art as Idea as Idea: an interview with Joseph Kosuth

Published in frieze *16, 1994.*

Stuart Morgan: *Your work is based on a critique, first of art, then of other disciplines: philosophy, anthropology, psychoanalysis . . .*

Joseph Kosuth: What is the nature of making art? If it is not simply about fashioning forms and colours, then it has to do with the production of meaning. My practice is based on that assumption. If you begin there, you realize that potentially everything is material for art, because at some point it has to have an aspect of concretion and must be framed in relation to people's lives. It does not need to illustrate or work with that, but it does need to have a connection to the community which produced it.

So art is about the making of meaning.

Yes, and that involves not only the assertion of meaning but also its cancellation, since one kind of meaning needs to be produced through cancellation or denial or erasure of a group of meanings.

Isn't that putting something forward to say nothing?

If you assume that you send a silver bullet of signification, yes. But within the context of lived lives, silence can also be meaningful. It is not necessarily a nihilistic act, like speaking in the wrong place; social and cultural context is important. Work like mine is concerned with an understanding of language which is pragmatized out of language. Certain artists who use words do not do so from that point of view.

You mean the words are used abstractly.

They're reified; they're used as objects. Such work begs a larger context, but the work is not reflexive of the larger context, so it deals with neither one nor the other. The words simply hang there as the signature style of a particular artist. A long time ago when I was reading about the philosophy of science, I found the theory of models in the sciences interesting because, according to that, there were models which were tests and models which were illustrations. For me, an artwork must involve a test. Art that doesn't work in this context consists of illustrations of what art might be. That work is best as a kind of product identification.

You're talking about work that defines Conceptual art.

Yes: first, second, third generation, whatever. Not neo-Conceptualism; those are younger artists with another agenda and that work has its own authenticity. It's the 'adults' who are to blame; they should know better.

This insistence on holding viewers responsible for making meaning has political ramifications, of course.

Certainly, but it is often depoliticized in the act of looking. Part of the problem with so much of our culture is that it prescribes passivity on the part of the viewer. Culture organized by official managers of culture is always about passive receiving, consumption. Add to that the tradition of painting and sculpture. The problem is that its forms become forms of authority. If I make a painting, it's not just that I go to an art space or buy the paint and canvas or a brush – which is a machine to make one kind of art – but that even doing that is so loaded with prior meaning that whatever I as an artist would say, as a form of authority it speaks so loudly that my voice could not possibly be heard. That's what I realized when I was twenty, in the sixties in New York. I love painting; I was a painter and began studying painting when I was very young. So when I gave that up it was very painful. But I believed in art and had to give painting up. The reason Peter Schjeldahl, in 1968, called me 'the Savonarola of Conceptual art' was that if I had a passion some then called dogmatic, it was a strong belief in the direction art could go if it was ever going to be more than decoration or neckties. Twenty-five years later we are even nearer to that critical point: whether art is going to be a serious and enriching part of our cultural life. And I still look and see which artists, first, but not just artists, share this sense of responsibility.

A responsibility for meaning. Is that why you write about your work?

What I learned from Ad Reinhardt was that he painted black paintings but he also taught, wrote texts about his works, drew cartoons, took part in panel discussions . . . His practice included an enormous production of meaning about what art was. You can't separate the paintings from the rest. It's the same with Judd and his writings. What we have now is a struggle over the meaning of art, between what I have called primary and secondary texts in relation to production.

Obviously you feel close to Ad Reinhardt, with his talk of endings. How does this place you historically?

He said he was making the last paintings he could make. So he really saw himself as the end of a certain art, but as he himself said, 'The end in art is always the beginning.' I've found myself in panel discussions about whether

I am at the end of modernism or at the beginning of postmodernism, but of course it doesn't matter because at any turn of a corner they are one and the same. When I first showed at Castelli I called my work 'post-modern' in a flyer for the exhibition because I felt I was at the beginning of a generation brought up in the shadow of Cubism but having as little relation to Picasso as it did to Velázquez.

One way in which you are postmodern is that you take on great modernists one after another by referring to them in your work.

One of the things my generation felt was that modernist art preserved the idea that with one work you could describe the world, with the limit on the element of play that that implies. All my works are focused on some aspect of my problematic but they deal with it in different ways. The example I always like to give is that if you have a superhighway or Autobahn and you're on one side buying cigarettes and a friend is on the other but is unable to hear you because of the noise of the traffic, you send the same message in different ways – by miming, by shouting, by hand-signals . . . And there are overlaps as the message comes through. And across the process of a life as an artist one can see connections between the gaps and say, yes, that whole activity means certain things but that's not the same as the attempt to make in one work that big picture of the world. It's simply that the integrity of the activity involves relations to a larger process which is dynamic, not static, because we can't depict the world like that. Nor can any grand system of philosophy. This attempt to totalize is all part of that world. That way our art continues to be an authentic activity which is not speculative, in the way that philosophy is speculative, and remains flexible and interacts with the world on that larger horizon where the consciousness of all of us is formed. And in this way art indirectly manifests philosophical 'pretensions'. That isn't to say one is trying to illustrate philosophy. On the contrary; precisely because it does not try to do so, it has the hope of being enriching as a cultural activity and, as well, inheriting the responsibility of being that which attempts to see questions rather than 'supply' solutions. Its product is to reveal the questioning process of the lives of specific individuals living at a particular moment.

You seem to be asking if art can be of any use. I wonder if you ask the same question of philosophy. Is there a postmodern philosopher?

Philosophy died such a particular death that philosophy begins again now as the history of philosophy. It's operating in the realm of the pragmatist, and finally you end up in a job in industry! Does that colour its meaning?

It's obvious artists have to resist the market, but not ignore it. For, not unlike Eisenhower's 'military-industrial complex', there is an art-historical market complex in which there's a validating process. There is a way in which forms of authority, the traditional forms of art, continue to appear to have a new life over and over again because of the conservative mechanisms of the market. The developments in art which question that are tolerated only up to a certain point. If, using the model of Chinese politics, you see the history of the early part of the century as a two-line struggle between Picasso and Duchamp you understand how the world regarded Duchamp as opposed to the painting tradition which Picasso represents. Check auction prices for the past fifty years and compare the 'value' put on their work.

What effect has the market had on you?

I can't ignore it. In the sixties I began by trying to work outside of it. It is that social zone of projected meaning. I take some pleasure in the fact that artists like myself are skipped in the Saatchi Collection, for example. From Minimalism it hops to Neo-Conceptualism. And even though Judd said, 'Everything sculpture has, my work doesn't,' in the end it became sculpture.

His did but yours didn't?

Well, I continue to fight for the meaning of my work, I haven't let the market define it. Individuals may support my work, but they're not buying sculpture. Besides the Saatchi collection, look at the recent survey of American twentieth-century art at the Royal Academy. One entire strand is missing. Minimalism and post-Minimalism are there, Conceptual art isn't. Perhaps finally they realized that Conceptual art had some subversive aspect and it got edited out so they could skip to neo-Conceptual art. In the long term, that ratifies Conceptual art, I suppose, but in the short term it's difficult, because in this politico-economic system cultural engagement is expressed in economic terms. People who buy art are also sitting as trustees on the boards of museums. And museums decide what young artists see. There's a teaching dimension to our museums and galleries; they tell the young what kind of art to make or not make.

What does the term 'neo-Conceptualist' mean to you? You were a Conceptualist and you are still working. Does that make you a post-Conceptualist?

If it's authentic it remains authentic as long as the work continues to be relevant. If I was twenty-two again, would my work be different? Certainly, but my work is framed by my own history. I can't avoid that and that's part of my material; that's the context I'm obliged to account for every time I make art.

Let me ask the same question in a different way. You teach, your students make art, yet the context for their work is entirely different. They have a much easier time. They don't have to fight the battles you've already fought.
I disagree. Students have said to me, 'You were so lucky. You could do all those things then, but see how difficult it is now.' I was in my early twenties in the mid-sixties. And we had had Abstract Expressionism, Pop art and Minimalism in rapid succession in a period of six or seven years. Not that one happened after the other, but when they had all arisen it really seemed that everything was used up. There was a lot of hand-wringing. It seemed like the most difficult time to be an artist. But look at all we did after that. You just apply yourself to the task at hand. These days I have advantages; my work has a context and there is the economic possibility to make it. Having money forms work just as not having money does. Much of my early work came out of the fact that I had absolutely no money. That wasn't the only reason it was ephemeral or used common objects or things that were not expensive, but what I believed in matched that situation. Now I have another job to do. At 48 I have other kinds of responsibilities, the 'play' of my work is less limited internally as well as externally, first, but I face my own location. Also, I can use what I've learned to try to make the situation more open for those who are forming their own questions, and are 'out of the loop'. But, yes, the economics are a factor.
Times are hard.
In the seventies in America a survey said that only 2% of artists could live from the sales of their work. I don't know how much worse it could be than that. As in the rest of society, a few get too much money and are hurt by it. If you are an artist – no, even if you are not an artist – and you know what to do with your life, having much more money than you need is almost the same as not having enough. Because you must cope with having that kind of economic power. Dealing with stocks and bonds and real estate takes away from what you want to be spending your time doing. It's equivalent to hustling around for money, trying to pay your studio rent. There's a very interesting relation between those two, time-wasting aspects of economic life.
Yet through your work you talk about the freedom of the artist. Your recent exhibition at the Brooklyn Museum was a major statement about the liberty of the artist, which is being challenged or eroded. Do you see this as one-off agitprop work, or some permanent strand?
My work is fragmentary. I want to be able to continue to play. Not enough

artists do that any more. The artists of my generation, for the most part, are producing 'signature styles'; there is no longer the spirit of investigation or intervention in their work. They seem to be stuck in a sixties moment. Whatever they meant as a radical intervention in the sixties, these signature styles no longer mean the same now. They are really there for purposes of product identification. I have tried to free my work from that. The causal nexus of all the ways in which my work functions on the surface is evidence of how tightly connected it is at its centre.

You talk about models taken from other disciplines – the anthropological model, and so on . . . What is your current model?

More and more I realize that my work exists in the gaps between models. This autumn I made a work at Margo Leavin in Los Angeles. And because it was in Los Angeles, I reduced the elements and used a different presentational format, so what it came down to was cartoons and quotes from philosophy: Thomas Hobbes, Blondie and Dagwood, Schopenhauer, whatever. People were surprised. They said 'You're stealing this cartoon and you could be sued.' They didn't worry about stealing the texts of Hegel and the others. Just the cartoons. So I said 'I'm not selling the cartoons. I'm not selling the text. My work is between the cartoons and the text. And that's what you're buying if you buy the work.' Of course, that hasn't been tested in court. I don't know if a businessman or a judge would see it from that point of view, but I think that's how it has to be regarded. Quite early in my career I realized that my work may be Conceptual but it wasn't Post-Minimalism; nor, on the other hand, could it be explained by the idea of dematerialization. There were very intelligent examinations of my work by Lucy Lippard, the most sympathetic critic of the time. But she was very much part of the generation of Sol LeWitt and others, so understandably she saw the work from that point of view. We were doing something else. It wasn't simply to do with 'the dematerialization of the art object'. Whether it consisted of a grain of sand or a block of granite was irrelevant. It wasn't about materiality at all. It was about meaning.

You talk about the 'between-ness' of your meaning. There are other types of between-ness, territorial and scholarly, and I'd like to ask you about those. You travel constantly between the United States and Europe, for example, and live in both places.

Yes, I'm caught half-way between Europe and America, something of an outsider in both and yet very much at home. They are the two sides of a dialectic; they need each other. America has the 'place' in time. Europe is the source, the discourse; it gives meaning to our experience of the century. You can't have one without the other. The problem is to get past that, to look at the world's culture, that's the real problem, because integration ends by being the domination of the stronger. Do you want that? If you don't, all the other problems have to be faced: that always leads to misunderstanding the other culture.

Wasn't there a danger of that when you showed in the Hungarian Pavilion in Venice at the last biennale?

I'm American, of course, but through my family I'm Hungarian in a nominal way, yet I was amazed to be offered that pavilion. When I asked them why, they said that my writing had been distributed underground and that my work had been known and used in the seventies and eighties as an alternative to Socialist Realism, so given the change of government it was important that I should be in their pavilion. The generation that was underground now begins to run things. The fact that I have a Hungarian family with a particular political history meant that the nationalists did not object to my selection – as uncomfortable as my anti-nationalistic statements made them – and the nature of that particular biennale made it feasible. So it was a combination which worked.

In general, you are very critical of curating, especially by the museums. But now you are curating yourself. You are here in Britain to show your work alongside that of Ad Reinhardt and Felix Gonzalez-Torres, who studied your work. Does that imply that you were Reinhardt's student?

Not exactly. He came to the Cleveland Art Institute as a visiting artist while I was a first-year student. Most of the audience left his lecture about halfway through. I stayed, asked the only question, and we continued to talk afterwards. Reinhardt gave me his address and said, 'If you ever come to New York, look me up.' So, of course, I eventually did and found myself in his studio on Broadway. He used to buy me lunch occasionally and one day took me to lunch with Rothko. I immediately recognized in Reinhardt a kindred spirit. I can't imagine how he got invited to that school, by the way – after I left there the director attacked me at a faculty meeting and said I was the most destructive freshman in the history of the school. I took it as a compliment at the time. But the idea of Reinhardt, Felix and myself is not about the passing of a baton; it's about a Conceptual practice.

Arguments for the Conceptual aspects of Reinhardt's work put you in an antagonistic position to art historians, not for the first time. In his catalogue essay for the Reinhardt retrospective in 1991, Yve-Alain Bois proposed a formalist approach.

Reinhardt was always misunderstood, which means not understood yet. His relationship with the Museum of Modern Art is, of course, legendary, as it was with Clement Greenberg. It is both unfortunate and appropriate that MoMA would be the place Bois's rather creative piece of revisionist history would find a publisher. I think it is rather scary for many artists to see the form ambition takes, now, for some of the younger art historians. Historical fiction has its place, but it should be correctly labelled. My essay for 'Symptoms of Interference, Conditions of Possibility' was a necessary response to Bois.

Are you talking about art historians or critics?

Art history is still the basis of the practice, but it is formed by criticism, and vice versa. Criticism tends to be less objectionable because it is just opinion added to the conversation, take it or leave it. Its subjectivity is defined. Opinion parading as 'objective' art historical writing is much more pernicious, and we can thank *October* for increasing quantities of that. But there is a need for writing which discusses the work's implications, so that both the work, and the writing on it, stands on its own.

The opposite would be some museum diktat.

Of course. As artists we object to the implication that museum choices are somehow an objective idea of 'the best'. In contemporary art that's impossible to assert. One can only introduce ideas into the conversation. I much prefer it when artists make exhibitions, take responsibility for the surplus meaning that the collectivity of individual works produces and don't try to validate with a list of 'importance'. That way the integrity of individual works remains intact and art is presented on its own terms.

The Story of I: an interview with Tracey Emin

Published in frieze *34, 1997.*

Stuart Morgan: *You return to your experiences again and again in your work. Will this ever stop?*

Tracey Emin: No. When people ask 'How much of herself can she keep digging out?', I say 'You've only seen the tip of the iceberg, mate'. The more confident I get, the more will rise to the surface. I've started writing love poetry, but I don't want to write fiction; I want to take from life. What travels through me is what I make. Something comes into me, spirals out, and as it spirals I pull it in, create something, then throw it back into the world. I want to move quickly; I need the confidence it gives. People think my work is about pain, but it isn't; that's just the part people hook on to. The part they choose to remember.

In your work you talk about daily life but also about spirituality. Why do you place these side by side?

First, in order to be open about it. It's like a light that's always switched on, so I can talk to like-minded people. The only thing I'm well-read in – and my friends take the piss out of me for it – is mysticism: moving into other dimensions through the understanding of time and space, whether it's levitation or astral projection. It's the only thing I've ever studied with any interest, but you get to a point where you have to cut it out because you end up wafting around. But now things are better; now I'm making sense of everything.

Is there something holding it together?

Definitely. I was talking to friends last night about reincarnation, and I said 'I'm not coming back here again. I mean it. This is my last one.' And they said, 'but if you believe in life after death, where are you going?' I said, 'I'm going to be part of the sun, that's where I'm going. I'm going to become light.'

Why?

I'm not going to become negative. Dark space is my enemy, and I've seen it ever since I was a child. It would come into the room and sweep over me, but now it doesn't come in its true form. It disguises itself as images which I might find attractive.

Temptation?
More like dreams in real time. I'm lying in bed, I wake up, someone is there and I have to rationalize the situation. A few weeks ago I didn't. I followed it into the hall, which became a sea-wall with me sitting on it, looking out to a Mediterranean-type sea. And as I looked, this person started stabbing me in the stomach and there was blood, like real blood. I was in genuine pain.
Does it have a face?
It does now. In 1987 I was living in Bell Street. One night a noise woke me and as I looked at the sofa there was a person on it, with skin like autumn leaves. She sat up and her eyes were red sockets and the hair was completely white as if it might break. Then she started to levitate and to walk towards me in a long purple gown. It was the most terrifying thing because it was me, walking towards myself as if I'd been buried for six months. I was so frightened, I said, 'Dear God, I promise I won't be afraid, please don't let it hurt me. Take it away. I'd confront it but I'm so afraid.' While I said this little prayer I knew it was really close. As I took my hands away and looked straight ahead – I couldn't really tell how far away – colours appeared, all the colours of the rainbow, and as they started to spin, every shade of blue you could imagine was there. Then it changed to aquamarine and every kind of green, every kind of blade of grass, every kind of leaf: the whole spectrum. It felt like hours, though it must have been only moments. I saw every colour there is, then just laid down and went to sleep. I think it was my reward.
Why do you think these things visit you in particular?
Well, I was talking to my mum the other day. In her house she has a white Formica table. I said, 'Why is this table so special?' She said, 'Because we used to do the seances, the ouija board, on it.' I said, 'On this table? Where was I?' She said, 'Under the table'. My family has always been psychic, especially Uncle Colin, who died. He was decapitated in a car crash. It only took a moment. He was holding a Benson and Hedges packet just before he died. It looked like real gold. In my family when we die we are cremated and our ashes are thrown into the sea amongst the seagulls. I love seagulls. I'd like to be one.
Is your family alive?
Yes, but my Nan died last Christmas. It was sad, but I still feel close to her. Two weeks ago I was here, crying, and I felt her touch my arm. That was the second time. The first was on a bus once in Sweden when I felt someone touch my back. She was behind me. I saw her hand on the edge of the seat.

People imagine that they see the dead because they really want to, but it isn't quite like that. You miss people, you have to see them, you are desperate to know what happened. So sometimes you feel them or imagine that they're sitting there. You see it, you sense it and then it's gone. I've had a few visitations from my Nan.

Will you pursue this in your work?

That and other things: travelling to parallel worlds, other dimensions. Now that Joshua [Compston] and my Nan are dead I reckon that when I go on my own journey they'll be there to help me. So I'm not afraid; I just have to expand my mind for the next place. It's one thing to be into sex, but I have to get kicks in other ways too. And art, in the generic sense, is never going to do it for me.

What more do you need?

Artists shouldn't just be making things; they should be having conversations like this.

What kind of conversations are you having at present?

Well, Sarah [Lucas] gave me this book called *The Other World*; it has descriptions of heaven from people who have died and come back in seances to tell us what it's like. There are people with silvery robes, some see-through. Different people reach different levels of spiritual attainment. Some who were mad about their jobs are there with their work. And there are animals in heaven, but only if souls were connected to animals they loved. People are wandering around in heaven in silver robes and every pet they ever had is walking along beside them.

How do you want to be when you are 70 years old?

Compos mentis but eccentric, with a massive house by the sea. I'd like to be a writer. And to have somebody to hold my hand.

And children?

I don't want to give birth.

You could adopt.

Or have a caesarean – I'd want to be unconscious. If I ever did get pregnant I wouldn't terminate it; I would have to go ahead. I've had a miscarriage and two abortions, and I can't do that again. People have family values – I don't, not in the conventional sense – I know I'll never be part of society, so why try? That's what's lovely about being an artist: I don't have to.

Much of your work involves violence towards women.

Because I am a woman, people have been violent towards me. It's something that should be discussed more. I was raped at thirteen by someone hardly older than myself. This happens to boys too. You must break that chain. Be aware of what's happening and stop it. In my work I continually re-address my youth, when I let things happen to me.

'Let them happen'?

I accepted them as part of life, but I was so nihilistic then that I didn't expect happiness.

How do you feel about that now?

I can stand up for myself.

When you depict sex and violence in your work I can't always tell them apart.

I hardly ever go to the cinema, but when I do go I choose masculine, violent films with plenty of blood. It must excite me. For me aggression, sex and beauty go together. Much of my work has been about memory, for example, but memories of violence and pain. Nowadays if I make a drawing I'm trying to draw love, but love isn't always gentle.

In your work you talk a lot about anal sex.

Yes.

Does it have to be pictured so violently?

I haven't had anal sex for a long time, but it can often be painful; it feels like a violation. But if you love someone and that's what you're really into, you feel brilliant. My anal sex drawings aren't recent; I am probably remembering what it was like. I had one relationship which was all about that. In the years I was with him I think I only had vaginal sex twice.

His choice or yours?

The sad thing is that it was probably his choice.

Why is that sad?

It's hard to say. I'm sitting here thinking, remembering it. Women are not allowed to enjoy anal sex. Well, a lot of women are never going to get it because they are not ready to accept the fact that they like it. They've probably never been with a partner who would face up to wanting it. A lot of people don't know how to do it properly, that's the other thing. But my Nan told me it used to be the major form of contraception. I'm sure that 100 years ago it wasn't a problem.

It's a short step from here to the artists who have inspired you, like Egon Schiele or the German Expressionists. Do you still want to be a German Expressionist?

No.

Did you ever?

Some people say the Beatles were only good between 1959 to 1963, and I was like that about art; only art from one period seemed important. Schiele was marvellous. So young – he made those drawings between the ages of 18 and 28. People forget he was only 28 when he died. He was sent to jail for his art. I like his lifestyle; it was open. My other favourite is Edvard Munch. He was free with his emotions, he was a socialist, and although people call him misogynistic he was quite female in the way he expressed himself. His titles and subjects were almost soft, yet he made this hard kind of mad painting. There are photographs that show him painting naked in the woods.

He seems to have been so lonely, particularly as he got older.

Even if you depict lonely things you have an audience in mind.

When you make art who are you talking to?

First, to me, questioning myself. Secondly, to society. I want society to hear what I'm saying. I'm not only talking to galleries, museums and collectors. For me, being an artist isn't just about making nice things or people patting you on the back; it's some kind of communication, a message.

What is that message?

It's about very, very simple things that can be really hard. People do get really lonely, people do get really frightened, people do fall in love, people do die, people do fuck. These things happen and everyone knows it but not much of it is expressed. Everything's covered with some kind of politeness, continually, and especially in art because art is often meant for a privileged class.

Do you mean rich people or educated people?

Educated people.

People like your work because it is honest. Like the video you made about your life in Margate. You had sex with men there – men older than yourself – and you enjoyed dancing. In fact you danced so well you entered a competition, only to find the boys you had slept with booing you off the stage. You knew you had lost the competition and that what you wanted most was beyond your reach forever. Is all of this true?

Yes.

Is it true that because you had slept with them they kept shouting 'Slag! Slag!' as you danced?

I'd slept with quite a few of them, yes. And I was fourteen and they were between 19 and 24. You could say that they should have known better than to sleep with a fourteen-year-old girl. Well, they certainly should have known better. They shouldn't have publicly humiliated me. But this story is very edited. Even when I walked down the High Street they used to shout 'Slag!' or 'Slut!' I never did anything wrong to them; all I did was have sex with them. Last year I met one of these men and we talked. He has daughters now. He said he'd thought of the way he'd treated me and felt bad about it. So the story is absolutely true. But I had such good fun making the film and I really do love dancing and their calling me 'slag' is never going to stop me fucking or making love with someone, it's impossible. But for years I felt very strange about sex.

The first time you had sex, was it against your will?

I don't think it was the first time I ever had anything put up me but it was the first time I'd had a penis there, yes. And it was against my will. But after that I was on some sexual exploration. After about six months I thought, 'This is great; we can just do it.' I was very free and I wasn't in love. I thought sex was great.

What did it give you that you lacked?

Power.

To do what?

Well, I had this idea. I left school at thirteen, but I was quite good at geography. I had to go back at fifteen and they said I could do geography O-level, but I said no, I didn't need to sit an exam; I'd rather study maps. I'd study the world and travel, that's how I'd learn about geography. And I had this idea that if you slept with someone it was like going to another country. I still talk about the springboard effect. Usually the biggest events in my life have coincided with a new sexual partner. It gives you a fantastic feeling. It's . . .

Confidence in yourself?

More. It's things coming together. It's a coming together with someone new. It's not about physical satisfaction; it's about being with someone, drifting. I would like to get into people's minds, to explore inside, not just outside. Sometimes that can happen when you make love.

The opposite would be if you were faced with surfaces and nothing else.

If I think about my mind or myself as a whole, a pomegranate is what I'd like to be. It's got that prickly helmet on the top, but when you open it there are tiny sweet seeds. And it comes out in sections, so it's also like a mind: split into layers, like my dreams.

All these things occur in your drawings. But what role do the drawings play?

They float like sections of my mind that materialize in drawing. It could be a sentence, could be figurative, might be anatomical, or could end up as a squiggle with crass writing on the top.

Finally, you have plans for a tent.

The idea came from the Tibetan exhibition at the Imperial War Museum. I want a tent with a sky blue floor. It will travel – anywhere with grass would do – and I'll perform inside, perhaps for a day. Not real performance; the important thing is the stories. I could do other things too. Recently I danced to one song for an hour.

What's the song?

Marc Bolan's 'Oh Girl'. But I assumed he was singing 'Oh God'.

Did you think he was religious?

No, but he might be now.

Thomas Demand: History Lessons

Published in Thomas Demand, *Kunsthalle, Zürich/Kunsthalle, Bielefeld, 1998.*

Though the corner of the archive is empty, signs of uses are evident: boxes piled up neatly, one on top of the other, a ladder propped against a wall to ensure access to the shelves. Peace and quiet prevail. But after all, don't archives most resemble mausoleums: places where time stands still? The nature of the subject suggests collecting, research and preservation, the forging of links between then and now. So it hardly matters that the room is in slight disorder while changes are being made. Perhaps the staff are taking stock or some new method of storage is being put to the test. One thing is certain: perverse though it may seem, the sheer blandness of those boxes requires greater attention than the viewer could possibly have anticipated. For that very reason questions spring to mind. 'Where am I?' 'How long has this been here?'

In no time at all those grey boxes will be closed again, but by then it will have become evident that something is amiss, partly of course because there are no labels, so none can be distinguished from the next. This discovery triggers a sequence of responses. For in this case instead of offering information, the opposite may be taking place: not exactly a deliberate attempt at obfuscation, but certainly a total refusal to negotiate with the user, if one exists. Snug to the point of being stifling, the interior sends shivers down the spine.

Begin again. On shelves that lie flat, square boxes of equal size and colour can be seen. From the viewer's point of view, one box is indistinguishable from another. The reason is simple: not enough information is available on the box to make any decision about what is going on. Possibly the problem is being examined from an unpromising direction. As the analysis continues, doubts set in. And since there are no titles to explain what should go where and what everything is called, the answers must be obvious. So for the employees an entirety must be recognizable, even named. And for people who matter, it is. In normal circumstances the correct way to reach a solution would be to examine evidence. In this case, however, evidence is scant. Luckily another strategy exists. Rather than believing everything that meets the eye, why not experiment instead with the idea of disbelief, just to find out what might happen?

The result is surprising; for a second, more sceptical glance the problem is clarified. Previously the state of the space in question gave rise to various doubts, none easy to dispel. The real difficulty, however, is how to locate the source of such fears. For while one involves order, or rather orderliness, another relates to materiality and how this is registered by the camera. Yet somehow this approach also fails to prevent the possibility of being wrong at least, perverse at most. Doubleness, one aspect of that perversity, results from lack of information but that is not the secret to be prised from this tableau. For the key to the puzzle may be the way information is presented. A short step distinguishes mere surface from display for its own sake. Why, then, the subtle suggestion of flimsiness? Could it be a lie or some other means of diverting viewers? Of what use are closed boxes on shelves, anyway? Perhaps the point is not what the boxes might mean but rather the very fact of their existence. Equally important, it seems, is their apparent blankness, as if they exist merely as tokens. In other words, since their actual value lies elsewhere they must remain unused – half-forgotten but in safe hands. Yet somehow those flat, blank, square untitled boxes have become so valuable that they have to be guarded.

In the world outside, those boxes command little belief; their existence may be merely symbolic. In each case these objects may be so valuable that they lack any name or description, for though on the one hand the untitled boxes are harmless, on the other an opposite reaction may be felt, for gradually these innocent items of evidence have come to seem sinister in the extreme. And perversely, as the image gains credence in one respect, in another it sacrifices the ability to summon sustain belief. The result could be pathos. On the other hand it could command respect for one reason: because it is so rarely subjected to examination.

Only a police examination would be sufficiently finely tuned to do justice to the detail of Demand's art. For example, *Archive* includes at least one sinister feature: among the shelves one box has been tampered with, a result that seems all the more heinous given the air of secrecy that Demand has worked so hard to create. The regular shape of the piled boxes serves to dramatize this absence, seen now as flagrant interference. Yet while the brain works overtime to solve the mystery, other references intervene. Isn't the shelf of boxes an obvious nod to first-generation Minimalism? Isn't there more than a whiff of espionage about the scene? And what is the connection between the two? After all, the empty rooms serve as a surrogate for an empty room and its habits. The two most disturbing suggestions made by Demand are first, that whoever does it, all looking is akin to policing, and second, that this state of bafflement has somehow become the norm.

For Demand revels in deception, almost for its own sake. One of his favourite images is the sequence in Fellini's film *Casanova* when the hero appears to row on water, an effect produced not with water at all but with plastic foil, inflated from below. Little wonder that his work reveals an interest in duplicity. Working from wartime photographs, for example, Demand has made maquettes from photographs of interiors. Here the idea could have stopped. But instead it was taken further when the notion of evil was introduced. For example, *Corridor* seems to describe a haunting or a dream. 'Why that space in particular?' we ask, realizing that no logical answer exists. But suddenly what was concealed rises to the surface. Indeed the two most important themes of Demand's work may be survival and memory.

Banners from Uccello's *Battle of San Romano* in the National Gallery in London reappear in Demand's personal image bank. But so does the image from his history lessons of the attempt to kill Adolf Hitler, a moment that could have changed the course of history. And so do image banks themselves. The figure who may have pondered most deeply on the value of the image in the twentieth century has been Bill Gates, the chairman of Microsoft and the world's richest man. Years ago he had begun purchasing the rights to certain key images of his choice which he correctly called 'the oil of the 21st century' and regarded as ideal.[1] An opposite, perhaps perverse reaction to the idea of image was that of L. Ron Hubbard, whose aim, like that of Chairman Mao, was to make people believe in an ideal, whether that ideal was the truth or not. Despite the fact that he founded Scientology, Hubbard led the life of a recluse who lived and wrote his books in hotels and was seldom photographed. (The result was that only seven or eight official photographs of him have survived.) All of these figures shared strong views about the role of the image in contemporary life. And they all crop up as absent images in Thomas Demand's work. Consider the significance of any main work, for example *Diving Board* from 1994, a concrete monument like a skeleton of a building. No matter how important athletics and sheer display became during the Third Reich and its aftermath, for example in that perverted form of American chic analysed by Susan Sontag in her essay 'Fascinating Fascism', or its dubious appearances in the late architecture of Philip Johnson. In this photograph heroism is presented for its own sake. Though the diving boards are empty, the lone figure can be imagined standing there, on display to the applauding crowds. Now, however, there is no one to dive or win prizes, no roar from the onlookers, above all perhaps no fame or adulation, for such acts were done to celebrate the power of the Third Reich. (We are a long way from *The Triumph of the Will.*) But perhaps the element that draws Gates and Hubbard together is their level of fear, an element that draws together some, if not all, the imagery and lifestyle, the fame and loneliness of people who want to excel. When Gates buys the sole rights to a perfect image of a hurricane, for example, he is trading in perfection, nothing less.

The fate of perfection is not only a matter for Gates, however. It is also the business of Thomas Demand himself. Slowly producing a body of images which he has directed in an almost theatrical way, he also strives to absorb them into his growing image bank, where they make new connections between themselves, each new image playing a part in producing the next. *Archive*, for example, offers an insight into the moral dimension of images, one that could be contrasted with the *Peg Board* as a piece of poker-faced humour on the subject of two and three dimensions. In contrast, the photograph of a remade model of the site of Hitler's headquarters, *Room*, is complex, crazed and operatic, resembling classic black-and-white film masterpieces in the lavishness of its effects.

Could the remaking of famous incidents, sites or situations be an exercise in confronting historical events from an unusual angle, in order to gain a different, more correct point of view? Or is this a misunderstanding of the traditional Brechtian *Verfremdungseffekt*? Is Demand mixing genres almost for the hell of it, simply in order to see what happens, as so many postmodern novelists have done? Is he the expected spin-off from film and its lighting techniques: untrue in every way but seductive in the extreme? Or is he setting out to make his own, permanently sceptical vision of what we laughingly call 'fact'? Or could it be that the very use of that word has become a waste of breath, given everything that we know now? And yet the procedural care Demand takes with his scepticism, if that is what we have decided it is, suggests a rumour of real things.

Among other things, Demand is a fine historian, making images in the tradition of the stage or even the cinema. Not true images, but something far more important than that. How else is it possible to describe the effect of power on the individual than *Zimmer* or the *Corner*? And as a historian he uses images with great poignancy. One of his most recent works, *Parlor*, is set not in Germany but in New York. Taken from a photograph of a massage parlour, it is truly international, and in New York, at least, less and less common. The bed is clean but decidedly small, in order to remind clients that theirs is not to be a two-way activity. The few tools of the trade lie around to indicate that attempts at conversation will not be welcomed. Most poignant of all the details is a red lamp on the wall. Is it to summon a bouncer in case one of the clients becomes excited? Does it serve to remind the clients of the time limit? The fact is that the artist does not know; at the time of making the photograph, he had never visited a masseuse. Despite this, when the imitation booth was finished, artificial though it was, Demand decided that something extra was necessary. The light on the wall was never part of the *mise-en-scène*; it was an inflated red balloon.

1. At the time of writing, Gates is involved in a legal wrangle of major importance. For a summary of the complex legal position of Microsoft, see John Carlin, 'Windows, Gates and Closed Shops', *The Independent on Sunday* (18 January 1998), section 2, p.5. *The Corner*, as presented by Demand, is where the young Bill Gates created Microsoft.

Contra Natura: on the writing and criticism of Stuart Morgan

Juan Vicente Aliaga

The most potent elements in a work of art, are, often, its silences.
– Susan Sontag

If there is something I've always hated in art criticism it is when it doesn't fulfil its function. That is to say when it uses the work of art or whatever other artistic manifestation to exhibit pedantic periphrasis or comments full of abstruse and incomprehensible terminology. Or when criticism stuffs its commentary or review with empty but, certainly, sonorous and resounding adjectives. All these defects occur frequently in French and Spanish art criticism but also, often, in the Anglo-Saxon variety.

To my judgment, the practice of art criticism carries with it the need to clarify the meanings of the artistic proposition, so that readers might figure for themselves a sense of place and obtain an understanding of the object analysed. For this, it is imperative that the handling of language be crystalline and transparent. There is nothing worse than an art critic whose expression is clumsy, confused, affected or equivocal.

This said, one shouldn't understand these words as a defence for a criticism that is merely didactic or short on intellectual flights. Writing is an act in which the understandings and the culture of the person who writes are overturned, in order to eviscerate and dissect the folds and darknesses of, in this case, a work of art.

I am not against brilliance, but against the sterile pomposity of reviewers or hacks.

None of this applies directly to the writing of Stuart Morgan. And that is probably one of the greatest lessons that can be extracted from the enormous pleasure of reading him.

In *Inclinations* (a title as of literary reminiscences, which though rather musty does allude to the formation of an aesthetic sensibility) a group of texts and interviews of greater or lesser range is collected, that cover an ample period, 1977 to 1998. Published in US or British magazines or in the form of short catalogue essays, or even unpublished, they form a heteroclite ensemble from which it is sometimes difficult to detach a definition of the kind of art that Stuart Morgan defended. And the thing is that Morgan situated himself generally as though perched in an observatory from which he looked avidly and curiously at the artistic manifestations that paraded before his eyes. It is from there that his acuteness can land on the work of two representatives of German Neo-expressionism such as Markus Lüpertz or Georg Baselitz without it stopping him from plunging into the eccentricities of Edward Allington or into the installations of Jonathan Borofsky. On the other hand, and though situated in the spirit of the decades about which he reflects, he does not forget to rescue the names of artists buried by the cruelty of the market or abandoned by a criticism alert only to fashion. This is the case, for example, of Alice Aycock or Rose English.

Similarly, in the asymmetric and zigzagging system that constitutes the gaze of Stuart Morgan, there are no scruples when the time comes to get involved in aesthetic manifestations beyond the exclusivity of the art world. His eye fixes itself as much on the experimental performances of the Theatre of Mistakes as on the dame of Wuppertal, the visionary dancer Pina Bausch.

Even today art criticism in the majority of newspapers or magazines manifests a certain fear when the moment comes to jump, without a net, from one discipline to another: criticism is too often incapable of seeing the osmotic language present in many artists. Stuart makes the leap rigorously, always accompanied by a first-rate intellectual armoury and by a cunning touch. Just as there is in his writing no hierarchy of artistic values according to the market or to fashionable tendencies, and I thank him for his subjective criteria, neither is there a temporal limit to his insatiable critical voracity, and along his scalpel parade those from the arch-consecrated Picasso to Jeffrey Dennis, an artist unjustly absent from the international scene.

All the above does not mean that in the subjectivity of Stuart Morgan there are no preferences or more pronounced leanings: there are and they are noticeable, very much so, in the detailed attention received by Louise Bourgeois or in the weight that he dedicates to an artist simultaneously conceptual and mystical such as Joseph Beuys. Both are also included in *What the Butler Saw* (1996), Stuart Morgan's first book. But that favouritism also manifests itself towards characters that are unusual, strange, according to the canon of the moment, such as Khlebnikov, known only to the erudite, a clairvoyant Russian who wanted to distance himself from the influence of Futurism, build houses of flowers and poplars, and make nudism the norm. And the thing is that deep down these outlandish characters, like the marginal and unknown Martín Ramírez, confined to a psychiatric hospital, are clearly the saints of his devotion.

This said there are two artistic cultures that Stuart Morgan knew best, that of his own country and that of the United States, and it is his education that was responsible for this. But being situated on both Anglo-Saxon shores of the Atlantic did not prevent him impinging on another ambit in which he felt comfortable: Germany. It may be observed in the many Teutonic terms of which he makes use, and in the number of German artists to whom he dedicated his time (among others, Martin Kippenberger, Thomas Locher, Thomas Demand).

All this could sketch an identikit portrait of a complacent writer, soft in his taste, but that is not the case. Without being a frenzied beater of the art he disliked, the questioning is frequent in his observations, acerbic even, and always tinged with a fine and subtle sense of humour. It appears, for example, and forcefully, in his analysis of the exhibition 'A New Spirit in Painting' (1981) in London's Royal Academy. An exhibition which delighted in celebrating traditional values such as individual creativity, good painting and the quality of the work, incongruities that sharpened Morgan's critical sense. Perplexed before an unfortunate exhibition, which harboured the Italian Transavanguardia as well as German Neo-expressionism, Stuart dedicated to it an exceedingly ironic title: 'Cold Turkey', for there was nothing new or refreshing in said exhibition.

Neither do two figures of the British establishment, Gilbert & George, save themselves. He cannot bear the way they glorify the working-class kids, turning them into heroes and patriots with an unfolding of abundant Nazi-tending iconography. This work by the famous Fournier Street couple earned from him hard epithets: simplistic and offensive, especially so, he thought, given the British context in which the work was first produced, against a backdrop of street disturbances stirred up by the racism of the country. And the thing is that the gigantic photographs of Gilbert & George, which supposedly redeem a disadvantaged youth, are in his judgment: 'a truly right-wing art, aestheticizing and self-indulgent'. But his sharp criticism did not stop there. Perhaps more surprising are the commentaries where he incises the weakness of one of the most famous and unsullied saints of contemporary art, Bruce Nauman. The essence of his work happened already in the seventies, Morgan tells us, as he looks enquiringly into the meaning of some of the works belonging, at the time of writing (1989), to Count Panza di Biumo. By contrast, the work of Judd married better with the cold and monastic arcaded halls of that old remodelled hospital that is today the Reina Sofia of Madrid, a museum that housed the collection of the Conde de Varese. All this permitted him to cast doubt on the equivocal name given to Minimalism, which frequently uses theatrical means or lighting (see Flavin) that are hardly plain, sober and minimalist. An acute observation, in line with others made by Morgan on Conceptual art, about which, in an interview conducted in Valencia in 1989, he offers an innovative and unusual prism when he highlights the humorous character of the movement which has passed into history for its cryptic hermeticism.

In all this crop of texts written with a language precise, concise and bulging with ingenuity (and with which he has studied themes and artists considerably differing from each other), one that is prominent is the treatment of a subculture, to use the term employed by Dick Hebidge (*Subculture: The Meaning of Style*, 1979), which has prospered in clubs and premises of ill-repute. The focus is quite unusual in this genre of writing that we call art criticism.

I am referring to the hybrid and porous subculture emerging from and associated with the cabaret, low budget theatre and transvestism, a very rich tradition in England (see establishments such as The Vauxhall Tavern or The Black Cap in London). In this field, which Stuart depicted in a splendid text titled 'English Drag' (1990), published in *Artforum* and considered for a cosmopolitan and international reader, both spectacle and biting language, which Stuart surely indulged in on more than one occasion, glitters. This subculture of strident make-up, steely and fast words, histrionics and conspiratorial laughs is that embodied by Regina Fong and her devout followers The Fong-ettes, and by Lily Savage: two stars, one of frills, buttons and bows and the other of a more shabby and proletarian vein.

Seen with affection and with the memory of shared nights these two nightbirds turn drag into an art based on British pantomime in which the sexes interchange the clothing which, according to good manners and strict norms, is appropriate to them. And it is the case that Britain, as Morgan recalls, has given us figures of the mettle of Bette Bourne, founder/foundress of the Bloolips company, an unclassifiable character who could be seen as having something of the Berlin cabaret but who connects more with a British spirit of vitriolic and subversive speech in which ambiguity reigns, even in the knowledge that it's just a game.

One of the aspects that most awoke Morgan's interest in these productions of cheap Vaudeville was the indomitable sexuality present in Bourne's performances. But this is not the only case. Morgan's writing, by way of the persistent question to artists such as the Spaniard Pepe Espaliú or the North American Nayland Blake, is hospitable to investigations concerning sexuality and art, drawing a map of the body (there would enter the allusions to the anthropologist Mary Douglas) in which anal practices and sadomasochist drives emerge with vigour. Few art critics dared so much in their moment, or even now, in these times ill named as post-Aids, poking about in these subjects with exquisite naturalness and with the eagerness of a child who formulates their first questions about the forbidden in the hope of experiencing its delights.

(Translated by Juan Cruz)

Index of Names

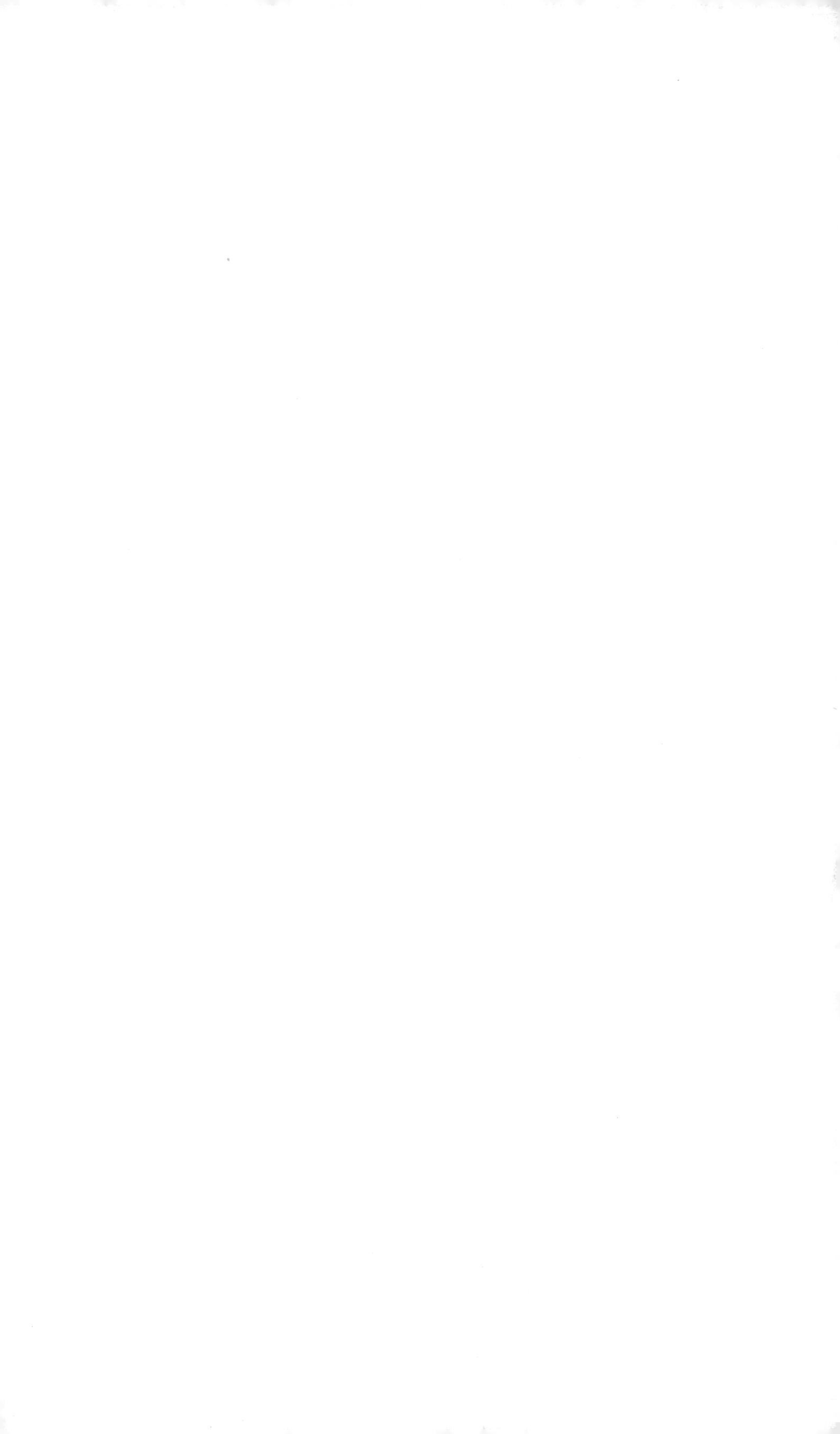